PICTORIAL
INTRODUCTION
TO THE BIBLE

PICTORIAL INTRODUCTION TO THE BIBLE

William S. Deal

Hendrickson Publishers, Inc.
P.O. Box 3473
Peabody, Massachusetts 01961-3473

Printed in the United States of America
ISBN 1-56563-296-6

Foreword

Two factors commend this book to me. First, it offers in readable form the kind of material needed in my private life and work. Often a book with solid content is unmanageable because it speaks only to the trained specialist in that field. It is important that laymen have good background material if their Bible study is to profit. In my work, there is also a constant need for a fast, accurate reference volume as speeches or articles are called for. It is of benefit to know the trends of the people during a certain period of history if we are to make accurate application to today's problems. This book gives vital information in terms which readers can grasp and use. You will recognize that the author and publisher worked together in producing this commentary-type aid so that it appeals to teachers as well as to young people and their parents.

The whole purpose of this *Pictorial Introduction to the Bible* is an acknowledgment that God sovereignly lives and acts today. It assumes the integrity and authority of the canon of sacred Scriptures. It is indeed unlikely that one could overstate the importance of such a perspective. We still face today the pseudo-intellectual whose creed is academic disbelief. Such a person will affirm that God does not exist, that the Bible is unreliable, or that Jesus Christ immortalized Himself in institutions, rather than allowing that Christ is alive today and ruling in the hearts of regenerate men as their Savior and Lord.

The other factor that commends this book to me is that it comes out of the heart and work of a man in touch with life. He invests the time that is necessary to learn truth as it is in Jesus. The spiritual insight he has gained is employed in the great service of counseling troubled people. His is a ministry of counseling youth, families, and fractured marriages in such a way that God's power is brought to bear on the dilemmas of men.

Mark O. Hatfield
U. S. SENATOR FROM OREGON

Preface
to the
New Edition

This book is the result of many years of intensive study and research.

The author is very grateful to God for the outstanding success of the former editions of this book. And he is deeply indebted to the publishers of Baker Book House for publishing the original edition and for their excellent promotion of it over the years.

Since the first edition of this *Pictorial Introduction to the Bible* appeared as a hardbound book in 1967, it has been reprinted many times, in a variety of formats. A special English edition has been published for distribution in Asia and the Philippines. Translations have appeared in German and Chinese, extending the usefulness of the book worldwide.

In this new quality paperback edition the text of earlier editions has been retained, but some of the illustrations have been updated.

From its very inception, God has had His good hand on this work. It has brought enlightenment, inspiration, and a much better understanding of the Bible to countless thousands.

Not only have many laymen been blessed by using this book, but many ministers and teachers have benefited from it as well. Several colleges have used it as a textbook in their Introduction to the Bible courses. It is hoped that this new edition will be used as a textbook in a series of correspondence Bible courses for laymen and young people who want to learn more about the Bible and its times, its peoples and customs, and its total message of salvation.

May God continue to shed forth His blessings on this work as it glorifies Him; lifts up His Son, Jesus Christ our Lord; and honors the Holy Spirit who inspired the Bible upon which this book is based.

Introduction

In presenting this volume several things should be mentioned.

First, it was prepared primarily for young people of high-school age, with their language, understanding, and thinking always in mind. It is the author's most sincere hope that multitudes of them everywhere will come to love and appreciate this book for its simplified, yet dignified, presentation of the greatest Book on earth.

Second, the book will naturally appeal to parents and other adults who like reading materials on this level. It should soon become an ideal Home Circle Reading Book, suitable for almost everyone in the home.

Third, Sunday school teachers and other Christian workers will find here an abundance of materials for their uses. For example, suppose the Sunday school lesson is from the Book of Ruth. In a short time one can get all the important facts about the Book of Ruth, plus other spiritual truths, from this work. This will make the Book of Ruth "come alive" for the teacher. People with neither the time nor research facilities needed for preparing Sunday school lessons or other talks, will find this volume a great boon. Ministers, also, will find it helpful for resource materials.

Fourth, Bible colleges and other religious schools will likewise find the work helpful for beginning Bible classes or for Biblical introduction classes.

More than two years went into the research and original planning of this work. Critical analysis of the original materials by several Bible scholars and their suggestions were most helpful in the final preparation of the work for the press.

It is now offered to the public with the most earnest prayer that God will bless its use to untold multitudes who read its pages.

Explanatory Notes

Quotations have been kept at a minimum in this work. The average youthful or adult reader does not care to have his reading cluttered with an abundance of footnotes, or filled with constant references to sources of quotations.

The author has received light from many windows and drawn deeply from innumerable fountains. The information derived from such research has been molded into the common language used here to express the limitless ideas thus gained. Care has been taken, however, to state all *facts* as nearly and closely as possible. Constant, further research has been made to assure that all data concerning the authors, dates, places of writing of the Biblical books, and other historical information are as nearly up to date and accurate as possible. The Bibliography presents a partial list of the research background out of which this work has come.

Matters of authorship, dates, places of writing, and other information given relative to the books of the Bible, together with their authenticity and trustworthiness, are all positions taken within the conservative theological viewpoint. An attempt has also been made to maintain an evangelical approach and appeal. Questionable positions have been kept to a minimum or excluded entirely. This is not an apologetical work for scholars but a Home Reading Book for youth and laymen in general. Its purpose is to inspire faith, rather than to place debatable questions into the minds of its readers.

Parents and teachers may rest assured that every vital position taken relative to any portion of the Holy Scriptures has been tried in the fires of careful research. Only the pure, refined gold has been presented here.

William S. Deal

Acknowledgments

To all the publishing companies whose books are listed in the Bibliography, I express deep appreciation. Few direct quotations occur in the work, but without these research sources this work would have been impossible.

To the fine number of excellent Bible scholars over the nation, who read various parts of the original manuscript and gave helpful critical advice, the author will forever be grateful. Their assistance was invaluable.

To Mrs. Ruth Coy, high school English teacher for many years, who holds the Master of Arts in English, and who patiently edited the whole original manuscript, goes most sincere thanks. To her goes an abundance of credit for the excellent readability of this book. The editorial work was done with a high-school-level readership in view. This makes for pleasant reading for both young people and adults. Also, to Mrs. Coy goes deep gratitude for finalizing the Old Testament copy for the press.

To Mrs. Opal Ruth Coy Fitzgerald, for her final preparation of the New Testament manuscript for the press after the editorial work was completed, finally is due my most sincere gratitude.

And last, to my wife, for her patience and assistance; to our daughter Evangeline Sue for her assistance as an elementary school teacher; and to a number of other people who have read portions of the original manuscripts and offered helpful suggestions, I express my most sincere appreciation.

William S. Deal

The publisher gratefully acknowledges the many individuals, organizations, and institutions which provided illustrations. Specific acknowledgment is made in the appropriate places.

Contents

Illustrations

How We Got Our Bible

HOW WE
GOT OUR BIBLE

The Bible is the oldest book in the world. The art of writing was well established long before Moses wrote the first five books of the Bible, known as the Pentateuch. From writings found in old tombs, on stone slabs, and on the walls of cities and tablets of those times, we know that writing was well developed in ancient Babylonia and Egypt. Modern archaeologists have deciphered these writings and from them have established many important facts.

Books and other writings possibly existed in those far away days, long before Moses' time. The so-called Laws of Hammurabi, an ancient king living about the time of Abraham, represent such writings. These laws were similar to some of the writings of Moses in the Pentateuch, but much inferior. No book of universal significance was written before the Pentateuch, and none other of any moral and spiritual value has survived from those times.

The content of the inscriptions referred to above were mostly of a business, social, or historical nature. They are important to us now largely because they establish the fact that writing was well-advanced by Moses' time, and they correspond with and support many Biblical facts. For instance, unbelieving scholars once denied that any such people as the "Hittites" referred to in the Bible ever lived. The name was pure invention, they said. But archaeologists discovered a stone on which there were found inscriptions about these strange people, whom secular historians had either forgotten or passed over. So, the Bible was proved to be correct. In this way many Bible references and claims have been proved true by archaeologists' spades.

THE OLD TESTAMENT

The Old Testament part of our Bible was originally written in the Hebrew language. This was the language of the ancient Jewish or Israelitish people, and of Canaan, which became their national homeland. They had left it as a mere tribe of about eighty persons, but under Moses and Joshua returned as a strong, young nation for those times.

This language had been developed by the ancient peoples, and by Moses' time was reduced to written form. Every language is first formed in spoken communication; then by using letters to fit the *sounds* of the speech, it is made into written form. Such societies as the American Bible Society and the Wycliffe Translators are still working on unwritten languages in various parts of the world, reducing them to written forms. They do this to get the Bible into the language of the people, as well as to give the people their language in writing.

Under the tutorship of Moses and others among them, the Israelites soon learned to be a reading people. Moses could then write for them God's words and laws, and they could learn them. As their great spiritual, moral, and political leader, he was considered by them to be the greatest man on earth in those days. And in every respect, his place in history has accorded him this honor, although not all modern people accept this.

God spoke to Moses face to face. He performed many mighty miracles, such as leading Israel out of Egypt, feeding them with manna for forty years, and bringing water to them out a rock in the wilderness. Moses himself did not do these miracles, but God used him as the human instrument through which He performed these great things. Since Israel's leaders knew that God spoke to Moses and gave him His word for the people, they were very careful to preserve all the writings of Moses so none of them would be lost. All through the centuries, they kept these as God's word and laws, adding to them such other writings as later men of God gave them from the Lord. But always, each prophet's or writer's works were kept separate as God's revelation to that particular person. In this way the books of the Old Testament came into being and took their place among the sacred writings of the Jewish people.

When God wished to reveal to His people, the Israelites, and leave for all men the record of how all things first began, by His Spirit He inspired Moses to write the account of these things. Now, from Adam's time until Moses' days, there were only about six or seven generations. Adam lived until just before Noah was born. Noah lived to see Abraham's grandfather, who in turn lived until Abraham was about seventy-five years old. Abraham was about one hundred years old when Isaac was born and lived until Jacob and Esau were at least well into their thirties, dying at the age of 175.

Joseph lived to be 110 years old, and by this time the oral traditions of all the stories of ancient times were well fixed in scores of minds, which in turn would carry them down until the days of Moses.

But Moses did *not* depend upon oral tradition for his information about the origins of all things. The Genesis account, written by Moses under direct inspiration of the Holy Spirit, is not the work of a traditionist, nor a copy of existing materi-

als. It is a fresh, new statement of the facts. Besides, there are many things about creation which no one could have been present to see or hear. Furthermore, the accurate and terse statement of scientific facts recorded in Genesis which would require an understanding of modern science. Only by inspiration from God could he have so correctly and accurately told these most remarkable stories of creation, our first parents, their sin, God's redemptive plan, and other matters.

In such matters as the origin of the Jewish nation and the covenant of God with Abraham, Moses could well have received aid from oral tradition. But here again are important details which only the Spirit of God could have supplied. Important matters in the Genesis account required divine inspiration for their correct statement.

As for the other four books — Exodus, Leviticus, Numbers, and Deuteronomy — Moses expressly states many times that the Lord spoke to him, telling him what to write or to say. Of their inspiration there can be no question.

Beginning with Joshua, the later books were written by leaders of Israel who were most certainly inspired by the Holy Spirit as they wrote. All these books or writings were faithfully preserved. They were carefully copied by later "scribes" of Israel when the old manuscripts would last no longer, thereby preserved in new manuscripts. This was repeated with the most exacting care until the Old Testament books were all completed.

Toward the close of Old Testament times, after many additional historical books and others had also been written, a final selection needed to be made of those books which were considered inspired of God. For this task a group of the most learned and pious Jewish leaders were selected, possibly under the direction of the

Courtesy, Oriental Institute

WRITING EQUIPMENT OF AN ANCIENT SCRIBE. *A palette, with two hollowed out sections, with writing reed and water jar.*

great and highly renowned scribe Ezra. Ezra is believed to have been the person who, more than any other, was responsible for collecting and arranging all the Old Testament books into an order which is nearly the same as that of today.

For this important work there had to be a *standard* set — a way to measure the worthiness of each book to be considered as inspired. It had to have certain characteristics which made it acceptable as an inspired book. It had to be true to the facts of the times and history; it had to be consistent within itself — it could not have within it any contradictory statements; it had to show that in its teachings it honored God and was true to all moral concepts of righteousness; and it had to be free from anything which would not be in keeping with a God-inspired work. It had to have a trustworthy author, so far as could be discerned. The test of the book itself, however, was even more important than its author. It had to bear the marks of divine origin, such as its claim by its author to be from God; its teachings about the nature and person of God, if any; true miracles, if any; and its truthfulness, purity and honor of God. When a book passed all these "rules" or standards, it was believed to be *inspired*.

It was then included in what was called the "canon." This word comes from a word which meant to measure something; also, a rod for measuring. In this way thirty-nine books were finally selected as the Old Testament. The word "testament" also means "covenant," and represents God's covenant or promises to His people.

THE NEW TESTAMENT

The "New Testament" simply means a new "covenant," or new promises which Christ brought to us when He came. He fulfilled the old covenant and brought to us the real meaning of that old covenant. His death was God's way of providing for all men to be saved. The New Testament is, therefore, God's new message of salvation for all men, through Christ. It is called the New Testament because it takes the place of the Old Testament in matters which relate to redemption, which is the most important part of the Bible, by far.

All twenty-seven books of the New Testament were written in the Greek language, which was the universal language of that day. Matthew may have been written first in Aramaic, the language which Jesus spoke in Palestine, and then translated into Greek. This is not known for certain now, but it is known that Matthew, as well as the other gospels, appeared in Greek.

The Book of Acts — the historical account of the early church and of Peter, John, Paul, and its other leaders — as well as all the epistles, was likewise written in Greek at first. The gospels tell the story of Christ and His work, Acts records the early beginnings of the church, and the various epistles give the rules and regulations, and set forth the doctrines of Christ and His church. The book of The Revelation properly closes the New Testament as God's last message to man and as the revelation of the final winding-up of all things on this earth.

THE SHRINE OF THE SCROLLS

Courtesy, Israel Information Service

QUMRAN WRITING TABLES

Courtesy, Palestine Archaeological Museum

THE DEAD SEA SCROLLS. *As far as is known no original writings, as they came from the hands of Bible authors (autographa), are in existence today. However, many ancient manuscripts have been discovered. The comparatively recent discovery of the Dead Sea Scrolls serves to confirm Christian confidence in the faithful transmission of the Bible.*

The scrolls are now permanently housed at Hebrew University in Jerusalem. Work on the identification of tens of thousands of manuscript fragments goes on, but it has already been established that the fragments contain writing from every book of the Bible except Esther.

EXHIBIT OF DEAD SEA SCROLLS

Courtesy, Israel Information Service

THE DOME OF THE SHRINE, WITH CYLINDER CONTAINING BOOK OF ISAIAH

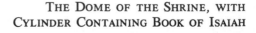

Courtesy, Israel Information Service

Within the first one hundred years after the birth of Christ, all the New Testament writers had finished their work and were gone. John, the last of the apostles to die, lived until possibly about A.D. 96.

The New Testament canon was finally fully settled about A.D. 325, after many years of earnest and prayerful discussions by great church leaders. The early Christians of the first century accepted almost all the books of the New Testament. The Revelation was the last written, close to the end of the first century. It especially, together with II Peter, James, and Jude, was held in question for sometime. After the first century, such writings as the Epistle of Barnabas, the Epistle of Clement (Bishop of Rome), The Teachings of the Twelve, and other books appeared. Some claimed inspiration for these works, and some of them were even read in the churches, but they were never given accord as Scriptures by the body of the church.

The canon of the New Testament was very similar to that of the Old in its rules or standards for accepting any book as inspired. Perhaps, in settling the New Testament canon, the fact that the churches as a whole had felt that these books were inspired by the Holy Spirit, and had so come to use and accept them, went as far as any single external evidence in their being accepted into the canon of Sacred Scripture. Once this canon was established, it remained with very little opposition.

THE APOCRYPHA

This term refers to some fourteen books written between the close of Malachi, in the Old Testament, and the opening days of the New Testament. It was never accepted by the Jewish people as part of their divine revelation. It was also rejected by the early Christian church as not being inspired as Scripture. However, much later the Roman Catholic Church accepted the Apocrypha as part of the Scriptures, and has included it in its present Bibles.

TRANSLATIONS AND VERSIONS OF THE BIBLE

Throughout the centuries many translations have been made of the Holy Scriptures into the languages common to the peoples of the world. The first of these was the Septuagint Version, made by about seventy scholars (from which it takes its name) at Alexandria, Egypt, around 250 B.C. It was a translation from the original Hebrew into the Greek, then the common language of the countries about the Mediterranean Sea and in Bible lands. It was used for several centuries and was most likely the Bible from which Jesus and His apostles made their quotations.

Several versions of the Bible or parts of

The Apocrypha

I and II Esdras

Tobit

Judith

Parts of Esther not in the
   Hebrew or Aramaic

The Wisdom of Solomon

Ecclesiasticus

Baruch

The History of Susanna

The Song of the Three Holy Children

The History of the Destruction of Bel
   and the Dragon

The Prayer of Manasses

I and II Maccabees

it appeared in the second century A.D., but none of them became popular. The first version to become popular was that of Jerome. He lived about A.D. 340-420, and was one of the Latin Fathers of the church. He was well known for his great learning. His translation was made early in the fifth century, possibly at Bethlehem, in Palestine. Here he spent the last years of his life in a monastery built by a wealthy Roman lady. His translation was known as the Vulgate and was in the Latin language, then fast becoming the common language of the areas of the Mediterranean and southern Europe. The word "vulgate" means *vulgar,* or *common*; not the same as our word does today — unrefined, or something ugly or of bad taste. It referred to the language of the common people. Except for a few Greek manuscript copies held by eminent persons, this version was the only Bible known to multitudes; it was a most popular and influential version for many centuries. A number of less-known versions were made from A.D. 400 to the sixteenth century, but none of them became popular.

The first English version, out of which our present English and American versions of the Bible grew, was probably that of John Wycliffe. It is not certain just how much of the actual work of translating Wycliffe did, but this has always been known as his translation. This work was completed about 1395 and remained in popular demand for a long time.

In 1523, William Tyndale began to translate the New Testament into English, working against much opposition from the English clergy. Finally he was forced to go to Germany, where he completed this work and published the first edition in 1526. Later, parts of the Old Testament were also translated by Tyndale. Some scholars contend that Tyndale's work, rather than Wycliffe's, was really the foundation of our present English versions. At least it played a very important role in foundation work.

Miles Coverdale's translation of the entire Bible into English was first printed about October 1535. In its entirety, his was the first of all *printed* English Bibles and is known as the Coverdale Bible.

Four less-popular versions followed: Matthew's Bible, the Great Bible (from its enormous size), the Breeches Bible (because it rendered "aprons" in Genesis 3:7, "breeches"), and the Bishops' Bible.

In 1609 the "Douai Version" appeared; it was a new English translation authorized by the Roman Catholic Church. With some changes, this is the same version used by that church today; it is now known as the Douay Version.

Perhaps the greatest undertaking ever ventured upon in any Bible translation of later times was the production of the King James Version of the Bible. It is known as the Authorized King James Version. It arose out of the proposal of the High Church, and the Low Church of England (the Anglican Church) together, appealing to King James I for a new version of the Bible. The king sketched out a plan to be followed. About fifty scholars worked on this version. It was completed after about two years and nine months of work which involved comparisons with all former translations of any merit, revisions and corrections, and then a thorough restudy of the whole work. It used the latest language of that time and was as up-to-date as possible. No pains were spared to make it the latest and best. An additional nine months was required for preparing the manuscript for printing.

When the King James Bible was released from the presses of Robert Barker,

The Latin Vulgate Bible

Until the 15th century copies of the Bible had to be prepared by hand. Most of these manuscripts followed Jerome's Latin Vulgate translation of A.D. 406, which became the authorized Bible of the Western Church. Until the invention of printing, most of the precious handscribed Bibles, such as the 13th century Bible pictured here, were unavailable to the general public.

The Wycliffe Bible

In order that Christians in England might be able to read the Bible in English, John Wycliffe translated the Latin Vulgate Version into English. It appeared in 1382. Although moveable type had not yet been invented, Wycliffe's translation was carried by his followers into many parts of England.

The Tyndale Bible

William Tyndale's English translation of the New Testament was published at Worms, Germany, in 1525. He translated from the original Greek, not from the Latin Vulgate. Six thousand copies of this first edition were printed. Tyndale suffered a martyr's death in 1536 near the city of Brussels, Belgium.

All Photos, Courtesy, American Bible Society

THE GREAT BIBLE

*This Bible is so named because
of its large folio size. It was
printed in 1539 and enjoyed immediate popularity. Notice that
the Bible illustrated includes
some of the Apocrypha.
The Old Testament ends with
the Second Book of Maccabees.
Under the reign of Mary, use
of this Bible was forbidden.*

THE BISHOPS' BIBLE

*Although this version of 1568 had
the support of ecclesiastical
authority, its inferiority made it
unacceptable both to scholars and
the masses. It derived its
name from the fact that eight of
its fifteen translators were bishops.*

THE KING JAMES BIBLE

*This version of the Bible, although
issued in 1611, still is a popular
version. It was the work of forty-
seven English scholars who
were appointed by King James I
of England and "translated . . .
by his majesty's command." The
King James Version is noted
particularly for its beautiful
cadence and its prose harmonies.*

```
┌─────────────────────────────────────┐
│                                     │
│         Books of the Bible          │
│                                     │
│   Old Testament            39       │
│   New Testament            27       │
│                          ─────      │
│                                     │
│   Total                    66       │
│                                     │
│    Approximately Forty Authors      │
│                                     │
└─────────────────────────────────────┘
```

London, England, in 1611, it became an instant success. Thousands of copies were purchased immediately, despite a short-lived wave of criticism from various quarters. Multiplied millions of copies of this Bible have been sold, and it remains today the best seller among Bibles in the world. It has become by far the most popular of all Bible versions and will doubtless remain in demand for a long time to come. All quotations and references in this work are taken from the King James Version.

A revision of the King James — the Revised Version of 1881, in England, and 1901 in America, is one of the most accurate versions ever made, but has not become so successful as the King James. The two latest revisions have been the Revised Standard Version of 1957, in America, and the New English Bible revision, of 1961. Neither of these will likely attain the fame of the King James Version proper.

Our Bible began to be written about 1500 B.C., and it was completed about A.D. 100 — about sixteen hundred years in the making. Some thirty-six to forty penmen wrote various parts of it. These men ranged all the way from Moses, the mighty scholar and law-giver, to kings, prophets, priests, common laborers, public servants, political leaders, and at least one physician. These writers were from almost every walk of life and represented both extremes — the very wealthy and the very poorly educated. The aged, such as Moses, Paul, and John, joined hands with the younger, such as David, who wrote many of his psalms while still reasonably young, and Luke, whose Gospel and Acts comprise almost one-half of the New Testament, probably written before he reached the meridian of life.

Every strata of culture was represented among the writers and they spoke the universal language of human need and understanding in their writings. The soldier and the statesman joined hands with the shepherd and the plowman; mighty men of fame, the lowly and unknown — each made his contribution to this sacred Book.

Above all, God by His Holy Spirit so inspired and guided the writers that, although they used their own styles and their personalities flowed out through their writings, they penned the truth without error. In this way we have both a human and yet a divine book — the Word of God, truly and fully conveyed *through* mortal man *to* mortal man, without error, and with the stamp of the Deity upon every page!

This is the story, told very briefly, of how we got our Bible. We hope every reader will enjoy reading all about each book of the Bible — when and how it came to be written, to whom it was written, its purpose, its author, and also the great things which each book teaches.

May God bless each reader and grant him an understanding of this greatest of books and the wisdom to put into practice the truths which he discovers as he reads.

The Pentateuch

Genesis

The word "Genesis" means *beginnings*. It comes from a Greek word, first used in the earliest translation of the Old Testament, that known as the Septuagint Version. In the Hebrew Bible, the word for the name of this book also meant *beginnings*.

Another Hebrew word, which also meant "beginnings," occurs ten times in Genesis, at the opening of each of the ten sections of this book, as follows:

"These are the generations of . . ." (1) The heavens and the earth, 2:4; (2) Adam, 5:1; (3) Noah, 6:9; (4) Noah's sons, 10:1; (5) Shem, 11:10; (6) Terah, 11:27; (7) Ishmael, 25:12; (8) Isaac, 25:19; (9) Esau, 36:1; (10) Jacob, 37:2.

We shall see a bit later that there were many *beginnings* in Genesis.

TO WHOM

The book of Genesis was especially written for the children of Israel. They were first to receive it; and they kept it for hundreds of years, preserving it for all men. But this book is also universal in its language. Its message is for all people of all time. It is also the foundation book. Without this book we could not understand the rest of the Bible.

PURPOSE

There were at least two reasons for this book: 1. It provided the correct historical background for Israel, its racial history and its national development. It also pro-

vided a prophetic forecast of Israel's place and work among the other nations, and Israel's final Messianic mission, that which God raised up Israel to do. 2. Genesis provides for all men the correct world view of creation, of sin, and of redemption, as these relate to God's first dealings with mankind. This is perhaps its most important message to man; it is the universal purpose of the book.

These two purposes help us today to understand both the place of Israel, or the Jews, in God's plan and in our own historical and religious background.

Genesis introduces us to the covenant God made with Adam (3), and with Abraham (12, 15, 17). In this covenant He promised to bring Christ into the world through the nation of Israel, to be the Savior of all men who would believe upon Him. Be sure to trace the development of this covenant, or promise, its fulfillment, and the prophetic mention of it as we go through the Old Testament. The whole Old Testament should be studied with this covenant and its relationships to Israel, and to us, in mind.

The main message of Genesis for us today, then, is to help us understand creation, sin, God's plan of redemption, and our responsibility to God.

TIME

Fragments of old writings, such as the Babylonian Creation and Flood Stories, and the Code of Hammurabi, have survived, but their main value is in showing how ancient was the art of writing, something of the character of that writing, and a glimpse of the civilization of that far-away day. Genesis, however, has brought down for all people and for all time information of the most vital importance. It is one of the world's most highly-valued books.

This book was most likely written during the sojourn of the children of Israel in the wilderness, after leaving Egypt. It may have been written during the earlier part of that forty-year span, and so could have been written somewhere around 1450-1420 B.C.

The time covered by the story of Genesis is roughly about two thousand years, maybe a little more. The writing itself may have required only a short time. It was possibly originally written either on clay tablets or leather rolls, or perhaps on papyrus — a heavy, crude form of paper. It was later copied onto more durable materials.

AUTHORSHIP

The most ancient Jewish records state that Moses wrote Genesis, which along with the other four books form the Pentateuch — the first five books of the Bible. The oldest historical references and traditions likewise declare that he was the author of this book. The church has also accepted this as true from the most early times.

The most important evidence for Moses' authorship, however, is that Christ Himself referred to Moses as the writer of these books, and so did the New Testament writers (see Matt. 19:7-9; Luke 24-27; John 7:19).

The vast amount of minor detail, as well as much historical material in Genesis, could not possibly have been known by Moses without some recourse to information. How did he get this information? Looking at it for a moment from the human side, consider the following: Adam lived until well over two hundred years after Methuselah was born, who in turn lived until Noah was about six hundred years old. Noah lived to talk with Terah, and the latter lived well into Abraham's days. Abraham lived to talk with Joseph, who also lived until Amram was a young man, and Amram lived to see Moses in his youth. According to this genealogy there is an unbroken line of seven men from Adam to Moses. Moses could have received much of his material from oral tradition.

In ancient times writing was not as easy as today; oral tradition was much more dependable. Much later among the Jews, the scribes are known to have memorized verbatim whole passages of the Bible. It is not unlikely that Moses had at hand much of the material from this oral tradition, in accurate form.

But interesting as this is, it is far more important to remember that Moses was *inspired* by the Holy Spirit to write this account. There are many details and facts here which he could never have gotten from any other source but directly from God by revelation. Whatever he may or may not have had from other sources, the final writing was inspired, superintended, and guided by the Holy Spirit, so as to make the account accurate, free from error, and fully dependable.

From the human standpoint, Moses was well prepared for his great task of writing. He was trained "in all the wisdom of the Egyptians" (Acts 7:22), as

→

NOAH AND THE FLOOD. *This engraved crystal composition of two forms — a boat shape resting against a mountain peak — symbolizes the story of the Flood. While the dove hovers above, signaling the abatement of the waters by the olive branch in its beak, Noah embraces his wife. Within their arms they shelter a young buck and doe. Giraffes, elephants, and lions are engraved below.*

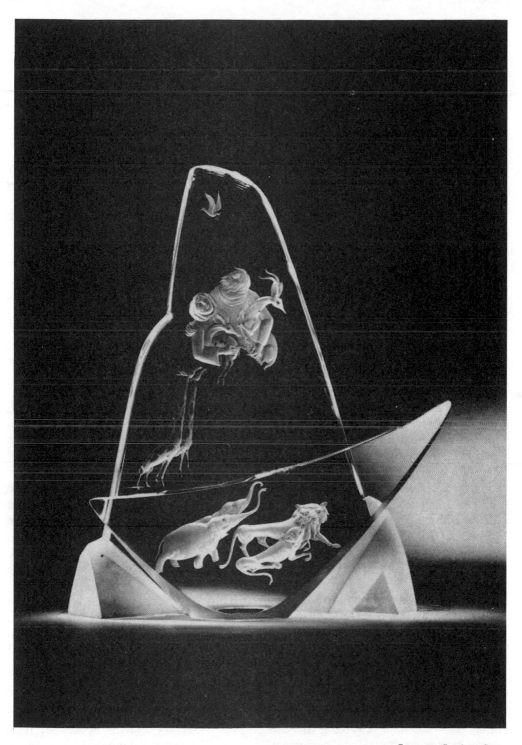

well as having excellent spiritual preparation in his forty years alone with God in the Midian desert. His great fund of knowledge was used to the best possible advantage. Although the words, "Thus saith the Lord," are not found here as in the other four books, Genesis is doubtless inspired as well.

Genesis is entirely different from the other books of the Bible. It deals largely with the early history of the race, and the covenant basis for starting of the Jewish nation. It lists few commands of God, and whenever moral precepts and statements of *ought* and *ought not* in conduct are made, they occur most frequently in the stories of the people, the actors in the historical drama which the book presents. The cultural progress, moral lessons, religious teachings, and redemptive truths are somewhat tied together in this great book.

Genesis is indeed the book of *beginnings*. It relates the beginnings of time, life, marriage, family, worship, human government, and civilization; also sin, sacrifice, sorrow, death, and redemption from sin. Crime, as well as the development of character, begins here. Cain and Abel (4), represent both of these facts. The beginning of nations, of war and of peace are also listed here, as well as the beginnings of industry, personal ownership of property, and the right of possession. Here, too, began the age-old struggle between good and evil (3) and the story of how God provided redemption for the first sinning pair. The basic redemptive covenant of all time is stated here (3:15); it was to be fulfilled in Christ long centuries later.

Genesis has been called the "seed-bed" of every important doctrine taught in the Bible. It would be a rewarding study for young people to trace the "beginnings"

of all the things listed above and also the first references to various Christian doctrines, such as faith, forgiveness, salvation, etc.

One might outline the book briefly as follows:

I. The Creation Story, 1:1—2:3
II. Human life before Abraham, 2:4—11:26
III. The beginnings of the Hebrew nation, 11:27—50:26

The first section has sometimes been called the "Creation Hymn," the "Epic of Creation," or the "Poem of the Dawn." This section, while strictly historical in the facts it relates, contains poetic elements in the original. Sometimes it has been also called the "Song of Creation," the oldest song in existence. Some scholars believe it first may have been revealed to Adam, and then passed down the ages by oral tradition.

At one time some questioned how Moses could have written the Pentateuch when writing was believed to be a much later invention. Long since, however, the archaeologists' spades came to the rescue and provided ample evidence that writing was in practice centuries before Moses' time. Stories of creation, of the flood, and the Tower of Babel were in circulation among the ancient nations long before the time of Moses. In fact, it is now quite certain that the people who lived before the time of the flood also had the advantage of writing, as seen from the many tablets believed to date back to this time.

An interesting study of Genesis is to trace the following major characters and the part they played in the book:

1. Adam — Father of the Race (creation and fall)
2. Noah — Preserver of the Race (ministry and the flood. See New Testament references)

3. Abraham — Father of the Faithful (covenant, faith, and faults)
4. Isaac — Son of Promise (consecration and following)
5. Jacob — Name of a Nation — Israel (children and flight from Padan-aram)
6. Joseph — Preserver of a Nation (character, fortitude, and reward)

Special attention should be given to the fact that not only was Abraham important because of his faith and obedience, but primarily because he was chosen of God to head the *race* which in turn was to produce the *nation* out of which Christ would come into the world!

Joseph's funeral instructions (50:24-26) are evidence of his faith in the covenant which God had made to give Israel the Promised Land, and his bones which Israel carried with them when they went up from Egypt were a symbol of that faith (Exod. 13:19).

Genesis is the introduction to Exodus, for Genesis ends in Egypt, while Exodus presents the new nation on its way back

to the land in which the stories of Genesis occurred.

GREAT THINGS IN GENESIS

The most *outstanding stories* of the book, together with the chapters in which they are found, may be listed as:

1. Creation, temptation, and fall, 1-3
2. Cain and Abel and their sacrifices, 4
3. Noah, the flood and the new beginning, 6-10
4. Tower of Babel and confusion of languages, 11
5. Call of Abraham, his faith and obedience, 12-18
6. Destruction of Sodom and Gomorrah; saving of Lot, 19
7. Birth of Isaac and his offering on Mount Moriah, 21-22
8. Marriage of Isaac and Rebekah, 24

SODOM. *A potash works and a salt mine are now in operation at the southern end of the Dead Sea, the traditional site of Sodom. It is thought to be buried under water.*

Courtesy, Charles F. Pfeiffer

Courtesy, Ashmolean Museum

9. Stories of Jacob and Esau, 25-28
10. Jacob in Padan-aram, 29-31
11. Jacob's wrestling; his new name, 32
12. Meeting of Jacob and Esau, 33
13. Joseph, his trials and triumphs, 37-50

In these stories and elsewhere in this book a number of *great truths* are taught, truths which every young person should learn well:

1. The sin of Adam and Eve, their loss of Eden, and Cain's terrible sin, making him the first murderer, show how fearfully expensive it is to sin. They illustrate the fact that one cannot "do wrong and get by"; they show something of the awful *cost of disobedience.*

If you will watch for it as you read through the Bible, you will see that disobedience to God and His laws always results in terrible cost.

2. A look at Cain's punishment and the story of the flood shows that God will not allow the wicked to go unpunished. God is bound to punish sinners who will not repent and turn to Him. He is a God of justice as well as of mercy. This is why only through Christ is there mercy and salvation for the sinful, for Christ took our place and satisfied the divine demand for justice. If we accept Christ, He stands between us and eternal punishment. If not, we have no other escape from punishment for our sins.

3. God also rewarded those who were righteous. God is not forgetful of obedi-

---

← THE SUMERIAN KING LIST. *This prism with its cuneiform writing (wedged-shaped) lists the names of Sumerian kings. It was compiled sometime between 2250 and 2000 B.C. and gives the earliest traditional rulers who reigned before the Flood.*

ence and loving service to Him. Enoch was "translated that he should not see death" (5:24; Heb. 11:5). Noah and his family were saved by obedience to God's command to build the ark, and were rewarded as the beginners of a new world order (6-8).

4. The lesson at the Tower of Babel is that man cannot work out his salvation nor build his own way to heaven. "For by grace are ye saved through faith . . . not of works, lest any man should boast" (Eph. 2:8, 9). Evidently this was an anti-God movement — a determination to concentrate man's power, rule the world as he wished, and ignore God. Read chapter 11 well.

5. God chose Abraham for a grand, universal purpose (12). He was to become father of "a great nation" (the Jews), as listed in the first covenant of God with him (12:2; 15:1-7). Later this covenant was expanded so that he was to become "a father of many nations" (17: 1-16; note v. 4). But in this covenant was another phrase, probably not well understood by Abraham; it concerned the universal aspect of it. His seed was to become as the "dust of the earth" (13: 16) and as the "stars of the heavens" (15:5). Scholars believe that these two statements have a twofold meaning. His seed would be as the "dust of the earth" — earthly children, the Jews — and as the "stars of the heavens" — spiritual children, all truly godly people of the Old Testament and Christians of the New Testament church. We are all the spiritual children of Abraham.

So Abraham's call was for the twofold purpose of beginning, and shaping the spiritual life of the Jewish nation, so that Christ might be born out of that nation, as the world's Redeemer. This is really the great place of Abraham in Bible history. He is called "the father of all them that believe" (Rom. 4:11), and Christians are said to be "blessed with faithful Abraham" (Gal. 3:9).

Faith and obedience are the twins of salvation. To walk with God, every Christian must have both, just as one must have both legs to walk normally. One cannot have the one without the other; they are inseparable.

6. Isaac is a beautiful type of Christ in his willingness to die at his father's orders (22:1-14). He was a child of faith, his birth having been a miracle, because his mother was an old woman (Heb. 11:11); his birth was entirely out of the ordinary. His name means "laughter," or happiness, because his coming meant joy to his parents. Christ was also a Son of miraculous birth whose coming brought "joy to the world."

7. Sometimes Bible students point out that Isaac and Rebekah's marriage has beautiful spiritual meanings (24). Abraham, representing God, our Father, sent his servant Eliezer, representing the Holy Spirit, to take a bride for his son, representing Christ. Their marriage is symbolic of Christ and His Church being united forever at His coming.

Another lesson for all young people is found in the fact that Isaac's bride was chosen from among the family of believers in God. No Christian should ever marry one who is *not* a Christian, however good the unsaved one may otherwise be (II Cor. 6:14-16). Believers and unbelievers must never be "yoked together" in marriage.

8. Esau's selling of his birthright for the "mess of pottage" (25:29-34; Heb. 12:16-17) is an illustration of people who are willing to sacrifice their souls for the sinful pleasures of life. Afterward, when they would turn and save those youthful

years, however bitter their remorse, there is "no way to yesterday," and the days once wasted are forever gone. Think twice before sacrificing the best you have for mere folly.

Jacob's deceitful trick in stealing the birthright blessing (27:1-29) shows something of the depths to which a man will stoop to have his own way and gain his ambitions. He used his mother, deceived and broke his father's heart, and invited his brother's wrath for all time, just to "get ahead." Although he got what he wanted, he paid a price far too dear for it, and blotched his good name. On the other hand, Esau reaped what he had sown in selling the birthright.

God intended for Jacob to have the birthright blessing, but He certainly did not intend for him to secure it in this lying, crooked way! It never pays to get ahead of God in trying to help the Lord work out His plans. God would have had an easier solution, graced Jacob, and doubtless made him a blessed example for the ages, had Jacob waited upon Him.

9. Jacob met God at Bethel (28), and he became a changed man in many ways. But it took the night of wrestling at Peniel (32) to bring him into the needed position with God, to be the man God desired him to be. Some twenty years later he met Esau again (33). Though not stated in the text, it is most likely that Jacob made some proper apologies to Esau at that time. Their fellowship seems to have been temporarily restored; but the hatred between the two resulting nations has never subsided to this very day. The Jews of Jacob's descendants and the Arabs of Esau's descendants, though tribal or national cousins, today still hate each other thoroughly. They have never ceased to war between themselves throughout the thirty-seven centuries

Courtesy, Matson Photo Service

since that day when Jacob by his deed of deceit set Esau against him.

What a lesson of warning against deceitfulness, getting ahead at other people's expense, and other evil things along this line! Life is too short and the consequences of one's deeds far too long to ever allow oneself to get involved in such petty things.

10. Jacob's wrestling match with God (32) is a most blessed illustration of what many Christians today need to experience. Jacob apparently loved God at this time, for the angels came to protect him as he journeyed (32:1, 2). The Bible does not say, "The angel of the Lord encampeth around about sinners, cutthroats, swindlers, and cheats." Such Jacob has been called by those who have not read their Bibles aright! No, God's angel encamps around about "them that fear him, and delivereth them" (Ps. 34:7). This simply means that Jacob was God's child; Jacob feared and loved Him. But evidently there was yet something lacking in Jacob's life. He could not meet Esau the next day in his present state, although he had met his father-in-law, and protested his honesty (Read carefully 31:37-42.)

Alone with God, Jacob wrestled with

RACHEL'S TOMB. *Genesis tells us that Jacob's wife Rachel "was buried in the way to Ephrath, which is Bethlehem." Traditionally, this site has been known as the site of Rachel's grave. The mosque-like building dates back to the fifteenth century, A.D.*

the divine Wrestler until he experienced a new touch of God, which was to result in the change of his name and a new disposition. He was no longer merely Jacob "the heel-grasper," ambitious, selfish, but *Israel* — "prince of the house of God." Ah, what a change! His whole life took on a new complexion from that day forward, and we do not see him again wobbling in his life for God as he did before. Whatever may have happened to Jacob there, the same thing or its equivalent needs to happen in the lives of God's people today if they are to be truly useful and blessed in His service.

Once again God was working out in Jacob's life, just as he had in Abraham's (17:1-16), the necessary spiritual qualities to make him fitted for his place in carrying on the covenant line. Through Jacob was to come the world's Redeemer, and He must have a worthy ancestor to spiritually guide the beginning nation from which He was to come. This story

SHECHEM. *First mention of Shechem is made in Genesis 12:6, where we are told that Abraham built an altar there. The activities of Jacob centered about Shechem. He sent Joseph to his brothers who were tending their father's flocks near the city.*

The first archaeological excavations at Shechem were made in the early 1900's. Recent work at the site has provided a wealth of information about the ancient city.

Shown here are remains of the "East Gate," indicating rebuilding from time to time (1); the combination of a vat, a platter-stone, and a store jar unearthed in a residential district of the eighth century B.C., suggesting the making of wine or olive oil, or perhaps the process of dyeing

(2); foundation lines of a residential dwelling (3); and a complex of walls at the East Gate, showing two pairs of large, carefully cut basalt blocks on each side, dating back to about 1575 B.C. (4).

All Photos, Courtesy, Drew-McCormick Archaeological Expedition

Photo by Lee C. Ellenberger

Photo by James T. Stewart

Photo by Lee C. Ellenberger

Photo by Lee C. Ellenberger

with its divine Wrestler — whom some believe was the Angel of the Covenant — is a very important one in the progressive unfolding of the redemptive plan of God for the ages. It also shows that God deals with those who will walk with and obey Him, making their lives no longer a series of defeats and disappointments, but lives of victory and usefulness.

11. Joseph is a beautiful type of Christ, although not so described in the Scriptures (37-50). One sees Joseph first in humility, unnoticed by his brothers, but beloved of his father and busy about his father's business (37). Then he is hated of his brothers and put away by them, and even betrayed and sold for the price of a slave, as was Jesus (37:25-28).

But God was with Joseph, and at last he comes out of his cruel treatment as ruler of Egypt, and saves his people from starvation (41-50), just as Christ came to save His people from their sins (Matt. 1:21). This, again, is God's way of preserving His people for the coming of the Savior.

SEMITES ENTERING EGYPT. *The Israelites who entered Egypt during the days of Joseph may have looked like these Semites of the nineteenth century B.C. depicted on the walls of Egyptian tombs.*

Courtesy, The Oriental Institute

Lessons of great value here may be these: First, the old adage, "You can't keep a good man down," is so well illustrated in this story. How true this is in life! "Truth, though crushed to the ground, will rise again."

Second, this story gives proof of the statement, "Surely the wrath of man shall praise thee" (Ps. 76:10). Although his brothers "in wrath" sold Joseph, God made it work to His purpose.

Third, when dear old Jacob, hearing the demands of his sons, cried, "All these things are against me" (42:36), he little realized that these very things were the means God was using to preserve both him and his family. How often we complain at the dealings of God, when for us it is the very best thing!

Fourth, how often, too, must these brothers of Joseph have reaped their evil deed in smitten consciences (42:21). And doubtless, during these sad years of missing Joseph, Jacob remembered his own deed of deceit toward Esau.

This whole story of Joseph is loaded with reminders: "Be sure your sin will find you out" (Num. 32:33); "Whatsoever a man soweth, that shall he also reap" (Gal. 6:7).

Genesis witnesses the beginnings of the covenant for Christ's coming (3:15) and

traces the progress of God's plan in the beginnings of the nation out of which Christ was to come, and its removal to Egypt. The whole story of Genesis may be said in a general way to be the story of God's purpose and preparation to bring Christ into the world to save men. If this thought is held uppermost in the reading, one will see this purpose working out at every major development in the whole book.

Beginning is the key word, and *covenant* the major thought of this book. Redemption, though not made as plain as in the following books, is nonetheless the major theme of this book. Here it is seen in the shadows of preparation — at sunrise, shall we say? There it is seen in the more full day of its symbolic revelation.

Significantly, Genesis opens with creation and life abounding, and ends with a "coffin in Egypt." It opens with a beautiful pair in Edenic paradise, but it closes with the divinely-chosen family in the shadow of bondage; but out of it all comes the slowly developing plan to save mankind, according to God's desire.

Genesis is the foundation book of the Bible, upon which the rest of the structure stands. As such it is broad, deep, and of bed-rock nature. Every major

truth of the Bible is in some way embedded here, though often in dim shadows only. But one must become well acquainted with this book and get a good, clear picture of all its teachings to truly appreciate the rest of the Bible.

Memory Verses

"And I will put enmity between thee and the woman, and between thy seed and her seed; and it shall bruise thy head, and thou shalt bruise his heel" (3:15).

"The scepter shall not depart from Judah, nor a lawgiver from between his feet, until Shiloh come; and unto him shall the gathering of the people be" (49:10).

Exodus

Exodus means "going out of," or "departure," and has special reference to Israel's going out of Egypt. This title was first listed in the Septuagint Version of the Old Testament.

TO WHOM

It was written for the Israelites as an immediate historical statement of their deliverance, and for their children who would follow them. Possibly the children and the generations to come were more in the writer's mind than the immediate group there in the wilderness.

As a book of early national history, this work would always have great meaning for the Jews, and later for the whole Christian world. It was in this sense universal in its scope.

PURPOSE

The major purpose of the book seems to have been to set forth God's dealings with His people in their deliverance from slavery, which is a type of sin; and, in the wider sense, to give the Jewish nation a correct background for their very own purpose for existence as a nation. The mere historical statement of their exodus from Egypt was only incidental to the over-all purpose of God for them in their lives and their place in the world about them.

Too often when reading the Bible, one fails to see the constant universal scope of its deeper meaning and over-all purpose. God apparently does nothing with only a local and personal purpose in mind. Even the salvation of the individual person has a far wider scope than his personal enjoyment of salvation and final escape from eternal punishment. This is made plain in Christ's great prayer for His disciples. Note that He prays for their oneness with Himself and His Father; first, that they "may be one in us," and second, "that the world may believe that thou hast sent me" (John 17:21). Here the ultimate purpose of the individual's salvation is God's glory, and through it the world becomes convinced of Christ's true mission in it.

The most important purpose of this book seems to be to set forth God's fulfillment of His covenant with Abraham and to show His progressive revelation of Himself in His plan for the final fulfillment of this covenant in the ultimate coming of Christ. This latter truth was not seen then by the Israelites, but in the light of its fulfillments, it is apparent to today's reader. The ancient Israelite, however, did see God's fulfillment of His covenant with Abraham in preparations to bring Israel back into Canaan as He had promised to Abraham (Gen. 17). Genesis, then, has as its primary and immediate purpose the tracing of this part of this fulfillment.

TIME

The time from Jacob's migration into Egypt to that of the Exodus was about 430 years (12:40, 41). The time covered by this book is believed to be about 145 years, as it covers the period from the death of Joseph to the setting up of the Tabernacle at the foot of Mount Sinai.

Beyond doubt, the book was not written until all its historical references had been accomplished and properly cataloged as they occurred. It was probably written during the first part of the sojourn in the wilderness.

AUTHORSHIP

There has never been any question among the most ancient Jews that Moses wrote the first five books of the Bible. The Christian church as a whole has also accepted this as historical from its earliest days.

With the beginning of Exodus, Moses wrote largely the story of his own life, bound up with that of Israel and its varied experiences, as recorded in this and

Courtesy, The University Museum, Philadelphia

STELE OF RAMESES II. *Rameses II (right) stands before his god Amon-Re. Between the two figures are various vessels, probably booty from his military exploits, now offered to his god. Although the evidence is not decisive, Rameses II is thought to be the pharaoh of the Exodus.*

the following three books. These four books alone constitute about one-seventh of the whole Bible; they are two-thirds as large as the New Testament.

Moses was well prepared for his great life work. His Egyptian training supposedly included all kinds of hardships, fastings, long marches, and military preparations, as well as learning in the classical lore and history of the past. Thus he was prepared for much that he needed to know in these fields while leading Israel through the wilderness.

Since much of the history recorded in the first part of this book occurred in Egypt, here is the place to note several Biblical connections with Egypt. Abraham once sojourned there for a while, as did Jacob; Joseph was once its ruler. The Hebrew, or Jewish, nation was born there from their descendants. Moses was the adopted son of one of its queens; he was trained in all its arts and sciences. The religion of Egypt was calf-worship, a religion into which the Northern Kingdom of Israel later lapsed. Jeremiah is believed to have died in Egypt, and from the Babylonian captivity to the time of Christ, a sizable Jewish population always lived there. The Septuagint Version was made there, and Christ Himself spent some time there in His infancy. Egypt finally became an important center for the early Christian church.

This book may be briefly outlined as follows:

  I.   Birth and persecution of a nation, 1-4
  II. Beginning of deliverance, 5-11
  III. The Passover and the Exodus proper, 12-14
  IV. Song of deliverance, 15
  V.   Wilderness travels, 16-19
  VI. Sinai and the Ten Commandments, 20

Courtesy, The Metropolitan Museum of Art

BRICKMAKING IN EGYPT. *This wall painting from an Egyptian tomb at Thebes shows slaves making bricks. Israelites performed such work while in Egypt.*

VII.   Laws and statutes of Israel, 21-23

VIII.   The Tabernacle, a house of worship, 24-31

IX.   Preparation of the people and the Tabernacle for worship, 32-40

This book abounds with revelations of the nature of God and His requirements of man. It may be said to tremble with mercies and bristle with the wrath of justice. It reveals to man a holy God and the requirements for man's spiritual life if he is to follow Him. It is strongly related to God's covenant with Abraham.

GREAT THINGS IN EXODUS

Among its *outstanding stories* are the following:

1.   Birth and training of Moses, 2:1-10

2.   A human attempt to do a divine work; its failure, 2:11-15

3.   Moses and the burning bush, 3:1-22

4.   The Passover story, 12-13

5.   Deliverance at the Red Sea, 13

6.   The Ten Commandments, 20

7.   Moses and the elders at the feet of God, 24

8. Aaron and the golden calf, 32

The latter part of this book deals with the consecration of priests for their service, the Tabernacle and its furnishings, and the order of worship.

Among the *great truths* found in this book are the following:

1. Israel in Egypt at first grew peacefully, but later felt the stern blows of persecution (1). God often permits us to prosper in ease, but to move us on into deeper spiritual depths, He may permit the hand of oppression to rest upon us, as He did in ancient Israel. Nothing happens to God's people by chance — it is all within the purpose of God.

Had Israel been at ease in Egypt, they likely would never have left under Moses' leadership. God often has to thrust out His people by strange experiences, to lead them into closer communion with Him and to help them find His highest will for their lives.

2. Moses was chosen of God long before Moses chose to follow the Lord. So, likewise, all men have been made God's choice, if not for special service, certainly for redemption (John 3:16, 17; Rev. 22:17).

When Moses was forty years old, he made his great decision (2:11; Acts 7:23; Heb. 11:24-27). This choice was just as definite for him that day as one's turning to Christ is this day. Although God had chosen Moses for a great work, only after Moses turned to God was he truly God's man.

3. Even at this juncture, Moses had much to learn. He was full of zeal in his new-found joy and determination, but "not according to knowledge." Moses' first attempt to reveal himself to Israel and become their leader ended in tragic and dismal failure (2:11-15). God had chosen him, but He had not yet *sent*

him. How well this illustrates the human attempts to do divine service, which so often ends in futility and despair. Only when one is conscious of divine sanction and presence, can he do a successful work for God. Always remember, a *call to service for God* is a *call to prepare* first! Moses was only half-prepared; he had his formal education, but not his heart and soul training.

4. Forty years later Moses met God at the burning bush in the Midian desert (3:1—4:17). It must have required much patience to understand the "silent years" when it seemed God did not speak; there was little evidence of any purpose in Moses' life. But he had learned his first lesson well — never venture where divine leadings have not promoted! One often wonders, too, what may have been the thoughts of our Lord in His human nature during His "silent years" from twelve to thirty, of which we know absolutely nothing of Him or His work. But they were as necessary to His redemptive work as His last brief years of flaming ministry and popularity, by which we now know Him so well. Possibly the most important part of Moses' preparation for his work lay within the forty silent years of development in the "University of the Desert."

Moses' commission at the burning bush was the greatest task any human leader ever undertook. He was to be forty years in accomplishing it, but behind him lay eighty years of training and preparation. He was now ready, but he was far more hesitant to go, even with God's command upon him, than before, without it. Youth needs to ponder this lesson well — the *greatest work* is only done with the *best preparation* possible.

5. The heart of Exodus centers in the Passover story and the deliverance that

1

THE TABERNACLE. *Notice the Holy of Holies in the partially completed tabernacle (1). Completely around the outside of the tabernacle were the "hangings of the court" (2). The ark (3) contained a pot of manna, Aaron's rod, and the Ten*

2

Commandments. Shown in front of the embroidered veil which separated the Holy Place from the Holy of Holies are the seven lamps burning olive oil, the altar of incense, and the table of show bread (4). Models by R. H. Mount, Jr.

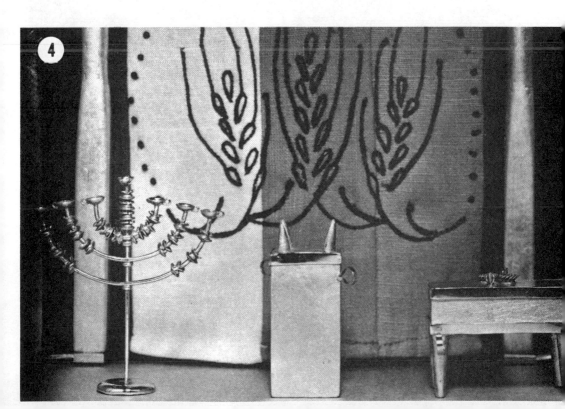

followed. This great story shows God's redemptive love for Israel, and His justice vindicated upon the disobedient Egyptians.

The Passover lamb foreshadowed Jesus, the "Lamb of God," and the sprinkling of the blood upon the lintel and door

MOUNT SINAI. *This mountain in the southern part of the Sinai Peninsula is the traditional Mount Sinai or Horeb where Moses received the Ten Commandments. Today it is called Jebel Musa (Arabic for Mount Moses).*

Courtesy, Matson Photo Service

posts speaks of obedience to God. Only as we accept Christ's sacrifice at Calvary in obedience to the command, "Repent ye, and believe the gospel" (Mark 1: 15), can we hope for deliverance from the wrath of God. "For even Christ our passover is sacrificed for us . . ." (I Cor. 5:7), Paul tells us, referring back to the Passover as the foreshadow of Christ.

6. The miraculous deliverance from the Egyptians at the Red Sea reveals another aspect of God's redemptive work. He not only had the *right* to redeem Is-

rael as His people, but also the *power* to do so. He could protect what He had purchased, finish what He had begun, and deliver those who trusted in Him.

The same sea which became a glorious victory for Israel in *obedience* became a tragedy for Egypt in disobedience. Life is filled with similar occasions. Victory or defeat often hinges not so much upon the thing itself as the motive and attitude toward it.

7. At Sinai God gave the people the Ten Commandments as the heart of moral law. While delivered for the first time in formal presentation, later to be made into a written code, this was by no means the beginning of moral law. In establishing human government and proper sanctions of moral law, God had declared to Noah, "Whoso sheddeth man's blood, by man shall his blood be shed . . ." (Gen. 9:6).

King Abimelech understood well the sin of adultery, and when he discovered he had mistakenly taken Abraham's wife, he trembled to think of the sin he had almost committed. (Read carefully Gen. 20:1-16.) In this same story he also reproved Abraham, as well as Sarah, for telling a half-truth.

The moral law, then, was "written upon the fleshly tables of the hearts" of mankind long before it was engraved upon tables of stone for Israel. Man has within his very nature a sense of the moral laws of God, as may be seen from the fact that all heathen people, however backward, have some sense of certain moral laws, as seen from missionary literature (Rom. 2:14, 15).

The Ten Commandments are no part of the law which was "fulfilled in Christ" except as His grace now gives power to keep and honor this code of law. The laws of sacrifice, rites, and ceremonies of the religious code of Israel were fulfilled in Christ, for He was the fulfillment of all they foreshadowed. The moral law is as binding as ever upon all men, and though we are not saved in the keeping of it, it is nonetheless required. One certainly cannot be a liar, an adulterer, and a profaner of God's name and yet be a Christian.

8. Moses and the elders of Israel were called to the mountain to meet God, and there they tarried for many days; they ate and drank in His presence. Yet, they did not "see God" in the physical sense but enjoyed the mystic presence of Him (24:1-18).

This story reveals God's ability to communicate Himself to His people. Although shrouded in mystery, God can become very real to His people. Christ has brought God to man in a new and closer way. "He that hath seen me hath seen the Father . . ." Jesus told Philip (John 14:9). In prayer we now have communion with God through Christ by the Holy Spirit. James exhorted, "Draw nigh to God, and He will draw nigh to you" (James 4:8).

9. How soon the human spirit's religious fervor can cool and its devotions change when not wholly set upon God, is seen in the story of Aaron's golden calf (32:1-14). Moses was on the mountain with God for forty days. The evil-hearted among the people wanted to go back to Egypt, so they persuaded good old soft-hearted Aaron to make a golden calf as a symbol of submission to the old Egyptian ways.

Egypt's religion was calf-worship. To go back bearing a golden calf would show the Egyptians that Israel had come back willing to accept Egypt's religion and way of life. Doubtless, with the pharaoh of the oppression dead, they

APIS. *The worship of gods in the form of animals was common in Egypt. The sacred bull was popular.*

A DESERT WADI. *Although dry almost the entire year, occasionally a heavy rain fills the riverbed with rushing water. Israel traveled through terrain such as this.*

hoped to fare better now upon their return.

Satan often tries to persuade the believer that living in the worldly way again would not prove as galling and disappointing as it once did. For them to "turn back to Egypt in their hearts" was as grievous to God as if they had gone back physically, for God looks upon the heart-life of man. God is displeased with every sinful wish and inward longing which is not in harmony with His will. This is why He demands that the Christian be "pure in heart" (Matt. 5:8; James 4:8). One cannot wholly follow the Lord with an impure heart.

Here again is the manifestation of "human religion," similar to that of Cain, who tried to have God accept *his* way, instead of accepting God's way himself. Man has ever been at this evil game. Many today have a religion that very well satisfies their own evil hearts, but

it is not the religion of the Lord Jesus Christ.

No form of religious life, however pious in appearance, in which self-will and stubborn determination to have one's own way prevail, is of God. Only when one has "perfect submission" to God can one's spirit truly sing, "All is at rest, I in my Saviour am happy and blessed."

The remaining portion of this book develops the manner of the Tabernacle worship, foreshadowing the work of Christ in atonement. It is the further extension of the idea of the covenant of God with Abraham, not only to give the land of Canaan to Israel, but to prepare the way for the Messiah's coming to redeem Israel and the world of lost men.

The key thought of this book is *deliverance* — physically from Egyptian bondage, and spiritually from sin's bondage. If studied in this light, Exodus becomes much more meaningful.

Memory Verse

"And the blood shall be to you for a token upon the houses where ye are: AND WHEN I SEE THE BLOOD, I WILL PASS OVER YOU, *and the plague shall not be upon you to destroy you"* (12:13, emphasis the author's).

Leviticus

The name of this book refers to the Levites and the laws and customs of the Levitical system, under which the Hebrew nation lived. The word originally came from "Levi," one of Jacob's sons, and the tribe which God chose to provide the priests, instead of taking the firstborn of various tribes (Num. 3:41). One family of the Levites, Aaron and his sons, was dedicated to the priesthood; the rest of the Levites were assistants in the duties of worship, singers, etc. In Canaan they were given forty-eight cities and were supported by the tithes of the people (Num. 35:1-8; Josh. 21:1-42; Num. 18: 20-25).

From this group came not only priests, but their assistants, who had the care of the Tabernacle, and later the Temple; and from their number came the scribes, musicians and officers of the Temple (I Chron. 23).

TO WHOM

This book was given to Israel in general, but to the Levites in particular, since it pertained to their work and offices. The common public of Israel, however, needed to read it that they might know the place of their leaders and so respect them, as well as to know their own places in matters of religious worship.

For us today, the main value in the book lies in its revelation of the moral nature of God, His demands for holiness and righteousness, and its beautiful symbolism of spiritual aspects of the Christian religion. It should be read in the light of both the Old Testament times and that of our day.

PURPOSE

The major purpose of this book was to set forth the laws, regulations, and customs for the priesthood of Israel, and the general plan of worship under that system. It was not to be a perpetual thing; it was to serve to finally lead the people to Christ.

It outlined the many and varied types of sacrifices and offerings the people were to make to God, and it showed the manner in which they were to be made. The major purpose of this system seems to have been to make the people continually conscious of their sinfulness and need of atonement, their dependence upon God for mercy and salvation; it pointed to the demands of God for holiness of life and purity of purpose on the part of His people. This could never be attained by their own work, but only by the sacrifices for sins, which were made obligatory upon every person.

We study Leviticus for the benefit of seeing how the Levitical system applied to the lives of men in its age, and for its symbolic truths for our day.

TIME

Almost all these laws and regulations were given while the people were encamped at Mount Sinai, where the Ten Commandments were also received.

ALMOND TREE. *When the rod marked with Aaron's name budded, it brought forth almond blossoms .*

This book may have been written about the second year after the exodus from Egypt. Its actual writing may have covered only a few days, or a few weeks at most.

AUTHORSHIP

The Mosaic authorship of this book was never questioned among the Jews in ancient times. The Christian church from its earliest days has also accepted it as the writing of Moses.

If one looks at this book as simply the catalog of Israel's religious and ceremonial laws, dietary and sanitation regulations, local diseases, and social welfare and services, it can be a very dry book indeed. But Christians must look beyond these to its symbolic message.

In its symbolism, types, and foreshadowings of Christ and His redemptive work for mankind, Leviticus is one of the richest books of the Old Testament. It is in this realm that its worth to us is found. All its offerings and feasts in some way prefigured Christ's atoning work.

This book may be outlined as follows:

I. The sacrificial system and its priesthood, 1-10
II. Laws of sanitation and health, 11-15
III. The annual atonement and its observance, 16-17
IV. Condemnation of abominations, 18
V. Civil and moral laws, 19-22
VI. The priesthood and its services, 23-24
VII. Special years; warnings and blessings, 25-26
VIII. Vows and tithes, 27

A still briefer outline of this book may be:

I. The *way to* God, 1-16
II. The *walk with* God, 17-27

THE HIGH PRIEST. *The elaborate dress of the high priest in his daily administration included an ephod, a sleeveless jacket made of linen; a breastplate, upon which were twelve precious stones, each engraved with the name of one of twelve tribes; an embroidered coat; a mitre, or headdress; and a sash. The use of footwear was not prescribed.*

Courtesy, Green Lake Bible Conference

BREASTPLATE OF THE HIGH PRIEST. *Worn on the breast, this piece of material of gold, blue, purple, and scarlet yarn and fine linen, was adorned with twelve tribes. The stones in the first row were a ruby, a topaz, and a beryl; in the second row, a turquoise, a sapphire, and an emerald; in the third row, a jacinth, an agate, and an amethyst; in the fourth row, a chrysolite, an onyx, and a jasper. Each was engraved with the name of one of the tribes.*

GREAT THINGS IN LEVITICUS

There are no *outstanding stories* here but many significant truths. From the many symbolical and factual things of this book, one can draw many *great truths,* a few of which will be pointed out:

1. One sees Christ's atoning work at Calvary in the Passover and its dying, sacrificial lamb. Tied to this fact was John's first announcement of Christ: "Behold the Lamb of God, which taketh away the sin of the world" (John 1:29, 36;

also I Cor. 5:7). The feast of Pentecost also foreshadowed the coming of the Holy Spirit, for it was on the day of Pentecost that the Holy Spirit first came dispensationally to the Christian church (Acts 2:1-4).

The feast of "first fruits" (23:10) foreshadowed Christ's resurrection. "But now is Christ risen from the dead, and become the *firstfruits* of them that slept" (I Cor. 15:20, italics by the author). This first sheaf of the wheat or barley was a figure of the Resurrection in that it was new life produced from the dead grain from which it had sprung.

The feast of tabernacles, or harvest ingathering in the fall, is also thought to foreshadow Christ's second coming and the ingathering of the saints to the heavenly home (23:39-43; I Thess. 4:13-18).

Almost every offering and feast of the whole book of Leviticus in some way prefigures or foreshadows something of spiritual worth in the New Testament. In this way the book has deep spiritual significance to Christians.

One needs to study the New Testament book of Hebrews along with Leviticus to appreciate the way in which the old system is fused into the New Testament thinking by way of figures and symbols.

2. The Levitical system was God's way of emphasizing the need for atonement for sin and the fact that without atonement there can be no forgiveness. Christ takes the place of this system in the New Testament, and the writer of Hebrews emphasizes His importance as the atoning Savior in the words, "Without shedding of blood is no remission" (Heb. 9:22-26).

3. The character of God is revealed in this system as one of holiness and justice. He will tolerate no sin or sinfulness under any circumstances. *Holiness* may be said to be the key word to this book; *worship*

is the key thought. Man cannot truly worship God in a sinful state; therefore, Christ came to take away our sins, that we may "serve him without fear, in holiness and righteousness before him, all the days of our life" (Luke 1:74, 75; also I John 3:1-10).

4. Another lesson from this system is that while it appears at first to be a national system of worship, it is very *individual* in its final application. No such thing as national religion really exists. Religion is a matter of the individual heart and life. Just as the ancient worshiper must bring his own offering, and in many instances take some part in its presentation, so the Christian must worship God personally and alone. In the matter of personal responsibility to God, no one can meet God's demands for another. God's personal care for His people may also be seen in this book.

It should also be noted that this book is but another expansion in the meaning and fulfillment of God's covenant with the forefathers. It was preparing the people for the spiritual as well as physical inheritance of Canaan. It was also a guide for the religious development of the nation from which the Redeemer would finally come in fulfillment of this covenant, as Jacob by the Spirit of God had so beautifully prophesied in his dying hours (Gen. 49:10). The word "Shiloh" here beyond any doubt refers to the Messiah; it was always so understood by the ancient Jews. The *Messiah* of the Old Testament is the *Christ* of the New Testament.

As far as its types and shadows of things to be fulfilled in Christ are concerned, Leviticus is the greatest book on redemption in the Old Testament.

Memory Verses

"For the life of the flesh is in the blood;

and I have given it to you upon the altar to make an atonement for your souls: for it is the blood that maketh an atonement for the soul" (17:11).

"Sanctify yourselves therefore, and be ye holy: for I am the Lord your God" (20:7).

Numbers

This book takes its name from the numberings of the Israelites. It was called "numerations" in old Anglo-Saxon versions of English Bibles. This came from the Latin Vulgate Version of Jerome, which he adopted from the Greek Septuagint Version. The numberings of the Israelites are listed in chapters 1-3 and 26.

TO WHOM

Numbers was written for Israel. Historically it was valuable to them and to their later national life. Its message was to all Israel, but more largely to the leadership of the nation, as it dealt with matters which would concern them more than mere laymen.

PURPOSE

The purpose of this book was to list the numberings of the people at various times and to record the places and times spent on their wilderness journey. It is a record from Egypt to Palestine, filled in with many details of their campings and movings and incidents which occurred as they went along.

It may serve for us today as a record of disobedience and failure, and as a

Courtesy, Consulate General of Israel

THE WILDERNESS. *The Israelites journeyed through this barren, mountainous terrain near Ezion-Geber. This area has been called "Israel's Badlands."*

picture of the defeated Christian, wandering long in this wilderness life. God never intended for Israel to wander in the wilderness, as seen from His attempt to have them enter the promised land at the end of two years (10:33-36; 11:1). According to God's Word, unbelief was the cause of their failure to enter Canaan at once (Heb. 4:6-8). The Christian may see in this book a warning against his failure to go on with Christ to full commitment and the way of Spirit-filled living. Israel's wilderness wanderings were only *permitted* by God; they were never

His first and highest plan for them (14:26-39).

TIME

The main portion of this book covers the time span between events at Mount Sinai to those in Moab, on the borders of Canaan. Within the first two years they were prepared to go into Canaan, but because of rebellion, God refused to allow them to enter (14:26-39). They then spent the remaining thirty-eight years wandering here and there, awaiting the death of those who had been above twenty years of age when they had left Egypt. (Numbers 14:29-34 should be read with care.)

It is interesting to note that at the second numbering of Israel, only Joshua and Caleb, who had "wholly followed

the Lord," were left of all those above twenty who came out of Egypt (26:64, 65). Let youth learn from this how *exacting* is the *justice* of God upon those who *reject* His mercy!

Chapter 33 records the circumstances of the wilderness journeys they made. It is one of the most pathetic chapters in the Bible! Yet, even in the midst of *exacting justice,* how great are God's untold mercies.

Probably this book was written progressively, as a log or record of the journeys, and then finished during the closing weeks or days of this long journey.

AUTHORSHIP

There can be no question that Moses wrote this book. Many references in the book itself show his authorship; from the most ancient times it has been accepted as the writing of Moses. Whether he kept records over a long time and finally compiled them, or whether he wrote it out as a fresh work during the last short while of his life, is not of importance. Whenever he wrote it, he wrote under the inspiration of the Spirit of God and therefore, without error.

This book more than any other shows Moses in action. Here his longest term of service stands out as one crosses the pages of this history of Israel's life for forty years. His battles with enemies of Israel, his trials with the stubbornness of his own people, and the complaints of even his own kin, as in the case of Aaron and Miriam (12:1-6), were not easy to bear. His underleaders, upon whom he depended to deal with the whole nation, sometimes proved unfaithful, as in the case of Korah and his conspiracy (16:1-50).

Once, too, the dear man of God lost his patience with Israel and grieved the Lord by striking the rock twice to bring out water (20:9-13). This rash act cost him the honor of bringing Israel into Canaan.

This is a difficult book to outline, as it is so nearly historical. One may use the following divisions:

I. Numbering and organizing the people, 1-4
II. Special laws, 4-5
III. Preparation for the journey to Canaan; its start, 6-10
IV. Rebellion; curtailment of the journey, 11
V. Sedition of Miriam and Aaron; the twelve spies, 13-14
VI. Korah's rebellion; various laws, 15-19
VII. Final start for Canaan, 20-21
VIII. Baalam's prophecy and folly, 22-25
IX. The last census, 26
X. Various regulations and events 27-36

One of the greatest miracles of continuous performance in history was that of God's care for His people in the wilderness. According to the best estimates of scholars there were about three million people in the nation of Israel during the forty years in the wilderness. They did not gain or lose much during this period; a fairly even balance was kept between the birth and death rates.

The wilderness over which they journeyed is known to have been very barren, rough, and rocky. It produced very little vegetation and except in a few places, it did not have much water. The "manna from heaven" which supplied their needs was brought by a direct intervention of God and continued for all this time.

Here again one sees the expansion of the covenant fulfillment. Israel, preserved as a nation, is to produce the Messiah. God's care of them in the wilderness must have been an unending source of fear to the heathen nations about them, who most certainly knew about this. These nations saw that they must finally reckon, not just with Israel but with the mighty God who had preserved and protected Israel all these years.

GREAT THINGS IN NUMBERS

The most *outstanding stories* may be listed as follows:

1. The murmuring of the people for meat; the coming of quails, 11
2. The sedition of Miriam and Aaron, 12
3. Journey and report of the twelve spies, 13-14
4. Korah and his rebellion, 16
5. The blooming rod, 17
6. Moses' loss of patience, 20
7. The fiery serpents and God's remedy, 21
8. Baalam and the lost cause, 22-24

Several *great truths* which may be observed here are:

1. Israel's murmurings against God occurred several times; they show a lack of faith and trust in God's loving care. Each time they were punished for this in some way. God is grieved today when His children complain about the circumstances by which they are beset, rather than trusting Him.

Quails were miraculously sent to satisfy Israel's hunger for meat (11:31, 32), but in the midst of their gluttony the curse of God blasted their pleasure (v. 33). God allowed them to have quail,

QUAIL. *"And there went forth a wind from the Lord, and brought quails from the sea, and let them fall by the camp. . . ."*

---

but He sent leanness into their souls. Many times God permits Christians to have things which they persist in praying for, but as a result, they suffer leanness of spirit and do not prosper spiritually. Christians should learn to "be content with such things as ye have" (Heb. 13:5).

2. Miriam and Aaron learned dearly that God demands respect for His chosen leaders (12). Only God's mercy saved Miriam from the fate of a leper's life.

A lesson must be seen, too, in race relationships. Moses' wife, over whom the contention arose, was likely his wife Zipporah, who was an Arab whom he had married in Midian (Exod. 2:21). Though in English here called an Ethiopian, this does not necessarily mean a Negro, as this term may vary in the Scriptures.

The real complaint was not so much against the woman as against Moses having all the governmental authority, which they seemed to desire to share. God made it plain to them at once that they were to complain no more, but to be content with their own positions.

3. One of the saddest scenes of Old Testament history is the report of the twelve spies. Only two of these men,

after seeing the good and fruitful land, believed that God could bring Israel into it; the others rebelled and turned away in unbelief, losing their lives and burying their names in disgrace (13:26-33; 14:1-38). Note especially the contrast in the faith of Joshua and Caleb; they alone survived, while the other ten men died (14:37, 38).

This was one time when the people should have believed the "minority report" and acted favorably upon it. It is often true that the *believing* group in any religious body is the smaller of the two. But it is only men of faith who ever accomplish any worthwhile thing for God. Unbelief always brings defeat and sorrow, both to the individual and the group.

Think what a responsibility those ten unbelieving men had — their report with its unbelief doubtless caused all Israel to reject the plan of God, resulting in thirty-eight years of wandering, sorrow, death, and heartache untold. Remember, as a leader your lack of faith can be most tragic!

4. Korah's rebellion against Moses' authority was a very costly thing. It probably arose out of jealousy and a desire to assume a greater place of leadership on Korah's part. Korah wished to take over more sacred duties and so accumulate to himself more high honors, but he was in no spiritual condition for such a promotion. He is constantly referred to in the Scriptures as unworthy, rebellious, and unholy.

God's punishment for this unholy ambition and unrighteous attempt to take authority not belonging to him was swift and sure (16:23-35). One may see here that God has no place for the religiously ambitious who would use His work as a cloak for their pride or as a means to

MACHTESH RAMON. *This site in the Negeb Desert may have been one of the camping grounds of the Israelites after they left Kadesh.*

their own selfish interests and promotions. How truly humble, then, ought those to be who would carry forward the work of God, seeking not their own honor but that of God!

5. Aaron's rod that was caused to bloom and bear fruit (17:6-13) was God's way of defending the leadership of Aaron's house in the priesthood. God has chosen leaders, today even as then, and we should never murmur against them. Many people are lean in soul because of such quibblings against God's chosen leaders; God is grieved with them, as He was with ancient Israel.

6. One of the most outstanding experiences in the later life of Moses was his tragic mistake at Horeb. The Israelites had murmured against God because of the lack of water. He had heard their complaints and prayed for their forgiveness so many times that his patience with them evidently became exhausted. God had told him to "speak" to the rock, out of which the Lord would then miraculously bring water (20:8). But in his heat and haste, Moses *smote* the rock *twice* (v. 11). This seems to have been the only place at which Moses disobeyed the Lord. What a costly disobedience! For this act he was forbidden by God to lead Israel into Canaan; he so lost this great and, doubtless, much desired honor.

Just *why* this disobedience was so sternly dealt with by God is hard at first to see; Israel had sinned so many times and been forgiven. Moses was pardoned all right, but the consequences were not to be removed. His sin was a blotch upon the "meekest man upon the earth" in his day; it is still remembered today.

Moses' sin seems to have consisted in the following: 1. He was impatient with the people, calling them "rebels." 2. Instead of speaking to the rock, he *smote* it in direct disobedience to God's command. 3. He evidently did not give God the glory for this miracle. Notice that he said, "Must *we* fetch you water out of this rock?" as if it were he and Aaron who would do this thing. 4. It is distinctly stated that he did not believe God at this point — "because ye believed me not, to sanctify me in the eyes of the children of Israel" (v. 12). Evidently he so expressed himself before Israel as to raise doubts in their minds about God performing such a miracle as this. Apparently for one small moment Moses took his eyes off the Lord and focused them on himself. How dreadful was this act and its consequences for him!

Paul explains that this rock symbolizes the Christ. ". . . They drank of that spiritual Rock that followed them: and that Rock was Christ" (I Cor. 10:4). In smiting this rock twice, Moses seems to show that he did not fully recognize the presence and power of God in this act as he should have done.

If we suppose that this *rock* typified Christ, and the water flowing from it was a type of the Holy Spirit, flowing from Christ to His followers (John 7:37-39), then this rock represented not the "smitten Christ" of Calvary, but the exalted Christ on His mediatorial throne. If this be true, when Moses *struck* the rock instead of speaking to it, he not only disobeyed God's plain command to "speak unto the rock," but he also broke this great type of the exalted Christ. The exalted Christ is to be smitten no more, but to be spoken to in reverence and intercession. Moses, therefore, dishonored God and Christ. Moses lost his entry into Canaan by this act of disobedience. It is evident from the very passage (v. 12), in which God pronounces His displeasure upon him that Moses would have led Israel into Canaan if he had been faithful and obedient.

Young readers should study this whole passage and connected Scriptures and let them sink into their hearts, noting how dreadful it is for believers to disobey God. Note: Although Aaron only stood by, he was apparently party to this act of Moses, and was likewise included in the prohibition to enter Canaan (see vv. 10-12). Not only must we not partake in another's disobedience, but we should disassociate ourselves from anyone who is knowingly disobeying God, and have no part in it. This may seem like a stern rule, but sin is a horrible thing, and one should have no part of it in any way.

7. The appearance of fiery serpents among the people as a result of their sin (21) illustrates for us the nature of sin. It is a fiery, poisonous, and killing thing. As in Eden when the serpent was seduced by Satan and used to tempt Eve away from God, this story brings us face to face with another illustration of Satan's attempts to ruin man.

The serpent of brass which Moses had erected upon a pole in full view of any bitten persons who would *look* upon it was God's remedy for the poisonous bite. Christ applied this to Himself; He is the remedy for sin. Just as they looked and lived that day, so those who will look to Christ, God's atoning sacrifice for sin at Calvary, will be saved (John 3:14, 15). Today this is the supreme lesson of this story for us.

8. Balaam, the false prophet who lived near the Euphrates River among the Ammonites, was called by King Balak to curse Israel, that they might not destroy his kingdom (22-24). Balaam, once a true prophet of God, seems to have added to his prophetic gift, sorcery, and divination. In this manner, he had departed from God, becoming a false prophet. Ancient kings often hired religious leaders to "curse" their enemies. God turned Balaam's curse into a blessing, however, and the disgusted prophet then proceeded to advise the Moabite women

---

BAALAM. *God sent His angel to stand in the prophet's way. Three times the dumb ass saw the angel and turned aside. When the ass spoke, Baalam's eyes were opened by the Lord.*

to attract Israelitish men to commit adultery with them and worship their idols. As a result, twenty-four thousand Israelites perished under the chastisement of God.

Balaam had cried very piously, "Let me die the death of the righteous, and let my last end be like his" (23:10), in his high moments of inspiration — for God did use him to prophesy the coming of Christ (24:15-19) as the "Star" and the "Scepter" that should rise out of Israel. But poor old Balaam did not fare quite so well at his end, for he was slain among the disobedient. When the Israelites found him after arriving in his adopted land, they killed him (31:8). To the end of the Bible, his name is connected with his wicked acts (II Peter 2:15; Jude 11; Rev. 2:14).

This story indicates how dearly men pay for their love of honor and money when they sacrifice principle and character to obtain these transient things. Nei-

ther is worth a ruined life. This, youth should well remember.

9. In addition to Moses and Aaron, two outstanding men, Joshua and Caleb, are worthy of special mention. These men "wholly followed the Lord" and brought a true report about Canaan and kept their faith, for which they were permitted the highest of honors, living to a very advanced old age in the land of Canaan. We shall see them again as our story progresses.

10. Every young person should memorize one passage of Scripture in this book: "But if ye will not do so, behold, ye have sinned against the Lord: and be sure your sin will find you out" (32:23). This was Moses' warning to the two and one-half tribes who wished to remain on the wilderness side of Jordan, but promised to help their brethren conquer the land of Canaan. It is a solemn warning against the breaking of promises made to God and to His people, with the fearful notation, ". . . be sure your sin will find you out."

Possibly there is no more well-illustrated Scriptural truth than these last words: *Be sure your sin will find you out!* This is not merely a text for preachers; it is a moral principle as unchanging as eternal justice and as true as the fact of God. People's sins will find them out by God's laws in the Bible, in conscience, in providence, in moral law, in social law, in the Spirit's dealings, and in death and eternity. Sin, like a dreadfully-awakened conscience, will never rest until it has somewhere, sometime, told its dreadful tale of woe. Youth should take this passage to heart, for when can it save more heartache and bring so much good than during the early years of a person's life.

This book is another expansion of the great covenant of God with His people.

It shows His struggle with a disobedient people, but his mercy in sparing them, indicating progress toward the fulfillment of this covenant in its first phase — that of giving to Abraham's seed the Land of Promise, Canaan. One should ever keep in mind the progressive development of this covenant as the leading truth in all these Old Testament books, pointing finally to the coming Redeemer of mankind.

Memory Verse

"But if ye will not do so, behold, ye have sinned against the Lord: and be sure your sin will find you out" (32:23).

Deuteronomy

This book takes its name from the old Septuagint Version and the Latin Vulgate Version, from the words meaning "second law" or "doubling," a *repetition* of the law.

In reality, however, Deuteronomy is not only a restatement of the laws given in Exodus, Leviticus, and Numbers, but much more. It is an amplification, an expounding, a rehearsal of them, as they are applied to the *settled* life of Israel in Canaan. Added to them is a more deeply spiritual application; the religious and personal meaning of each is developed.

TO WHOM

This book was produced for what might be called the "New Israel." All of the old generation who had come out of Egypt, those above twenty years of age at that time, were dead. The new generation was about to enter Canaan. They needed the laws of God impressed upon their hearts and consciences anew. This book is the answer to that need.

PURPOSE

The purpose of Deuteronomy was to restate to the new nation of Israel, many of whom had not been born when Moses received the Ten Commandments and the laws at Sinai, the moral and spiritual purposes of the laws which they had been taught to observe. Sanitation and health matters were now not as important to them as the application of the laws to the new moral and social situations in which they would soon find themselves, though the former were not set aside or changed. They had lived quite apart, for instance, as a people in the desert. Soon they would be living in closer contact with other peoples and cultures.

Deuteronomy brings the law of God into personal play in the life of the believer, as a spiritual force. For a good example of this, look at the explanation of the first commandment. The "Thou shalt have no other gods before me" of Exodus is now expounded as ". . . The Lord our God is one Lord: and thou shalt love the Lord thy God with all thine heart, and with all thy soul, and with all thy might" (6:4, 5).

Not only did they need this new restatement of the laws, but they also needed *warnings* against unfaithfulness, idolatry, and acceptance of the conditions of the land where they were going. Moses took particular pains to vividly set forth all this. They were not only reminded of the stiffnecked position of their fathers, but they were warned against the peril

of following their example. Deuteronomy is sprinkled well with such references that the Israelites would be constantly reminded and placed on guard by reading this book.

Today the message of Deuteronomy can be read by all Christians, with much profit. Its message is a spiritual one, and from it one may draw many lessons. It has some of the finest statements of doctrine and conduct in the Old Testament, and some of its passages are said to be unsurpassed for beauty and eloquence in literature.

TIME

This book was written during the last part of the fortieth year after the exodus (1:1-3). Its production took place in the plains of Jordan, near where the Israelites later crossed over into Canaan.

If the exodus from Egypt occurred in 1491 B.C., as some scholars have thought, then this book was written about the last part of the Jewish year, in the year 1451 B.C. There is some difference of opinion as to the exact date of the exodus. Some have placed it as late as 1300 B.C., under Rameses II, pharaoh of Egypt at that time. It is certain that the book was written at the end of the wilderness journey.

AUTHORSHIP

The Mosaic authorship of this book has been accepted from the earliest times by both the ancient Jews and the Christian church. Only in the last century has there been any serious questioning of his authorship; sound Biblical scholarship and modern scientific research favor the traditional viewpoint.

The style of Deuteronomy differs from the other four books, just as Genesis differs greatly from the remaining four books of the *Pentateuch*. But this naturally would be so, since the purpose of this book is entirely different; it was also delivered under very different circumstances. The particular *purpose* of Deuteronomy accounts for what might be called its *slant*.

It will be noted that this book speaks of *conditions* which would exist in the land of Canaan of which Moses, as an ordinary person, or even religious leader, would not have known at this time. But this poses no problem, for Moses was a *prophet* (18:15-19), and as such he certainly was inspired to forewarn Israel of conditions they must face. Considerable portions of the warnings of this book are of the prophetic nature.

As to *how* this book was produced, we are not told, except that it is apparent from its introduction that Moses *spoke* this message to the people (1:1-5). That it was originally delivered in lecture or teaching form can hardly be questioned. Since Joshua was Moses' faithful assistant and successor, it is not unreasonable to hold that he would have made a *verbatim* record of these addresses, aided perhaps by able scribes, as they were delivered. After Moses had rechecked them for accuracy, the book would then have been placed together as one whole volume. Or, it is possible that after the lectures were delivered Moses himself wrote them out; there is nothing to hinder the supposition that he may have written them *before* he delivered the lectures, afterward giving them by memory or reading to the people. However it was done, the main thing to remember is that these lectures were *inspired* by God; they are the inerrant Word of the Lord.

It is most likely that someone other than Moses wrote the introduction (1: 1-5), possibly Joshua, as the book fell immediately into his hands. Very likely the same one wrote of the death of Moses and also the words of praise in the last part of the book (34:1-2). He most certainly had to be inspired, as he records things which he could not have known in any other way than by inspiration (34:1-6, especially vv. 5 and 6).

Deuteronomy is especially important in its relation to the covenant of God with the forefathers, as it further expands and *spiritualizes* the meaning of that covenant. Moses here prepares Israel to inherit the Land of Promise and to become the nation out of which the Messiah would come. Had Israel heeded completely Moses' farewell address, they would have, beyond a doubt, become the most powerful nation in the world! It is entirely possible that Christ's coming would not have been delayed as long as it was; Christianity would have succeeded far beyond our present scope of understanding, had this been true.

Moses was preparing the nation to become not only God's earthly people, but His heavenly people as well. They would have been as "the sand of the seashore," the "dust of the earth," and as the "stars of the heavens" had they been true to their commission to bring all nations to know the Lord their God. This was the ultimate aim of the covenant (Gen. 17).

The following outline of this book may be used. It consists largely of addresses:

I. First address, 1-4
II. Second address, 5-26
III. Third address, 27-30
IV. Final words: farewell address, 31; song of Moses, 32; ordination of Joshua, 33
V. Moses' death and burial

GREAT THINGS IN DEUTERONOMY
There are no *outstanding stories* in this

MOUNT NEBO IN MOAB. *From this mountain Moses viewed the Promised Land, which he was not allowed to enter.*

book, except the one of Moses' death and burial.

As for *great truths,* it merely reiterates those presented in Exodus, Leviticus, and Numbers, with added spiritual emphasis and future warnings to Israel. Certain things which stand out may be noticed with profit:

1. The first address calls attention to God's faithfulness, despite Israel's sins; it is a great lesson in the mercy of God (1-4). God hates sin but loves the sinner.

On some occasions, however, had it not been for Moses' intercessory prayers and true meekness, God would have destroyed the rebellious Israelites and begun over again with Moses alone (Num. 14:11-24; especially vv. 11, 12). Only God knows how great is the power of true intercessory prayer. Oh, for more young people who will become "intercessors" in prayer!

2. In this same passage the glory of humility and self-forgetfulness is shown by Moses' attitude toward the prospects of becoming a mighty nation himself (Num. 14:13-19). God could have destroyed Israel, started over with Moses alone, given him children, and out of them produced a new nation, still keeping every word of His covenant with Abraham, Isaac, and Jacob. Only God's mercy, evidently brought upon Israel by Moses' prayers, saved them from this fate. What humility and love for his people Moses displayed!

3. Possibly one could say the "heart" of Deuteronomy is in chapters 5-26, where the moral law is amplified, explained, and applied to daily living. This section should be read with care, looking for high peaks of spiritual application. The highest point of spiritual life is presented in the words, "And thou shalt love the Lord thy God with all thine heart, and with all thy soul, and with all thy might" (6:5). Jesus cited this passage in His exposition of the Ten Commandments (Matt. 22:37-40), adding, ". . . Thou shalt love thy neighbor as thyself," to complete a summation of all Ten Commandments.

Perfect love to God and the love of one's neighbor as himself embraces all that the moral law demands. This is only possible when the love of God has been shed abroad in one's heart by the Holy Spirit, when life is fully devoted to God (Rom. 5:5; I John 3:1-4, 14).

4. Moses constantly warned Israel not to forget that ". . . thou wast a bondman in the land of Egypt, and the Lord thy God redeemed thee . . ." (15:15). This was to keep their attitudes right when dealing with other less-fortunate persons among themselves, and even the "stranger" who may chance to come among them.

It is always a fine thing for Christians to remember that they were once sinners with many bad traits and much about them which was undesirable. When tempted to scorn someone who is drinking, swearing, or acting very ugly, remember, but for the grace of God, *you* may have been in his very same condition!

5. A passage which every person should know is found in Deuteronomy 29:29, where Moses explains, "The secret things belong unto the Lord our God: but those things which are revealed belong unto us and our children forever, that we may do all the words of the law." Often young people especially wonder *why* certain things are not revealed to us in the Bible. There are some things which God does not see wise to reveal to man; these will never be known. These include all technical problems

Courtesy, Moissaye Marans

MOSES. *This contemporary sculpture by Moissaye Marans is entitled "The Ten Commandments." The Pentateuch closes with the account of the death of Moses, "whom the Lord knew face to face."*

THE PROMISED LAND. *These postage stamps, issued by Israel in 1958 and 1959, portray the produce of the land. Deuteronomy 8:8 speaks of "a land of wheat, and barley, and vines, and fig trees, and pomegranates; a land of oil olive, and honey."*

FIGS

WHEAT

BARLEY

GRAPES

OLIVES

POMEGRANATES

DATES

which have no answer in the Bible, such as: why God permitted evil in the universe; why, if He is all-powerful He did not *prevent* sin from happening in the first place; why He created Lucifer in such a way that he *could* sin, and so become Satan as we know him, bringing all the sorrow and trouble it has cost, when He could just as well have made him so that he could *not* sin, and then sorrow would never have been known. One can think of many unanswered questions which, in frank language, are "none of our business." These things belong to God.

For its spiritualization of the laws of God, and its clear views of the character of God and His purpose in relation to His covenant people, Deuteronomy is one of the most important books in the beginning of the Old Testament.

TRIBUTE TO MOSES

As a fitting close to the Pentateuch, we pay this tribute to Moses:

Moses was last seen (physically) on the foothills of Nebo as he ascended that mount to view the Promised Land and then lay down in the tender arms of Deity, entering eternal bliss. Angelic pallbearers laid his mortal remains to rest in an unknown valley of that mount, to await the sounding of the trumpet at the Savior's glad return. Funeral attendants must have consisted of hosts of seraphim and cherubim, angels and arch-angels, who welcomed his redeemed spirit to paradise with everlasting joy.

He is next seen on the Mount of Transfiguration with Elijah and Jesus (Matt. 17:2-6), discussing the details of Christ's redemptive mission at Calvary; he is last mentioned in the song called the "song of Moses, the servant of God, and the song of the Lamb" (Rev. 15:3).

No final estimate of the contribution of Moses' work to mankind's well-being has ever been made. He was a sublime statesman, a powerful general, a remarkable organizer, a profound legislator, a tremendous leader, a voluminous author, a great prophet, and a grand intercessor.

Towering over all Old Testament worthies from his time onward, he stands without a peer in the ancient world of men. Although stern as the law he received, yet he was called the "meekest man on the face of the earth." Enduring almost unbelievable strains of mind and body, with one exception he remained poised in spirit and gracious in manner, throughout his long life as a leader of his people. Patient and understanding, brilliant and fearless, he was the most outstanding of all ancient world leaders. Among intercessors in prayer, no one stood nearer to God nor was more self-effacing than he.

His mighty, monumental work, the Pentateuch, is the foundation stone upon which the whole structure of divine revelation rests. It contains the germ of every truth revealed in the Bible; beyond doubt it is the greatest literary production of all time. Moses was entrusted by God with the sublime task of all ages — laying the foundation for all future revelation concerning the covenant of God with His people and the coming of Christ to be the Savior of the race.

Deuteronomy is the crowning work of this great task, the acme of Moses' divinely-inspired pronouncements.

Memory Verses

"Hear, O Israel: the Lord our God is one Lord: and thou shalt love the Lord thy God with all thine heart, and with all thy soul, and with all thy might" (6:4, 5).

The Historical Books

Joshua

This book is named for Joshua, the great hero of faith who was consecrated as Moses' successor just after the latter's death. In the Old Testament Hebrew Joshua means "he shall save" or "salvation of Jehovah." In the New Testament "Jesus" is its Greek equivalent. The name probably refers to the fact that Joshua led Israel out of the wilderness into Canaan and delivered them from their enemies in this new land.

TO WHOM

It was written for all Israel as a history of the conquest of Canaan. As the generations of the future came, the youth of the nation would need its message. It is, as part of God's Word, also of universal interest to the church and all peoples of the world.

PURPOSE

The writer probably intended to provide an accurate history of God's dealings with His people in leading them out of the wilderness into Canaan. He also provides accounts of the conquest of the Promised Land, the settling of the tribes in the land, and the establishment of their boundaries. In later discussion of boundaries between tribes, this book was of untold value as the original source book from which to draw.

It may be that he further intended to set forth a record of God's power in granting many great victories to His people as they fought to establish themselves in their new land. While the land was given to Israel, it was not given to them without many battles of conquest on their part.

This may serve to illustrate for all God's children in times to come that no moral and spiritual victories are ever won without battles. Satan and his forces will contend to the last stand for every inch of territory possible and will only give in as forced by divine intervention to do so.

Joshua also shows the progressive unfolding of the fulfillment of God's covenant with Abraham, that of giving the land of Canaan to his children after him. Israel was now well on its way toward becoming the nation of divine origin and destiny to bring into the world its coming Redeemer, Jesus Christ. There were some three million Israelites spread over the land at this time, and they began to multiply and grow as never before. By the time described in the end of this book, there had been a great population increase, and the surrounding nations were filled with a justifiable fear of Israel's expansion.

One should keep his eye upon the idea of this divine fulfillment of the covenant, as every story of triumph is geared in some way to this onward marching thought.

TIME

Joshua's conquest of Canaan is thought to have taken about six years. The remaining years were spent in settling the land and developing the civil and religious government, together making about twenty-five years of his leadership.

From the internal evidences, such as references to places, times of conquest and development, and the like, it is evident that the book was written near the close of his leadership, probably not long before he died. The book covers a span of some twenty-five years.

AUTHORSHIP

The authorship of this book has been assigned to Joshua by the most ancient tradition of the Jews; it was accepted by the Christian church as his production, without hesitation.

There are some references in Joshua to incidents, names, and places of apparent-

ly later times, which have caused some scholars to think that possibly Samuel or even Ezra may have written this book. This is hardly plausible. Besides, the book reads as if it were the writing of one who was present and taking part in the activity it records. As for the tribal boundaries and other similar matters, these would naturally have been quite largely set during Joshua's day. Joshua seems to have written the book in basically the same form as we now have it.

As far as later references are concerned, this poses no problem. It is well known that the "scribes" copied all the Old Testament books, keeping accurate, up-to-date copies of them. It is likely that such simple notations as the changed name of a city, or that of a city which

---

HAZOR. *These relics were found at the site of a pagan temple in an area thought to be Hazor. The inhabitants of the city were slain and the city burned by Joshua and his men.*

"continues unto this day," were made by the scribes as they copied the book and were added by later copyists as part of the book. This in no way disturbs the pattern of the whole, nor does it damage the book as an inspired writing.

Joshua is in one sense a continuation of Deuteronomy; there are facts in its earlier chapters which no one would have known so well as Joshua himself. The account of his divine challenge is stated as a personal account in the first chapter, although he does not name himself as its author. Further, as Moses' secretary, army general, and *aide-de-camp,* Joshua naturally would have followed Moses' pattern of recording everything of value in his own campaigns and other labors.

Again, expressly stated is the fact that "Joshua wrote these words of the book of the law of the Lord" (24:26). While this may have referred particularly to the code of the law and the covenant given by Moses and recited by Joshua, it doubtless means to convey to the reader that Joshua had written the whole book in which this code occurs. Since almost the entire book refers to matters of his own conduct and the conquest under his leadership he was the logical person to have written this book.

As a man, Joshua was outstanding. He was of the tribe of Ephraim (Num. 13:8). He was Moses' personal attendant and minister throughout the forty years in the wilderness: at Mount Sinai (Exod. 24:13), as one of the twelve spies (Num. 13:8, 16), and as a companion in his last days, possibly writing the last words of tribute to him (Deut. 34).

He is supposed to have been about eighty-five years of age when he succeeded Moses as Israel's leader; he died at the age of 110 (Josh. 24:29). Joshua was one of Israel's greatest leaders after Moses. Leading Israel into Canaan and freeing them from their enemies, he became the prototype of Jesus the Savior, who came to deliver His people from their sins (Matt. 1:21).

Joshua was revered by Israel as one of their greatest leaders. He was buried in Ephraim, his own tribal land (24:30). He was a mighty man of faith, heroic courage, and great military skill.

This book may be outlined in the following brief way:

    I.   Introduction and qualifying of Joshua, 1:1-18

   II.   The conquest of Canaan, 2-12

  III.   The division of the land and the settling of Israel, 13-22

  IV.   Joshua's farewell address and last instructions, 23-24

This book contains the most outstanding military conquests of all Biblical history. Its feats of faith and daring accomplishments were never surpassed, especially when one considers the conditions of Israel and the odds against them and compares them to the same circumstances in the later years of conquest.

GREAT THINGS IN JOSHUA

Outstanding stories may be listed as follows:

1. Joshua's preparation, 1
2. The rescue of Rahab, 2
3. Israel's crossing into Canaan, 3
4. Joshua's angel visitor, 5
5. The fall of Jericho, 6
6. Achan's sin and Israel's defeat, 7
7. The trickery of the Gibeonites, 9
8. Stopping of the sun, 10
9. Caleb's reward, 14:6—15:20
10. Joshua's farewell, 24

Note the *great truths* pointed up by these stories:

1. God never commands us to do any-

thing for which He does not provide strength. Joshua's commission was not greater than his God-given qualifications. Yet, Joshua had to make the necessary preparations (1:1-9). God did not just qualify him automatically; he had the faith, courage, and obedience to perform.

2. The rescue and redemption of Rahab has become a thing of spiritual meaning (2:1-24). Some scholars think the word harlot (2:1) may mean simply an "inn keeper" and not an immoral woman, as evidenced by the fact that the Israelite spies had stopped there for entertainment, as at a hotel, certainly not for immoral purposes.

By her act of daring kindness to them, she showed her faith in Israel's God and became a convert to the new way of life. She is listed as a heroine of faith (Heb. 11:31), and her act made her immortally famous. By simple obedience to God we will gain everything in the end. Just as she escaped the sure doom of Jericho, so we who believe and obey God will escape the doom of this sinful world.

3. Israel's crossing the Jordan was a miraculous act however it may be interpreted (3:1-17). Whatever the means used to stay the waters, it was a divine intervention for Israel's sake to bring them into Canaan.

The people came to the river in faith. When the feet of the priests touched the water, the river parted for them. Faith and obedience, without present evidence, were the order here. God would teach us that we are to obey and trust Him for the outcome, without regard to the present circumstances.

4. God's manifestation to Joshua as "captain of the host of the Lord" near Jericho notified him of how to invade and destroy this strong city (5:13-15).

So far this stubborn city had held out against them and had not been attacked by Joshua.

We often need divine reassurance in times of supreme testing or when spiritual advance seems impossible. God is faithful to help us. He never requires of us that which He does not help us to accomplish. Before every Jericho of our lives will be the divine visitation, granting us strength in some way.

5. The fall of the wicked city of Jericho represented the first major victory of Israel in Canaan. It was a task for which they were not humanly prepared. The city was walled up with a high, strong wall all around it. Israel had no battle arms for such warfare. It would have required either some type of battering ram to beat down these walls or great numbers of powerfully armed forces to enter and overpower all the people in the city.

God's orders to have the priests march around the walls with the people, bearing the ark of God, once daily for six days, and seven times on the seventh day, the last journey during which they were to blow rams' horns, seems very simple indeed to us today. Several explanations have been offered as to why the walls fell down, but it is certain that a half-million men walking around a city thirteen times, blowing rams' horns, and giving a great shout all at once, would never of itself cause such huge walls to "come tumbling down." There had to be supernatural power to cause this to happen as it did.

The walls of Jericho were probably double walls, wide enough so houses could be built upon the walls, as was Rahab's house (2:15). The walls were most likely made of bricks one to two feet long, laid in mud mortar.

Some believe there may have been an earthquake at the time, which God could

have used, as any other means, to perform the miracle.

Of the many possible lessons, here is one: When God commands His people to do anything, He goes before them to prepare the way. Again, although He prepares the way, personal faith and obedience are required of us in each venture for Him.

6. Achan's sin disgraced Israel at the peak of their victories for God (7:1-26). God will not allow and condone sin in His people at any time. Achan was only one of the great mass of people who had invaded the cursed city, but his sin caused much suffering and shame.

Sin is an *individual* thing, but it often does immense *collective* damage. It is an individual thing, for example, for one to betray his country in time of war, but one betrayal may cost untold lives before it is over. This is why treason is such a

ACHAN. *This old engraving depicts the destruction of Achan and his family in the Valley of Achor.*

horrible thing. Sin is treason against God, and this is why it brings such far-reaching results. No one can sin individually by breaking God's laws without affecting others; he lays himself open for divine punishment. Sin is individual in the *act* but collective in the result. Young people should always remember this.

7. The fearful Gibeonites tricked Israel into a league of peace (9:1-15). Upon discovery of this piece of trickery, Israel made them, as a people, bond slaves for menial tasks the rest of their lives.

This story reveals how the fear of Israel was spreading everywhere. It also irked the kings of surrounding cities, causing them to go to war with Israel. This

VALLEY OF AJALON. *This area was assigned to the tribe of Dan, but the Amorite inhabitants were not expelled. Here, following the long day during which the sun stood still, Israel defeated a coalition of kings.*

JERICHO. *Archaeologists have excavated the site of old Jericho on several occasions (above). The "Mount of Temptation" is seen in the background.*

The city of Jericho was located on an oasis (left). It became known as "the city of palm trees."

was only their loss, however, for these kings lost all and were made subjects of Israel.

8. In the midst of a furious battle, Joshua and his forces needed extra daylight to accomplish their battle aims. For them to stop fighting at dusk would possibly have meant that the enemy kings would regroup their forces and stand a better chance of becoming victorious.

In response to Joshua's prayer, one of the greatest miracles of the Old Testament was performed. The "sun stood still in the midst of heaven" for about a whole day (10:13), while Joshua wound up one of the greatest victories of the Canaanitish campaigns. This story (10:1-43) shows not only God's power and willingness to intervene in the realm of nature when such is needed, but the power of prayer and faith in the hour of crisis.

It should be noticed, however, that Joshua did not pray for this for any personal glory or fame, but rather that Israel might have her inheritance as God had promised. His prayer and motive were utterly unselfish.

Again, the archaeologists' spades have proved that these cities fell during the time of Joshua's conquest of Palestine; all below their ruins was Canaanitish, while all above these remains is Israelitish in nature.

Just *how* this miracle of the sun standing still is to be explained is not so easy. Some think the earth was slowed in its rotation upon its axis sufficiently for this to have occurred; others have differing explanations. That it did occur by God's direct intervention we cannot doubt. God may also have provided some special arrangements to preserve the earth and its relationships to itself and the sun. There are records in other nations of a long day having occurred about this time, and there is also a day missing from the calendar of time, according to the calculation of some.

9. Caleb, it will be remembered, was one who, with Joshua, "wholly followed the Lord" in the matter of entering Canaan after the ten spies brought back the evil report (Num. 13:26-33). Now, after the conquest of Canaan, he asks for his reward (14:6—15:20).

At eighty-five years of age the old warrior was asking for a mountain location to conquer (14:12). He received it, cleared it of its evil inhabitants, and lived there in peace the rest of his days, enjoying his old age in beautiful, fruitful Canaan. One can easily imagine the old man going to the top of the hill above his house many times and looking out over the vast country about him with delightful joy welling up in his heart. Old age, prosperity, plenty of friends, and the abundant blessing of God had come to him for his "wholly" following the Lord.

These particular temporal blessings may not always follow us as God's people, but it is certain that those who will "wholly follow the Lord" can live the life of victory and peace with God and have the abundant blessings of God upon their lives. It will be noted, too, that Caleb made this great decision to wholly follow the Lord in his youth and that he never backed down from carrying it through, even in the most difficult times and under great pressure from others. This is most certainly an excellent lesson for youth today. It pays big dividends to begin living for Christ when one is young and continuing in this commitment to the end of life.

10. Joshua's farewell address contains, among other beautiful things, this great

home. Youth is the most ideal time to start.

In this book we again see the broadening stream of fulfilled prophecy concerning the covenant. Here Israel, after nearly five hundred years, takes her place as a nation, in fulfillment of God's promise to Abraham (Gen. 12:2, 3). Israel is now on the way to becoming the *great nation* of that promise. God is invading history with His plans for the coming Redeemer's appearance among men.

Memory Verse

"If it seem evil unto you to serve the Lord, choose ye this day whom ye will serve; whether the gods that your fathers served that were on the other side of the flood, or the gods of the Amorites, in whose land ye dwell: but as for me and my house, we will serve the Lord" (24:15).

Courtesy, Matson Photo Service

JUDEAN LANDSCAPE. *This modern photograph gives a clear picture of the terrain in which Israel lived. It was taken in the Valley of Ajalon.*

Judges

challenge: "As for me and my house, we will serve the Lord" (24:15). This should become the motto of every young person, and especially of every *couple* who start out together in the bonds of Christian marriage.

No home can ever be what it should be without Christ as its head. Parents need His guiding counsel and the help of the Holy Spirit in times of crises, when grave decisions have to be made, when children are to be instructed, and in untold other times. "Christ is the Head of this house" should be the motto of every

This book is so named because it describes the rule of the judges of Israel between the close of Joshua's leadership and the rise of the prophet Samuel.

During this time Israel was still under what may be called a *theocracy* — meaning rule by God — as she had been from Moses' day and the exodus. Each judge was raised up of the Lord to direct the national affairs and give the people guidance during his reign.

TO WHOM

Judges was written for all Israel as

well as all future generations of people who would come to read the story of Israel's early history.

PURPOSE

The main purpose of this book seems to have been at least two-fold: First, listing the several judges who ruled the people, it records a progressive history of the period, including those periods of depressions under enemy oppressors whom God allowed to chastise Israel.

The second purpose appears to have been to show both God's faithfulness to His people and His punishment of them for their sinfulness. Each successful rule of a good judge came to an end in peace and prosperity. After the death of a judge, Israel would invariably turn to some form of idolatry practiced by the surrounding evil nations. Upon their idolatry, God would permit a nation to invade the land, capture control of the people, and oppress them as slaves until they would turn to God in their distress.

This pattern of sinning and repenting, of God raising up a judge, after which the nation again fell into idolatry, is repeated many times in this book. There are ten periods of oppression, each followed by a time of deliverance by the Lord.

After Joshua's day there was no central government in Israel. No great leader arose, who was strong enough to command total national support and weld the people into one national group. God seems to have tried to prove Israel and show them that there could be a supreme rule of God, in which men would be governed by inward guidance; but Israel would not reach this high level of devotion, so this type of highly spiritual leadership under God failed. It did not fail because it *could not* work, but because

Israel *would not* be submissive to God and His laws. It is possible that had Israel wholly followed God as a nation, the world would have seen the greatest example of God-rule of all time. It is tragic that Israel failed God then, just as the governments of the world have continued to fail to carry out His will on earth.

Possibly, too, there is for us today a purpose in Judges. Its unfolding shows quite clearly God's desire to lead His people by His Spirit and the written Word of God, under the leadership of spiritual men. It also points out to us that when churches as local societies or as larger denominational groups forsake the ways of spiritual life, He will chastise them, just as John warned the seven churches of Asia (Rev. 2, 3).

There is always the individual lesson, too, in the Scriptures. Each person may see here reflected in some form his own spiritual life. Judges would represent the rather low state, if it should be applied to today's Christian experience. There is a higher plane of living for Christians, just as there was for them in that land, had they accepted and fulfilled it. It does show another principle in Christian living — that God chastises His children when they disobey, thereby drawing them back to Himself.

TIME

It is rather difficult to know just how much time may be covered by the book itself. Some have set the estimate at about four hundred years; however, a closer reckoning would make it nearer three hundred years. From the death of Joshua to the death of Samson seems to have been about 317 years. This is the major period covered by the book, even though the times of the judges extends well into the book of I Samuel to about chapter 8. The book itself was likely written shortly after the close of the age of the judges.

AUTHORSHIP

Some believe this book was originally composed in two separate sections, chapters 1-16 having been done first, and 17-21 some time later — possibly by two separate authors. However, the weight of evidence favors one author, probably the prophet Samuel. He is the most likely person to have written this book, living as he did at the close of the period and being familiar with the history of the period.

As Judges is based more upon God's dealings with His people than upon a straightforward chronological history of the times, not too much attention is paid to the connection between each judge and his period of rule. This makes the connective history a bit more difficult to follow.

This book is divided into six cycles of backslidings, oppressions, and deliverances. It may be outlined as follows:

- I. Introduction, 1-2
- II. First cycle, ending with Othniel as deliverer and judge, 3:1-5:11
- III. Second cycle, ending in the rule of Ehud, 3:12-21
- IV. Third cycle, ending with the victory of Deborah and Barak and their associated rule, 4:4—5:31
- V. Fourth cycle, ending with Gideon's victory and rule of the land, 6:18-32
- VI. Fifth cycle, which records Jephthah's deliverance and rule, 10:6—12:15
- VII. Sixth cycle, beginning with Shamgar's deliverance and ending with Samson's death, 13:1—16:31
- VIII. Israel adrift, 17-21. This section shows Israel filled largely with civil strife and religious confusion, without a central leader. It reveals how far Israel had drifted into idolatry and is a sad commentary upon the sinfulness of man without God.

The key expression of Judges, found several times, is: "In those days there was no king in Israel, but every man did that which was right in his own eyes" (17:6; 21:25).

GREAT THINGS IN JUDGES

The *outstanding stories* are listed as follows:

1. Deborah and Barak's deliverance of Israel and their famous song, 4-6
2. Gideon's mighty victory with the famous three hundred, 6-7
3. Jephthah's victory and rash vow, 11:29-40
4. Samson's remarkable story, 13-16
5. The wickedness of the men of Gibeah, 19-20

From these stories are found *great truths* of much worth today:

1. The episode of Deborah and Barak reveals how God often uses women in His work. Some would condemn the "spineless Barak," saying that if he had done his duty, there would have been no woman ruler in Israel. Perhaps so. But have they realized just how great and towering was the personality of this most remarkable woman Deborah? Did she not in humility offer to forward Barak's cause? She was also a "prophetess," which meant she had the call of God upon her to proclaim His sacred truth.

Perhaps Barak was well overshadowed by her much superior personality. At any rate, she did not take the lead until he refused to do so, making her doing so an absolute necessity.

One of the shames of the church today is that less than thirty-five per cent of its actively participating membership are men! This is not because the women have taken over and pushed the men out, but rather because the men, like Barak, have failed to "come up to the help of the Lord." The good women have been left no other choice than to carry on the work of the church as did Deborah.

Possibly, too, this story may serve to teach us that God chooses both men and women to carry on His work, that in spiritual matters He is no respecter of sexes. Yet it must be remembered that women are not to "teach, nor to usurp authority over the man" (I Tim. 2:12). She is not to take the authority away from the man and proceed to lord it over him. Most assuredly, the apostle is not condemning here the simple fact that in their proper sphere ladies may teach God's Word to others. Hardly; he heartily commended a gospel worker named Phebe as "a servant of the church at Cenchrea" (Rom. 16:1), and in all probability, its pastor. He commended "those women which labored with me in the gospel" (Phil. 4:3) and worked shoulder to shoulder with Aquila and his wife Priscilla (Acts 18:2-19).

He most certainly would not have condemned Philip's "four daughters, virgins, which did prophesy" (Acts 21:9). The original word from which "prophesy" comes can mean either to *preach, pray,* or *proclaim* by testimony of religious truth. Perhaps God has had no other choice but to employ godly women to help carry out His work when men have failed Him so largely.

2. In the story of Gideon's victory with the three hundred men there is a remarkable, spiritual lesson. At first, 32,-000 men responded, but God told Gideon he had too many men; they would take the glory to themselves. God knew these men were not spiritually minded enough to be trusted with a great victory. When all the faint-hearted and fearful were asked to turn back, 22,000 walked away (7:3).

Following another special test, 9,700 more men walked off because they could not stand the test. This left Gideon with only three hundred men, with which God told him he would deliver the Midianites into his hand.

Now, note *how* this army was recruited and then reduced. First, upon the call of Gideon, they responded of their own accord — they were not *drafted.* At the first test, the men who turned back did so of their own accord. But the second test was a bit different. Only the soldiers who lapped up the water as dogs, lifting their hands to their mouths with the water, while in all probability watching toward the hilltop for the enemy who might appear, were set aside. Those who fell down and drank to their hearts' content were sent home (7:5-7). *Why* was this test so peculiar? It appears that only the three hundred who were *dead to self-interest* and totally dedicated to the need of the hour were truly qualified for this great task. The others were good men, but they placed *self-interest* ahead of God's work, revealing thereby a weakness which disqualified them for this important assignment for which God alone was to have the glory for its accomplishment.

Is there not here a supreme lesson in

spiritual qualifications? Only those people who are totally committed to Christ, who have renounced the ways of the world and the sinful, fleshly, carnal life are truly prepared to do God's work. Granted, multitudes of Christians are not so totally committed, and many workers are far below this standard, but is this because God wills it? Such a condition exists because of their unwillingness to fully commit themselves to Christ in a life of the Spirit's fullness, not because it is God's will for them. Youth is the time to determine to be among the inner circle of the truly trustworthy, the fully committed, the Spirit-filled Christians.

3. Jephthah, in a moment of great distress, in his efforts to win his battle against Israel's enemies, made a very rash vow. He promised the Lord that He would sacrifice to Him whatever of his household first came to meet him upon his return. He did not expect that it would be his own darling daughter who would come skipping to meet him, but alas, this is what happened (11:29-40). How saddened his heart must have been as he realized the meaning of his rash vow!

Since Israel was forbidden to offer human sacrifices, it is not likely that Jephthah actually *killed* his daughter and offered her in sacrifice. It is more likely that he bound her to perpetual virginhood, never allowing her to marry. This was almost as bad as death to an Israelitish girl. This seems to be the meaning of the passage in chapter 11:40, where she was yearly mourned by her close friends.

What a lesson against rash vows! How few people there are who are strong enough to refrain from some kind of rashness in times of crisis. But one should remember from this lesson that rashness

Courtesy, Gertrude Levy

PHILISTINES. *A reconstructed scene of Philistines in battle, showing swords, shields, and armor. Designs were copied from actual objects from the periods in which the Philistines lived.*

is never justified and is always dangerous to both the person indulging in it and for those whom it may finally affect. Never act in haste and make outrageous statements or promises, no matter what the pressing occasion may be.

4. Samson is one of the most pitiful characters of the Old Testament. Brought up by godly parents, he was a *Nazarite* from birth. He was set apart and dedicated to God's service from birth or before. But when he became a man he failed to carry out those noble plans for which he had been consecrated (13:1-25).

Samson had great physical strength. It is not likely that he was a huge giant, but rather that his great physical powers were given him by God, supernaturally, upon necessary occasions. But his great physical strength was not the supreme

secret; it was his dedication to God that gave him this strength. It lasted only as long as Samson obeyed those Nazarite principles of drinking no wine and allowing no one to cut his hair. This may seem strange to us today, but it was a sacred rite in those days, and for one who had accepted it, to break it spelled his spiritual ruin.

Samson was too much inclined toward the love of the world. His first marriage to a Philistine woman was clearly out of his range. He should have married an Israelitish girl. In today's language, in marriage it is a "Christian for a Christian." Christians and unbelievers have no business marrying. This was Samson's first downward step.

His second foolish step, after that wife was taken from him, was to repeat the first bad act. How very like weak humanity this is. The first wrong generally leads to the second, and so on. His marriage to Delilah only served to weaken his resolve for the right. Delilah means "delicate." Doubtless she was beautiful,

CANAANITE CULTIC OBJECTS. *From left to right: an image of Baal, an object with snakes and birds, and an incense stand.*

winsome, and clever — all the more dangerous to him.

Read carefully the story in chapter 16:6-20 and note how cunningly Delilah works upon Samson's affections with her wits and her tears to get him to reveal to her the secret of his great strength. Note, too, how much *nearer* he comes to telling her "all his heart" each time. Finally he comes so close as to say that his hair may be placed in a weaver's beam and that this will weaken his strength. How frightfully near he has come to telling her *how* to *ruin* him! Only one more step is needed — her hypocritical tears.

At last comes the fearful break — Samson tells Delilah the secret (v. 17). What a tragedy that the man had no more sense nor self-control than this. But this is the end for which he started when he married the first Philistine woman. Sin leads one on, ever so imperceptibly, to the final brink of eternal ruin. Samson had tampered with the truth and with his conscience until he had deceived his own heart. He thought when he awoke he would "go out as at other times, and shake myself, but he wist [knew] not that the Lord was departed from him" (v. 20). Now read what follows (16:21-27). How sad to see the poor blind creature of his own folly grinding away at the mill of the Philistines while they make sport of him. Those who meddle with sin will pay such a price in the end.

There is only one bright spot in this dark picture. It comes at the close of the story (16:28-31). It shows God's great mercy to his erring children. In his deep grief and sorrow of heart, Samson had doubtless repented. He had returned to keep his vow to the Lord and was willing to die that he might correct his evil mistake and win a mighty victory for the Lord. His life did not end in suicide, as it may appear at first, any more than does that of any soldier who gives his life for the cause of his country. He is listed among the heroes of faith (Heb. 11:32), doubtless indicating his restoration to favor with God at the last. How kind and merciful is God to those who will repent and turn.

What a lesson for youth in the cost of disobedience! Think what a mighty man of immortal renown Samson might have become — instead of the pitiful, weakly creature which he did become, all because he tampered with sacred things. How important that one learn in youth *not* to follow this example of weakness and folly. Ungodly women have ruined more men than any other thing on earth!

5. The blood-curdling story of the wickedness of the men of Gibeah (19-20) pictures the depths to which Israel had fallen in her drifting away from God. It reflects the social and moral conditions of the times, but it also shows that there were left in Israel men of heroic courage who would not allow national morals to drift any lower without attention to justice.

Here again, though shining somewhat dimmer, the progress of the fulfillment of the Abrahamic covenant must not be lost sight of for a moment. Judges, in some sense, shows the exceeding weakness of Israel, but it also *shows* the great mercies of God as He ever leads His people on toward the final fulfillment of the ancient promise, the coming Messiah.

Memory Verse

"In those days there was no king in Israel, but every man did that which was right in his own eyes" (21:25).

Ruth

This little book is named for Ruth, the Moabite daughter-in-law of Naomi. Naomi and her husband had gone to Moab during a famine in Israel. Their two sons married Moabite girls. About ten years later, following the death of Naomi's husband, both sons died. Naomi decided to return to Palestine, and at first both daughters-in-law were going with her. But Orpah turned back. Ruth, however, held steadfast in her purpose and came with Naomi to her home town of Bethlehem.

TO WHOM

The book was written for all Israel and for universal reading among all peoples of the world. It is one of the ᵣmost beautiful stories of romance ever recorded. It is said that Benjamin Franklin charmed the godless literary critics of Paris by reading to them this book without announcing what he was reading. After their applause, when one asked the source, he replied, "Gentlemen, I have read to you the book of Ruth from the Bible." They were stunned into silence.

PURPOSE

This may have been twofold: It shows the ancestry of King David, his tribal lineage, and background. Here again the matter of the covenant of God with Abraham comes into play. It should be remembered that "Shiloh" — the Redeemer — was to come out of the tribe of Judah (Gen. 49:10) and that David also came out of this tribe. As the expanding kingdom grew, the eyes of the old prophets seem never to have lost sight of the covenant and its relationship to Israel. Although not stated in so many words, this may well have been part of the purpose of this book. Certainly the book had a more important purpose than merely to tell of an Israelitish romance.

Again, it points up the beautiful devotion of Ruth to her mother-in-law, and her conversion to Israel's God. It also shows God's impartiality toward all people; He accepted her into His peculiar people as part of them. It reveals also how Israel accepted strangers who wished to come and accept the Lord as their God, and Israel's way of life. It forever secures Ruth's niche in history as the ancestor of King David and of his far more important, though then distant, Son in the flesh, Jesus Christ. Ruth, although a Gen-

MILLET. *The King James Version tells us that Ruth gleaned "ears of corn" in the fields of Boaz. This phrase is more correctly translated "ears of grain". Several kinds of grain were grown in Palestine. Millet, pictured here, was one of the common grains.*

tile, then, comes into direct line in the fulfilling of the covenant, showing that "God is no respecter of persons: But in every nation he that heareth him, and worketh righteousness is accepted of him" (Acts 10:34, 35). Peter was to learn this much later.

TIME

The incidents of the story occurred many years before it was written, as seen by the last part of the book. It certainly was not written before the days of David. Some think the events of the book probably occurred during the reign of Shamgar, judge of Israel. The time covered by the book may represent about fifteen years, hardly over twenty at most.

AUTHORSHIP

Who wrote this beautiful book is not known for certain. Some have attributed it to Ezra, the great scribe who did much of the Old Testament historical writing and probably arranged most of the books in their chronological order.

The book of Ruth, however, serves as a kind of introduction to the books of I and II Samuel and gives the historical background to the birth of David. As he was living much closer to the times, it is far more likely, therefore, that the prophet Samuel wrote this book than that Ezra did.

GREAT THEMES IN RUTH

This book may be called a *pastoral idyll*. Its main setting is near Bethlehem. It is an interesting sequel to the book of Judges and an opening insight to I Samuel, between which books it serves as a connecting link. Its historical trustworthiness is confirmed by David's friendliness to the Moabites (I Sam. 22:3, 4) and by the genealogies of Christ in the New Testament (Matt. 1:5; Luke 3:32).

This *outstanding story* may be outlined as follows:

   I. Naomi's flight to Moab and her sorrow there, 1:1-13
   II. Orpah's return to Moab and Ruth's faithfulness to Naomi, 1:14-22
   III. Ruth's introduction to Boaz and his care of her, 2:1-17
   IV. Ruth's plea to Boaz for her redemption, 3:1-18
   V. Boaz's redemption of Ruth and their marriage, 4:1-17
   VI. Historical conclusion, 4:18-22

From this outline the following *great truths* may be pointed out:

1. When in great distress we are some-times driven into what may appear to be unfortunate circumstances, such as happened to Naomi in Moab (1:1-13). Often out of these conditions, however, God will bring about abundant blessing, teach us great lessons, and work out His plan in our lives. Had there been no trip to Moab for Naomi, there would have been no Book of Ruth with its many blessed lessons.

2. True love always shows its depth in crises. Orpah loved Naomi, but not more than her homeland. Ruth's love proved stronger than material attachments and may be called "unselfish devotion" to what she saw as duty (1:14, 15).

3. Ruth's choice to go with Naomi, however, reveals a deeper devotion to Naomi's God, whom she came to love and serve. Ruth made a decision to serve God and accept His land as her homeland forever (1:16-18). It is one of the most beautiful, tender, and touching passages of all the Old Testament, one of the most sublime pieces of all literature.

Ruth's choice to break with old homeland ties and go with Naomi and serve her God may have been a little painful at first. But see what greater happiness it afforded her even in this life, and what immortal fame blossomed in that decision! Surrendering the old life to follow Christ may at first seem like a trial, but the sufferings of the Christ-way are not to be compared to the glory that shall be revealed to those who follow Him to the end of the way.

4. Naomi had nothing to promise Ruth, but Ruth's trust in God was not to be disappointed. God never fails those who truly trust in Him and commit all to Him for time and eternity. Ruth's wonderful reward of faith in her marriage to Boaz was a striking illustration of Christ's reward to those who leave all to follow

Him, expecting nothing but the rewards of right living.

5. Another lesson is that we must not sit and wait for God's plan to be worked out in our lives. We must also work with God in working out His plan, just as Ruth gleaned in the fields of Boaz (2:1-23).

6. Ruth's meeting of Boaz (2:5-15) shows becoming humility for a stranger and reveals both something of the customs of the day and the character of Ruth.

7. It may seem very much out of place for a young woman to visit her boy friend's lodging place at night and ask him to marry her (3:1-18)! It was very different in that day, especially when we consider Ruth's particular circumstances. Ruth was left without children by her first husband. The law provided that the "nearest kinsman" to such a bereft widow could marry her and so give her a family. Except for one other man, Boaz was her nearest single kinsman (3:12; 5:1-8). In this light Ruth was perfectly within her rights in asking Boaz to *redeem* her, which also meant to marry her, provided the nearest kinsman did not wish to do so. One can imagine how Ruth's heart must have trembled as Boaz went to ask the nearest kinsman if he would redeem her, for by now she was in love with Boaz, not the unknown kinsman. The man finally renounced his right to redeem her, giving Boaz the opportunity to do so (4:6-10).

Here again one sees the hand of Providence: The nearest kinsman fails to redeem Ruth, giving her to Boaz. Only by so narrow a margin did the girl escape dropping into oblivion as just another Jewish proselyte unknown to history. But the purposes of God stand sure, regardless of how close they may seem at times to failure.

8. It is very interesting to note that the fields in which Ruth gleaned may still be seen at Bethlehem today, just across from the famous "Shepherds' Field," where the angels announced the birth of Christ to the shepherds eleven hundred years later. Further, it is interesting to know that Boaz was a direct descendant of Rahab, the Canaanitish innkeeper who was saved by faith in God and His people (Heb. 11:31), and her Jewish husband (Josh. 2:1; I Chron. 2:51; Matt. 1:5). One sees here that outside blood from at least two Gentiles flowed in the veins of the family from which the Messiah and Savior for all nations was to come. Christ was definitely from the tribe of Judah and the house of David. (See Matthew's genealogy in chapter 1:1, 2, and 5 for confirmation of this.)

There is a tradition that Christ was born in the very place where David's home was in Bethlehem, which also was the ancestral home of Boaz and Ruth. There is no historical proof of this, as there is of the Fields of Boaz and the Shepherds' Field, but it is interesting to note that in the little town where Boaz married Ruth and the Davidic family began, Christ was born of the same family lineage some eleven centuries later. It paid Ruth great dividends and gave her immortal fame to decide for the Lord instead of turning back as her sister-in-law did.

Memory Verses

"And Ruth said, Intreat me not to leave thee, or to return from following after thee: for whither thou goest I will go; and whither thou lodgest I will lodge; thy people shall be my people, and thy God my God: where thou diest will I die, and there will I be buried: the Lord do so to me, and more also if aught but death part thee and me" (1:16, 17).

I Samuel

This book takes its name from the prophet Samuel whose life and influence occupies much of it. Originally the four Books of Samuel and Kings were all called the Books of Kings. Later the Books of Samuel were separated from Kings as a single book; it was further separated for convenience in common reading.

TO WHOM

This book was written for all Israel, but probably especially for the scribes and leaders who needed accurate records of all the historical happenings of Israel. There is much in it of value for Christians today as well.

PURPOSE

Its main aim was to set forth a correct record of the historical events of the times and to show God's dealings with His people. The first part of the book is a continuation of the period of the judges, furnishing a background for the setting up of the kingdom of Israel.

Throughout the book the thought of God's supreme leadership in national affairs is uppermost. The writer apparently

←

GORGE BETWEEN MICHMASH AND GEBA. *It was in an area like this that David met Goliath.*

had in mind to give his readers the *reason* for the *failure* of the leadership of King Saul. To all leaders who afterward would disobey God, it is a warning that their kingdoms could end in miserable failure.

In relation to the need for complete obedience to God, there is much counsel for Christians in this book. It may well serve to illustrate what happens to the Christian church, both as a whole and locally, when there is not total obedience to God upon the part of leaders and individuals. There is also the *individual* lesson in King Saul's personal life which teaches us that sin is expensive and does not pay in the end. Self-will and stubbornness are strongly condemned (15:22, 23).

TIME

The time covered by I Samuel is that roughly from the close of the period of the judges to the end of King Saul's reign. This period was about 115 years.

AUTHORSHIP

No definite authorship is assigned to anyone in this book. It is therefore impossible to know just who the human author was. I Chronicles 29:29 refers to Samuel the seer, Nathan the prophet, and Gad the seer and seems to indicate that the larger portion of the book was composed by Samuel himself. The last four chapters could have been the work of either Nathan or Gad, prophets of a later time.

This seems much more likely than to suppose that either King Hezekiah or Ezra may have written it; Samuel was so well acquainted with all the major events of this book. Whoever the human author was, God, the true author of all the Bible, by His Spirit, inspired and guided him. This is the most important thing to remember about its authorship.

Three major characters are portrayed in this book: Samuel, Saul, and David. Almost everything in the book is in someway related to these three men.

A brief outline of the book may be as follows:

I. The rise of the prophet Samuel and his reign as judge, 1-8
II. Saul's rise to power and the beginning of the kingdom, 9-17
III. Saul's decline and David's struggle for survival and rise to power, 18-31

Samuel's birthplace was Ramah, about six miles north of Jerusalem. It was also his judicial residence and the place of his burial (1:19; 7:17; 25:1).

About five miles north of Ramah was Bethel, Samuel's northern office while judge. It was one of the highest points of the land. Here, eight hundred years before, Jacob had seen the heavenly ladder (Gen. 28). Mizpah, three miles west of Ramah, was his western office. Here Joshua had seen the sun stand still. Gibeah, about half way between Ramah and Jerusalem, was Samuel's home. Bethlehem was only twelve miles south of Ramah, while Shiloh, the site of the Tabernacle, was some fifteen miles north of Ramah.

This was the scene of the prophet's main ministry, though his influence reached into all the land.

Samuel was of Levitical parentage (I Chron. 6:33-38) and was thus both a priest, prophet, and a judge. He was both a religious and a civil leader. He turned out to be one of the noblest and purest characters in all of history. The last of the judges and first of the prophets, his main mission was the organization of the kingdom, starting with Saul.

VIEW OF GIBEAH OF SAUL. *The name Gibeah means "hill". It was the home of King Saul. Tell El Ful has been identified as Gibeah.*

Courtesy, Matson Photo Service

GREAT THINGS IN I SAMUEL

Following are the *outstanding stories* of this book:

1. Hannah's prayer for Samuel and his dedication to God, 1-2
2. Samuel's call and beginning as a prophet, 3
3. Israel's defeat and Eli's death, 4
4. Israel's request for a king and Samuel's warning, 8
5. Saul's anointing and coronation, 9-10
6. Saul's first sin, 14
7. Saul's failure in punishing Amalek, 15
8. Anointing of David as future king, 16
9. David and Goliath, 17
10. Saul's tragic end, 28-31

Note the following *great truths* in this book:

1. Hannah's silent prayer did not impress poor old backslidden Eli. He rebuked her for her drunkenness, only to be greatly embarrassed when he discovered his error. Mumbling in his beard, he pronounced a blessing upon her and retired to his place of watching the crowds. How sad that some men high in ministerial circles are so far from God that they have no spiritual discernment anymore!

Silent prayer is as effective as vocal prayer. After all, it is the *heart*, not merely the lips, which prays. Earnestness and faith are the two main elements of any prayer. Hannah's prayer was answered. God gave her a son (2:24-28).

Eli's chief sin consisted in allowing his sons to profane themselves and God's work (2:17; 3:13, 14). Young parents should take warning that they do not fail to rear their children correctly.

2. How quietly God often speaks to one's soul, and yet, how plainly may be seen in Samuel's call of God (3:1-10). Although he was very young at this time, he manifested true, characteristic prophetic boldness in telling Eli exactly what was to happen to him and his household (3:11-18). While still young, all Israel recognized that Samuel was becoming established as a prophet of God (3:19-21).

It is very important that young people keep their hearts open to God so that He may speak to them. Youth is the ideal time for a call to any Christian work. A call to any work is a *call to prepare;* one should begin his preparation at once. The ministry, in any form, should require the best and most adequate preparation possible for one to secure.

3. Eli's death at news of Israel's defeat was the close of a corrupt leadership and the beginning of a loftier reign under Samuel (4:12-21).

At this time a grandson was born to Eli. He was named Ichabod, meaning "the glory is departed from Israel." Whether that of nation, church, or individual, God will visit sin with sure punishment, and the glory of success and blessing will certainly depart from those who do not repent.

4. It seems Israel needed a king; this was largely because they had rejected God's way in theocratic government. Men always miss God's best when they choose a lower level than His highest will for them.

5. No young man in history ever started out better than did King Saul. He had God's approval, a strong ally and wise adviser in the prophet Samuel, and the hearts of most of Israel as his loyal followers. While his kingdom was not large, he had the advantage of being the first monarch and could have laid down one of the best possible platforms of government (9-13).

At his coronation Saul showed great humility and gentleness of spirit (10:21-23). Even his enemies he treated with most gracious concern (10:26, 27; 11:12, 13). It is too bad that he did not continue in this attitude and way of life. After only two years there came a breach between God and himself, and between him and Samuel.

6. Saul's greatest downfall throughout his kingly life was his constant *fear of people*. This caused him to commit his first trespass against the Lord, and was possibly his most outstanding weakness thereafter (13:8-12; 15:20-24; 18:6-9).

It was Saul's fear of losing the support of his soldiers which caused him to lose his patience with Samuel and "force" himself to make the offering. Saul was not a priest; therefore, God's law had forbidden him to make an offering to God, for this could be done only by a priest. Saul committed a grave error in forcing himself to do that which he had no right to do. It would be similar to a layman today going into the pulpit and throwing the minister out in a fit of rage and taking over. Saul knew very well he was doing wrong, but, to forward his cause and save face with the soldiers, he did it anyhow. In doing so he lost the favor of God and started on his downward drift toward a sad end.

7. The next major disobedience of Saul was his refusal to carry out the order of God to destroy all the Amalekites (15:1-23). It may seem difficult today to understand *why* God would order this seemingly cruel thing. But the Amalekites tried to destroy Israel in the wilderness; God then promised that when Israel was in Canaan, these merciless, wicked people should be destroyed (Exod. 17:8-16; Deut. 25:17-19).

One thing we must remember in this connection — and throughout all the Old Testament times — is this: The Old Testament Israelites were God's *earthly people*. They fought and won *earthly victories* over *earthly, human enemies*. All their relationships to the kingdom were largely in an *earthly context* and under *earthly conditions*. In our times, the Christians are God's *heavenly* people. We fight and win *spiritual battles*, not with fleshly instruments, but with moral and spiritual means. We use *prayer*, the *Word of God*, the *influence of good character*, the strength of *resisting evil* and evil things, and the use of the *voting ballot* to root out evil practices wherever we can.

Again, many of the Old Testament peoples apparently had become utterly unsavable by any means of God's economy. Their continuation, as in the case of the Amalekites, would therefore only mean more people born to live in sin, die, and be lost. If the whole people, therefore, were destroyed, it was best for all the unborn generations of them and for the moral conditions of that age. God destroyed the people of the world at the time of the flood because it was a *moral necessity* (Gen. 6:1-8). Had this not been done, the race of godly people would have become extinct, and there would have been no possible way God could have reached man by sending His Son to save man. The world would have become a vast bestial jungle in which supreme heathen savagery, far beyond our ability to imagine, would have reigned. Man would have destroyed himself in time. With all that God has done for man, it even now seems at times that man will yet destroy himself in his own sinfulness.

All the wars against evil people, and the Psalms in which the writer prays for the destruction of evil people must be

Courtesy, Steuben Glass

DAVID AND GOLIATH. *This engraving upon glass depicts the encounter between David and Goliath.*

looked upon in the light of this explanation — that it is the *sin* of people against which God fights, not merely people.

8. Upon the divine rejection of Saul and his line from kingship of Israel forever, God sent Samuel to anoint a new king. David, who proved to be a man who followed God with all his heart, was chosen (16:1-13).

Of all Jesse's sons, none seemed fit for the new task. Samuel seemed a bit discouraged and asked if there were not another. The little, ruddy-faced chap out in the sheep pasture was finally ushered into the famous prophet's presence, and the Lord said to Samuel, "Arise, anoint him: for this is he" (16:12).

God looks not on the outward appearance but upon the heart (16:7). He saw that David would be the top choice of all Israel. David proved successful, as the years revealed. Only God can know the future and choose the right persons for His great work. To be chosen of God for any work is the highest honor one can ever have come to him.

9. David's slaying Goliath is one of the great victories of faith in the Old Testament (17:32-58). Refusing Saul's cumbersome armor, the lad chose the weapon he knew best how to use — his trusty sling.

Out of long practice during his boyhood, with deadly accuracy David could put a stone where he wanted it to go.

Courtesy, Matson Photo Service

TOMB AT KIRJATH-JEARIM. *This tomb is located in an Arab village called Abu Ghosh, thought to be the site of Kirjath-jearim. The ark remained in this area for twenty years. Note the stone which rolls in front of the opening to the tomb. It was such a stone that the women feared they could not move after Christ's burial.*

Had he chosen Saul's armor, he would have been defeated before he started. David did not match battle gear with the giant nor try to show himself a great soldier or hero. He simply employed the means he knew best how to use, prayed to God, ventured in complete confidence, and won the victory. Some have said there was a small hole in the Philistine's helmet, for which David aimed successfully the first time. Be that as it may, the first blow downed the giant, but David did not stop here to "shout" his victory, or he may have lost it. While the giant was knocked out, David made sure of his victory by using the giant's own sword to cut off his head! He did not intend to score a half-victory.

Bringing this lesson into spiritual life,

one should never stop at a half-victory but make sure of total commitment to God. The simplest approach of faith toward any problem is far better than the most sophisticated reasoning. Our faith stands not in men's wisdom but in the power of God.

10. Saul's tragic end (28-31) is one of the saddest pictures of failure, defeat, and ultimate ruin in the Bible. From the most noble start to his suicidal end on Mt. Gilboa (31:4-6), Saul plunged from a height of fame, which could well have made him one of the greatest kings in history, to a shameful end in disgrace.

Perhaps it is best to allow the young person to trace for himself the strange and heart-breaking career of King Saul. Note the following steps:

1. His good beginning (9:25—10:27). Please read each passage carefully.

2. His first sin (13:8-16).

3. His second great sin (15:1-23, especially v. 23. See also chapter 28:15-18, especially the last verse). He utterly refused to obey God; he listened to the people.

4. His jealousy of David and his attempt to murder him (18:5-11). Again, his fear that David would undercut him and get the kingdom drove him to a dreadful state of mind and wicked actions.

5. His oppression of David. He continually haunted, hunted, and persecuted David, much as a disgruntled teen-ager tries to pick a fight with someone who has outmatched him but whom he considers inferior to himself (19-27).

6. His visits to the witch at En-dor to try to secure information from the now-dead Samuel (28). Witchcraft had been forbidden and Saul had punished witches before. Now, in his state of desperation, he turns back to what he had totally for-

saken. How like every person on the downward way!

His last sad confession to Samuel — who it appears by divine intervention had been permitted to speak to Saul, even from the dead — is indeed frightful to read: ". . . I am sore distressed; for the Philistines make war against me, and God is departed from me, and answereth me no more, neither by prophets nor by dreams . . ." (28:15). Note carefully Samuel's reply (vv. 16-18), reminding Saul *why* God had departed from him and had become his enemy. His refusal to obey God's orders regarding the destruction of Amalek was said to be God's reason for departing from him. Disobedience is the greatest evil in the world, and next to it is stubbornness and rebellion (15:23).

In this sad manner ends the life of one who could have been a flaming example of righteousness and faith for all time to come.

Notice in this book two important things relative to the covenant which we have been tracing throughout the preceding books. In this book the nation of Israel blooms out into a kingdom which placed it on its way to becoming one of the truly great nations of all time. Had Israel only remained true to God and His revealed will for them, they would possibly have in time become so powerful a nation that the world would have been brought under their control. In this way, the covenant would have been fulfilled as to its expansion, as the "dust of the earth." In so reading the message of salvation, had Israel been true to the evangelization concept, it is probable that great sections of the world would have turned and become Jewish proselytes, accepting the Word of God and the promised Messiah.

The other important point is that with the switch from Saul to David, there was the formation of the kingly line right down from Judah to Christ. Christ was of the descent of David, who in turn was from the tribe of Judah, from which Moses said "Shiloh," the Redeemer, would come.

This is a very important and noteworthy development. Saul's fight to destroy David was likely the result of Satanic opposition by which he tried to eliminate David from the Messianic line, not mere human jealousy.

Keep in mind all the time that the whole purpose of Israel's mission in the world was to spread the message of God's Word, to prepare the way for the coming Savior of mankind. Every story in it, then, in some way is linked with godly living and the Messianic progress of fulfillment of the covenant.

Memory Verses

"And Samuel said, Hath the Lord as great delight in burnt-offerings and sacrifices, as in obeying the voice of the Lord? Behold, to obey is better than sacrifice, and to hearken than the fat of rams. For rebellion is as the sin of witchcraft, and stubbornness is as iniquity and idolatry. Because thou hast rejected the word of the Lord, he hath also rejected thee from being king" (15:22, 23).

II Samuel

This book, like the former one, takes its name from the prophet Samuel. It was formerly part of the first book, but was evidently separated for convenience in handling and reading, as the original paper rolls were quite large.

TO WHOM

It was for all Israel but in particular the officers of the nation, as part of its basic historical records. It has come down to the Christian church as a part of God's Word for universal reading.

PURPOSE

It served both as a historical record of Israel's leaders and outstanding events, and the story of the unfolding of the kingdom of David. The lessons set forth in this section under I Samuel would be profitable here. (See PURPOSE, under I Sam., p. 87).

TIME

The time covered by this book is about forty years. Most of it is devoted to the establishment and reign of David as Israel's second king, his life, and his acts thereafter.

AUTHORSHIP

The authorship of this book is not stated in the book; it is somewhat uncertain. Certainly the author could *not* have been Samuel, as he died before Saul and quite some time before David's reign began.

The ancient Jews believed that Jeremiah wrote the books of Samuel from records left by Samuel, Gad the seer, and Nathan the prophet. It is thought he completed the books, adding the last materials and filling in details as they now stand. If this is true, it is still likely that Samuel, Gad, and Nathan did the original works of both volumes (I Chron. 29:29), especially when we know the books were

originally all in *one* volume. The most likely person to have prepared the original of what is now II Samuel would have been Nathan the prophet, who was David's personal prophetic and religious counselor (7:1-17; 12:1-14).

This book is another step in the progressive unfolding of the covenant made with Abraham. As the story unfolds it shows more of how God would make the Hebrew nation a blessing to all nations, and it is revealed that God is establishing a family line from which the Redeemer is finally to come. The King will live forever and establish a kingdom of endless duration.

One of the most outstanding chapters of this book is the seventh. Here God unfolds to David His purpose in making his family the royal line from which Christ should eventually come. "Thy throne shall be established forever" (7:16) is the first promise. This is followed by many more of such significant promises of God to David. They are recorded in the various historical books (I Kings 2:4; I Chron. 22:8-10; II Chron. 7:17, 18).

One should also read carefully Psalms 89:3, 4, 27-29, and 34-37, as part of this covenant promise to David. These covenant promises continue to be strewn throughout the Old Testament in many places: Psalm 132:11; Isaiah 9:6, 7; 11:1, 10; Jeremiah 22:29; 23:5-6; Amos 9:11-12; Micah 5:2; Zechariah 3:8-9; 6:12-13; 9:10; 12:8; 13:1. This covers a period of some five hundred years in the Old Testament. In the New Testament the fulfillment of these promises is recog-

→

NOB. *David First stopped at Nob, "the city of the priests," as he fled from Saul. This site, thought to be that of the Biblical Nob, is near Jerusalem.*

nized in the birth of Christ fully (Luke 1:30-33).

To the keen eye of the prophet in the Old Testament and the alert Bible student today, much of the Old Testament was the unfolding of this divine purpose of God, in its redemptive meaning and progressive fulfillment. The Old Testament worked out the *earthly pattern* for the fulfillment of the *heavenly plan* of redemption. This whole national process of development, despite its many unfortunate backslidings and necessary divine chastisements, was part of the total redemptive program of God, promised to Abraham. God's original plan as announced to Abraham, making him a "father of many nations" (Gen. 17:4), in whom "all families of the earth shall be blessed" (Gen. 12:3), was *not* a merely human, national, secular thing. Indeed, God's thought was that through Abraham and this nation the Redeemer promised in Genesis 3:15 should be brought into the world. It was a *spiritual goal* toward which God worked throughout the Old Testament. This was often overlooked by national enthusiasts, but it is the heart and core of the entire Old Testament program.

From here onward in the Old Testament there will be seen a more spiritual meaning attached to the idea and fulfillment of the covenant. Its scope is enlarged and made more spiritually applicable. This is what is meant by the *progressive unfolding of divine revelation.* Readers will need to keep this term well in mind. It means that God *adds more and more meaning* and gives *new light* and *new concepts* of His revelation as the Old Testament age advances. The age of the kingdom which is described in I Samuel, and that of the prophets which began with it and extends to the close of the Old Testament, gives a greatly expanded view and meaning to the covenant and its spiritual relation to Israel and to the world. Keep in mind that the *covenant* — the set of original promises God gave to Abraham — had both a material and a spiritual meaning, both a national and a universal meaning. It is the *spiritual* and *universal* meaning and application of this covenant which constitutes the *progressive unfolding of divine revelation.*

This is the first book in which there has been such a forward lunge, as it were, in this progress of revealing God's intended spiritual purpose in the covenant. This is because in this book we see founded, not only the kingdom and also nation, but the royal family, out of which the Redeemer was to come. This is the *key* to the rest of the historical and prophetical sections of the Old Testament; it should be kept in mind as these sections are read and studied.

This book may be outlined briefly in the following manner:

I. Coronation of David and establishment of his kingdom, 1-10

II. David's sin with Bethsheba and its bitter consequences, 11-18

III. David's restoration to divine favor, the re-establishment of his kingdom, and the events which signalized the latter part of his reign, 19-24

GREAT THINGS IN II SAMUEL

Outstanding stories in this book include the following:

1. David's tribute to Saul and Jonathan, 1:1-27

2. David's coronation in Hebron and his future course, 2

3. David's transfer of the ark to Jerusalem, 6

4. David's sin with Bathsheba, 11:2-27
5. The cost of disobedience, 12:18
6. An act of supreme devotion by David's three mighty men, 23
7. David's sin in numbering Israel, 24

Great truths which these stories point up are as follows:

1. David's unselfishness and devotion to God are shown in his behavior after the news of Saul's death reached him. The wicked Amalekite who had finished killing the king, expecting reward from David, was put to death out of regard for Saul, God's anointed king (1:1-16).

David's tribute to Saul and Jonathan is among the finest pieces of literature in the Bible (1:17-27). The true David, in his own personality and nobility, is here shown in full portrait. Saul had been his worst enemy; yet he lauds him as a close friend, showing his high regard for God's choice of him as king.

2. After Saul's death the tribe of Judah crowned David king in Hebron, where he reigned for seven and one-half years (2:1-11). During this time there was much warring between David's men and Saul's household and followers, but finally Saul's house faded away and David's influence gained over the whole nation. Without Saul's tricking and scheming, the nation finally turned to David and crowned him king over all Israel (3:1-5:12). As a ruler David proved his justice, mercy, and purity of life and God solidly established his kingdom.

3. For a long time the ark of the covenant — the wooden chest which held the Ten Commandments, a pot of manna, and

---

ASHKELON. *These Roman columns now adorn the Antiquities Park in Ashkelon. In Old Testament times Ashkelon was one of the five leading Philistine cities.*

Courtesy, Israel Office of Information

Aaron's rod — had been kept at Gibeah. David now desired that it be moved to the capital of the nation, Jerusalem. A group of men were dispatched by David to bring the ark home, and King David accompanied them.

The ark was carried on a large cart drawn by oxen. Sometime after they were on the way, the cart hit a rough place, and it looked as if it might overturn. Uzzah, to steady the ark, took hold of it. He died almost instantly as a result. God was displeased with his action, for the ark was a holy thing, representing the meeting place between God and man. Uzzah's act profaned the ark and grieved the Lord; as a result He took him away (6:3-8).

This lesson was hard for David to take, but it may have been intended to teach all Israel that sacred or holy things are not to be treated as secular and that everyone must have proper reverence for all divine things. There grew up, as a result, a much more reverential fear of God and of sacred things.

Finally, after some while longer, the ark was brought to Jerusalem amidst great rejoicing. King David did a special kind of religious dance that day in expression of his great delight that the ark was now at its proper resting place. His wife despised him, later condemned him, and was made to suffer for her untimely rebuke of her kingly husband (6:20-23). We should never make fun of or criticize the religious actions of others. They may be very sincere, though they may seem strange to us.

No one knows what finally became of this ark. It is supposed that it was lost at the time of the Babylonian captivity of Judah and never discovered.

4. The blackest spot on all of David's life was his sin with Bathsheba, virtually having her husband murdered (11:1-27). Every young person should read chapters 11-18 with utmost care. Study the tragic events of chapter 11 and see one of the greatest men of his times stoop to the lowest possible form of sin, hypocrisy, and cheapness. Then read carefully Psalm 32 and see David in the anguish and trouble of a sin-convicted, guilt-troubled soul. Turn then to chapter 12 and see how Nathan, the faithful prophet of God, rebuked David for his sins (12:1-14). Finally read Psalm 51 — the *Penitential* Psalm, as it has been aptly called — and hear David's bitter anguish and prayer for forgiveness of his awful sins. In this way one will get a true picture of his horrible wickedness and how David finally was restored to God. It is quite certain that he wrote Psalm 32 during his inward struggle over this awful sin, before his confession of it and his prayer for forgiveness. Psalm 51 is the prayer for forgiveness which he wrote later.

But this is only the start on the road to the long, dark, awful payday. Nathan's fearful sentence, "The sword shall never depart from thy house" (12:10), was literally fulfilled. After this David often was a broken-hearted and desolate man. Oh, how terrifying was the dreadful *cost of disobedience* for such a short duration of sinful pleasure! Read carefully and watch the frightful drama of trouble and sorrow unfold itself to this poor, suffering, troubled man:

1. His loving daughter was raped by her brother, 13:1-22.

2. Amnon, his son, is slain for his wickedness, 13:23-29. Note David's heartbreak, 13:30-33.

3. Absalom's rebellion again broke David's heart, 15:1-37. He had to stand and see his wives violated, immorally mistreated, right before his own eyes, and he was helpless to do anything about it. Oh,

how he must have thought of his own sins with Bathsheba, and having her loving but helpless husband put to death. These awful things must have stuck like daggers in his heart and mind as he was driven out of his home by his own rebellious, sinful son.

4. At the death of Absalom, his beloved son, his heart was torn again; he wept and cried (18:5-17; 29:33).

5. Following this, another bloody rebellion led by Sheba, against David broke out (20:1-22). War with the Philistines came again; to the end of his life David had nothing but sorrow and trouble.

Finally, as if he had not seen enough trouble, David grieved God by numbering Israel when told by Joab not to do so. This was followed by dreadful pestilence. Again David was heartbroken (24:1-25).

This section of this book speaks in fearfully loud terms of that Scripture which Paul was to pen about a thousand years later, when he said, "Whatsoever a man soweth, that shall he also reap" (Gal. 6: 7). Young people should let this great though dark and sad lesson sink deep

HEBRON. *This town, about twenty-eight miles south of Jerusalem, is one of the oldest towns in the world. David reigned here for seven and one-half years.*

down into heart and memory, never allowing sin to rule at any time in life.

We have already seen in the book how the covenant relates itself to Israel in a new and larger way than ever. It may be well to remark that despite the dim and sad picture just presented, God wrought His purpose. He will never fail to carry out His plan through those who will be obedient to Him.

Memory Verses

"Wherefore, thou are great, O Lord God: for there is none like thee, neither is there any God besides thee, according to all that we have heard with our ears. And what one nation in the earth is like thy people, even like Israel, whom God went to redeem for a people to himself, and to make him a name, and to do for you great things and terrible, for thy land, before thy people, which thou redeemest to thee from Egypt, from the nations and their gods?" (7:22, 23).

I Kings

The two Books of Kings were so called because they deal with matters concerning the kings and kingdoms of Judah and Israel. Originally they formed one book, but were separated for convenience in handling and reading at the time the Septuagint Version was made.

TO WHOM

These books were written for the Hebrew people in general. They still have valuable lessons today and should be read with two things in mind: God's dealings with Israel and Judah, and the spiritual lessons which may be drawn from the stories in these records, for application to our own lives.

PURPOSE

There seems to be at least a twofold purpose in the books before us: first, the accurate recording of the history of Judah and Israel, providing all Hebrews a continued story of their history and the background from which they had come. It tended to give a sense of unity to the Jewish cause, even though the people were divided into two kingdoms. A complete history is not provided, but the major outlines provide dates, events, and outstanding persons around which the story is told. The kingly lines are kept in view and the major events are related in interesting fashion.

Second, throughout there is a *religious* history interwoven into this story. It is the history of increase of godliness under some reformer, such as King Asa, and decline again during the reign of a sinful, careless king and his court, such as Ahab. Also threading through the scenes are incidents of personal piety, heroic faith, and daring action, such as those seen in the lives of Elijah and Elisha. These personal accounts were helpful to Jewish believers in those days; they served as inspiration, warning, and illustration of God's mercy, power, and His judgment upon evil. They serve the same purpose for us today (I Cor. 10:11, 12).

TIME

I Kings roughly covers about 120 years, from the close of David's reign to the death of King Jehoshaphat of Judah. It opens with the rising prosperity of Israel under Solomon and closes amidst the gloom of Israel's ten tribes in decline toward their final captivity in Assyria. Judah is also seen as a declining, sinful kingdom, drifting farther from God.

AUTHORSHIP

The authorship of both these books is not certain. An ancient tradition among the Jews assigns the authorship to Jeremiah. The author, whoever he was, makes reference to other works then in existence, such as "the book of the chronicles of the kings of Judah" and of Israel, and the "book of the acts of Solomon" (I Kings 11:41; 14:19, 29; 15:7, 23, 31; 16:5, 14, 27; etc.). At least there seems to have been an abundance of records of the historical facts from which to draw. It is evident from the nature of the two books that they were both written by the same author, who was inspired by the Spirit of God for this important task.

However, in the latter part of II Kings there are references to times much later than those of Jeremiah, especially those which refer to the period of Babylonian captivity (II Kings 25:25-30). Before this writing, or at its time, Israel was in Assyrian captivity (II Kings 17:6-24). Furthermore, certain portions which seem to be from Jeremiah are recorded here (II Kings 24:18; 25:1, compared with Jer. 1).

In this light, it is believed that possibly Ezra, a great Jewish scribe and leader, living about the time of the Babylonian captivity, most likely wrote these two books. He seems to have been the best qualified person to have done the work. Whoever the human author was, it is important to keep in mind that he was inspired for his task by the Holy Spirit and therefore produced a correct and dependable work.

From ancient times Ezra has been almost universally named by the Jews as the person who collected and arranged the Old Testament books in their present order, giving us the Old Testament canon. He could certainly have written the book of Kings.

One might outline this book briefly as follows:

    I.   The rise and splendor of Solomon's kingdom, 1-10
   II. Solomon's apostasy and decline; division of the kingdom, 11-12
  III. Story of the divided kingdom, under two kings, 13-25

The main stories cluster about the kings and the prophets, with the kings generally holding the limelight. After the division of the kingdom, Israel, the northern kingdom, principally followed calf and Baal worship, despite powerful prophets, such as Amos, Hosea, and Elijah, warning against their sins. The southern kingdom of Judah, though more godly, often fell into idolatry also. Samaria was the capital of Israel, and Jerusalem the capital of Judah.

The covenant which we have been tracing looms larger than ever toward its fulfillment under Solomon. After his death there is a decline, but David's line holds firm to the end of the story. Sin, tragedy, and general darkness show the utter sinfulness of man's nature, and that without the spiritual fulfillment of this covenant in Christ, there can be no permanent prosperity, even in that nation which God chose to bring the Messiah into the world. Despite the spiritual dimness of the age, prophets never lost sight of the coming glory of Israel and the Messiah's manifestation.

This may be also seen in the prophecies of Hosea, Isaiah, and Jeremiah.

GREAT THINGS IN I KINGS
Outstanding stories of the book are:
1. Solomon's coronation, 1, 2
2. Solomon's dream and God's promise to him, 3
3. Solomon's greatness and power, 4
4. Solomon's temple, 5-7
5. Solomon and the Queen of Sheba, 10
6. Solomon's sin and God's prediction of punishment, 11
7. A kingdom split asunder, 12
8. Tragedy for a man of God, 13
9. Elijah and Ahab's contest for fire from heaven, 17-18
10. Elijah at the juniper tree, 19
11. Ahab and Naboth: sowing and reaping, 21, 22
12. The reign of a good king, 22

Among the *great truths* which stand out in these stories are the following:

1. Despite David's sin, God in mercy gave him a son to reign in his stead and carry on the covenant line. Although this son was from Bathsheba, with whom he

Courtesy, Oriental Institute

SOLOMON'S STABLES. *During the tenth century B.C., Solomon fortified Megiddo and made it one of his chariot cities. This model indicates how these stables may have looked. The model is based on ruins and archaeological research.*

sinned, this does *not* place God's sanction upon his sin! It may show, however, that when God forgives the past, it is forever forgotten and never held against one. But this in no way should encourage youth to sin!

Solomon's coronation as king of Israel reveals God's overruling providence in carrying on His program, looking toward men's redemption, in spite of man's sin. Keep ever in mind that God *never* sanctions man's sin, however merciful He may be to him afterward (2:1—4:45).

2. Solomon's dream and God's promises to him (3:3-15) show again God's mercy, granting him the promise of the "sure mercies of David," which had relationship to God's determination to fulfill His covenant promises to Abraham.

In these Old Testament characters it is necessary for us to see God's overall purpose being worked out in their lives as part of a great master plan and purpose which courses through divine history. If this is kept in mind, the whole purpose of any book, and the whole of the Old Testament, in fact, can be much better understood and appreciated. Solomon, for example, is God's fulfillment to David in an immediate sense, but His fulfillment of the covenant in both a backward look to Abraham, and a forward look to Christ. David's prayer for Solomon (Ps. 89) is in reality a prophecy of his greater Son, Jesus Christ, for the petitions and praises of this prayer could not be applied to a mere human king, however great.

3. Solomon's reign made Israel a famous nation all over the ancient world. Although very small, Israel's glory was far-flung, and the nation became known for its riches and Solomon's glory and wisdom (3:1—4:35).

This may seem unimportant from a mere historical standpoint. Its importance is largely seen in the fact that it was another step in the fulfillment of the famous covenant of God with Abraham. At this point, Israel came nearer to being like the "dust of the earth" and the "sands by the seashore" in number than at any other time previous to this. Had her spiritual light been what it should have been, she could have ministered the knowledge of the true God to the whole world! This was doubtless God's original purpose for Israel.

4. Solomon's mightiest feat was his building of the Temple (5-7). In wealth it far exceeded any building of the times, because so much of it was overlaid with or made of gold. The Architect's Association of Illinois estimated in the 1930's that in modern times it would cost about eighty-seven billion dollars!

It would be unthinkable for any nation today to undertake such an expensive building! Gold then, of course, was not as important nor as costly as now, but even at the best figures, the thought is staggering.

This temple resembles in some sense the worthiness and importance of the worship of God. As an earthly structure it resembles for us today something of the divine values. It is rich in religious symbolism, if studied from this standpoint. The most important things of life are not the human, but the divine and spiritual values.

5. The story of the Queen of Sheba's visit to Solomon represents the fame of Israel's king and court (10). His wisdom was God-given; his glory the result of divine blessing. Only in his wisdom is Solomon a type of Christ; his kingdom in temporal glory may represent the church at its best in spiritual matters.

The modern Ethiopians trace their national leadership back to this event. It is claimed that their famous queen who visited Solomon begged him for a child by him, which he granted her. From this son came the royal line for all the centuries since then. Whether this is fact or fiction is certainly an open question, but its presence in Ethiopian tradition helps to establish the historical fact of her visit, recorded in the Biblical narrative. Here again one sees the spreading fame of Israel and the covenant promises coming ever nearer to fulfillment.

6. Solomon's sinful drift toward idolatrous women, who turned his heart away from God, is one of the saddest pictures of all the Old Testament (11:1-13). His sun set at noonday, so to speak, and his great fame was blasted and cursed by the wickedness of idol worship. The very thing Israel had become famous for — the worship of the true God — was publicly disregarded and virtually denied. His sins in this respect became internationally known, and he ruined a world-wide influence for God and for good. In this it may be seen that no one can sin without damaging others and hurting God's work. The more widely known the person, the greater the folly of his sin.

God's punishment of Solomon was almost immediate. God told him that He would rend the kingdom from his descendants, leaving his lineage only the one tribe of Judah "for David my servant's sake, and for Jerusalem's sake which I have chosen" (11:11-13). God also allowed other nations to rebel against Solomon (11:14-27).

7. When Solomon's son Rehoboam was to become king of all Israel, he was requested by the national leaders to lighten the burdens of taxation his father had imposed, but he refused with scornful pride and hard words (12:1-11). Israel revolted: the ten tribes went away with

Jeroboam, who finally turned them completely away from Jerusalem as a religious center. He built an abominable golden calf in northern Israel and directed the people to offer sacrifices there to the Lord. But it turned them back to Egyptian calf-worship and was the cause of Israel's ultimate ruin (12:12-33).

While the rendering of the kingdom from Solomon's line was a divine chastisement, it did not have to result in this wicked and heathenish thing. Oh, what a price Israel paid for its sin! Solomon himself may have been lost at last, as there is no record of his repentance. Some think, however, he did repent. (See Notes on Ecclesiastes: AUTHORSHIP.)

8. The story of the tragedy which came to the man of God who was called to prophesy against the idolatrous worship at Bethel (13:1-32) stands by itself in the sacred record. We do not know this man's name nor anything about him, except what is here stated.

He was told by the Lord to go preach against this evil work and that he should neither eat nor drink in this wicked place, but leave immediately. He obeyed the first part of his mission and made a profound impression upon the people. But finally he yielded to an old prophet who lived in Bethel and came back to his house to eat and drink. Then God's Spirit came upon this old prophet, and he cried out against this "man of God," telling him he would lose his life on his way home. Sure enough, on his way home he was slain by a lion (13:24).

This is a fearful lesson in the cost of disobedience. It seemed so natural, proper, and correct that he should return to the *home of another prophet*, possibly a man in whom he had great confidence. But it was contrary to God's plain word to him. Herein is often an awful snare

— the things which Satan suggests that we do are many times so natural; they seem harmless; others do them and appear to be all right, but for the truly devout person, they are wrong. We must obey God's Word as it is revealed to us and not follow the examples of others, often worldly in their ways. Certain things look so attractive and one is tempted to think, "What harm can there be in this?" The better question is, "What *good* is there in this? Will it help me to be a *better* Christian?"

9. One of the most interesting stories of the Old Testament is the contest between wicked King Ahab of Israel, and Elijah, a fiery, uncompromising prophet (18). He shut up heaven for three and one-half years by prayer and faith (James 5:17-18), until wicked Ahab was calling for a meeting with him to get matters straightened out and the famine stopped.

When Elijah and Ahab met again, Elijah called upon him to meet at Mount Carmel and let God show who was the true, supreme deity of Israel. At this meeting the false prophets utterly failed to bring fire down from heaven as Elijah had demanded, to prove that Baal, the sun-god whom Israel had been foolishly worshiping, had supreme power. This was the nearest and easiest test he could possibly have offered them. Was he not said to be the god of *fire,* the sun-god? Could he not produce his *own* kind of *element?* Nothing could have been more fair than this test. Elijah safeguards his proposition by having his sacrifice drowned with

SHISHAK. *During the fifth year of Rehoboam's reign, Shishak, an Egyptian pharaoh, invaded Palestine and took temple treasures as tribute. His exploits, including capture of cities in Judah and Israel, are depicted on this wall in Thebes, Egypt.*

water, until *false* fire, produced by Elijah, would be seen to be an absolute impossibility. Then in a little sixty-three word prayer, he asks for fire from heaven, which God granted to the amazement of all (18:32-38).

In this way God convinced Israel of His supreme reality and of the utter folly of idol worship. The 850 false prophets were put to death, showing God's wrath against idol worship. The God of the covenant here again shows His glorious power to keep His word and bring His plan to pass upon earth.

10. Even the greatest of God's saints are subject to great discouragements at times. Note Elijah's plight when Jezebel notified him she intended to kill him. Elijah, the mighty prophet of fire and power, whose prayers had so lately turned

---

ELIJAH. *While hiding by the Brook Cherith, Elijah was fed by ravens.*

Courtesy, National Gallery of Art, Samuel H. Kress Collection

Israel back to God and caused remarkable changes, was now lying under a juniper tree in a lonely desert in a pitiful plight of discouragement and despair, (19:1-9).

God did not scold Elijah; rather, he fed the weary prophet and sent an angel to encourage him. God knows the weaknesses of the saints. He does not wish to condemn, but to lift, deliver, and encourage one when he is in supreme difficulty and depression. When you are in distress and you are tempted not to trust in God, never make any important decision. Wait for the reassuring Holy Spirit, who will always come to help you.

11. Ahab was an utterly wicked, selfish, and unprincipled man. He wanted Naboth, a certain poor man, to give him his vineyard for a garden. This was contrary to the Jewish land laws, and Naboth refused, preferring to obey the law of God rather than the king's order. Pouting, Ahab reported this rebuff to his even more wicked queen, Jezebel. She in turn plotted Naboth's death and then told her husband the vineyard was his. Going down to see his new possession, Ahab saw the rugged old prophet Elijah standing right in the middle of the garden. Pointing his long index finger right into the sinful king's face, Elijah told him he would pay for this horrible sin with his own life (21:1-24).

All seemed well enough as Ahab proceeded to carry out his plans, despite Elijah's stern warning; but his heyday was short-lived. Though God spared him much sorrow for his repentance, which followed Elijah's rebuke (19:27-29), he paid in the end as Elijah had said (22:33-38). See chapters 19:19 and 21:38 for the prophecy and its fulfillment.

Here again one sees the frightful price of disobedience to God. The principle which Paul was to announce centuries later rings out again: "Whatsoever a man soweth, that shall he also reap" (Gal. 6: 7). This is one of the most unalterable laws of the Bible. Every young person should learn this lesson well and avoid disobedience.

12. This book closes with the long reign of Jehoshaphat, a good king (22: 41-50). Here again, despite all the evil, God is bringing His purpose in the covenant promises ever nearer fulfillment. The house of Israel declined steadily until it was wiped out by an Assyrian invasion and captivity in Nineveh, from which Israel never returned. But God prospered Judah, keeping the royal lineage of David alive. Even though Judah was later carried to captivity in Babylon, the tribal line was never to become extinct until the Savior's birth.

Memory Verse

"Yet have I left me seven thousand in Israel, all the knees which have not bowed unto Baal, and every mouth which hath not kissed him" (19:18).

II Kings

This book, like the former, was so named because it relates the story of the kings of Israel and Judah. We have already discussed its authorship and audience. (See these sections under I Kings.)

TIME

The period covered by this book is about 434 years, from the death of Ahab, king of Israel, to the Babylonian captivity of Judah. The general decline of both kingdoms and their final banishment from Palestine by the Lord, Israel to Assyria, and Judah to Babylon, are related here.

The matter of the progressive unfolding of the covenant is seen in the preservation of Judah, even in captivity. The royal line of David was kept constantly alive and never lost sight of, despite the scattering of the Jews over much of the Babylonian Empire. This is another evidence of the divine purpose and progress toward man's final redemption by Christ.

It is interesting to note here the following facts:

The Northern Kingdom of Israel lasted from the split of the kingdom, 933 B.C., to its captivity in Assyria in 721 B.C. Nineteen kings, all of whom were idolators, reigned over them without one single case of a godly king. The longest reign was that of Jereboam II, forty-one years; the shortest was that of Zimri, seven days.

Judah, the Southern Kingdom lasted from 933-606 B.C. when they were carried away to Babylon. Twenty kings reigned over this kingdom, of whom seven were good, or mostly good, and thirteen were bad. The longest reign, fifty-five years, was that of Manasseh, one of the worst kings; the shortest, three months, was that of Jehoiachin, also bad.

Israel's leadership was totally wicked and idolatrous, while Judah's was mixed: some good, some bad. On the whole, much more devotion to God was seen in Judah than in Israel.

In this book the ministry of Elisha is prominent in the first half.

One may briefly outline the book as follows (This outline clusters around the prophets.):

I.   Final work and translation of

Elijah, 1-2

II. Ministry and work of Elisha, 3-13

III. Decline and captivity of Israel, 14-17

IV. Decline and captivity of Judah, 18-25

GREAT THINGS IN II KINGS

Outstanding stories of this book are as follows:

1. Elijah's translation, 2
2. The miracle of water in a dry valley, 3
3. The miraculous saving of a poor widow, 4:1-7
4. The prophet's chamber and the woman's reward, 4:8-36
5. The healing of Naaman the leper, 5:1-19
6. Gehazi's sin and his fate, 5:20-27
7. Miracles of Elisha, 6
8. The rout of the Syrian host by a strange noise, 7
9. Jezebel's fate, 9
10. Resurrection power in Elisha's bones, 13:2-22
11. Destruction of Sennacherib's army, 19
12. Hezekiah's healing, 20:1-12
13. The book of the law and the great reform, 22, 23

Great truths in these stories may be seen as follows:

1. God seems to have had a purpose in Elijah's translation alive into heaven. He is seen coming back to talk with Christ on the Mount of Transfiguration (Matt. 17:1-6). He may be one of the two witnesses which are to come to the earth and die during the great tribulation. (Rev. 11:1-13 should be read carefully.) Power to "shut up heaven" in his day seems to refer to Elijah's great prayer miracle (I Kings 17:1-8; James 5:17, 18).

Beyond doubt, Elijah's translation was used for some redemptive mission. Coming as it did before the frightful disaster of the captivity of Israel and Judah, it may signify or illustrate the coming of Christ for His church before the great tribulation breaks upon the world in its fury (I Thess. 4:13-17).

Elisha's receiving the mantle of Elijah is a good illustration of the fact that Christians receive spiritual power from God only as they are faithful to God, just as Elisha was to his master Elijah. It may also be a type of the Holy Spirit coming from Christ to the believer after the Savior's ascension, as He did at Pentecost. Most Old Testament occurrences of this

ELISHA. *Returning to the River Jordan, Elisha smote the waters with Elijah's mantle, as Elijah himself had done. Again the waters parted.*

kind have in them some rich symbolism of deeper New Testament truths. The lesson for us today is one of faith and obedience.

2. The miracle of the waters for the dry valley was a supreme test of Elisha's prophetic calling. If he were going to be a successful prophet, he must be able to perform miracles. When needed most, the water was there, as Elisha had predicted (3:12-23), and the heathen were defeated by their own hands.

God's intervention here was not for sinful Israel's sake so much as for His own glory. The miracle demonstrated that God was able to perform whatever miracles were necessary for the preservation of His people.

3. The miracle of the increasing oil, by which the poor widow was able to save herself and her sons from being sold into slavery (4:1-8), reveals God's love and protective care for the helpless. Even though the story of the Old Testament is largely the progressive unfolding of the Messianic purpose and plan, yet it is filled with incidents of the individual and personal care God bestowed upon His people.

4. The woman who had kindly provided Elisha with a special room for his convenience upon his usual visits in that vicinity had been blessed with a son as a result of Elisha's prayers. This son became sick and died. What, now, could the poor woman do but go to the prophet whose prayers had first helped her? Here again God's personal care of even an infant shines through this story of His raising him from the dead (4:8-36).

5. In the healing of Naaman the leper, who was a great general in the Syrian army, we have revealed the compassion and love of God for all men. He is not just the God of the Hebrews, but of all men. He would have all men to come and be saved (5:1-19). Here again the universality of God's love and His claims are shown; another step is made in the revealing of God's overall purpose in the fulfillment of the covenant with Abraham.

If one looks for this redemptive truth, it shines out through every major story of the Old Testament. While Naaman's healing may have served no immediate purpose in God's plan with Israel, it certainly shows this larger truth of His love and interest in all men.

6. The tragic cost of disobedience is again seen in the sin and punishment of Gehazi (5:20-27). His greedy heart devised a lying way in which to secure the soul's desire, but at what fearful price! (v. 27). Little did Gehazi realize when he made his plans, that in less than an hour, his life would be blighted for all time to come. Oh, the blindness of sin!

It seems that the punishment for this type of crime was unduly heavy and that the prophet was relentless, mixing no mercy with the punishment. Although Elisha and Gehazi were doubtless good friends, the prophet would not compromise with Gehazi's sin in the least.

Perhaps Gehazi's sin was greatly amplified by the fact that it made the prophet appear as a spineless, greedy, unprincipled man, whose word could be changed at any whim (5:22), thus reducing him to a mere charlatan in Naaman's eyes. This damaged the cause of God and brought disgrace upon the whole country of Israel and upon the name of God and all that Naaman thought of God as standing for. Gehazi's sin was against universal redemption and the successful fulfilling of the covenant. In some sense, the total cause of mankind's welfare was at stake.

7. Three miracles of Elisha: causing the iron axe head to swim (6:1-7), smit-

ing of the Syrians with blindness and delivering them to Samaria (6:8-23), and giving famishing Israel food by routing the Syrians (7:1-20), show God's great personal and national care for His people.

Possibly Elisha worked more miracles than any other Old Testament prophet, yet he was a very quiet, unassuming man. His natural gifts seem to have been much less in evidence than those of Elijah. One may see in this the lesson that faith is not necessarily accompanied with fanfare. Often the most remarkable evidence of spiritual life and power is not spectacular at all.

8. The deliverance Elisha had forecast in his promise of food within twenty-four hours (7:1) was accomplished in a rather strange way. The Syrians were camped near Israel, planning to strike with a gigantic force. Israel's only hope was in God. During the night a strange noise began to sound. The Syrians heard it and believed Israel was planning a master counter-attack. In terrifying superstition, for which many of the ancients were noted, they fled without a battle, leaving untold bounties behind them (7:6-7).

Perhaps these miracles were God's means to bring Israel back to worship and serve Him, thereby averting their disastrous captivity. But they would not listen.

9. Although the judgment of Jezebel was long delayed, her fate was finally sealed. After Ahab was dead and Jehu was anointed king, he had her executed in a most frightful way (9:30-37). Her trickery and deceit had finally failed. She had decked herself out for carnal, lustful appeal to Jehu (v. 30), only to reap a harvest of swift destruction. The dogs licked her blood as they had done her husband's, fulfilling Elijah's dreadful prophecy (I Kings 19:19) and allowing all Israel to see its fulfillment (9:35, 36).

Courtesy, The Oriental Institute

ANNALS OF SENNACHERIB. *On this clay prism Sennacherib, the Assyrian king, describes his attacks upon Hezekiah. Although Sennacherib received tribute from Hezekiah, he was not able to take Jerusalem.*

The lessons of sowing and reaping and of the cost of disobedience are seen again.

10. Elisha had now been dead for some time and his bones were lying in a cave. Certain men, going out to bury a man, were surprised by a small group of their enemies, and they hastily placed the dead body in the cave with Elisha's bones. Touching the bones of the prophet, the man instantly came to life. Imagine the

consternation of these men, seeing their corpse immediately standing up and looking at them! (13:21).

The prophet seemed to have resurrection power, so to speak, in his very bones. Possibly one can draw from this story the truth that God's true saints have a living, vital influence long after their lives end on earth.

11. Sennacherib, the Assyrian king, was determined to destroy Judah as his predecessor had Israel. He was encamped against Jerusalem with an army of about 185,000, planning to invade it (18:13—19:37). Isaiah the prophet sent a message to King Hezekiah to have no fears; the Lord would deliver Israel. That night almost the entire army perished in a fearful plague (19:33). It is not known what this plague was, but for Judah it was a miraculous intervention of God.

God had purposed to remove Judah to Babylon, as this nation would preserve them, whereas Assyria may have destroyed them. While the sure fate of Judah was captivity, God would not allow Assyria to be the instrument of His chastisement of Judah. It may be interesting to note two things here: first, that God was working out His covenant purpose, even in this disastrous intervention against Judah's enemies; second, that even though God may be compelled sometimes to chastise His children, *He* will choose the means of our chastisement, not allowing Satan to do so!

12. Hezekiah's sickness and healing (20:1-11) are a lesson to us today. He had so lived that he was not ashamed of his life (20:3). This is always a gracious comfort in times of distress and sorrow. His healing seems to have been connected in some way with the sparing of Jerusalem (20:6). Here again the very mention of David reminds one that this miracle was also connected with the fulfilling of God's covenant to Abraham, renewed again to David.

13. One last, great effort to swing the tide and avert captivity was made in Judah. Under the reign of young Josiah, the lost book of the law was discovered — possibly a copy of the first five books of the Bible (the Pentateuch) or perhaps just the Book of Deuteronomy — was discovered. The reading of this book by the high priest and the king's proclamation of a religious reform movement produced a temporary turning to God. But it was short-lived. The people had sunk into such deep-seated sin and idolatry that they found permanent turning to God well nigh impossible, because they would not pay the price of separation from its evils.

This story ends in utter tragic darkness and failure. Both kingdoms had sinned away their day of grace and there was nothing left but God's justice to be meted out to them for their sins. Not all the people had sinned in this manner, but here, as in many other cases, the innocent had to suffer with the guilty. Despite their chastisement in captivity, it worked for them a great good. Never again after their restoration from captivity did Judah ever worship idols. Captivity in Babylon made of them ardent believers in the Lord, the Jehovah-God, the Redeemer. Since then they have always believed in the one true and living God, the God of all the universe.

Memory Verses

". . . *Elijah said unto Elisha, Ask what I shall do for thee, before I be taken away from thee. And Elisha said, I pray thee, let a double portion of thy spirit be upon me. And he said, Thou hast asked a hard thing: nevertheless, if thou see me when I am taken from thee, it shall be so unto thee; but if not, it shall not be so*" (2:9, 10).

I Chronicles

The two Books of Chronicles were so named because they are largely records of the kings of Judah and Israel. The word chronicle comes from the Greek and is related to our word chronology. A chronicle was a detailed account of history arranged in order of time. The term was first used in the Septuagint Version.

Like the two Books of Kings, these books are thought to have been originally in one volume, but were later separated for convenience in reading and handling.

TO WHOM

These chronicles were prepared more largely for the kings and religious leaders, but they were also placed into the hands of the common people for reading. They may be read by Christians today with much profit also.

PURPOSE

There must have been a two- or three-fold purpose for these books. First, they provided a fresh review of Israelitish history for the newly returned captives from Babylon. The rising generation would possibly read a new edition of these stories, written by a later author, with more zest than the older copies, such as Samuel and Kings provided. Again, there was more material which needed to be added to bring the historical survey of Israel and Judah up to date, so a new history of the nation was evidently thought wise.

Finally, there was here a new reminder for the people of the mercies of God by which they had been brought back to their present state. Both the sins of Israel and Judah, and God's punishment of them, as well as the mercies and goodness of God, were set forth anew in this work. Israel, like the church of Christ today, needed new and fresh presentations of God's love and mercy, as well as fresh reminders of His expectations of His people. One will find much for meditation, devotional outlook, and spiritual help in these remarkable books. They serve well in our day to emphasize many great truths.

TIME

Everything in these books points to the time of the return from captivity as the period in which they were written. The expressions used, the references made to several places known by these names at this time, and those of some special words point to this period.

At the very end of II Chronicles reference is made to the decree of Cyrus, King of Persia, for the return of the Jews to Palestine (II Chron. 36:22, 23). This indicates that the books were written either at this time or shortly afterward.

AUTHORSHIP

It is not known just who wrote these two books. That they were the work of one person rather than several is evident, however, from their style, continuity, and their unity of language expressions.

For a long time both Jewish and Christian authorities have held that they were written by Ezra. This man was one of the most outstanding scribes at the end of the Babylonian captivity.

There seems to be more evidence in these books of Ezra's authorship than that of any person known. There are a number of similarities between his book Ezra, and the Chronicles. In all three books the writer's use of certain terms, not known to have been in use before the return from Babylon, for instance, is a good example of evidence in favor of Ezra's authorship. For these and other reasons, scholars have generally assigned these books to his pen. Whoever the author, it is well to remember that he was inspired of God and therefore wrote a true record, as directed by the Holy Spirit.

Several differences in the historical events of these books from that presented in I and II Kings, for instance. These do not amount to discrepancies or inconsistencies so much as to *omissions* of certain facts. David's sin with Bathsheba will not be found in the Chronicles, nor will the unfortunate case of Tamar's having been raped by her brother Amnon be found. The writer of the Books of the Chronicles makes little mention of the kings of Israel; of the wars of these kings just before they were carried away captive to Assyria he writes not one word! This part of the record apparently had no appeal to the new generation returned to Palestine.

Differing from the Books of Kings, the Books of Chronicles enlarge upon Jewish ceremonies and genealogies — nine chapters are given. Much is also said of the proper order of the priests, Levites, and religious ceremonies. A short genealogy from Adam to David is also given in these records.

The long absence of the Jews from Palestine required a new statement of many basic things which concerned them; these books provided these in a sort of orientation for the new generation who must now take up where the older one left off in the Jewish national life. These books set forth many of the finer things of Israel's inner life and provide important details not found in other historical books. Jerome, Church Father of the fourth century A.D., considered them the "epitome of the Old Testament." They provide a good *commentary* of much in the Books of Samuel and Kings.

It will be remembered here that the Books of Chronicles are almost entirely confined to presenting and bringing up to date the Southern Kingdom and the

PAPYRUS. *Writing material, also called papyrus, was made from the papyrus plant which was very common in Egypt and Palestine. Sheets were formed from split stems, then glued together and rolled on wooden rods. Undoubtedly Old Testament scribes used papyrus as writing material for their chronicles.*

Courtesy, Israel Office of Information

line and descent of King David. This was because only Judah had survived; Israel had been carried away to Assyria and had never returned. Therefore, it was necessary to start with Judah and rebuild as much as possible of the whole of the Israelitish nation, but the emphasis is still upon Judah's kingdom and place in the program of God.

The author of the Books of Chronicles draws his information from many sources, some of which are mentioned here: chronicles of King David (I Chron. 27:24); Samuel the seer; Nathan the prophet; Gad the seer (I Chron. 29:29), the prophecy of Ahijah; visions of Iddo the seer (II Chron. 9:29); the story of the book of the kings (II Chron. 20:34); book of the kings of Israel and Judah (II Chron. 32:32); and others not here given. All these sources, plus his inspiration by the Spirit as to what to choose and present from these many sources, provided the writer with a rich background for his work.

As a brief outline for I Chronicles, the following may be used:

    I.   The genealogies, 1-8
    II. Re-establishment of the ancient inheritances, and settlements, 9:1-34
    III. Connected history of the Kingdom of Judah: David to the captivity, 9:35—29

There is little or no Messianic insight in this work, for it is really a reconstruction of historical data, which has little relation to the future *purpose* of Israel as a redemptive nation. The covenant relation seen in this book is merely the preservation of Israel as God's people, in keeping with His purpose for them.

GREAT THINGS IN I CHRONICLES

Most of the *outstanding stories* of the historical period have been listed in the former Books of Kings and Samuel. We shall here point up a few *great truths* from two incidents listed in this book:

1. Three of David's mighty men risked their lives to bring him a drink from his home well (11:15-19). David was so touched that he refused to drink this water; instead he used it as an offering to the Lord. True greatness is more often revealed in the little incidents of life than in the great.

2. It is not fully understood just *why* David's numbering of Israel was considered a sin (21:1-4), when Israel had been numbered before at different times. Perhaps it was the pride of David in doing so; it pointed to his reliance upon human might instead of divine power and love. At any rate, it was a costly blunder.

Note that David was warned against this, but he persisted in his plan (21:4). Either he purposely ignored this warning or did not believe he was doing wrong. Gad the seer told him of God's anger and His offer of mercy. David hastened to repent and offer sacrifices for his transgressions, but this did not keep many from suffering for it.

Two things stand out for attention: No one can sin without affecting others (21:7, 14). Others, too, must suffer for our sins, even today. The criminal brings shame and sorrow to his loved ones; the drunkard, to his family; the prostitute, to her loved ones; and so on. All sin ultimately brings suffering to others.

David refused to accept the offer of free grounds for his sacrifice (21:22-25). There is a price to be paid by those who disobey God. All sin is expensive. Even though forgiven, many suffer for a lifetime for the sins of youth. Sometimes, too, innocent children suffer because the sins of their parents have brought either disgrace or physical handicap upon them. Long after the parents thought they were entirely cured, blindness, or other physical or mental handicaps may occur in children who have contracted venereal disease because of the immoral practices of their parents. Sin is too expensive to be fooled with in any form!

Memory Verse

"Thine, O Lord, is the greatness, and the power, and the glory, and the victory, and the majesty: for all that is in the heaven and in the earth is thine; thine is the kingdom, O Lord, and thou art exalted as head above all" (29:11).

II Chronicles

This book is in reality a *continuation* of the former book. What was said about purpose, time, authorship, and intended audience in the introduction to I Chronicles, also applies to this book.

Two Chronicles is occupied largely with the reign of Solomon and the history of the kingdom of Judah. It is entirely silent regarding Israel's history after the kingdom was divided. Particular attention is given to religious ceremonies, the work of the priests and Levites, and the particular tribes of Judah. This book would properly form a fourth section of the total work, beginning with Solomon's reign and going right on down to the edict of Cyrus, the Persian King, for the return of the Jewish exiles from Babylon to Palestine.

A singular evidence that this book was written for the captives returning from Babylon is found in the fact that no mention is made of the kingdom of Israel. By that time it had been extinct as a nation for more than two hundred years, although it is thought that some of the Jewish Assyrian captives had also returned with those of Judah. Many of the weaker and poorer had been left, so that the whole twelve tribes could be reconstructed again as part of the nation which grew up after the Babylonian captivity. This, in some sense, cemented the nation back together. The Jewish nation had no kings after the Babylonian captivity. The facts of this book were needed in the re-establishment of the Jewish nation.

This ends the historical period of the Old Testament, as far as history proper goes. The books of Ezra, Nehemiah, and Esther, while historical in some sense, are fragmentary stories of history rather than historical progression as such.

Like I Chronicles, the only pattern of the Messianic covenant traceable in this book is the orderly progress toward the redevelopment of the Jewish nation, out of which that fulfillment would ultimately come. This is seen in Judah's remarkable preservation in Babylon and restoration by divine decree to Palestine, as Jeremiah had prophesied would occur.

This book may be outlined in very brief form as follows:

   I.   Solomon's reign, 1-9

  II. The reigns of the kings of Judah, with supplemental materials for reconstruction of the Jewish nation, 10-36

The closing note of hope in the edict of Cyrus for the return from Babylon indicates the end of an era of punishment and the beginning of one of blessing. So closes this long story of Israel's history from Egypt to the restoration of the Jews to Palestine — a sort of second exodus and beginning again, in the kindness and mercy of the ever-loving God.

Outstanding stories and great truths of such stories have been covered in the Books of Kings.

Memory Verse

"If my people, which are called by my name, shall humble themselves and pray, and seek my face, and turn from their wicked ways; then will I hear from heaven, and will forgive their sin, and will heal their land" (7:14).

Ezra

This book carries the name of its author, one of the most famous of Old Testament scribes. The name Ezra simply means "help," probably implying that he received the help of God.

TO WHOM

It was prepared for the Jewish nation which had resulted from the captives who had been returned and settled in Palestine. Even since the days of the return from captivity, a new generation was arising. It had now been over sixty years since the *first* group had returned to Jerusalem. A new nation was fast developing. To them and their descendants, this book would prove invaluable.

PURPOSE

Ezra is a continuation of the history of Judah in a different form from that of the true historical books such as Kings and Chronicles. This book states facts about one of the most important events since the exodus from Egypt — the restoration of the Jews to Palestine from Babylonian captivity. It is a personal account of the two stages of this return and is therefore in two sections, as will be seen later.

The writer passes over the long period between the beginning of the restoration, nearly sixty years earlier, and the second large movement which he led. He does so without even a notice of anything which happened during this interval. He seems to focus attention upon the matter of the total restoration, ignoring the fact that there were two separate groups involved.

The purpose seems to have been to set down in proper order the manner in which the Jews were restored to Palestine. He lists the great religious awakenings, revivals, and reforms which had gone into the restoration period, as well as the outstanding families and the chief leaders who took part in the work.

Evidently another purpose was to show that this restoration was the hand of God at work among His people. Nothing less than divine intervention in the affairs of mankind could have taken a slave people, most of whom were not even acquainted with their fatherland, and brought them back into it. When one considers the iron grip ancient kings held upon enslaved peoples, the slow and awkward modes of travel, and the lack of determination of

STAIRWAY FROM DARIUS' PALACE AT PERSEPOLIS. *This palace was an indication of the might of Persia. The stairways depict, in relief, twenty-three nations bearing tribute to the Persian ruler.*

a people enslaved for almost three quarters of a century, it seems to have been a miracle alone by which they were returned to their home land. In fact, it was only a remnant which did return, leaving untold multitudes in heathen lands.

TIME

The story of the book covers a period of some sixty years. The date at which the book was written has been placed between 457 B.C. and 444 B.C., the earliest and latest possible dates it could have been done. Likely it was written nearer the earlier date, as the events would have been fresher in the writer's mind.

AUTHORSHIP

There is every reason to believe that Ezra wrote this book. Some have thought that since it covers such a span of time, possibly several persons wrote parts of the story, which Ezra later compiled, but there is no evidence of this. There are passages in the book in which the first person is used and others in which the third person is used; this causes some to favor the theory of different authors, but this is not necessarily so. Any author is free to change the style of his writing where he considers the best interest of his readers may require it. Doubtless, Ezra used public documents such as genealogies and other historical accounts, which he inserted as he found them, and then went on with his own personal story.

From the most ancient times, Jewish authorities have assigned authorship of this book to Ezra. There is no other known writer to whom this book could be successfully ascribed; it is quite conclusive that Ezra wrote it.

EZRA, THE MAN

A number of interesting and important facts about Ezra may be drawn from this book, as well as from what his friend and co-laborer, Nehemiah, recorded in his book, and from Jewish traditions.

RELIEF FROM THE STAIRWAY AT PERSEPOLIS. *Shown are Babylonians and Syrians bringing tribute to Darius.*

Courtesy, The Oriental Institute

He was a priest, a descendant of Eleazar, Aaron's son (7:5). He belonged to that branch of Eleazar's family which had recently furnished the high priests of Judah. He was a direct descendant of the high priest Hilkiah, of King Josiah's days (II Kings 23:4), and of Seraiah, high priest when Jerusalem was destroyed and the last captives taken to Babylon (II Kings 25:18).

Ezra was also a scribe — a teacher or interpreter of the laws of Moses and other Old Testament Scriptures. He es-

pecially taught and explained the Pentateuch as part of his daily duty. He was, therefore, well educated in the Old Testament law and Scriptures.

He had obtained a remarkable position at the Persian king's court as a very young man. The king showed great respect for him. He was employed by King Artaxerxes, who was then ruling. The Persians had conquered the Babylonians and taken over the rulership just about the time the first captives were returned to Palestine some sixty years earlier.

Through his acquaintance with Artaxerxes, Ezra obtained permission to visit Jerusalem (7:6). He was also permitted to take with him all the Jews who would like to return to their home land (v. 13). The king gave him a commission which made him supreme ruler over Judea (another name for Palestine) for several years, along with Babylon in 458 B.C. He arrived in Jerusalem with about eighteen hundred men and their families (8: 3, 4, 14, 21) about four months later (7:9).

In Jerusalem Ezra's authority was immediately recognized. He deposited in the temple, which Zerubbabel had rebuilt many years earlier, the vessels returned by the Persian king. He began religious revival and reform on a large scale (8). After this he possibly returned to Babylon for a short time, but he is seen again assisting Nehemiah in Jerusalem in 444 B.C. This time Nehemiah had been made governor, and Ezra assumed a secondary place as the religious leader (Neh. 8:1-18). He taught, directed, and blessed the people, continuing there until the dedication of the new wall around Jerusalem, built by Nehemiah in 441 B.C. He took a leading part in this ceremony (Neh. 12:36). There are no other Scripture notices about him or his work. He is not mentioned as taking part in the religious revival under Nehemiah, probably because he was not then at Jerusalem.

The following statements are dependent purely upon Jewish tradition. Several of these are quite trustworthy, while others are not so certain. (It may be well here to look up the meaning of the word *tradition*.)

Ezra is supposed to have instituted the Great Synagogue — a group of one hundred older wise men who assisted him in finding and correctly placing together all the books of the Old Testament. Ezra is generally credited with this work, although he may have been assisted, as here stated. He secured all the books of the Old Testament then written and placed them in much the same order as they are now, with a few exceptions. This is what we know as the Old Testament canon of Scripture. Ezra, as well as those who may have assisted him, is believed to have been guided by the Holy Spirit in his selection of these books. Certainly he was the best-fitted person of those times for this work, for he was a "ready scribe in the law of Moses" (7:6). He had "prepared his heart to seek the law of the Lord, and to do it, and to teach in Israel statutes and judgments" (7:10). He was a very gifted man, well-learned, and very pious. If he wrote the Books of Kings and Chronicles, which seems more likely than anyone else, and his own book, there is no justifiable reason to suppose he may not have been used of God for this work of forming the Old Testament Canon.

Some believed that he wrote the prophecy of Malachi, writing his own book under his own name and that of Malachi under his prophetic title. This, however, is far from certain.

The personal character of Ezra stands out as pure and noble in all Scripture references to him. Nehemiah held him in highest esteem. His gifts and graces were recognized by the Persian monarch who gave him an honored position. His intense devotion, earnest prayers, trust in God, spirit of humility, and strength of character all commend him as a great man of God. He was simple, candid, devout, and sympathetic, yet filled with energy, unselfishness, and a burning patriotism, mingled with true kindness for all. As a religious leader, civil and ecclesiastical administrator, and historian, he left behind him, among the Jews of later times, a reputation second only to Moses.

It is said that after leaving Jerusalem, while journeying toward Babylon, Ezra died at Samarah, on the Lower Tigris River. His tomb is said to have been pointed out here as late as the times of Benjamin of Tudela, although this tradition is not absolutely certain.

This book is really the story of two restorations and so contains separate accounts. The book may be outlined briefly as follows:

I. The first restoration, 1-6
II. The second restoration and matters of revival and reform, 7-10

GREAT THINGS IN EZRA

Ezra presents one long, running story of part of Israel's restoration and re-establishment in Palestine, instead of several *outstanding stories*. To appreciate it, the young reader should at first skip the genealogies and read the whole connected story to get it well fixed in the mind; then, coming back, pick up the genealogies and see how they fit into the picture.

The book is very like Chronicles, Daniel, and Haggai, all of which were written about the same time. Like Daniel, it has some Chaldean language in the original. Ezra tells his story in plain and simple language, moving onward with speed. Only once does he leave his story to burst forth in praise to God (7:27, 28).

Some *great truths* which stand out in this book are:

1. God never forgets His people, although He may have to punish them for their sins. In Babylon God raised up prophets, such as Ezekiel and Daniel, to encourage and guide His people and finally lead them back to their land. God chastises His children today in a different manner, but for the same love's sake — that He may bring them fully to Himself, to stray no more.

2. God will restore those who repent. It took Babylon to break Israel of idolatry. When there was sufficient humility and repentance, God moved the necessary elements for their restoration. God loves even the erring ones and will restore them to full peace and joy as soon as they repent of their evil ways.

3. World governments are not left to themselves. This is revealed in His dealings with the Persian monarch. It may have been so much "foreign policy" to him, but it was God's way of securing His ends with Israel. God still rules among the nations in His own sovereign way, although His plan is hindered by the sinfulness of man. But His ultimate purpose will be realized.

4. Not all the Israelites took advantage of this opportunity to return to their home land. Many were satisfied to remain where they were. Had they all returned, how much greater could the nation of Israel have become! Too many times those chastised by the Lord do not profit thereby and return to Him.

5. From the small remnant which did

return, God developed a mighty people. To this day, though scattered the world over, the Jews represent a distinct people who have never lost their identity! Once, when an ancient king demanded that one of his counselors give him in *one word* the best evidence of the truth and inspiration of the Holy Scriptures, the counselor answered, "Jew."

"Who hath despised the day of small things?" (Zech. 4:10), asks the prophet. "Not by might, nor by power, but by my Spirit, saith the Lord of hosts," cried the same prophet (Zech. 4:6).

The progressive unfolding of the covenant is seen in this book, not by reference to it, but by God's restoration of His people to carry out the originally intended purpose. This is seen in the restoration of pure worship of God, the Temple cleansing, and the corrections of priests, Levites, and leading men from idolatrous connections with the heathen about them.

Memory Verse

"Now when Ezra had prayed, and when he had confessed, weeping and casting himself down before the house of God, there assembled unto him out of Israel a very great congregation of men and women and children: for the people wept sore" (10:1).

Nehemiah

This book was also named for its author. The name Nehemiah means "Jehovah comforts," probably referring to his great sorrow at seeing Jerusalem in its sad plight, as he found it. It is a companion volume to Ezra, and like Ezra, in part it is a personal narrative, setting forth a historical event of great interest to Israel.

TO WHOM

It was written for the newly established Jewish nation and for their descendants as a picture of Israel's condition at this time. It also serves the church as a fine piece of Bible literature, pointing up a number of important lessons for our age.

PURPOSE

The writer desired to set forth a true historical account of one of Israel's greatest events — the rebuilding after the restoration. As part of the recorded history of the Jewish nation, this would prove of great interest to future generations.

This book also reminded the people that this great work was done both at the direction of God and under His protective care. They were never to lose sight of the fact that all things which had any divine connection in Israel were done under God's protecting, directing care. The writer wished to make Israel more and more God-conscious in their new life as a nation. It was the God whom their forefathers had served who had done these marvelous things for Israel. They were to love, serve, and glorify Him in return.

Much in Nehemiah is of great value to the church; it is a pattern for progress in spiritual things. It also contains truths which have excellent personal application.

TIME

The time covered by this book is some twelve to fifteen years, perhaps 444-432 B.C., or 431 B.C. It is a natural sequel to

Ezra. In fact, at a very early time the two books were placed together as the first and second parts of one volume. However, for many centuries they have stood separately, as they should. The book was most likely written at the close of Nehemiah's ministry at Jerusalem, after the dedication of the great walls and his commission as governor had expired.

AUTHORSHIP

There is every reason to believe Nehemiah is the author of this book, especially those parts which are of the most interest and give it its true characteristics. These would be chapters 1-7; 12:27-47; and 13, all of which are written in the first person. It has been argued that chapters 8-10 were written by someone else, probably Ezra, since they are in the third person. But there is no evidence of this, except an old tradition that Ezra was also the author of Nehemiah. This section could have been drawn from public records and simply inserted by Nehemiah as a necessary part of his book. Or, he could simply have changed persons in recording these facts of an impersonal nature. Either way, he was inspired by the Spirit and so gave us a true account from whatever sources.

Chapter 11 is the account of his own census, and chapter 12 may likewise be that or a public record. The last chapter sparkles with his personal touch.

The book in some ways resembles Ezra in its straightforward personal account of a great event in Jewish history, told in moving form and with warmth. Unlike Ezra, the style of which is smooth, Nehemiah is rough and terse, as from the pen of one not too well educated.

Those parts of the story which carry the main thread are vigorous, strikingly dramatic, and often highly devotional.

Nehemiah often expresses himself in strong, emotional language, stamping his individuality firmly upon the book. Here and there are short prayers, as if the man were praying as he went. He certainly carries a moving sense of action throughout the personal parts of his writing. This again favors his authorship of the book.

NEHEMIAH, THE MAN

Nehemiah was the son of Hachaliah of the tribe of Judah and was likely born in Babylon during the captivity. Probably he had never been to Palestine in his youth, though he considered it his native land. While still a youth, he had secured the very popular and well-paying position of "cup-bearer" to the Persian king. In this position he became well acquainted with Artaxerxes and his queen, Damasia. He was well liked at the royal court, as shown by the granting of his request to return to Palestine.

A burning interest in Jerusalem was created in Nehemiah's heart by his brother Hanani, who had just returned from Jerusalem. After hearing of the dilapidated condition of Jerusalem, Nehemiah was in mourning for several days, praying for the restoration of Jerusalem.

Upon his return to court, the king asked him about his sadness, and Nehemiah explained about conditions at Jerusalem. The king was very sympathetic, granting him a leave of absence to go to Jerusalem and work on the walls of the city. He also furnished him with the necessary equipment and gave him a royal commission to undertake the work, sending letters to the nearby governors, ordering them to assist in the rebuilding of Jerusalem's walls (2:11). He left Persia in the summer of 444 B.C., arriving in Jerusalem some four months later.

He quickly surveyed everything and

was ready to begin work before giving the nearby governors the letters from the king. He expected persecution and interference from the obstinate governors, but the Jewish people worked unceasingly until the work was finished. The task was completed in just fifty-two days! The governors hardly had time to make any successful moves against him. They worked around the clock (4:21-25) to perform one of the greatest feats in later Jewish history.

Nehemiah launched a population increase drive for Jerusalem, bringing in many families from the surrounding country to make the city strong enough to withstand its enemies. He remained governor for thirteen years.

During the latter years of his rule, he sought to promote a genuine revival of religion. He also instituted great social and moral reform, demanding Sabbath observance and the breaking off of all re-

REBUILDING OF THE WALLS OF JERUSALEM. *Under Nehemiah's leadership the walls of Jerusalem were rebuilt even though opposition existed.*

lationships with the sinful heathen about Israel (10-13).

One of his last public acts was the solemn dedication of the walls of Jerusalem. This was perhaps the highest point of his service there. For the occasion he had invited Ezra, his old friend and co-laborer, to take a leading part in the ceremonies (12:27-47).

Nehemiah left the city in a state of good repair. He was a very gracious and amiable man, self-denying, hospitable, and active in deeds of mercy and kindness (5:8, 14, 17; 13:14). How old he lived to be and the place of his death are unknown. He had no tomb, but as Josephus well observed, "The wall of Jerusalem constituted his best and most enduring monument."

The book may be outlined as follows:

I.   Rebuilding of Jerusalem's walls; new genealogy, 1-7

II. State of religion during Nehemiah's administration, 8-10

III. Enlargement of Jerusalem's population; lists of priests and Levites, 11—12:36

IV. Dedication of Jerusalem's walls; religious reforms, 12:27-13.

GREAT THINGS IN NEHEMIAH

This book constitutes a long, *outstanding story* in itself, in which several *great truths* are suggested by the following episodes:

1. Nehemiah's pleas and a king's commission, 2:1-9

2. Nehemiah's first opposition, 2:17-20

3. Ridicule of his work by enemies, 4:1-6

4. Offer of compromise and its rejection, 6:1-9

5. Great awakening, revival, and reform, 8-9

6. Dedication of Jerusalem's walls, 12:27-43

1. Nehemiah's spiritual understanding of conditions at Jerusalem resulted in a deep desire to go there and restore the walls of the city. His prayers opened the way. The king's heart was touched by Nehemiah's pleas for his city and he received a commission to repair it.

When God wishes to accomplish a special work, He first finds a suitable man for it. When a young person develops a deep concern for some phase of God's work, he should pray seriously about it and seek to know if God is calling him to this kind of work. He may be (1:4-11).

The king's confidence in Nehemiah was the result of his godly life as he served the king. Others know of our dedication to God. or the lack of it, by their association with us (2:1-9).

2. Opposition to God's work can always be expected. Satan still raises up enemies to hinder, just as he did then (2:17-20). These men had orders from the king of Persia to *assist* in this work, but they did just the opposite. Sinful people will sometimes assist in religious work outwardly, but more often both inwardly and outwardly they will oppose it. Sometimes not by outward opposition, but by cold, indifferent neglect, they throw their influence against it. Young people must learn early that opposition is no reason to cease service to God.

3. If outright opposition will not win a new convert back to the worldly ways, often ridicule and making fun of will prove very effective in hindering the young Christian. These men made fun of Nehemiah's work and made laughing-stock of it, trying to discourage him, but without success (4:1-6). Among other ridiculous things, they said a fox, trotting upon his fast-built walls, could shake them down. Nehemiah paid no attention to them.

We must learn to take our stand for right, no matter what the others call us in the way of silly names and slogans which ridicule. They will soon stop when they see it does no good.

4. When Nehemiah's enemies saw they could not ridicule him out of his work, they tried "compromise" tactics on him. "Come, let us meet together," they invited ever so soothingly (6:2), intending thereby to stop him.

This is an old trick of Satan. If he cannot get God's people to give up and stop their service for God outright, then he resorts to compromise. By this means he can often get them to so weaken their position that their influence is hurt and the work hindered just the same. It has happened all too often, and young people need to be on their guard against this trick.

5. Awakening and revival came only when the Word of God was presented to the people and took hold in their hearts. Today's greatest need in the church is a revival of reading and obeying the Word of God — the Bible. Youth should master as much of the Bible as possible. Revival is always followed by moral reform and a higher way of life.

6. Nehemiah wanted to give proper reverence and thanksgiving to God for the remarkable work of erecting this wall. He planned a great public ceremony in which this would be done. Ezra was invited to participate, and the whole country was invited to attend. This again made the people conscious that God had helped in this marvelous feat. Otherwise it would not have been possible. This was doubtless the crowning public act of Nehemiah's life.

Here again the Messianic unfolding of the fulfillment of the ancient covenant is seen only in the further development and preparation of Israel for this great event in all its fullness. There are no Messianic passages here; yet, at this same time the prophets were heralding this message, as we shall see, for instance, in Haggai, who was a contemporary of Nehemiah.

Memory Verse

"And I sent messengers unto them, saying, I am doing a great work, so that I cannot come down; why should the work cease, whilst I come down to you?" (6:3).

Esther

This book was named for its heroine. Her name means "Ishtar" or "Venus," probably from her great beauty. This was the Persian name given her; originally her Hebrew name was Hadassah, and it meant "myrtle," from the myrtle wood trees, which are probably in some way associated with the thought of beauty.

TO WHOM

This book was doubtless prepared for the Jews scattered over the huge Persian kingdom, as well as for those in Palestine. The story would be of intense interest to both groups of people, as much news of the events it relates had undoubtedly been scattered everywhere among the Jews.

For the Christian, too, it presents a very striking case of divine intervention in behalf of God's people.

PURPOSE

Esther contains a very important episode in Jewish history, unconnected in any way with the regular course of such history. But for this book and the Feast of Purim, instituted to memorialize the tragic event, it would have long since been forgotten.

The purpose of the book is probably twofold. First, it provided the Jewish peoples of the Persian Empire, Palestine, and elsewhere, with the correct story of the great providence by which they were spared. This was a very important event

Courtesy, Oriental Institute

THE MOUND OF SUSA FROM THE AIR.
*Archaeological excavations began here
more than a century ago. Nehemiah lived
here as servant to Artaxerxes I. It was
to Susa that Esther was brought in the
days of Ahasuerus. It is located in the
present-day country of Iran.*

in their history and well worth preserving
for all time to come.

Second, it was doubtless written to
show that divine providence had been
thrown around the Jews, by which they
had been most miraculously spared from
destruction. It was received at Jerusalem
in this spirit and was read widely among
the Jews in that day. It was so highly
recognized to be a work of inspiration
that it was included in the Old Testament
canon of the Holy Scriptures.

Furthermore, it shows how silently God
may work for His people; the world
about may never recognize His workings.
It is another solemn, though unan-
nounced, demonstration of God's intervention in the affairs of men in the carrying out of His purpose. In this way one
may see the Messianic purpose of the covenant being worked out even in this book.

It provides the Christian reader with
a remarkable demonstration of the courage, faith, and heroic action of the persons involved in the story. Besides, it encourages faith in the working of God

among men, though it is not recognized by such persons as God's work.

TIME

It is quite certain that this event did not occur during the reign of King Darius, the Persian king, nor as late as the reign of Artaxerxes Longimanus, under whom Nehemiah served. From the best of evidence, it occurred during the rule of the king who is known in secular history as Xerxes. In Esther the name used for this king is Ahasuerus — the Hebrew form of the Persian name, *Khshayarsha.* The Greeks turned this name into *Xerxes,* as recorded by Herodotus, the great Greek historian. The Hebrew name corresponded letter for letter with the Persian.

The nature of the court, social customs, and state of affairs described in Esther fits perfectly into the picture of the secular history of the times, as does the very date itself, leaving no question as to the identity of the period. The events of this book may have occurred about the year 473 B.C.

AUTHORSHIP

The authorship of this remarkable book has never been fully established. Some among the Jews assigned it to Mordecai; others to the men of the Great Synagogue who helped Ezra in establishing the canon; but neither among the Jews nor the early Christians was there a definite statement. It is apparent, however, that the book was written by a Jew, who understood Jewish customs and people, one who was a long-time resident in Persia, also understanding the customs of that land. The fact that Mordecai never used the first person, if he wrote it, does not mean he *could not* have written it, although the high praise of him makes this questionable by some. The writer must

have been intimately acquainted with both Esther and Mordecai to have obtained the information related in the book. Therefore, the author of this beautiful book must have been either Esther herself or a younger contemporary of both Esther and Mordecai. It is not impossible that Esther may have written it. If either of them did, the likelihood inclines more toward Mordecai. The ancient Jews were convinced that it was inspired by the Lord and so included it in the canon of Scripture.

It is likely that the reign of Ahasuerus was over when this book was written. Xerxes (Ahasuerus) died in 463 B.C. Its language and descriptions are much like the period of Ezra, Nehemiah, and Chronicles. It may therefore have been written as early as 460 B.C. or as late as 450 B.C.

Esther's importance in Jewish history cannot be appreciated until her influence has been weighed. Though in order this book comes after the book of Nehemiah, she made her contribution to the cause of saving the Jewish nation from obliteration some thirty years before his days. Had there been no Esther, the Jewish people may have been wiped out, Jerusalem never rebuilt, and Jewish history a very different story. Her influence upon the Persian monarchs was very great. She was probably still living in the reign of her step-son Artaxerxes, under whom Nehemiah rebuilt the walls of Jerusalem. She doubtless was influential in furthering the cause.

About the Book of Esther there are several things of special interest. One remarkable feature is the absence of the name of God. There is no name of the Deity nor any reference to God, either in the original language or in any translation in English. The *fact* of God is certainly implied throughout by His intervention in saving the Jews as a result of fasting by Esther and the Jews. Mordecai's mention that if Esther refused to intervene for them, "then shall there enlargement and deliverance arise to the Jews from another place" (4:14), also indicates a belief in divine intervention.

The word prayer is likewise absent from the book. Although strongly inferred in the references to the *fasting* of Esther and the Jews, prayer is not specifically mentioned. Neither is there any direct religious teachings in the book. The story is allowed to speak for itself, without preachments or moralizations of any kind.

Why this is true is not known. Some have thought that the writer did not wish to use the name of God since the story is told in secular form, and there had been no special miracle wrought in saving the Jews, but rather by the courses of providence. Or, perhaps as the story was lifted from secular sources and not given by immediate divine inspiration, the writer did not feel he should use the name of God. The Jews held the name of God in such high reverence that it came to be used only by the high priest, once a year on the day of atonement, and that only in a *whisper*. Whatever the reason, the absence of God's name or a reference to Him does not mean the book was not inspired.

The book may be outlined as follows:

I.   Introduction of the main characters; dethronement of Vashti, 1

II. Choice of Esther as queen, 2

III. Haman's decree and final destruction, 3-7

IV. Deliverance of the Jews; Purim, 8-9

V.   Mordecai's greatness, 10

GREAT THINGS IN ESTHER

This book lends itself to an overall narrative of one continued story, as did Ezra and Nehemiah. There are, however, some high points in the story which may be pointed out:

1. A courageous queen — Vashti, 1
2. Choice of Esther as the new queen, 2:1-18
3. Mordecai's discovery of a plot against the king, 2:19-23
4. Mordecai's refusal to bow to Haman; Haman's plan for revenge, 3:1-15
5. Mordecai's notification to Esther; Esther's pleas for intervention, 4:1-15
6. Esther's great decision, 4:16
7. Esther's invitation to the king and Haman, 5
8. A sleepless night for the king, 6:1-11
9. Haman's humiliation, 6:12-14
10. The uncovering and punishment of a scoundrel, 7, 8
11. A new decree and a delivered people, 9:1-16
12. Institution of a great feast, 9:17-32

Great truths in the incidents above are:

1. Queen Vashti was justified in refusing to submit to the brutal request of her royal husband to disrobe herself before the leering eyes of the drunken spectators at the royal banquet. Perhaps no other king in ancient times ever made so cruel a demand of his queen (1:1-19). Had she obeyed, she would have lost the respect of the Persian empire, her husband, and herself. She certainly manifested queenly reserve, even in the face of possible death.

This is a rare and gracious lesson to all young ladies — never, for anyone, on any occasion, descend to the depths of displaying your body for lustful purposes. Your body is sacred and no man has the right to see it disrobed except your *husband* alone.

2. Esther's choice as the new queen was doubtless providential. She was chosen, not only because of her beauty and intelligence, but probably for her other graces too (2:15-18). It paid her well to be a virtuous young woman. Had she been less than this, the king would not have chosen her, though ever so corrupt himself.

3. Mordecai was faithful to his royal master; upon discovering a plot against the king's life, he revealed it without hesitation. The culprits were brought to speedy justice, and the chronicler made a special note of it on the king's daily chronicle or record (2:21-23). Then the matter slipped from memory for a time — but not for always, for kindnesses and loyalty to duty have a strange way of surviving.

4. Haman could not stand the unbending Mordecai, who would not stoop to do him obeisance — a type of homage often paid by bowing down very low to oriental persons of fame (3:1-5). Mordecai's refusal to do this was probably based upon his strict Jewish background and religious conviction. Haman hated him for this and determined to destroy him. Mordecai was such an outstanding person at the king's court, however, that Haman had to be careful how he went about this matter, lest his plot be discovered and it backfire on him.

Since Mordecai was a Jew, it would be simple enough to create the impression that the Jewish people were fast becoming a menace to the empire, and therefore should be exterminated. One day, as casually as possible, Haman suggested this to Ahasuerus, who took to the story

and ordered the matter made a royal decree. The date was set for about twelve months later. In this way Mordecai would be eliminated and out of his way (3:7-15).

What a lesson in the wickedness of the human heart! How could a man be so low and cruel as to wish to destroy a whole people — untold thousands of them — just to satisfy a fiendish whim! But recent times have proved it possible, even in our enlightened day. Adolph Hitler, the German ruler, is a classic example of such wickedness and criminality.

Haman had not the slightest idea how soon the tables would be reversed. Things moved swiftly once Mordecai read the decree. Esther was contacted and implored for help. Only a few days and it was all over for Haman.

5. One of the most touching events of the whole story is that upon which the story really hinges. When Mordecai made the issues known to Esther and explained her duty to her people, she made the supreme decision of her life (4:1-17). Between the disclosure by Mordecai and the decision of Esther there were possibly several hours of intense thinking and planning. Finally her decision was made. She would invite the king and Haman to a banquet. When she had the king fully under her tender touch, she would reveal Haman's wicked plot and the *motive* which was behind it, plus the fact that she, too, was Jewish and that the decree which had been effected would even cost her life. She would then depend upon the king's love for her to devise a plan by which the decree would be negated. She requested Mordecai and the Jews to fast; she and her attendants would also fast in preparation for her venture. Then she would approach the king, and, "If I perish, I perish" (4:16). This was sublime

language, but a far more sublime decision. To enter the throne room of the king without being called meant that if the king did not hold out the scepter of welcome, one could be instantly seized by the guards and hastened away to death. In this way she imperiled her life to present the matter to the king. This, in turn, was another venture for life or death. If King Ahasuerus had not believed her story and listened to Haman, who, of course, would plead his innocence, then she may have lost her life in the attempt. The king graciously accepted her and also the banquet invitation.

The first banquet went off smoothly. Haman was much gratified, never suspecting that his own head was the one so near the executioner's noose. Pressed by the king for her secret, Esther prevailed upon the two to return the second evening for another banquet, at which she would reveal it (5:1-8).

6. Here the story takes a curious turn. For the king, sleepless night followed the first banquet. His servant read the court chronicles to him for passing the time. The episode of his near assassination was read, and the king asked what had been done for the person who saved his life. Learning that nothing had been done for Mordecai, he ordered that the very next day Haman lead a procession through town, with Mordecai riding in royal style. Haman was to proclaim that Mordecai was the man whom the king wished to honor for his gracious deed. Truly mortified, Haman could but carry out the

---

←

A MEDE AND A PERSIAN. *This relief appears in the ruins at Persepolis.*

Courtesy, The Oriental Institute

order. It was an unhappy Haman who came to the second banquet, but he did his best to shield it (6:1-14).

7. At the end of the second banquet, Esther in a few well-chosen, deft but powerful words revealed to the king Haman's plot. Hardly able to believe it, the stunned king went out of the room for a moment. Seeing he was ruined and that only Esther could have helped him, Haman came crouching like a dog to her. Upon returning to the room and finding him in this position, the king instantly supposed he had made immoral overtures toward the queen. Flushed with anger, the king ordered his immediate execution (7:1-10).

Unwilling to wait until the decree eliminated Mordecai, Haman had prepared a high "gallows" — actually a "cross." The Persians did not hang men as is done now, but placed them upon a cross-like timber, *impaled* them, cutting open their stomachs, and leaving them to die in this manner! Haman had erected such a scaffold in his own yard just before Mordecai's special honor by the king, that with pleasure he might see him executed there.

As soon as King Ahasuerus ordered Haman's execution, someone turned up the evidence that he had prepared a scaffold for Mordecai's execution. Immediately the king ordered him put to death upon his own instrument of brutality and cruelty (7:9-10).

What must have been the thoughts of Haman as he was dragged away to his own house, and in his own yard was lifted upon the very cross he had prepared for the innocent Mordecai! How surely he must have felt the wrath of justice being vented upon his own head.

In this we have another Old Testament

lesson of that fearful truth the Apostle Paul was to set down centuries later, "For whatsoever a man soweth, that shall he also reap" (Gal. 6:7). It has ever been so since the dawn of man's day upon earth and will remain to its close. There is no better time to fix this unvarying truth firmly in the heart than in youth.

The story sweeps on to its climactic close with the issuance of a counteracting decree by the king, the Jewish settlement of the issue by battling their way to a great victory, and the institution of the Feast of Purim to commemorate this tragic event. In this way the writer shows how God makes even the wrath of man to praise Him, and out of seeming defeat, brings triumphant victory.

The Messianic covenant, while not mentioned, is again seen in triumph in the saving of the Jewish nation, that it might go on expanding to the fulfillment of the ancient promise of God to the forefathers.

Memory Verse

"Go gather together all the Jews that are in Shushan, and fast ye for me, and neither eat nor drink for three days, night or day: I also and my maidens will fast likewise; and so will I go in unto the king, which is not according to law: and if I perish, I perish" (4:16).

The Poetical Books

THE POETICAL BOOKS

The poetical books of the Bible are listed as Job, Psalms, Proverbs, Ecclesiastes, and Song of Solomon. Sometimes these are called the wisdom books of the Bible. Most of these books were written in poetry, although not all of them. Except Job, most of them may be grouped about the days of David and Solomon; Job is considered older than the rest.

Hebrew poetry had no meter or rhyme, as modern poetry does. It consisted, instead, of parallelisms or thought-rhythm. It is said that the rhythm is in the thought. The first line states a thought or sentiment; the next line repeats much of it, usually adding something. It is in couplets, being doubled, sometimes tripled, or even quadrupled, making as high as eight lines in this type of expression.

The poetic beauty of these books cannot be seen in English. If one will read them, however, with this rhythm pattern of repeated lines in mind, much of the poetic nature of the material can be gleaned.

Job

This book bears the name of the famous patriarch about whom it is written. The name probably meant "one persecuted," from the old Hebrew. The meaning is a bit obscure, but possibly was taken from the fact of Job's trials.

TO WHOM

This strange book is introduced to no specific nation or people. Since it was found among the earliest sacred books of the Jews and was included in the Old Testament canon as inspired of God, it is assumed that it was first written for the Jewish people. But the book is universal in its scope. It has no racial connections and no national barriers or limitations. In the very nature of its message it is for all men. It is timeless in its application and carries its grand teachings to every place where human need exists.

PURPOSE

There may be two or three aspects to its purpose. One of its main objectives seems to be to reveal that human suffering of itself is no evidence of the displeasure of God. Using Job, one of God's choicest men, as an example, it shows that the best of men may suffer every kind of sorrow and loss and still be true servants of God. As seen from the counsel of Job's three friends, ancient people thought physical suffering, financial reverses, or the loss of social standing were signs that one had sinned and God was punishing him. This wrong view of human suffering was to be corrected by Job's life and experiences.

Even Elihu condemned this harsh view and offered a milder view, though not completely vindicating Job (32:2-37). God condemned the notion of the three friends toward Job as entirely wrong (42:7-9). Elihu is not included in this indictment, but he may be unfavorably referred to when God asks Job, just as Elihu had finished speaking, "Who is this that darkeneth counsel by words without knowledge?" (38:2).

It is clear, then, that God sometimes uses testings and trials in dealing with even the best of His people. In this way He helps them to develop the best qualities they possess, as well as to rid their lives of other qualities.

A further purpose of the book may be to teach the lesson that God is with His people at all times. Sometimes His presence is manifested to them; at other times it is withheld; but He is always with them. In the most severe trials, God is near. When one is in the "furnace of affliction," God presides over the heating and the work of the furnace. Although He often purposely withholds the *manifestation* of His presence, He never leaves His people when in trouble. God can often test one's faith best when the person is unaware of His presence.

JOB. *The first Chapter of Job describes Job as a man of great wealth. Included in his possessions were thousands of sheep, camels, oxen and asses.*

Courtesy, Cathedral Filmstrips

Job relied upon the moral character of God and his own personal integrity. He could not understand *why* God had permitted him to suffer so, but he could cry out in his darkest hour, "Though he slay me, yet will I trust in him" (13:15).

Again, the story proves that suffering may be permitted by God, but it is brought about by Satan. God is not the author of suffering, misery, and trouble. He may well permit these, and often He uses them to test His saints, but He is not the author of them. All forms of suffering and sorrow are the result of the sins of the race, though most often not of personal sin. This book points out how Satan, working behind the scenes, tries to destroy God's servants, but is always stopped short of his purpose. God turns this work of Satan into blessing, by which His cause benefits in the end.

These seem to be the three main lessons of Job.

TIME

The time at which the events of the book occurred, or even when it was written, is not definitely known. The style, tone, and language of the book seem to mark it for a very early date. This also may be seen from the mannerisms, institutions, customs, and modes of life seen in the book. References to city life and legal documents are said to be pretty much on a level with the civilization seen in Genesis times. Job's long life also seems quite well suited to the times of the patriarchs. Job's mention of writing being *engraved in rocks* reminds one of the early Egyptian writing or even writing of an earlier period (19:24).

No mention is made of the law given to Moses, nor of anything about the Levitical system of sacrifices, nor any reference to priests and other Hebrew leaders; there is no reference to anything about the Jewish nation or people.

From these and other inferences, some scholars have believed this book to be among the oldest — if not the oldest — book of the Bible. It is thought by some that Job may have lived about the time of the exodus or just before it. Everything in the book most certainly points to a patriarchal age — such times as those in which Abraham and Moses lived.

Other scholars, however, think Job lived at a much later date and assign him a time about the days of David and Solomon. They think he lived outside of Palestine under the patriarchal conditions which largely prevailed in lands east of Canaan, even until late in the Jewish age. But the weight of evidence seems to favor an earlier day as pointed out above.

AUTHORSHIP

The matter of authorship is also uncertain. No author is mentioned in the book. Some conservative scholars have suggested that it seems likely that Moses may have written this book. Job could have met Moses during his sojourn in the wilderness, just before his going to Egypt to deliver Israel. Moses, with all the records of Job at hand, and by hearing Job relate his story could very well have recorded it in its present form. Likely a man of Job's wealth would have had a record of the speeches and all the historical facts. Compared to moderns, the ancients had profound memories, as a rule, anyway; Job could well have furnished Moses with all the facts. Under the guiding inspiration of the Holy Spirit, Moses could have written the book, then, in original Hebrew. Or, it could have been translated about this time from a former copy in some other ancient language.

Those who hold to the later period believe that a learned Idumean from the country where Job had lived, originally prepared this book in his native language. They think that this version was made about the days of David or Solomon, and likely translated by Solomon into Hebrew, as a worthy classic to be conserved by the Jewish people. But here again arises the difficulty of reconciling the times indicated in the book itself with the times of the later period.

It will be remembered that whoever wrote the book, and whenever Job may have lived, this book is beyond doubt inspired by the Holy Spirit and is God's truth for us today.

THE MAN JOB

Job was a true historical character. The prophet Ezekiel associated him with Noah and Daniel (Ezek. 14:14, 20), as a true historical person.

The land of Uz (1:1) is believed by

some to have been located along the border between Palestine and Arabia, northerly and easterly toward the Euphrates River, on the caravan route between Egypt and Babylon. Tradition assigns a place called Huran as Job's home, in a region just east of the Sea of Galilee. Once rich in fertile soil and heavily populated, it is now in ruins. At one time there were some three hundred small cities in this area.

A note in the Septuagint Version refers to a tradition that Job was the Jobab, second king of Edom, mentioned in Genesis 36:33. If this is correct, and yet Huran is Job's home, it is plain that those ancient Edomite kings sometimes lived outside their famous cliffdwelling homes. But this tradition is not supported by any certain historical facts.

Job was certainly one of the richest and most popular men of his times (1:1-3). He was a man of great mental will. Otherwise, he could not have stood this supreme test. He was a man of deep piety and dedication to God, or he would never have been able to come through as he did. His wealth and popularity had not hindered him in God's service.

The dreadful disease which Job had is now thought to have been a form of leprosy, complicated with elephantiasis. This was one of the most dreaded and painful diseases known to the Oriental countries. His sickness perhaps lasted for about a year or so.

The Book of Job is one of the most interesting in the Bible. It is a historical poem — based on an event that actually occurred. Some have said that Job was a fictitious character and the book merely a fictitious poem, portraying the matter of human suffering and its relation to life, to God, and to good and evil. But this will not stand the test of investigation.

This book was beyond doubt based upon a true historical fact. The persons listed in it are historical persons. Take Job's three friends: It is pointed out that Eliphaz was a descendant of Esau (Gen. 36:11); Bildad was a descendant of Abraham and Keturah, his second wife (Gen. 25:2). Zophar, though from an unknown locality, was nonetheless a real person. Elihu is thought to have been a descendant of Nahor, Abraham's brother (Gen. 22:21).

The land of Uz has been located, as seen above, in a definite place. Also, the first two chapters are straight historical material, without a hint of anything fictitious. The matter of Satan and God conversing about Job is, of course, a *revelation* of things taking place out of the physical realm, but no more striking than many revelations of God to the prophets and others, which also were truly historical. The whole setting of the book breathes a definite historical atmosphere. The last chapter is certainly historical. Job is a solid piece of historical poetry and has been proclaimed by great literary minds as one of the greatest masterpieces ever produced.

The book is in three major parts:

   I.   Historical prologue, 1-2

  II.   Cycles of speeches, 3-41

 III.   Historical conclusion, 42

The main body of the book, then, may be outlined:

   I.   Speeches between Job and his friends, 3-31

      A.   First dialogue, 3-14

      B.   Second dialogue, 15-21

      C.   Third dialogue, 22-31

  II.   The harangue of Elihu, 32-37

 III.   Discourse of Jehovah, 38-41

 IV.   Job's reply and confession, 42: 1-6, followed by the conclusion

Job has some strange Messianic passages, although there is no reference to the covenant of God with Abraham. It is evident that Job knew of the divine promise of the ages past, since Eden, that God would send a Redeemer to save mankind. His insight into this truth may seem extraordinary for one living outside the Jewish nation. The knowledge of God, however, was not merely a matter of the Jews alone, but was universal. The *revelation* of God in His fuller understanding was made to all men, through Israel, not merely for Israel alone.

Two outstanding Messianic passages are the reference to the resurrection of the righteous (14:14, 15), and Job's reference to the Redeemer and the final resurrection and glory with Him, with even a glimpse of glorification (19:25-27). This latter passage is one of the great gems of the Old Testament, one of the brightest expressions of hope found there.

GREAT THINGS IN JOB

Outstanding stories of the historical parts:

1. The character of Job, 1:1-8; 20-22; 2:7-10
2. Satan's character, 1:6-12
3. Satan's swift destruction, 1:13-19
4. The folly of Job's wife, 2:9
5. The position of Job's friends, 2:11-13
6. God's rebuke of Job's friends, 42:7-9
7. Job prays with his friends, 42:10
8. Job's restoration, 42:11-17

Several *great truths* are pointed up in these stories and other passages:

1. God chose Job to demonstrate what the love of God in a man's heart could help him to endure without knowing the source of his troubles, still remaining true to God. Some think the name Job was given him after his great struggle, as it means "to be hostile; cruelly or hostilely treated; persecuted."

God described him all the way through, even after the struggle had ended, as being "perfect," meaning fully devoted to God and not blameworthy. Job was not faultless. Under pressure he spoke out of turn (42:1-6). But he was what Paul later referred to as "blameless and harmless" (Phil. 2:15) as a son of God. He was mature, grown up in the knowledge and love of God. He was "upright," resisting evil. It is supposed he was one of the most godly men of his age.

Evidently, God wishes to impress upon men that there is in this life a certain degree of relative perfection possible, which is obtained by obedience to God through faith in Him. He made Job an example of what all should strive to reach through grace.

2. Satan's character is described in few words. He is a wicked person, the arch-enemy of God and man. He is wise, cunning, and powerful, but his power is limited by God. His first act is to accuse Job before God of being selfish and insincere (1:9-11). This has been one of his old tricks (Zech. 3:1, 2; Rev. 12:10).

Then he accuses God of being unfair in unduly protecting Job. "Hast thou not made an hedge about him . . . ?" (1:10). Here is seen the bold audacity of the devil — he will even accuse God Himself! He will stop at nothing to destroy man if possible. He is destructive, even using the elements of nature when *permitted* by God to do so, stirring up evil men to steal, lie, and cheat (1:13-19). He will not hesitate to afflict in the most dreadful manner, when permitted (2:7). This is a small portrait of Satan at work. But remember always that he can go no further in his wicked plans than God will allow him. God's grace is sufficient for all men, and none need yield to the evil one. This is made abundantly plain in Job. If we lose sight of the *devil in the shadows* in this book, we lose some of its most valuable lessons.

3. The folly of Job's wife in siding with Satan and advising her husband to "curse God and die" (2:9) is a sad story. It shows a deep-seated weakness on her part and a total lack of complete commitment to God, such as Job had.

Satan may have suspected that Job would fall into this trap, as Adam had done long before, but he missed it there. Satan had told God that Job would curse Him to his face (1:11). Now, he set about using the dearest person Job had to influence him to do this very thing. Doubtless, unknown to her, Satan inspired the very words in her mind to suggest to him.

We must not be too quick to condemn Job's wife. Remember, she, too, was under attack from Satan. She was weaker than Job, and no doubt her heart ached to see him in such misery. For his affliction, Satan had chosen one of the most corrupt, stinking, and painful diseases of the ancient world. She felt he would never be well again, so why not die soon and have it over. Like Job's three comforters, she possibly also believed he had secretly sinned and that his hope of recovery was past.

One of a man's hardest blows in life is to have his bosom companion turn against him and side with his enemies. Job's case seems extreme, but remember God was allowing him to be tested to the absolute extremes that a man could be tested in this life, to show what God's grace in his life could do.

Christians should take a lesson from this incident about Job's wife. It may often occur that Satan uses good people to tempt and try others. When tempted to criticize another, or say some cutting word, hold the tongue in the mouth and save yourself from being Satan's instrument.

4. Job's friends completely misunderstood him. In those times prosperity was taken as evidence of God's approval of one's life. Calamities, especially when occurring by acts of providence, or sickness, such as in Job's case, were believed to be God's punishments for some sin the person had done or some secret evil which he was not willing to confess. This is the line of attack which these men took to bring Job to repentance. They were likely devout men and very sincere in their advice to Job.

After hearing of his calamity they came to visit him. Their sitting in grief seven days was an Oriental custom. Time meant nothing to Orientals, as it does to us.

Elihu's harangue against the three older men was intended to defend Job to some extent (32-37). He saw that God might use sufferings, not necessarily as punishment for sin, but as *chastisement* by which to draw the godly person nearer to God, or as correction when he erred. But still, Elihu's speeches had nothing of real value in them. God said they merely "darkened counsel" (38:1, 2). Job remained, to the last, true to his claim of integrity.

5. God rebuked Job's friends, telling them they were all wrong about Job. They had not spoken correctly about him, and were under divine displeasure for their position against him (42:7). He reminded Job that he had not spoken according to knowledge; this Job confessed in humility (42:1-6). But not once did God condemn Job as having sinned or in

any way displeased Him. Besides, He told Job's friends they were to go and ask Job to pray for them, for He would hear Job's prayer — final proof of God's approval of Job's life (42:8, 9).

6. Job's prayer meeting with his friends was doubtless a most interesting experience. These dear men had preached at him almost constantly for many days. Now, coming with their bullocks and rams, they are asking him to pray for them, that God might restore them to favor with Him. How humiliated they must have been. Yet Job never embarrassed them for a moment. He was not this kind of man, or God would never have asked him to pray for them.

One can imagine the men saying, "Brother Job, we are very sorry — we were wrong. Please accept our apology."

But Job must have replied, "Think nothing of it, brethren; we all often have been wrong. Let us ask God to bless us, and forget the past. You were very nice to come and sit with me during my sickness."

JOB'S WIFE. *This wood engraving depicts Job's wife urging him to curse God and die.*

7. Job's restoration was complete and very beautiful. In fact, God doubled His gifts to him after his great trial and endurance. His reward was rich (42:10-17). Job's last days were his best. His fame spread all over the ancient world of those times. His name became a standard word for patience.

Through his great experiences of faith for the testing, Job became a "world example of righteousness." His testimony was doubtless a powerful force for God and good in his days following the great trial.

8. There are other passages in which precious truths stand out, one of which is Job's great trust in God. "Though he slay me, yet will I trust in him" (13:15), he cried in one of his darkest hours. Although Job could not understand what God was doing, nor why, yet he would trust Him to the end. This is true faith.

9. Job's powerful will, not to surrender to Satan's suggestions, stood him in good stead. "I will maintain mine own ways before him," he cried out (13:15). Only those who have been through some deep sorrow and found themselves alone with mental and spiritual darkness, without an answer to *why,* can appreciate Job's position. When his wife and his friends tried to convince him he had sinned, he knew in his own heart that he had never turned away from God.

It was part of the supreme test that he was *not to know* what was happening, nor *why.* Otherwise, he could have seen through the scheme and his faith could not have been tested at all. God often hides from us His purposes in the hour of our supreme testings.

10. It may be too much to say that Job *understood* the future resurrection and glorification of the body, but he certainly expressed this grand faith (14:14, 15). The word "change" in this passage actually means "renewal." Christ has made this passage alive with blessed hope (John 11:25).

11. The great Redeemer passage (19:25-27) expresses the most sublime faith and expectancy. Job seemed to get a glimpse by spiritual insight into the future and see God's redemptive plan for man.

12. Job was quick to apologize when convinced of his error (42:1-6). Evidently he was a man of strong will and powerful determination. Otherwise he would have given way under the sledgehammer blows of his friends and supposed he *had* done something wrong.

His confession, "I abhor myself, and repent in dust and ashes" (42:6), does not indicate that he had been sinning and now turned to God in repentance. There is no such record anywhere in the book. He was innocent when he entered the trial, and God pronounced him so at the end (42:7). Of what, then, did he repent? It is made clear in his own words (40:4, 5). He had spoken out of turn — said things in his speeches beyond what he knew. But he had not willfully sinned against God; he had only complained in his sickness because he did not understand. Even when it was all over, God said of him, "ye have not spoken of me the thing that is right, as my servant Job hath" (42:7). This is God's standard of excellence for Job.

13. A final lesson from Job is that of patience, gathered from his great experience of suffering and yet enduring faith. "Ye have seen the patience of Job" (James 5:11), cries the apostle, and "seen . . . that the Lord is pitiful, and of tender mercy." James was exhorting to patient endurance of life's difficulties. One needs much patience even in this day.

Job, more than any other person of all time, has become the classic example of patience, endurance, faith, and fidelity under extreme pressures and hardships. Had he lived for no other purpose than to provide this great example, his life would have been well worth it.

When you are in trouble or difficulty, recall that Job had been this way before you, showing you that the Lord will "never leave thee nor forsake thee" (Heb. 13:5).

Memory Verses

"For I know that my Redeemer liveth, and that he shall stand at the latter day upon the earth: and though after my skin worms destroy this body, yet in my flesh shall I see God: whom I shall see for myself, and mine eyes shall behold, and not another: though my reins be consumed within me" (19:25-27).

Psalms

In Hebrew this book was called "Praises," "Book of Praises," or "Prayers." Later it became known as the "Book of Psalms." In the New Testament it is called by this name by our Lord (Luke 24:44), by Paul (Acts 13:38), and by Luke (Luke 20:42). This name was used by those who produced the Septuagint Version of the Old Testament and by Jerome in his translation of the Latin Vulgate Version.

TO WHOM
The Psalms were written to the Jewish people. They are expressive of much of Jewish history and personal experience, all the way from the wilderness, where one of them was most certainly written, to the last days of the Old Testament times. Some were prepared for special groups, such as singers in divine services. Others were dedicated to outstanding persons. Many are the expressions of personal praise to God, much like a personal testimony in our times.

But the Book of Psalms by its very nature has a universal appeal and application. Anyone who has drunk deeply at the fountain of the Psalter has found there the expression of every human emotion and the answer for every human need. God meant this book for all peoples, wherever the message of salvation should go.

PURPOSE
Many of the psalms are believed to have been written for the use of the temple singers in periods of worship. Others were written for the public of Israel, that they might praise the Lord under many varying circumstances.

This book formed the Israel's hymnal for worship, both collectively and privately. Many of the psalms or songs are of the nature for public use, in praise to God, such as Psalms 8, 16, 23, 24, 37, and scores of others. Some fit into private worship as personal confessions of weaknesses, sins, and prayers for deliverance, such as Psalms 7, 32, 38, 51, 52, 130, and 143. These are penitential psalms — prayers of repentance. Many are filled with the noblest meditative passages, such as Psalms 8, 19, 50, 90, 91, and many others.

The church in all ages has found in the psalms its most profound expressions of faith, hope, love, and courage. Christ loved the psalms and often quoted them. His dying agonies were expressed in a Psalm (Luke 24:44).

There was likely no distinct purpose in the minds of the several writers, as in the average book. Some were written for public use, others for personal use. Some, indeed, may have been dedicated to certain people. But there can be little question but what the overall purpose was to aid in man's worship of God.

TIME
The time covered by Psalms is a long span. They reach from the days of Moses in the wilderness to the days of the prophets Haggai and Zechariah. While the range of writing extends over many hundreds of years, it is remarkable how little variation there is in the general expressions of the writers and the truths they taught.

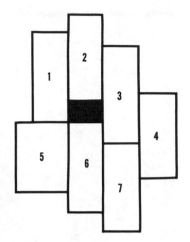

Postage Stamps from Israel. *These festival stamps quote Bible texts which speak of the part music played in the life of ancient Israel. Inscriptions which appear on the stamps are as follows:*

1. *In the day of your gladness, and in your solemn days, and in the beginnings of your months, ye shall blow the trumpets. Numbers 10:10.*

2. *And David and the entire House of Israel played . . with sistron and bells. II Samuel 6:5.*

3. *Praise Him with timbrel and dance, praise Him with resounding cymbals. Psalms 150:4, 5.*

4. *Praise Him with lyre and harp. Psalms 150:3.*

5. *An joy of heart as one going with a flute. Isaiah 30:29.*

6. *Praise Him with a harp. Psalms 150:3.*

7. *Sound the shofar on the new moon, on the full moon of our Festivals. Psalms 81:3.*

Courtesy, Dame Kathleen Kenyn

EXCAVATION TRENCH IN JERUSALEM. *Kathleen Kenyon discovered the remains of King David's Jerusalem in this trench on the eastern slope of Ophel in the 1960s. Excavations revealed the city wall about 160 feet below the crest of the ridge.*

AUTHORSHIP

Unquestionably, David, King of Israel, was the author of more than those of any other one writer. At least seventy-three are ascribed to him, and there may have been others written by him, but whose authorship is in question.

The earliest writer of any of the psalms is Moses, who most likely wrote Psalm 90. Twelve psalms are ascribed to Asaph, eleven to the sons of Korah, two to Solomon, and one to Ethan. Fifty have no author assigned. It is thought that some of these anonymous psalms may be ascribed to David. In some cases, too, an anonymous psalm may be ascribed to the author of the psalm which precedes it.

The New Testament writers recognized David as the principal writer of the Psalms. His name is more largely associated with the Psalms than any other; this has been true from his days onward. He did more to organize them and get them into use than any other person. Indeed, there was only a small collection before his day. He is said to have had an orchestra of four thousand players, and he made many of the instruments they used (I Chron. 23:5). Such instruments as the harp, psaltery, flute, pipe, horn, and trumpet, as well as timbrel and cymbal, were in use during David's lifetime.

David was a great warrior, a military genius, and a brilliant statesman. He led his nation to the pinnacle of power and glory for that day. The building of the kingdom was a great work, but his contribution in forming the Book of Psalms was his grandest monument of all.

INTERESTING FACTS ABOUT THE PSALMS

There are several groupings of the Psalms:

1. Songs of Degree, possibly sung when going up to the temple, 120-134
2. Hallelujah Psalms, beginning with praises to God, 106, 111-113, 135, 146-150
3. Penitential Psalms, 7, 32, 38, 51, 52, 130, 143
4. Imprecatory Psalms, 27, 49, 109, and others, which are prayers for calamity or destruction upon God's enemies. The writers are not voicing *personal* ill will in these, but vindication of the justice of God in punishing sin.
5. The Messianic Psalms, in which Christ is portrayed or prophesied in some way. These eleven psalms are so important that we here give captions to them:

    Psalm 2, Deity and universal reign of the Messiah

    Psalm 8, Man as lord of creation through the Messiah

    Psalm 16, Prophecy of Christ's resurrection from the dead

    Psalm 22 and 69, Christ's sufferings — the cross described

    Psalms 45, His royal bride and eternal throne

    Psalm 72, Glory and eternity of His reign

    Psalm 89, God's oath for the endlessness of the Messianic throne

    Psalm 110, Eternal King and Priest — Christ's official titles

    Psalm 118, Rejection of the Messiah by His nation's leaders

    Psalm 132, The Eternal Inheritor of David's throne

Next to Isaiah, the Book of Psalms is the most expressive of the Messianic prophecies and message in the Old Testament. The light of the covenant, to be fulfilled in the coming Messiah, here shines with an extra brilliance. It will be remembered that most of these psalms were written about one thousand years before the birth of Christ. Yet, the Holy Spirit so inspired the writers that their descriptions are almost like one writing of what he saw happening. Take Psalm 22, for example, which describes Christ's crucifixion. Read this carefully, noting how many references there are to things just as they happened. It opens with the cry, "My God, my God, why hast thou forsaken me?" It continues with several references to Christ's suffering: the mocking of Christ on the cross (v. 7); the saying, "let God deliver him" (v. 8); His heart-break, blood and water coming out where the spear pierced Him, and His bones coming out of joint, as in crucifixion (v. 14); the soldiers' gambling for His garments (v. 18); His tongue and mouth so dry from thirst (v. 15).

Many other passages of Scripture which concern Christ's life, death, and resurrection are made very plain in the Psalms.

Perhaps the key words to the Psalms are "trust," "praise," "rejoice," and "mercy." These words occur hundreds of times throughout the book. It is truly a book of trust and praise.

A brief outline of the book may be noted, keeping in mind that it is divided into five books or sections. Each of these *ends* with a doxology of praise, varying in length but similar in character.

I. Section One: 1-41
II. Section Two: 42-72
III. Section Three: 73-89
IV. Section Four: 90-106
V. Section Five: 107-150

Several further divisions are possible, but the outline above will serve to guide for general study. Each section begins with a letter of the Hebrew alphabet.

GREAT THINGS IN THE PSALMS

There are no *outstanding stories*. There are far too many *great truths* to point out all of them individually, so a few general observations will be made.

NATHAN AND KING DAVID. *Psalm 51 is David's prayer of repentance after Nathan pointed out his sin by means of a parable.*

1. The Psalms furnish mankind, especially those who love God, with a sort of emotional guidance. They plumb the depths of man's nature and bring up almost every color of feeling and expression. They serve as a guide in the emotional patterns much as other portions of Scripture do for faith and actions. The emotional appeal of the Psalms is certainly strong. As this is one of man's strongest elements, it applies to his deepest needs, his sense of guilt, futility, and unworthiness, as well as those of confession, trust, praise, and rejoicing. There is no feeling in all the range of human emotions or feelings which is not in some way portrayed here. From this viewpoint alone, the book is of untold worth to the human race. God's understanding of man's emotional needs and His supply of grace for them is abundantly shown here.

2. The Psalms also abound in devotional warmth and energy. One can always find there the inspiration for deep meditation, high resolve, and the finest of noble ambitions. No other portion of the Scriptures is so filled with devotional materials and expressions as this book. Whatever phase of work one may wish to pursue in God's kingdom, or whatever problem one may have in his Christian experience, he will find inspiration and help here.

3. In the Psalms there are little additions to great historical facts — for instance, that of Joseph being bound in fetters while in prison and being tried by God's word (105:17, 18). Apparently the rock from which Moses got water in the wilderness was a "flint" rock (114:8). Many examples of additional information about historical events are in this wonderful storehouse of truth.

4. Another great area is the deep psychological insight into the nature of

Courtesy, The National Union of Christian Schools, from HYMNS FOR YOUTH © 1966

THE CEDAR TREE. *This tree is mentioned in the Psalms several times. A few giant cedar trees may still be found in Lebanon.*

mankind. For instance, one can observe David's deep guilt-complex (32) or his confession of sin and restoration — after forgiveness — to joy and peace (51:1-19). Almost every psychological problem in normal life may be found in the Psalms.

5. Every great doctrine in the Bible is either *taught, expressed,* or *implied* in the Psalms. Such basic doctrines as sin, atonement (by sacrifice), guilt, forgiveness, justification, restoration, repentance, confession, cleansing from sin, personal witness to forgiveness and cleansing, faith, and the mercy of God are found in this great fountain of truth.

6. Every attribute or characteristic of God as the Divine Being is found here. The moral attributes of holiness, justice, mercy, truth, goodness, and righteousness, as well as the personal attributes of eternity of being, spirituality, omnipotence (all-powerfulness), omniscience (infinite knowledge), omnipresence (presence ev-

erywhere), immutability (unchangeableness) are ascribed to God in many places.

7. Every phase of religious experience is either described or anticipated in the Psalms. Such experiences as sin, guilt, repentance, confession, forgiveness, cleansing, restoration, faith, joy, peace, grace, hope, love, and witnessing to others are all found in abundance.

No other book in the Bible makes a more universal appeal to mankind than Psalms. It speaks a universal language to people of any age. It is by far the longest book in the Bible.

Memory Verses

"Thy word have I hid in mine heart, that I might not sin against thee" (119:11).

"Thy word is a lamp unto my feet, and a light unto my pathway" (110:105).

Everyone should memorize such psalms as 1, 19, 23, 24, 37, 90, 91, 103, 117, and others if possible.

Proverbs

The name of this book describes the nature of its contents. A proverb is defined as "an allegorical saying, where more is meant than meets the eye." It is a short saying which stands for a whole discourse or lecture.

TO WHOM

The book was intended for all Israel, and probably for many beyond the national bounds of Israel. In Solomon's day the influence of Jewish thought and literature was beginning to spread widely over the surrounding nations. Proverbs, by its very nature, is universal in its appeal and application. It is not national in its scope or concepts.

Proverbs, more than any other, is the *young people's* book of the Bible. It addresses youth and deals with matters of youth more often than any other of the sacred books. Almost the entire pattern of the book is arranged for the instruction of youth. Its most important sections are addressed directly to youth. If such a book were written today, the reviewers would say it was "slanted for youth."

As used here, "youth" does not mean merely children and teen-agers. The ancient Greeks considered youth lasting until the age of *forty*. Some groups today consider youth to be those whose ages are from ten or twelve to thirty or thirty-five years. Proverbs appeals to those from the early teens to this more advanced age.

Since Proverbs is the youth book of the Bible, young people should read and study its content and message thoroughly. It contains some of the richest gems of wisdom and good advice found in any literature in the world. Its pithy, spicy statements are loaded with the best admonitions and wisest counsel that centuries of experience and observation can offer.

PURPOSE

The purpose of the book, beyond doubt, was to give youth the necessary instructions, information, counsel, and advice which they needed to make good in life. It has a message, likewise, for older people. All will profit from its pages. The rich and poor, learned and ignorant, the wise and the foolish alike need messages of this book.

One of its chief purposes was to instruct the young in morals and proper standards of conduct. All through it one finds advice and counsel by parable, story, and statement. This is one of the most outstanding contributions to life; moral and social guidance are of the highest importance.

It was likewise intended to give advice regarding ethical conduct, matters of social graces, and even matters of money and its relationship to life. In fact, there is hardly an aspect of life for which Proverbs does not have some specific message or counsel.

To aid the young in getting the proper views of life and making the necessary adjustments to make life God-fearing, successful, and happy, seems to have been the main purpose of the writer of this book.

TIME

Solomon reigned as king of Israel from about 970 B.C.—930 B.C. The largest share of the work of Proverbs was probably done during this period. Something further of this matter will be discussed under the next division.

AUTHORSHIP

From the most ancient times since Solomon's day, the Book of Proverbs has been received by the Jews as work done by him. Certain parts in the book are said to have been written by others, but Solomon was doubtless responsible for their collection into the original volume. The whole work has been received as inspired by the Spirit of God, and therefore, as Scripture.

Some have suggested that Solomon *col-*

lected and arranged from many sources more of the proverbs than he wrote, since they cover so wide a range of truth, but there is no proof of this. It is true that all ancient peoples had their proverbs. Such works as *Aesop's Fables* are but ancient proverbs amplified by modern writers. The ancient Sanscrit language is filled with proverbs; so are the Arabic and Persian languages and the languages of China and India. But to say that Solomon collected these and placed them in his book is to assign to him an almost impossible task. Modes of communication and transportation and difficulties of language in those ancient times would have made this practically impossible.

Again, the *time element* is an even greater barrier to this theory. Taking 970 B.C. as Solomon's date of ascension to the throne, he would have reigned from 440 to 400 years *before* Cyrus, King of Persia, reigned. It was during Cyrus' reign that the *seven wise men of Greece* lived. This was about 640 to 600 years before Alexander the Great, during whose reign lived the three greatest early Greek philosophers — Socrates, Plato, and Aristotle. Since Solomon lived centuries before all uninspired ethnic writers of history began to write, it is evident that he could have borrowed nothing from them! Nor is it likely that he could have gained much from the heathen Gentile world of that day.

Scripture tells us that Solomon had a "wise and understanding heart" and that there was none before nor after like him (I Kings 3:12). He was a prolific writer of natural history: on beasts, fowl, and fish; but his other works are all lost, except Proverbs, Ecclesiastes, and Song of Solomon. He was the wisest man of the earth in his time and was certainly qualified by natural talent, mental acumen,

and proper training to have written Proverbs. Besides, his writing was inspired by God. God could just as well have given unusual wisdom in such matters as those in Proverbs, as to have inspired prophets to prophesy of untold events hundreds of years in advance.

The book itself tells us that certain parts were written by other writers than Solomon. Chapters 25-29 are a selection of Solomon's proverbs which the "men of Hezekiah copied out." Now, Hezekiah was a godly king who lived long after Solomon's day. The prophets Isaiah, Hosea, and Micah, all flourished during Hezekiah's reign, and these are believed to have been the "men of Hezekiah" referred to (25:1). Evidently Solomon wrote the proverbs at different times during his long life and this section had not been added to the original book. These men copied out this section, adding it to the original collection. Chapter 30, written by Agur, was directed to his pupils Ithiel and Ucal and is intended for youth at large. Chapter 31 contains the instructions of an unnamed mother to her son called Lemuel (vv. 1-9). The last part of the chapter is the description of a "virtuous woman," or the picture of an ideal wife.

Some believe the first part was Solomon's mother's instructions to him, Solomon here using "Lemuel" rather than his own name; they also believe that the last part is Solomon's tribute to his own mother, a word picture of a remarkable woman. In any case, the last part is a guide for every young woman in becoming an ideal woman and for every young man looking for a true companion for life. It is thought by some scholars that either Isaiah arranged the collection in its present form or that it was finally done by

SOLOMON. *Interested in literary pursuits, Solomon composed many proverbs. Two psalms are also attributed to him. His writings indicate that he was an avid naturalist. People came from all parts of the world to hear his wisdom.*

Ezra, who formed the Old Testament canon of Scripture.

In this light, without question, Solomon was the author of by far the most of the proverbs, although some were collected and arranged long after his day. He probably collected those credited to other authors in his original collection. That all are inspired of God is the most important thing.

There are several interesting things about the nature of this book. Much of it is allegorical — written in symbolic stories or parables. There are numerous instances when the writer used one of these methods to portray some moral evil, social misconduct, truth, virtuous deed, or way of life.

Proverbs also abounds in *metaphors* — figures of speech, in which one word stands for something else. An old rabbinical saying from the Jewish teachers illustrates this: "I have given thee my lamp; give me thy lamp." Here God is represented in the first instance as giving the "lamp" of divine knowledge and revelation to man. The second use of "lamp" was meant to mean "Give me thy *heart* and *life*," as these represent the *lamp* of life. Once you get the key word in the sentence, you have solved the problem of the meaning. "Put a knife to thy throat, if thou be a man given to appetite" (23: 2) does not mean to commit *suicide,* but simply to *cut down* on your eating! "In a multitude of counselors there is safety" (24:6) simply means that with a lot of good advice, you are likely to be sure of doing the right thing. Many such examples could be cited. Watch for them as you read this book. The words "My son," which occur many times, may simply mean "young friend" to us.

Proverbs contains a wide range of subject matter; many different persons are addressed. Helpful counsel is offered to sons, daughters, husbands, wives, fathers, mothers, and friends; their duties to each other and relationships with each other are discussed. Subjects include religion, character, honor, integrity, money, interest, love, fear, natural affection, friendship, justice, mercy, truth, and judgment. The fear of God and reverence for sacred things is the key thought. The writer also shows the evils of injustice, laziness, wastefulness, drunkenness, dishonesty, impiety, immorality, idleness, imprudence, laziness, impurity, greed, filthiness, lust, avarice, and almost every vice known to man. The writer points out that the "path of the just is as the shining light, that shineth more and more unto the perfect day" (4:18), while "the way of the transgressors is hard" (13:15). His constant theme is that the ways of righteousness lead to wisdom, virtue, and happiness, while those of sin lead to corruption, folly, and ruin.

His stories or short parables about indolence, dissipation, laziness, idleness, the results of bad companions, and involvement with lewd women are razor-sharp in description, forcefully brought to the point.

There is no Messianic message in this book. Its message has to do with moral, social, and civil righteousness, by means of pithy bits of wisdom. It does not deal with the matter of redemption as such, but rather with practical righteousness applied to daily living.

The book falls into five major sections. Keep in mind that much of Proverbs is on the teacher-pupil level and that the teacher is represented as giving his pupil private instructions, as was the general method of ancient education.

One may outline the book as follows:

I.   Admonitions, directions, and cautions, given in an attempt to excite the desire for the higher wisdom, with life-giving powers and qualities, 1-9

II. General instructions to youth on righteous living, 10-16

III. More admonitions to pupils to study for wisdom, to acquire learning, and to seek understanding of life, 17-24

IV. Solomon's proverbs copied out by the "men of Hezekiah." General instructions, with warnings against rejecting the truth and going one's own way, 25-29

V.   Advice to a son by his mother; description of an ideal woman, 30

The final section most fittingly closes this greatest of all young people's books of the Bible.

GREAT THINGS IN PROVERBS

There are no *outstanding stories* here, but rather a number of short, pithy parables and allegories. From these and other passages pointing up valuable lessons, our section of *great truths* will be taken:

1. The industrious ant, 6:6-11
2. The foolish young man and the wild young woman, 7:6-27
3. The ruin of a young man by a sinful young woman, 9:13-18
4. The drunkard and his ways, 23:29-35
5. The way of the sluggard, 24:30-34
6. Lessons from four small creatures, 30:24-28
7. A virtuous woman, 31:10-31

1. For its foresight, industry, and economy, the ant is a remarkable creature. Ants collect food at the proper time and store for the coming season. They sleep through the winter, needing no food, but at harvest time they evidently feed heavily. Hibernation is possible because of immense industry and the storing of energy in their bodies.

The writer of Proverbs would teach youth to labor through life and to *save* against the times of *need*. The theory, "Live only for today, enjoy the present, spend as you go, leave nothing behind," is plainly the philosophy of a *dunce!* He who would have something *tomorrow* must learn to live within his income and save something over, *today*.

2. The picture of the foolish young man and the harlot (7:6-27) is one of life's saddest scenes. This evil woman

tries to make herself as attractive as possible and to convince the young man that he will be "safe" within her home. Possibly pretending to be married, she thereby convinces him that there is even less danger of his being exposed by sinning with her than with a single girl. She presses her case further by saying she really *loves him,* offering her kisses freely.

To this pretense of safety she adds yet another — religion! She has "paid her vows," guaranteeing further the safety and health of her companion in this evil. The rest of the language is intended to excite every sexual passion and destroy whatever moral resistance the young man had left.

The young man goes after her as a stupid ox is led off to the slaughter. The rest of the picture is but the final ruin, downfall, and anguished end of those who take this way of least resistance and sin. The sins and miseries connected with the illicit use of sex are beyond description.

This kind of life destroys virtue, kills noble aspiration, and leaves the persons engaged in it little more than beasts. Let none deceive you: they who once contract certain social diseases cannot easily be cured! At least one type of such disease may lie dormant within the system until age has advanced considerably, then break out as a smoldering fire and burn the victims to the end of life. Softening of the brain, paralysis in varying forms, and other dreadful effects are sometimes traceable to them. In some instances children are cursed with blindness or deformity from birth! The price for promiscuous sexual indulgence is *far* too high for the very little and limited satisfaction gained from it.

The writer of Proverbs here intends to

ANCIENT LAMPS. *The writer probably had such a lamp in mind when he wrote, "For the commandment is a lamp; and the law is a light" (Prov. 6:23) or "The lamp of the wicked shall be put out." (Prov. 13:9)*

show the youthful lad how easily he may be taken in by a conscienceless young woman who is out to ruin him. The picture could be reversed, showing the lying deceit, fair promises, and hypocritical pretenses of young men who try to persuade girls to become their victims. Such persons find that this life is "the way to hell, going down to the chambers of death," (7:27).

3. This very brief picture of the wanton woman seducing the giddy, thoughtless young man is basically the same as the above description (9:13-18). It is not as extended, but it is intended to remind youth that death and hell are in the future for those who tamper with unlawful sexual relationships.

The Scriptures strongly warn against the sins of sex: illicit relationships between the opposite sexes and also homosexuality. These are very old sins of the race, and some of the most dreadful curses and warnings of their results are attached to these statements. The destruction of Sodom and Gomorrah is an example of God's wrath upon people who practice such immoralities.

Some argue that since sexual indulgence is a "natural thing" and that since

God placed the biological urge within human beings, to give way to this "natural impulse" cannot be sinful. This is all wrong. There are many experiences in life which are "natural," but forbidden to us except within legitimate, or lawful, bounds. The appetite for food is natural, but we are forbidden to "steal" to satisfy it. The desire to have nice things is natural, but we are forbidden to take them away from others without paying for them. God has provided within every person the ability to behave himself and keep his natural passions in proper check at all times.

To tamper with sex experience *outside* the marriage bond is to sin against something which God from the beginning has made most sacred. It is not satisfying a mere human, natural desire — it is *degrading* and *unhallowing* the *highest experience* two human beings can have, aside from religious experience. It is a crime against God and humanity; it is a serious blotch upon the highest law of God to man — the marriage law. It will most certainly be visited with divine vengeance. Do not allow anyone to tell you to the contrary. He has no authority from God's Book to tell you so. Though he may be a college professor, a medical doctor, a psychologist, or a psychiatrist, he is out of harmony with God's Word and is *dead wrong!*

4. The writer's very apt description of a "drunk" (23:29-35) shows that the effects of strong drink have not changed across the long centuries. It still makes "babbling fools" out of people who otherwise are intelligent persons. It has not improved with time. Man may be far more intelligent today than long ago, but the drunken are just as stupid, senseless, pitiable, and as much a laughing stock now as then.

The lesson is very clear — leave strong drink alone if you want peace and a worthwhile life. If not, your future is one of sorrow, poverty, and disgrace. The binding habit will burn life and at last bring a fearful death. Drinking is a stupid habit. The appetite is not native; it must be cultivated. It is contrary to every principle of health and decency and leads only to the most selfish ends. One who drinks is willing to inflict sorrow, disgrace, poverty, anxiety, and other troubles upon his loved ones, just so that *he,* big *selfish one,* may have *his* pleasure!

Once the wicked drink habit is formed, it is very difficult to break. If one does not become a drunkard, he is slowly poisoning his body, brain, and influence just the same. In spite of all the arguments to the contrary, drinking in *any form* is entirely uncalled for. It is a silly, senseless, selfish, sensual, filthy, dangerous, disgraceful, and devilish habit! Let all who hope to lead a decent and useful life avoid it in all forms — in youth, and forever.

5. Among the other vices which Solomon condemned in Proverbs is that of laziness or idleness. He drew a very graphic illustration of what happens to the "sluggard" or lazy man (24:30-34). It is an Oriental description of a field which a man proved too lazy and indolent to care for *properly*. Instead of the crop growing, only weeds, briars, and nettles grew up in its place. Agriculture was one of the most honorable of all types of work, especially among the Hebrews. To neglect one's fields and produce no harvest because of idleness or indolence was disgraceful. Such a person was despised and had little standing in society. Honest, hard work has always been honorable. The person who earns his living by honorable work, be it of whatever kind, is

always happier than he who cheats his way through life. The idea that "The world owes me a living, and I mean to have it without hard work" is the criminal's attitude. He who takes this path will soon be into more trouble than he imagined. It is the way of the sluggard, the lazy no-good; it can only lead to disgrace. No sensible young person will entertain such a view of life.

Jeremiah said, "It is good for a man that he bear the yoke in his youth" (Lam. 3:27). Idleness for the first fifteen or twenty years of life can ruin a person for life. Nothing tends to develop better character and make a more successful, happy life than to have work and responsibility early in life. Young people who have work and responsibility almost *never* turn up in criminal courts. "An idle mind is the devil's workshop" and "Satan finds some mischief still for idle hands to do" are true proverbs.

If you would be successful find something worthwhile to do as early in life as you can. Many famous men started out as newspaper boys. Every young person should have to do some work in obtaining his education, no matter how wealthy his parents may be. No one can become well adjusted to life and appreciate its problems without a good solid introduction to work in his youth. No one is fitted to become a leader of men whose hands have not known the meaning of toil in some form or another.

One of the major lessons of Proverbs is that of work and its relationships to life. One has not tasted the best in life, nor can truly master it, until he knows the sweetness of rest from honest toil. When God placed Adam and Eve in the Garden of Eden before the fall, He said that they were to "dress it and keep it" (Gen. 2:15). From the beginning God intend-

ed for mankind to work. This order was given to both Adam and Eve. There was to be no idleness or indolence on the part of either of them. There can be no complete happiness in life without some form of useful, wholesome work.

6. Four lessons from small creatures are pointed out (30:24-28). These lessons show that even the smallest of all creatures are busily engaged in some form of useful, wholesome work.

First, the *ant*: The ants are said to be "a people." They act like people and live much like people. They have houses, build towns or cities, and have public passage ways or roads. They work in colonies and use adroit wisdom in their work and relationships. It is very interesting to watch how they labor. See the notes under No. 1.

Second, the *rabbits*: The "coney" likely refers to a rabbit-like creature of the Orient. It does not live in burrows as some Western rabbits do. It makes "houses" in clefts and holes in the rocks. They use exceedingly cunning ways in gathering their food, protecting their young and managing their affairs.

Third, the *locusts*: These little creatures, something like the Western grasshoppers, only much larger, are one of the fastest-multiplying insects known. Although they have no known leaders among them, they go forth in troops, sometimes miles in circumference, when they take to the wing. They devour the countryside like fire. It is almost impossible to rid an area of them because they work so closely together and know nothing about retreating once they set upon an area.

Fourth, the *spider*: It is most curious in its ways of building its house, collecting its prey, and setting its nets or traps.

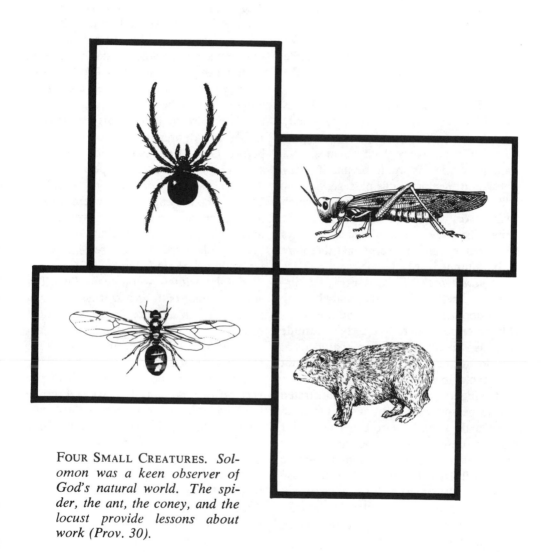

FOUR SMALL CREATURES. *Solomon was a keen observer of God's natural world. The spider, the ant, the coney, and the locust provide lessons about work (Prov. 30).*

The spider is ever alert, ever watchful, and is constantly on the job.

These four creatures are said to be "wise." They teach four lessons: the *ants* — preparation for the future; the *conies* — cleverness of adaptability; the *locusts* — successful cooperation; the *spider* industry. Man can learn many valuable lessons from his smaller neighbors, the insects and animals.

7. The virtuous woman (31:10-31) is the picture of what every young lady should wish to become. It is also the portrayal of what every young man should want in a wife. It would be fine if every girl would memorize this passage.

8. There is one other passage which gives a very valuable lesson for life. The writer lists seven things which he says God "hates," and he warns that these are to be shunned (6:16-19):

A proud look: Exalted eyes, looking only for selfish interests, and looking down upon the rest of mankind are probably referred to here. A certain attitude such as, "I am better than that person, and do not need to consider him," is not acceptable to God.

A lying tongue: This may be illustrated by the person who will not tell the truth when a lie seems "more convenient" for his purposes. Lying is a horrible sin that often fastens itself to its victim so that he can hardly tell the truth. One may also lie in his actions, as well as in his words. Lying destroys all foundation for honesty and integrity. It is a most detestable, useless, and wicked vice.

Hands that shed innocent blood: God hates any destruction of life, whether by outright murder or by other means which will end in fatally wounding the person. One may "shed innocent blood" by so mistreating, bullying, villifying, and abusing another that he may be driven to

despair and commit suicide. One who does so is a red-handed murderer in God's sight, though he may escape justice.

A heart that devises wicked imaginations: A heart allowed to harbor evil imaginations will often break out in open sins, in keeping with its devising. One cannot keep thoughts of evil from crossing the mind, but he can keep them from lodging in his heart. One who sits and ponders how to indulge his passions or satisfy evil desires is guilty of vicious sin before God. Evil imaginations will poison the mind if allowed to persist.

Swift feet in running to mischief: Those who are eager to go where wickedness is being practiced or where they may indulge in various forms of sin are here condemned. To desire, follow after, or practice sin is hateful to God.

A false witness who speaks lies: This is lying under oath as a witness in a case at law. From the most early times there have been courts of law and justice, and men have been called upon to witness for and against each other.

To tell a falsehood under oath to pervert justice is indeed a wicked crime. God hates it and will punish those who commit this fearful sin. It is not only breaking the commandments of God, but in addition, committing *perjury* — lying under oath to pervert and hinder justice from being done. It is even more wicked than ordinary lying because its purpose is to upset the process of justice.

Is a lie ever justified? Never, under any circumstances. What one may think about this is not the rule by which we are to be guided. A lie is a sin against God and is never permissible under any circumstances. God can defend the innocent; and if the innocent must suffer from the truth, it is no more than that which happens every day in the world about us. An honest man would rather have the truth told, and suffer, than to have a lie told to shield him.

There are many things in life which are honorable, but often honor is at stake. One can well afford to suffer rather than to become dishonest and dishonorable. Remember Joseph, about whom Potiphar's wife miserably lied and had him unjustly imprisoned? (Gen. 39). Did Joseph try to evade the issue or accuse this wicked woman? Did he have her imprisoned or punished after he became the prime minister under the king? If he had done so, it would most likely have been recorded. There are some things in life which are to be suffered for honor's sake.

He that sows discord among the brethren: In some other versions this reads: "Six things doth the Lord hate, and the seventh is an abomination unto him" (vs. 16). In other words, sowing discord is set apart as an abominable thing to God. This means it is highly displeasing, something very low down, mean, and cheap in God's sight.

No one has much respect for a person who is always tattling, telling tales, and stirring up strife among people. Tattlers and gossips are obnoxious people, whose nefarious traffic both God and man despise — and with just cause! Such people can stir up contention in families, among relatives, in churches, in communities, and among friends. They are the devil's friends and co-workers, the enemies of peace among men. There is hardly a worse enemy of mankind than a gossip who continually keeps trouble stirred up by his evil reports and by crossing up things and distorting the truth.

This sin has caused the work of God to suffer untold injuries and has been the cause of many turning from the Lord. It is a great evil, and all young people must learn to shun it as one would shun a poisonous snake.

Since Proverbs is the young people's book of the Bible, and since they are so very important, it is suggested that each person learn by memory the following proverbs:

"The fear of the Lord is the beginning of knowledge: but fools despise wisdom and instruction" (1:7).

"My son, if sinners entice thee, consent thou not" (1:10).

"But the path of the just is as the shining light, that shineth more and more unto the perfect day" (4:18).

"Keep thy heart with all diligence; for out of it are the issues of life" (4:23).

"Can a man take fire in his bosom, and his clothes not be burned?" (6:27).

"A false balance is abomination to the Lord: but a just weight is his delight" (11:1).

"Where no counsel is, the people fall: but in the multitude of counsellors there is safety" (11:14).

"The fruit of the righteous is a tree of life; and he that winneth souls is wise" (11:30).

"A virtuous woman is the crown to her husband: but she that maketh ashamed is as rottenness in his bones" (12:4).

"There is a way that seemeth right unto a man, but the end thereof are the ways of death" (14:12).

"The backslider in heart shall be filled with his own ways: and a good man shall be satisfied from himself" (14:14).

"He that is slow to wrath is of great understanding: but he that is hasty of spirit exalteth folly" (14:29).

"Righteousness exalteth a nation: but sin is a reproach to any people" (14:34).

"A soft answer turneth away wrath: but grievous words stir up anger" (15:1).

"Better is little with the fear of the Lord than great treasure and trouble therewith" (15:16).

"Pride goeth before destruction, and an haughty spirit before a fall" (16:18).

"The hoary head is a crown of glory, if it be found in the way of righteousness" (16:31).

"He that is slow to anger is better than the mighty; and he that ruleth his spirit than he that taketh a city" (16:32).

"A merry heart doeth good like a medicine: but a broken spirit drieth the bones" (17:22).

"A brother offended is harder to be won than a strong city: and their contentions are like the bars of a castle" (18:19).

"A man that hath friends must show himself friendly: and there is a friend that sticketh closer than a brother" (18:24).

"Wine is a mocker, strong drink is raging: and whosoever is deceived thereby is not wise" (20:1).

"An high look, and a proud heart, and the plowing of the wicked is sin" (21:4).

"It is better to dwell in a corner of the housetop, than with a brawling woman in a wide house" (21:9).

"Whoso keepeth his mouth and his tongue keepeth his soul from troubles" (21:23).

"A good name is rather to be chosen than great riches, and loving favor rather than silver and gold" (22:1).

"Train up a child in the way he should go: and when he is old, he will not depart from it" (22:6).

"He that oppresseth the poor to increase his riches, and he that giveth to the rich, shall surely come to want" (22:16).

"Withhold not correction from the child: for if thou beatest him with the rod, he shall not die. Thou shalt beat him with the rod, and shalt deliver his soul from hell" (23:13, 14).

"If thou faint in the day of adversity, thy strength is small" (24:10).

"A word fitly spoken is like apples of gold in pictures of silver" (25:11).

"He that hath no rule over his own spirit is like a city that is broken down, and without walls" (25:28).

"Where no wood is, there the fire goeth out: so where there is no talebearer, the strife ceaseth" (26:20).

"Boast not thyself of tomorrow; for thou knoweth not what a day may bring forth" (27:1).

"Let another man praise thee, and not thine own mouth; a stranger, and not thine own lips" (27:2).

"The wicked fleeth when no man pursueth: but the righteous are bold as a lion" (28:1).

"He that covereth his sins shall not prosper: but whoso confesseth and forsaketh them shall have mercy" (28:13).

"He, that being often reproved hardeneth his neck, shall suddenly be destroyed, and that without remedy" (29:1).

"Where there is no vision, the people perish: but he that keepeth the law, happy is he" (29:18).

"Favor is deceitful, and beauty is vain: but a woman that feareth the Lord, she shall be praised" (31:30).

Special Memory Verse

"Keep thy heart with all diligence; for out of it are the issues of life" (4:23).

Ecclesiastes

The present title of this book is derived from its opening word in the Hebrew language, which referred to "one who called an assembly." By way of the Greek and Latin languages, it became "Ecclesiastes." It is therefore understandable that it is sometimes called "The Preacher."

TO WHOM

Likely this book was also intended for youth more than persons of any other age. Its appeal is almost entirely to youth. Such passages as 11:9-10 and 12:1-7 indicate that the whole book is directed largely toward youth. Remember that by the term youth here, as in Proverbs, we mean from the teens to thirty-five or so.

It was originally given to the Jewish people, but it is so universal in its scope that it was hardly intended solely for them alone. Solomon had become so widely known in the ancient world by this time that his writings would naturally be read in all intellectual circles. There is very little in the book, in fact, which emits a distinctly Jewish flavor. It breathes the atmosphere of universal appeal and speaks a language of human experience which all can understand.

PURPOSE

It is evident that it aims to show the futility of life without God's love and grace in the heart. But it also represents one of the most baffling subjects occupy-

ing the most brilliant minds through the ages — the "why" of human existence. *Why* are we here? For what purpose? The writer shows that one may have every physical, mental, and social pleasure amidst riches, honor, fame, and every worldly joy, and yet never come to know the real purpose of life nor gain any really solid, lasting joy.

God prospered Solomon until he was considered the richest and wisest man on earth in his day. He allowed him to drink of every pleasure of earth to his satisfying full. Riches, honor, fame, friends, and every food and drink known to man at that time were his. He had seven hundred wives and three hundred court women — all available to him at any time. He added that which appealed to his eye, until not a choice could be left that he had not made. Apparently no human pleasure he had not enjoyed to its depth with abounding health and vigor. But he cries at last, "Vanity of vanities, all is vanity and vexation of spirit" (1:2, 14).

It seems that God permitted Solomon to experience this that he might warn others of the emptiness of life without God in the heart and life. After having burned out all the avenues of sensual pleasure and having tried out every human way to find lasting happiness, without finding it, he gives the world the results of his findings in this most remarkable book. His conclusion, given to youth at the close of the book, is that if they wish to find the permanent joys and satisfactions of life which will produce lasting happiness, they must "Fear God and keep his commandments: for this is the whole duty of man" (12:13). This pretty well sums up the purpose of the book.

In reaching this conclusion, he points

out some most interesting facts. The key thought of the book is expressed in the term "under the sun" (1:14). This phrase may be taken to mean *apart from God* — living life without serving God. This term occurs twenty-eight times in the book; and in most cases, if the reader will substitute *apart from God* for "under the sun," he will see that it gives a better understanding of the whole book. The key word to the book is "vanity" (or vanities) and this occurs thirty-seven times in the twelve chapters. This word suggests *futility, vainness, uselessness, nothingness.* With this as a reading guide, the book's purpose is not hard to see.

TIME

Most scholars think Solomon wrote this book toward the close of his life. Some believe that this book was written after Solomon was drawn away from the Lord by his sinful wives. This, it is contended, is his testimony of his return. Others are of the opinion that such a book could not have been produced in the old age of a man whose life had been burned out by sensual living.

AUTHORSHIP

Since ancient times the Jews have traditionally thought Solomon to be the writer of this book; it is so received today. Its language and nature are more befitting to Solomon than to any other Old Testament person. The philosophical turn of the book and its wide acquaintance with the ways of the extremely wealthy, as well as its depths of wisdom, all point strongly to Solomon as the writer.

There is this rather sad note which history forces us to face: If Solomon ever returned to the Lord in the pure and noble way in which he served Him in his earlier years, there is no mention of it in all the historical records of the Bible.

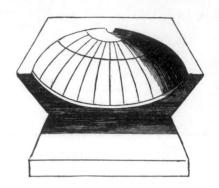

ANCIENT SUN DIAL. *A sun dial such as this may have been in use in Solomon's day. "To everything there is a season, a time to every purpose under heaven . . ."*

Some think he is referred to in the faith chapter (Heb. 11:33 — "subdued kingdoms"), but this is by no means certain. It seems that the sun sets upon his life after a fearful storm which had broken his boat from its moorings and taken it far out to sea, with no report of its return. Despite this fact, however, there is a persistent tradition that Solomon was converted in his extreme old age. Ecclesiastes may have been written at this time, just prior to his death.

However, it is more likely that Solomon wrote this book toward the decline of his meridian years, when he was still in vigor of health and favor with God, and under the inspiration of the Holy Spirit. There is nothing whatsoever to have kept him from writing this book then, for he had tasted every pleasure of life worth mentioning. This is probably the safest position to take concerning its authorship.

This book may be outlined as follows:

I. Proposition one: Neither labor or the world, nor riches, success, nor prosperity can render mankind happy, 1—5:13

II. Proposition two: Earthly possessions, instead of bringing happiness, become an obstacle to it and bring a snare to ruin life, 5:14—6:12

III. Proposition three: Man knows not what is good for him, either from ignorance or unmindfulness of life, and seldom does what is best, 7:1—11:10

IV. Conclusion: From youth to old age, there is only one sure way to happiness — to "fear God and keep his commandments," 12:1-14

This book has no Messianic message nor reference to the covenant. It is a wisdom book, showing mankind the follies of sinful life and pointing to the better way. It does not deal with redemption as such, but it is still worthy of a place in the Bible for the contribution it makes to life.

GREAT THINGS IN ECCLESIASTES

There are no *outstanding stories* or parables. There are some *great truths*, which may be mentioned briefly:

1. Several subtitles have been given to this book in an attempt to qualify it: "On the Meaning of Life," "The Disillusions of Worldliness," "The Philosophy of Self-Quest," and "The Book of the Natural Man." All these have merit but do not seem to fit the book. They do point out that this book uncovers one of life's most vital questions — the real meaning and value of life.

2. It has been pointed out that Job concerns itself with the problem of suffering, Proverbs with formulas for success and happiness, and Ecclesiastes with the meaning of life. This meaning can be found only as it is related to God and His righteousness in the individual life.

3. This book, perhaps more than any other in the Bible, takes the form of ancient philosophical argument. In reality,

there is but one great truth taught, although by references to several units of truth; the whole book is spent in presenting this truth. This truth is that *life apart from God is a mere vanity of futile existence,* not worthy of the name of life.

4. Ecclesiastes is the most melancholy of all the books in the Bible. It is permeated with an atmosphere of stagnant life, life gone sour — without meaning. Everywhere there is the constant complaint of "vanity of vanities;" nothing seems to satisfy. It is very much like the cynicism of despair in modern literature or the wailing howl of much that passes for music and song in this day.

5. This book points up the fact that the *absence of God* from life spells the *presence* of every kind of *unhappiness.*

6. Here is an utterly worldly atmosphere — of getting and giving, gaining and losing, fighting to become wealthy and famous without knowing what to do with it after its achievement. Here are the gloom of the grave and the shadow of the tomb — the worldly man does not look to life beyond the grave.

7. The writer closes his work with a description of old age with all its inconveniences and disillusions (12:1-7). His last words are to the effect that youth should so prepare that this sad state may not find them unprepared for the certain death which all must meet.

So ends one of the most peculiar books in the Bible, yet to the understanding youth, one of the most helpful.

Memory Verses

"Remember now thy Creator in the days of thy youth, while the evil days come not, nor the years draw nigh, when thou shalt say, I have no pleasure in them" (12:1).

"Let us hear the conclusion of the whole matter: fear God and keep his commandments: for this is the whole duty of man" (12:13).

Song of Solomon

This book draws its name from the nature of the book. In the original Hebrew it was "The Song of Songs" or an "Ode of the Odes," much like other Scripture superlatives such as "heaven of heavens," "King of kings," or "Lord of lords." These mean the highest, best, supreme. Solomon wrote 1,005 songs in all (I Kings 4:32). Only this one survives. The name "Canticles" has sometimes been attached to the book; it is derived from Jerome's Latin Vulgate Version.

TO WHOM

Some think this love poem was written to celebrate the marriage of Solomon to his favorite wife. This is without positive proof, although certainly not beyond possibility. It seems very fitting for such an occasion, as it describes dramatically an Oriental courtship and marriage upon the vast scale which Solomon was capable of executing.

It was, of course, left to the Jewish people as part of their great heritage of literature, and in some sense may have been written for them. It may well be adapted to the youth of the times as a love poem.

PURPOSE

Since the writer has neither stated his purpose nor given inferences of it in the book, for centuries it has been a subject of considerable debate. In this light, the *interpretation* of the book has varied considerably. At various times it has been considered as:

1. A plain congratulatory song or poem of the historical events of the courtship and marriage of Solomon and Pharoah's daughter. It may have been used as a drama for this occasion.

2. An *allegory* of God's dealings with Israel in bringing them out of Egypt into Canaan.

3. An *allegory* of Christ's relationship to His church, under the imagery of an Oriental love-making situation.

4. A description of the love and joyous experiences of true lovers in romance and in marriage, intended to show the ideal relationship of marriage.

Earlier among the ancient Jews much consideration was given to the first theory as the correct one. Later, however, there was superimposed the idea that this poem represents God's love for and dealings with His ancient Hebrew people. This spiritualization was first sponsored by Josephus, the learned Jewish historian of later Jewish times.

Sometime early in the Christian centuries some of the Church Fathers developed the theory that holds that this poem represents Christ and His church and the love relationship between them. This theory was based upon Paul's speaking of Christ and His church in the husband-wife relationship of love (Eph. 5: 22-33). On this basis these early Fathers completely spiritualized everything in this book. This theory has stood through the centuries and is still held by many, as will be seen in many Bibles where titles of this nature are given in the various chapters.

Lately it has been quite popular to interpret the book as a collection of Oriental wedding songs. The Syrians, for instance, until quite recently, considered a

THE LILY OF THE VALLEY AND THE ROSE OF SHARON. *The hyacinth (left) is likely the flower to which Solomon refers in Song of Solomon 2:1. It is still common in the Middle East. Few agree as to specific flower Solomon had in mind when he named the Rose of Sharon. Recent work in Biblical botany suggests that the tulip (right) may be the Rose of Sharon associated with Christ.*

newly wedded couple as king and queen during the marriage festival which followed the ceremony.

There are Bible scholars who believe that as a love poem, describing the loving and tender relationship which should exist between the married, this book is worthy of a place in the Bible.

TIME

This book has generally been assigned to Solomon's early days as king of Israel. The very nature of the writing calls for youthful vigor and imagination.

AUTHORSHIP

This book has been credited to Solomon by most of the ancient Jews and by the early Christian church. The book is also ascribed to Solomon in the opening words (1:1), which settles this question.

GREAT THINGS IN SONG OF SOLOMON

This is an *outstanding story* of poetic drama. While there are few *great truths* such as we have seen in most books, we may look at the following important facts:

1. Concerning the *persons* portrayed in the book, there is a variance of opinion. Some consider the hero to have been King Solomon himself and the heroine a young woman of northern Palestine. This young woman, a widow's only daughter, lived with her mother and shepherd brothers. She was engaged to a handsome shepherd boy, but was not yet married.

On a tour of her country, King Solomon met her, immediately admired her, and wanted her for one of his royal wives. He made love to her but failed to win her. Then he brought her to Jerusalem, hoping to win her affection by the affluence of his court and promises to make her his head royal wife. But she spurned his offers, remaining true to her shepherd lover. Solomon then released her to go home to her lover.

2. Others contend that this is a poetic description of the historical event of the wedding of Solomon to Pharoah's daughter. It is written, so they contend, to fit the seven days of the royal feast. Each of the seven nights brings some new discovery and proposals of love to each other.

3. The fact that the name of God does not appear in this book and the fact that the book is nowhere referred to in the New Testament make the theory of its representation of Christ and His church a bit difficult. This does not mean, however, that the book is not divinely inspired; other Old Testament books also are not mentioned in the New Testament. Despite this, however, there are many things in this book which may be used as symbols, both of Christ and His relationship to His people, and of other Christian truths.

4. Here is romantic and marital love in full bloom and in its most blissful state. Although its descriptions are suited to its times, the principles are universally basic to love-making. If husbands and wives today lived in each other's love as did the lovers portrayed here, there would be no divorce courts operating!

5. Taking certain passages to represent spiritual truths for our day, one may note:

(a) As the Rose of Sharon and the Lily of the Valleys (2:1), Solomon may be taken to represent Christ, the supreme Lover, to the redeemed soul.

(b) The little foxes which spoil the vines (2:15) may represent the little sins of life which, while seemingly small, nevertheless, eat the heart out of Christian experience, just as foxes ruined the vines then.

(c) Under pressures of the "north wind" of cold conflict, trials, and the like, the sweet spices of true Christian life often are sent forth (4:16). Saints under extreme trial often shine as at no other times.

(d) She that is "fair as the moon, clear as the sun, and terrible as an army with banners" (6:10) may well represent the Christian church in her most spiritual and aggressive times. In lesser form it may also portray the individual whose commitment to Christ has made him well nigh invincible.

(e) Some would see in the quotation, "Who is this that cometh up from the wilderness, leaning upon her beloved?" (8:5), a prophetic note, descriptive of Christ taking His church in the rapture of the saints at His coming (I Thess. 4:13-17).

Unless it is seen in the symbolism of this book, there is no definite Messianic message here. Taken symbolically much of Christ and of the fuller meaning of the covenant's fulfillment in Him is revealed.

Except for two ideas — the prophetic portrayal of Christ and His church, and a description of ideal married love — this book has little meaning. But with either, or indeed both, of these in prospect, it is filled with beautiful imagery and meaning.

Memory Verse

"Who is she that looketh forth as the morning, fair as the moon, clear as the sun, and terrible as an army with banners?" (6:10).

The Major Prophets

THE PROPHET AND HIS WORK

With the opening of this section, we come to a new type of book — the prophetical book. Before presenting these remarkable books, we should see something of their nature.

Prophets were a special class of God's servants, quite distinct from all other workers. The work of the prophets throughout the centuries has gone far to bring to us the present revelation of God in the Bible.

Some of these men, like Moses, called the first of the prophets, held other positions. Prophecy was only a minor part of their work. So also with Samuel, the last judge of Israel.

Some were mainly *preaching* prophets, such as Elijah and Elisha, who left no written records of their messages. Others, such as Isaiah and Jeremiah, gave their full time to the ministry and left their books for the peoples of following generations. Some wrote longer books, such as the two just mentioned, which are referred to as the major prophets. Others wrote much shorter books, such as Amos, Joel, or Hosea; they are known as the minor prophets. This classification has to do with the *length* of their ministry and books — not with the *quality* of their books or work. As far as their moral and spiritual work and value is concerned, the minor prophets are equally as important in their places and times as are the major prophets.

The word prophet comes first from an ancient Hebrew word which meant to "bubble up," to "pour forth," or to "run over," as from a living fountain of water. In its official sense it meant to *fore-tell,* or to *tell forth* truths under divine inspiration. To "foretell" is thought of more

as prophecy, but to "tell forth" is also part of the prophet's work. He not only foretold events, but also preached, proclaimed, and exhorted the people to repentance and obedience. The word also meant to *instruct, preach,* and to *proclaim as a divine message.* It also may have included the act of *testifying.* In the tenth chapter of Samuel, Saul is said to have *prophesied.* It probably meant that he prayed, supplicated, and testified; so also in I Kings 18 the prophets of Baal are said to have prophesied. The Greek word for prophet also meant to foretell events which were yet to happen; at other times it referred to telling others of secret things which had been revealed. It likewise carries with it the idea of prayer and supplications, as well as edification and exhortation. In I Corinthians 14, Paul uses the word to mean *prophesying, edifying,* and *exhorting.*

One form of the Hebrew word also appears to mean *moving about from place to place* and may indicate something of the migratory, itinerant type of life lived by many of the prophets. This would be much like the minister of today who moves from charge to charge or the evangelist who travels about preaching.

In ancient Israel the prophet was sometimes also called a "seer," or a *seeing person* (I Sam. 9:9; II Sam. 15:27). They saw visions and sometimes were divinely directed by dreams. The prophets were also called *men of God, messengers,* and sometimes *angels of God.* These divine messengers received their revelations from God in various ways and under differing circumstances, but they always proved to be God's true messengers.

However, there were *false* prophets in those days, just as there are people today who are insincere. In these cases, the false prophets *made up* their messages and pretended that God had spoken to them. Some were very good imitators of the true prophets. Elijah had to deal with about 850 such prophets at Mount Carmel (I Kings 18:17-40). False prophets in the ancient nations around Israel may have copied much from the true prophets of God in Israel.

The position of the prophet in ancient times was one of great honor among the Jews, the Arabs, and even the Greeks. In some instances the power and influence of the prophet was far greater than that of the king. For this reason kings often sought to obtain the benediction of the prophet on their plans.

As time progressed the Hebrew prophets became not only *foretellers* of secrets and events, but *forth-tellers,* the foremost preachers of their day. They were the ministers to whom the people looked for spiritual and moral guidance, both nationally and individually. The king and the prophet, as David and Nathan, were sometimes close friends.

The Jews listed as many as forty-eight prophets and prophetesses — women prophets such as Deborah — in their traditions. There are only sixteen *writing* prophets of the prophetic period, of which four are known as major prophets and twelve as minor prophets. The remaining ones, with rare exceptions, such as Elijah, Elisha, Nathan, and Gad, were little known beyond their days. However, there was an almost endless succession of prophets from Moses' time down to that of Malachi, so that the Scripture writing and even the formation of its canon was almost constantly under the guiding hand of some inspired prophet of God. How greatly this shows the mercy and kindness of God to Israel and His watchful care over them.

The *work* of the prophets may be briefly summed up as follows:

1. They conveyed God's messages — their most important duty — to the nation, the surrounding nations, and to the individual. They spoke to their contemporaries and to those in the far distant future God's messages of the ages — of justice, mercy, Christ's coming redemptive work, and the final conclusions of all things on earth.

2. They offered spiritual guidance, lifted the moral standards, rebuked injustices, offered social reforms, stood sternly against all sin (I Kings 17-18), stood as God's watchmen over Israel (Ezek. 3:17-21), and offered gracious encouragement and support in times of distress and trouble.

3. One of the great ministries was that of prophetically pointing to the future. Almost all of them had something of this element in their ministry, but Isaiah was by far the most outstanding of the *futuristic* prophets. Many of his most famous passages have to do with Christ and His redemptive work. See Isaiah 7:14; 9:6-7; 35:3-10; 53:1-12, for just a few of the most important ones. Many such passages can be found in the books of the prophets.

The Old Testament prophets stand alone as a class of men, without peer, both in the Bible and in all the literature of ancient times. Indeed, a large portion of the New Testament is made up of selections from these great writings or references to them in some manner. Today we are living in the amazing fulfillment of some of these centuries-old prophecies.

Let us enter into this section of the Bible with the reverence and respect due these great men of God.

Isaiah

This book is named for its author. In the original Hebrew Isaiah means "salvation of Jehovah." It was a common name in his day. It is the largest of all the prophetic books and properly stands at the gateway to this section.

Isaiah is called the "evangelical book of the Old Testament," and its author is called the "evangelical prophet." At times it reaches sublime heights of present day evangelical concepts, and much of it compares favorably with parts of the New Testament.

TO WHOM

Its primary and immediate appeal was to Judah and the Jewish nation. Much of the latter part has the future comfort and instruction of the Jewish people in view. This section applied largely to the post-Babylonian Jews and their needs. But the book also has universal appeal for all God's people.

PURPOSE

The Jews of Isaiah's day needed correction, reproof, and admonition as well as instruction for righteous living. Much of the first section of the book is addressed to these needs. A considerable portion of it is also directed against the enemy nations around Israel, foretelling their coming doom. Throughout the book there is also much comfort, encouragement, and inspiration to faith in God.

The larger purpose of this work was to point up God's redemptive plan for mankind, using Israel as the means through which this was to be accomplished. This redemptive note runs throughout the book, from the promise of the coming virgin-born Redeemer (7: 14), His glorious reign (9:6, 7), and the suffering Savior (53), to the final triumph of His kingdom (35:1-10; 65:17-25). From the universal and redemptive viewpoint, this latter purpose is by far the most important part of the prophetic ministry.

The final purpose of Isaiah may have been to prepare the Jewish people for the Babylonian captivity just ahead of them. This seems to loom largely in the prophet's thinking. While he strove to head this off by calling them to repentance, he realized finally that it was inevitable, and he became reconciled to it.

TIME

Isaiah is thought to have lived about 780-695 or 690 B.C., a period of eighty-five or ninety years. He lived during the reigns of Uzziah, Jotham, Ahaz, Hezekiah, and Manasseh. These were among the last kings of Judah before the Babylonian captivity. It is most likely that the writing of this book was in process for a good number of years. The work was evidently begun when the prophet was very young; the latter parts may have been composed near the end of his life.

AUTHORSHIP

From the most ancient times, this book was attributed by the Jews to the prophet Isaiah, and it was so accepted by the early church. Some modern writers have questioned his authorship of the last part because Cyrus, king of the Per-

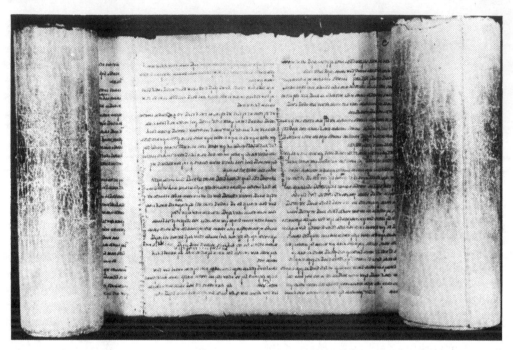

ISAIAH SCROLL. *This scroll, which was discovered in one of the caves near the northwestern end of the Dead Sea, contains the complete text of the Book of Isaiah. The scroll is made of parchment and dates back to the second century B.C. The total length of the scroll is almost twenty-four feet. The darkened portions in the center, on both sides, are the result of many hands holding the scroll at these points.*

sians, is mentioned by *name* in this section, when it is known that this king was born about one hundred years after Isaiah's time. Isaiah also makes certain references to post-Babylonian conditions, which it is argued, he could *not* have known.

There seems to be two definite sections in this book: chapters 1-39, composing the first; chapters 40-66, the last. The first part of the book is much more historical, relating to times and conditions of Isaiah's immediate day. Prophecies con-

cerning nearby nations relate generally to matters of more immediate concern, although some of these were not fulfilled for many years. The second section is much different in that much of it seems to relate to *future times,* those well beyond Isaiah's day. Here King Cyrus and descriptions of what are thought by some to be post-captivity conditions and times are mentioned. This has provided the ground of contention on the part of some modern writers. These critics do not always accept the *total inspiration* of the Bible and so find difficulty in reconciling the *miraculous* element in Isaiah with the historical portions of the book.

The explanation lies in these simple facts: Isaiah was inspired by the Holy Spirit, who guided him. The Spirit revealed to him future conditions, and facts so that he wrote them much as if they had been *history.* Prophecy, it must be remembered, is really *history in broad outline,* written *in advance* by the inspiration of the Holy Spirit. Sometimes, too, there can be a lot of *detail* in prophecy, as we shall see in the rest of the Old Testament books. When one accepts the total inspiration of the Bible, there is no problem regarding prophecy.

Now note the following: There are some prophecies listed in this book which were fulfilled very soon, such as those referring to the Babylonian captivity of Israel. Others, like those about Cyrus and post-captivity conditions, were fulfilled some one hundred years or so later. But there are also others which were not to be fulfilled for many more years, such as those regarding utter destruction of the city of Tyre, which was not fully accomplished until the days of Alexander the Great. But more than this: There were numerous prophecies about the coming of Christ which were not fulfilled for nearly seven hundred years. Sections of these prophecies are *yet awaiting fulfillment* — those regarding conditions at Christ's return to earth and those following it. There are others relating to the "new heavens and the new earth," which will not be fulfilled until much farther into the future, even after Christ's return. Some of these will be noted later in this book.

Now, if Isaiah, inspired by the Holy Spirit, could write prophecies which were not fulfilled for hundreds of years, and some which may not be fulfilled for two or three thousand years, or maybe much more, what would have hindered him from writing those which would be fulfilled within some one hundred years? *Nothing!* In fact, the *fulfillment* of these earlier prophecies strengthens the faith of God's people in the sure fulfillment of those yet to come.

What about the differences in the style and certain other factors in the second portion of the book? It should be remembered that Isaiah lived for many years. He began his prophetic ministry early in life, and likely also his ministry of writing. The second portion of this book was most likely written in his later years, which may account in part for these differences. Again, this section deals largely with matters of the more distant future; this accounts for his difference in outlook and even in certain features of style in writing.

Acceptance of the total inspiration of the Bible by the Holy Spirit and also the miraculous in prophecy, as all true believers in God's Word do, removes all obstacles. There is neither any room nor need for the theory of First and Second Isaiah's, written by two different men, the latter living far beyond Isaiah's day.

But to turn the screws down a little tighter on the true position which holds that Isaiah the prophet wrote this whole book, consider the following:

1. The New Testament quotes more from Isaiah than from all other Old Testament prophecies combined, and it always attributes the prophecy to Isaiah. There are 308 quotations from or references to Isaiah in the New Testament.

2. Jesus Christ and His apostles often quoted from Isaiah; they generally referred to its writings as those from the prophet Isaiah. To say that Christ, the Son of God, partook of the ignorance of the fact that Isaiah did not write the whole of this book would be the height of sacrilege and blasphemy! The apostles were inspired by the Holy Spirit. They referred to this prophecy as the work of Isaiah. Would not the Holy Spirit have checked and corrected them, had this not been so?

3. But the final clincher is this: Many

of the references in the New Testament are from that *second section,* disputed by some to be Isaiah's writing. And what is more, almost always the New Testament writers do *not* refer to just the *Book* of Isaiah, but specifically to "Isaiah, the prophet," "the prophet Isaiah," "Isaiah," and "the prophecy of Isaiah." There was evidently no question in their minds as to Isaiah's authorship of the whole book.

Isaiah was the "son of Amoz", who must not be confused with the prophet Amos. His father seems to have been little known, though some have thought he was King Amaziah's brother —a tradition without foundation.

Isaiah was married. His wife was referred to as a prophetess (8:3). He had two sons (38:1), and tradition asserts that his daughter was married to Manasseh, son of King Hezekiah.

Since he "saw visions concerning Judah and Jerusalem" in the days of Uzziah, Jotham, Ahaz, and Hezekiah (1:1), it is likely that he was about twenty years old when he began his prophetic ministry. These kings reigned about 780-695 or 690 B.C. In this case, if he lived well past the fourteenth year of Hezekiah, he may have been eighty-five or ninety years of age at his death.

He was held in high esteem by the Jews at Jerusalem during this period, and he lived on a high social level (7:3; 16:37; 21:35; 38:1-22; 39:3-8).

He does not record his prophetic call at the beginning of this book, as many do, but alludes to it in chapter 6. Whether he attended the "schools of the prophets," where young men were trained in the Law, Levitical Codes, and historical writings of the Jews (II Kings 2:3-25), is not known, but he was well trained for his work.

Courtesy, Moissaye Marans

ISAIAH. *This contemporary sculpture by Moissaye Marans is entitled "Swords and Plowshares." It is based on Isaiah's prophecy in Isaiah 2:4, ". . . and they shall beat their swords into plowshares. . . ."*

Isaiah was at the royal court during a portion of his ministry and seems to have recorded certain historical facts (II Chron. 26:22; 32:32). His prophecies contain some poetic parts of the highest type, together with prose sections of high literary excellence. Penning this work, together with his many duties in preaching, teaching, comforting, and counseling must have required much of his time.

It is believed that his prophetic career extended over some sixty-five years, if estimates have been computed correctly. Chapters 1-5 were written early and have the touches of youthful zeal and dogmatic firmness in them. His cleansing and commission (6), may have come in the last days of Uzziah, and it made a remarkable change in him. To the period of the next fifteen years, no other writing except chapter 6 has been assigned.

He may not have been very active during the reign of wicked King Jotham, and possibly many of his greater prophecies came during the reign of his good friend Hezekiah, a good king. He may have prophesied some during Manasseh's reign, but there is little evidence of it.

Tradition places his death during the reign of the wicked King Manasseh. It is said that for resisting some of the king's idolatrous acts, Isaiah was seized at the king's orders, placed between two large planks, and "sawn asunder" (Heb. 11:37) by the king's officers.

Isaiah was of the highest personal character. His style of writing portrays a more correct and majestic manner than that of any of the other prophets. Great earnestness and plainness of speech are seen in his writings. He rebukes king and people equally (7:13; 38:1; 1:10-23; 2:11-17; 3:15-19; 28:7-15). He calls Jerusalem a sinful nation and an "harlot" (1:4, 21) and denounces hypocrisy and rebellion (29:13; 30:9). Yet he weeps over her with bitterness and prays for her protection from a foreign invader (22:4; 37:22).

He is deeply reverent (6), and of a strong spiritual character (1:11-13; 56:2-8). His oft repeated expressions of reverence were "The Holy One of Israel" and "The Holy One." God is called "the high and lofty One who inhabiteth eternity" (57:15). This is the only time the word "eternity" occurs in the Bible. Perhaps some of the most lofty descriptions of God are in Isaiah.

The book may be outlined as follows:
  I.   Prophetical section with local applications, 1-35
  II. Historical section concerning local Jewish situations, 36-39
  III. Prophetical section concerning future matters relating to Israel, the Messiah, and the coming kingdom, 40-66

Another more extensive outline is:
  I.   Concerning Jothan and his reign, local situations, 1-6
  II. Concerning the reign of Ahaz, seige of Jerusalem by Pekah and Rezin; birth of Immanuel, and the calamities of Syria and Israel, 7-12
  III. Concerning Babylon, Philistia, and the Moabites, 13-18
  IV. Concerning nearby nations and their judgments, 19-35
  V.   Concerning Hezekiah's reign, Sennacherib's defeat, and the fulfillment of preceding prophecies (historical section), 36-39
  VI. Concerning the existence of God, truth of the Jewish religion, vanity of idolatry, return of Israel from captivity, and

Courtesy, The British Museum

THREE CAPTIVE LYRE PLAYERS. *This relief sculpture of captive musicians under the guard of an Assyrian soldier is found on a wall of Sennacherib's palace at Ninevah. The captives pictured may have been Jews.*

the coming of Messiah, 40-45
VII. Concerning personification of the Messiah — Christ: His sufferings, death, and burial; prediction of the return from Babylonian captivity and the glory of the latter days, 46-56
VIII. Concerning the coming of the Messiah, call and salvation of the Gentiles, disgrace and confusion of false teachers, etc., 57-66

There may be other methods of outlining it, but these serve as guides to its major contents.

GREAT THINGS IN ISAIAH

There are only a few *outstanding stories* in the book, as it is mostly prophecy:

1. Sennacherib's defeat, 36, 37
2. Hezekiah's sickness and healing, 38
3. Hezekiah's foolish act in showing off his treasures, 39

Great truths pointed up here are:

1. No matter how great the forces of evil, God's purposes will never be defeated by them. God is still upon His throne, and He still has power over the nations today, just as when in answer to prayer He destroyed Sennacherib's army and sent him away totally broken and defeated (36, 37:33-36).

2. Hezekiah's sickness and God's healing touch upon him show God's mercy in times of need and distress. It was wonderful that Hezekiah had so lived that he

could remind the Lord of how he had served Him in his hour of deep distress (38:2, 3). God did not heal Hezekiah only because of his good life, but because of His infinite love and mercy, and for His own glory. When in distress or sorrow, one must never plead his *own goodness,* however well the Lord has helped him to live; as one prays, he must plead the *mercy* and *grace* of God. However, it is a great encouragement to faith when one is able to look back upon a life well lived for the Lord.

3. After Hezekiah's healing, the Babylonian king sent messengers and presents to him (39:1-2). In showing off his treasures to these heathen messengers, He made one of the worst mistakes of his life. Isaiah delivered a stinging rebuke to the king, foretelling him what would happen as a result of his soft, sentimental act (39:3-8).

Perhaps there is a lesson here for us. Whatever God has done for us, we are not to try to *show off* to the public how well we have prospered or to act so as to build up or display pride. We should witness humbly to what God has done for us; we should never *boast.*

Some feel that the fifteen years which the Lord added to Hezekiah's life were poorly used by him. One should see to it that any extension of life be used only to God's glory, not for selfish ends. How many people hasn't the Lord kindly raised up from deathly sicknesses, who have failed to live for His glory thereafter!

Let us note further *great truths* in this remarkable book:

1. God's great invitation to all sinners (1:18) is one of the most beautiful anywhere in the Bible. Everyone should memorize it. It reminds one of Jesus' words centuries later: "Come unto me, all ye that labor and are heavy laden, and I will give you rest" (Matt. 11:28). Isaiah 1:18 is God's "whosoever" of the Old Testament to all men to come and be saved.

2. The promise of the Savior (7:14) is one of the most outstanding prophecies of the Old Testament. The "virgin birth" of Christ, here prophesied, has been the subject of much debate. Some have denied that the Hebrew word here signifies a "virgin" as such, but Christian scholars have shown that this is the *true meaning* of the word used in the original Hebrew. This has been accepted throughout the Christian centuries.

3. An outstanding Messianic passage relative to Christ's birth (9:6, 7) not only shows the birth, but the *kingdom* work of the Savior. Here is one of the most prominent "prophetic gaps" of the Old Testament. A "prophetic gap" refers to a place where a prophecy lists something as *occurring,* then immediately lists something else in some way connected, but far removed in *time* from the first part of the prophecy. Here Christ's birth is predicted. Then the church age is completely overlooked. In the next breath the prophet speaks of the glory of Christ's work in His coming *kingdom.* The church age, then, is said to be between Christ's birth and His glorious kingdom reign. It fills in the "time gap" between these two events.

4. Isaiah was the great "salvation" prophet of the Old Testament. His reference to drawing water out of the "wells of salvation" is a figure of speech, of course. But it reminds one of Jesus' words about the "water of life" (John 4: 13-15) and the last invitation to the world to "come and take the water of life freely" (Rev. 22:17). Water thus becomes

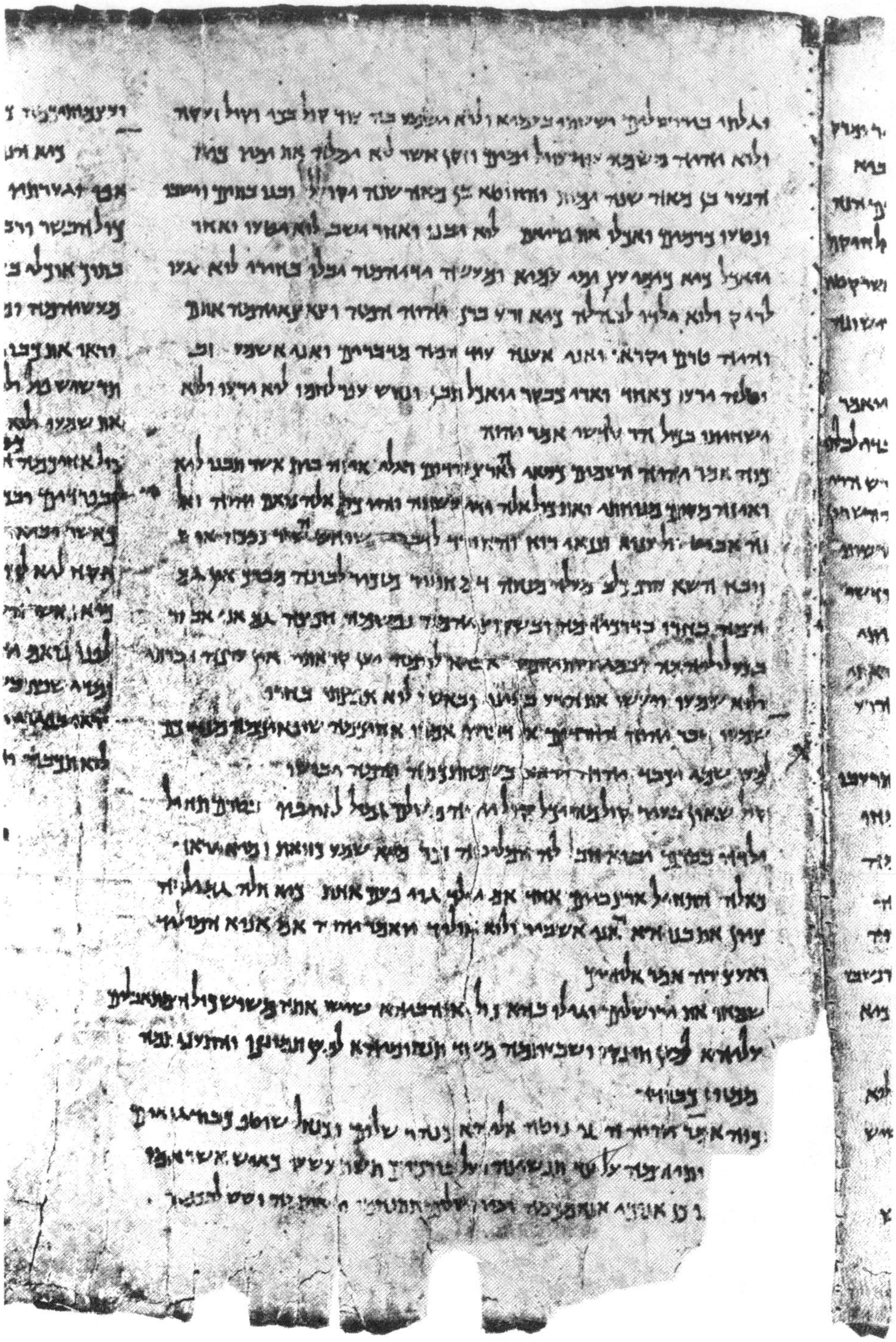

Courtesy, American Schools of Oriental Research

a "type" of salvation. Remember the explanation of "types" earlier in this work?

5. Complete peace of mind and rest in God comes by reposing trust in God (26:3). This is a most excellent memory passage. It is a sure cure for worry and anxiety. There is no peace like that which comes from completely trusting God for all things.

6. The short bed and the narrow blanket (28:20) may well be a parabolic saying, illustrating man's weakness and inability to please God in his natural state. Only by complete reliance upon the Savior are we safe.

7. The statement, "bread corn is bruised" (28:28), may be taken to illustrate a great truth. Just as corn or wheat must be ground before it can be made into meal or flour for bread, so we often must be *bruised* in some way before we can be useful in the Master's hands. Some of the most devout and useful Christians have been those who were allowed by God to suffer afflictions, privations, and sorrows. After they had learned their lessons through sufferings, they were mightily used of God. It was after Job, Joseph, David, Daniel, Paul, and many others had suffered considerably that they did their best work. Suffering is no sign of God's displeasure. It may be His means of drawing us nearer to Him and so fitting us for better service to Him.

8. The position of the righteous is secure and peaceful (32:17-19; 33:15-16)

←

SECTION FROM THE ISAIAH SCROLL. *Note how the parchment leaves were sewn together. The language is Hebrew, which is written and read from right to left. The complete scroll is shown on page 172.*

as he commits his way to God and dwells with Him.

9. The blessed way of the righteous in their heavenly journey is portrayed in rapturous language (35:1-10). Everyone should commit all or parts of this to memory.

10. Strength for the Christian journey of life is beautifully portrayed (40:31). Here is the divine recipe for strength in Christian living. Commit it to memory and it will be a blessing to you. Also, add 41:10 to this.

11. Hope for the sinner is held out again in a beautiful passage (45:22), and warning to the wicked is added (v. 23).

12. Perhaps the most significant of all the Messianic prophecies of this book concerning the Suffering Messiah, our Lord Jesus Christ, is chapter 53. The sixth verse shows the utter perversity of mankind — *"We have turned every one to his own way."* The last portion of this verse is the only hope of mankind for redemption — *"And the Lord hath laid on Him the iniquity of us all."*

This chapter should be studied with utmost care by every young person. It is the heart of both the Old and New Testament message of redemption, prophetically stated.

13. Another invitation to sinners to seek and find the Lord, together with *how* this is to be done (55:6-7), should also be memorized.

14. A description of the wicked (57:20, 21) and of their pitiable mental and emotional state shows that their *restlessness* results from the lack of being anchored in Christ.

15. The righteousnesses of unregenerate man are as filthy rags before God (64:6), and man has nothing in his

natural state to commend him to God. However good one may be morally and socially, only God's grace through Christ can bring him into an acceptable relationship with God.

Many more passages in this wonderful book point up other important truths, but those discussed represent some of the most outstanding. Every young person should memorize these passages and the truths which they teach.

It might be noted that in a way Isaiah represents the whole Bible. In the first major section of the book, there are thirty-nine chapters, just as there are thirty-nine books in the Old Testament. In the second section there are twenty-seven chapters, just as there are twenty-seven books in the New Testament. The first section is more immediate and historical, as is the Old Testament, while the last part is more prophetic and spiritual, just as the New Testament is more evangelistic than the Old.

The covenant of God with Abraham is given by far the largest and most expansive treatment found so far in the Old Testament. It is here pointed out that the *Gentiles* are to be included in God's redemptive plan in the coming of the Messiah (11:10; 42:1, 2; 45:22; 52:13-15; 54:2, 3). The covenant is seen here in its progressive fulfillment, marching ever onward toward complete fulfillment in the New Testament.

Isaiah's contribution to the Messianic prophecies and future fulfillment of the covenant constitute the largest portion from any one prophet in the Old Testament.

Memory Verse

"All we like sheep have gone astray: we have turned every one to his own way, and the Lord hath laid on him the iniquity of us all" (53:6).

Jeremiah

This book bears the name of its author. His name means "Jehovah has appointed." He was God's appointed prophet for the times preceding the Babylonian captivity and part of it. His messages are filled with predictions, rebukes, denunciations of sin, encouragement, and comfort for God's people.

TO WHOM

The writer had in mind mainly the Jews of the kingdom of Judah as his immediate readers, with a special emphasis for the people of Jerusalem. His Messianic passages, however, reach out to all Israel, and finally, to the Gentile world. His message is primarily for the Jews, but the universality of the prophetic message of the Messiah makes the book of universal interest and concern.

PURPOSE

Doubtless, Jeremiah hoped to bring Judah to repentance and so avert the disaster of Babylonian captivity, just as Isaiah had helped Judah to avoid Assyrian captivity some one hundred years earlier. His message was directed to the leaders in the hope of producing repentance and a stay from the captivity. This, however, failed, as the people were hopelessly steeped in idolatry and would not give it up. He warned against idolatry and sin, rebuking both with all his might. He encouraged the people to believe that God would be merciful if they would

Courtesy, Matson Photo Service

AIR VIEW OF ANATHOTH. *The present-day village of Anata is the approximate site of Anathoth, Jeremiah's home town. The hill of Mizpah can be seen in the extreme upper portion of the photo.*

repent, but they refused to heed his message.

At this time Assyria, to the north of Palestine, had been the world-ruling power for about three hundred years. Egypt, for some one thousand years be- fore Assyria's rise to power, had been the world power but was now dormant. Babylon, to the south, on the Euphrates River, was fast becoming the world's ruling power as Assyria's sun was sinking. For some twenty years before it happened, Jeremiah had consistently prophesied that Babylon would become the next world power. It broke Assyria's power in 607 B.C. and two years later crushed Egypt again, becoming the world's mistress. Jeremiah's ministry occurred under these circumstances.

With this in mind, he naturally tried to avert the captivity and its disaster, but when he saw there was no hope to do so, there was a change in his ministry. Invasion was assured. Captivity was certain to come. Only death and destruction could result from resistance. Knowing this, Jeremiah recommended surrender to the Babylonian forces as God's way for Israel. God was determined to punish His erring, sinful people, and this was the means He chose. "Submit and live," Jeremiah was virtually crying.

Because of his advice to surrender, he was naturally termed an unfaithful deserter of the national cause and a friend of the invading enemy. Because of this he suffered, as we shall see later.

Again, another purpose of Jeremiah's writing was to prepare the people for the sad fate to which their sins had brought them. He showed them that even in this fate there was tenderness and mercy, in that God was even sparing them at all. They must, therefore, accept their punishment, reform their ways, and prove themselves worthy of restoration.

Furthermore, he purposely points out in the more far-reaching portions of his prophecy the coming and work of the Messiah. This gives his work its universal touch and makes it especially appealing to the church and to this age.

Finally, his last purpose was to encourage and help the Jews during their captivity in Babylon. Part of the latter part of his work seems to have been written to them after they had arrived there, encouraging and strengthening them to trust in the Lord.

TIME

The prophecies of this book cover something like forty or forty-five years. The actual writing of them into book form, of course, covered much less time; possibly it was done toward the end of Jeremiah's life. This period may be listed as that from about 626 B.C., the time of Jeremiah's call to be a prophet, to 586 B.C., the year Jerusalem was finally destroyed and burned by the Babylonians.

AUTHORSHIP

Jeremiah's authorship of this book has been established from the most ancient times, and it has always been accepted by the Christian church as his work.

Baruch, Jeremiah's secretary, did much of his writing (36:1-5, 18). It is possible that Baruch may have written much of this book as Jeremiah dictated it to him, just as Paul's various secretaries wrote his numerous books as he dictated them.

The Book of Jeremiah contains many historical references to the prophet and his various experiences. It would be next to impossible to doubt the Jeremiah's authorship of this book.

Jeremiah is one of the most colorful of all the Old Testament prophets. More is known about his personality and character than any other of the writing prophets. This leader received his prophetic call when very young — some think about fourteen. His ministry lasted some forty to forty-five years, during a time of trouble and tragedy for the kingdom of Judah, of which he was the leading prophet of the time.

Like Isaiah, he belonged to the higher class of his society and was probably a man of some financial means, as evidenced by his ability to hire a private secretary. He was also a person of education and culture, as will be seen from his book. In many of his expressions he was elegant, although not as much as Isaiah. His book, expressing so much grief, sorrow, and trouble, however, did not lend itself to elegance as did Isaiah's book.

Sometimes, under extreme discouragement, he seems to have been tempted to give up his ministry, but the inner compulsion forced him onward (20:9). He has often been properly called the "weeping prophet," because he often expressed himself with tears. His book of Lamentations is especially given to this ministry of sorrow.

Born near Jerusalem, he was the son of a priest, Hilkiah — possibly the same one who discovered the lost Book of the Law (II Kings 22:8). He may have taken part in King Josiah's reform in his early days and so have made many enemies. Most of his prophecies likely were given during the reigns of King Jehoiakim and Zedekiah, during which he suffered much persecution. Even his own home village plotted against his life (11:18-23).

Jeremiah suffered persecutions from kinsmen (12:2-5), false prophets (14:13-16; 28:10-11), and the general public (15:10, 15, 18). Once he was arrested, beaten, and placed into stocks by a Temple officer (20:1, 2), against whom he predicted a tragic end (20:14-18).

During imprisonment under Jehoia-

DECORATED FACADE OF THE THRONE ROOM OF NEBUCHADNEZZAR. *The Ionic columns indicate Greek influence. Recent archaeological study has revealed many contacts between the Aegean civilization and that of the Middle East. Jeremiah's ministry occurred during the time of Nebuchadnezzar.*

kim's reign, God directed Jeremiah to write a book — possibly of his prophecies. He was to be assisted by Baruch, his secretary. When the wicked king read a few lines of it, in anger and disdain, he cut it to pieces and burned it. Directed by God again, Jeremiah reproduced the book with Baruch's aid. Jehoiakim tried to kill both Jeremiah and Baruch, but God defended them (36).

His bold preaching against the people's sins resulted in his imprisonment several times (26, 32, 33). Later, during an ex-

tremely tough situation, King Zedekiah had him brought into the king's court for prayers and consultations. But under strong pressure from the people (38:5), he was finally placed to die in a cistern under the prison (38:6). Shortly afterwards he was rescued by a Negro servant of the king.

After the overthrow of Jerusalem, he was permitted to remain with the new governor and the remnant of Jews. He was soon taken captive, however, and carried into Egypt. Tradition reports that Jeremiah continued to rebuke the people for their sins during the two years he lived there, until at last, thoroughly angered at his preaching, the people stoned him to death.

Few, if any, prophets ever suffered so much for a people. He appears never to have been at complete peace after his ministry began. Oppressed inwardly by the people's sins, he was constantly harassed by them for his rebukes of their evil ways. Suffering, sorrow, anguish of spirit, and outward persecution made up much of his lot. His ministry was characterized by three things: stern rebukes of sin and sinners, tender-hearted intercession and supplication for his people to God, and his weeping lamentations, which came more and more to the fore as time passed. He was a man of deepest affection, but he was completely misunderstood by many in his day.

The book may be outlined for study as follows:

I.   Jeremiah's call; warnings and predictions of Judah's fall to Babylon, 1-33

II. Historical and biographical section, 34-45

III. Predictions of the fate of nations surrounding Judah, 46-51

IV. Historical appendix: Zedekiah's

rebellion; Jerusalem's destruction, 52

The latter portion of the book contains some beautiful prophecies relative to the further fulfillment of the old covenant of God with Abraham. This covenant truth never gets out of sight again in the prophets. They see the day ever nearer when its fulfillment in the Messiah — the Christ of the Gospels — will occur. When studying the prophets, this must be kept uppermost in mind to gain the complete view which they held.

Figs. *The twenty-fourth chapter of Jeremiah contains a parable about good and bad figs. The fig tree is still a common sight in Palestine.*

GREAT THINGS IN JEREMIAH

The *outstanding stories* have largely been listed above in connection with Jeremiah's life, work, and persecutions.

There are certain *great truths,* however, to be drawn from these and other passages:

1. Jeremiah's youthful call (1:1-19) teaches that God often calls young people into His work, as He did Samuel, David, and others. Youth should always keep the heart and ear open to the voice of God through His Word, His Spirit, and in any other ways by which His call may come.

Whether or not Jeremiah attended the *schools of the prophets* we do not know. His priestly father could have taught him much that he needed to know in this line.

2. His early entry into the ministry gave him two things: a good beginning and an opportunity to see the Lord's miraculous workings for a long time in his life and nation's history. The earlier one starts, the better equipped he is to carry on successfully.

3. The persecution of Jeremiah by his kinsmen (12:2-5) reminds us of Jesus' words, "A prophet is not without honor, but in his own country, and among his own kin. . . ." (Mark 6:4). For some strange reason, this has always been the case. To the home folk, the "little fellow from around the corner" who has made good in any great work is still just an ordinary Joe. Young people who find themselves in this predicament should take courage — so have the truly great of all time, including Christ Himself. It was said of Him, ". . . neither did His brethren believe in Him" (John 7:5).

4. Persecution from "false prophets" was a normal reaction. Jeremiah's message of warning was a stern blow to their false prophecies of "smooth things." These false ministers were willing to deceive the people for their support and applause. True men of God in all ages have had to battle opposition from the popular, common herd. Only a casual glance at the towering spiritual figures of the past will prove this.

5. His feeling that the public was "cursing" him (15:10, 15, 18) shows that Jeremiah, too, had his melancholy days when it seemed that everyone was against him. While this was not literally

true, he felt as keenly about it as if it *had* been! We each need encouragement to meet life's problems which tend to depress us. The loss of friends is always depressing. Jeremiah was no exception.

6. Jeremiah's prison experience (26, 32, 33, 36) did much to test the metal in his character. The hardships of life show up what is really in people. Soft places and easy-going times may tend to weaken, or in some instances, actually undermine one. Jeremiah was so concerned for his people that even imprisonment could not stop his work. So he called Baruch and dictated his prophecies. After these were burned, God instructed him to write another copy of them. Baruch faithfully prepared this second scroll, and it was preserved. A good lesson here is that if our work is done in God's will, He will see that it is preserved.

7. The king of Babylon presented Jeremiah very enticing offers to come over to his side. Since the prophet knew captivity, he easily could have rationalized that he could have a very profitable ministry there among his people. Many a weaker man would have fallen for bait like this. But not the staunch and unrelenting Jeremiah! He had sternly rebuked his countrymen for their evils, but he would have no part in collaborating with their enemies, even though they were God's instruments to punish his people. He preferred to suffer ignoble treatment, and even death, with his people rather than go over to the enemy's side in the time of national distress.

Great truths found in *special passages* in this book are as follows:

1. A severe warning is listed in the distressing cry of the people, "The harvest is past, the summer is ended, and we are not saved" (8:20). Because God rejected Judah, a heart-breaking wail follows. So it has ever been with sinful humanity. Man tends to put off his salvation until it has become too late for him to recover from the fearful effects of sin.

2. The sinful state of the natural, unregenerate man is set forth in strong language: "The heart is deceitful above all things, and desperately wicked: who can know it?" (17:9). One does not "know his own heart" until he has seen a picture of it through God's sunlight-clear X-ray. There is no hope for changing it except through forgiveness and cleansing in Christ.

3. A stern warning to false pastors is given (23:1-4). It is a reminder to every young Christian worker: In the proclamation of His Word to others, above all else, God expects absolute obedience to Him, sincerity in the work, and complete compliance with Bible instruction. Christian leaders have a very serious obligation to duty and must never shun it. The whole chapter is given to this kind of warning and exhortation.

4. The parable of the good and bad figs (24) shows God's desire to reward and bless the obedient, and His determination to punish the wicked and disobedient. This truth is as much in force today as ever. God's principles of dealing with people never vary, though His methods sometimes do.

5. God's willingness to forgive and restore (29:12-14) and the conditions of this forgiveness are made very plain. "Ye shall seek me and find me, when ye shall search for me with all your heart." This kind of search for God on the part of the unsaved never fails to bring peace to the heart. If one does as instructed, he may be assured of the promised results.

6. The promise of ultimate restoration of Israel to Palestine is listed (31:36-44). This Scripture is in process of fulfillment in the restoration of modern-day Israel to Palestine, and the statehood of that nation. It is a partial fulfillment of the ancient Abrahamic *covenant,* seen all through the Old Testament.

7. A promise of sure answer to prayers is seen in chapter 33:3. "Call unto me, and I will answer thee, and show thee great and mighty things which thou knowest not." Prayer and faith unlock the storehouse of God.

8. The fifty-second chapter, with its story of the final deportation of Judah to Babylon, graphically illustrates for us that tremendous truth expressed by Paul: that "Whatsoever a man soweth, that shall he also reap" (Gal. 6:7). This is a universal principle and was in operation long centuries before the apostle Paul spoke it.

However much one may try to avoid it, whatever he may do to convince himself that he is the exception to the rule — sooner or later everyone will find that it is everlastingly true that what a man *sows* he must *reap*. This is not merely a maxim but a principle of life in the moral world.

Perhaps one of the chief lessons to be learned from Jeremiah is that to be faithful to God and God-given convictions often *does* cost one something. But it also *pays* large dividends. Had the prophet become soft and given in to the pressures of his times, we would doubtless never have heard of him. God can only use those persons who will be "true until death," whatever the cost. People of less strength and determination cannot qualify as real workers in the kingdom.

Memory Verse
"Call unto me, and I will answer thee, and show thee great and mighty things which thou knowest not" (33:3).

Lamentations

The name of this book reflects the fact that the book is a sort of funeral dirge, a song of heartbreak, over the destruction of Jerusalem. In the most ancient Hebrew groupings of Scripture, this book was listed with Ecclesiastes, Song of Solomon, Ruth, and Esther, which were known as "The Writings." It was listed there because, like these books, it was used for special readings in the synagogues.

TO WHOM

Lamentations is thought to have been written especially for the captive Jews carried to Babylon; it was written to be sung by them in their captivity and sorrow. In this way they would be reminded of their homeland and of their sins which had separated them from God and their land. It was doubtless also intended for the Jews at large, that they might see that which had befallen their homeland, as many now lived in other countries into which they had wandered. And, of course, the prophet intended that those Jews which had been permitted to remain in Palestine would read this description of Jerusalem's ruin with repentance.

Courtesy, George A. Turner

THE WAILING WALL. *Today devout Jews come to the Wailing Wall in Old Jerusalem to mourn and pray for the restoration of Jerusalem.*

OLD JERUSALEM. *The Dome of the Rock appears in this photo of Old Jerusalem. It is a Moslem shrine on the site of the ancient Temple.*

Courtesy, Israel Office of Information

PURPOSE

The purpose would naturally be tied into the above plan. Behind the writing was the intention to produce in the sinful Jewish people that element of true repentance necessary before God could work out their restoration to their homeland. Jeremiah had prophesied that there would be a return. He must now set about helping to prepare them for this fulfillment.

One sees in this book, also, the personal heartbreak and deep sorrow of the prophet *personally,* for his love for his city never ceased to well up from within him. No patriot has ever lived in whom burned the fires of true patriotism more deeply nor brightly than in Jeremiah.

TIME

It is quite probable that this book was written during the three months between the time the first group of captives were taken to Babylon and the time when the second group left Jerusalem, fleeing into Egypt in 586 B.C., taking Jeremiah with them.

AUTHORSHIP

Jeremiah's authorship of this book has never been seriously challenged. Even if there were not tradition assigning it to him since the most ancient times, the very nature of it would point toward his authorship. Many passages in this book show kinship to the book of Jeremiah.

One tradition says that this book was written in what is now known as "Jeremiah's Grotto." This is located under the hill near Jerusalem now known as "Golgotha," where Christ was crucified. Thus the prophet wept bitter tears and composed this poem of sorrow where later the Savior died for the sins of His

people. Probably a number of copies of this book were made by Jeremiah or Baruch his secretary, some being sent to Babylon and others being taken with the fleeing group to Egypt. At any rate the book was divinely preserved for the Bible record.

Lamentations consists of five poems. In the original Hebrew, four of these are in the acrostic form; that is, each verse begins with a letter of the Hebrew alphabet. Chapters 1, 2, and 4 each have twenty-two verses, the number of letters in the Hebrew alphabet. Chapter 3 has sixty-six verses, each third verse beginning with an alphabetical letter. Chapter 5 is not alphabetical, although it is poetry very similar to the rest.

Of course, these mechanical facts cannot be observed in the English, as it does not follow this pattern. Since it was apparently intended to be sung, the writer placed it in alphabetical order for easier memorization.

The book may be outlined as follows:

I. The desolation of Zion, 1
II. God's anger against Jerusalem for her sins, 2
III. Jeremiah's grief and his prayers of sorrow, 3
IV. The sufferings of the seige, 4-5

There appears to be no Messianic vision here. The matter of the covenant and its progressive unfolding is dimmed by the sorrow and trial of the present affliction. But the purpose of the affliction is clear — to bring Israel back to God and their homeland. In this sense, even here the idea of the covenant shines through, for God still intends to use His people Israel to bring about its fulfillment. The very purpose of their captivity was to teach them obedience to God and break them from idol worship. Perhaps the highest point of the book is reached in chapter 3:21-39, in which hope for restoration is seen (3:22, 26, 31-36).

GREAT THINGS IN LAMENTATIONS

There are no *outstanding stories* in this book, but several *great truths* deserve attention:

1. The unfailing truth, "Whatsoever a man soweth, that shall he also reap" (Gal. 6:7), pointed up so often in the Old Testament, is forcefully illustrated in the destruction of Jerusalem and the captivity of her people. God will deal with sin with dreadful justice when it is not repented of and forsaken.

2. There come times when prayers are *not* answered, despite the earnestness and faith accompanying them. Jeremiah's prayers for the sparing of Israel from captivity were not answered. God had another plan. When Jeremiah knew of this, he was content to take *no* for the answer. This must ever be the attitude of God-fearing people.

Often God must *hurt* the sinner in punishing his sin. Sometimes this is the only way he can be made to see the "error of his way" and repent. It was so then; it is often so today.

3. Youthful yoke-bearing is a great blessing. Youth need to learn early to shoulder their share of the responsibilities, at home, school, church, and in the community. "It is good for a man that he bear the yoke in his youth" (3:27), Jeremiah sighed, perhaps remembering how well his own youthful start had prepared him for his great life's work.

A glance over Bible history will reveal that the greatest men God used were given responsibilities when relatively young: Joseph, Moses, Joshua, Samuel, David, Paul, and Timothy, to mention a few. No great achievements have been made by older men who did not *definitely begin to achieve something in youth!*

4. Amidst the most darkening shadows of gloom, the prophet held on to faith in God. Somewhere every dark cloud has its silver lining. Nothing is so bad but that it could be worse, while we still live and have opportunities for amending things. God often works behind the clouds to produce His most glorious rainbow when the sun breaks through again. "Have faith in God," however dark the present hour may seem. This is one of the great lessons of this book.

Memory Verse

"It is good for a man that he bear the yoke in his youth" (3:27).

Ezekiel

This book also carries the name of its famous author. In the ancient Hebrew the name Ezekiel means "whom God will strengthen." Ezekiel was commissioned to minister to a "stiff-hearted" people, or people "of a hard forehead," and so would need the "strength of God" to face them (2:5; 3:7, 8).

TO WHOM

It was written primarily and immediately for the captives in Babylon, but it had a message for all Israel, wherever they were found. Certain parts of it were apparently directed toward the end-time

EZEKIEL'S VISIONS. *Ezekiel, like the apostle John, received visions from the Lord. Here the artist attempted to portray Ezekiel's vision of the chariot throne, related in chapter one.*

in which we live. It has much truth in it which is very applicable to our times. It should be read today with this in mind, as well as the thought of understanding something of Ezekiel's times and the message which God sent by him to the captives.

PURPOSE

Ezekiel's first purpose seems to have been to inspire in Israel faith that there could be a restoration; that God had not forgotten them and that if they would only be "willing and obedient," they would yet see the goodness of the Lord in their future return to Palestine. To accomplish this purpose, his message was not always pleasant. Sins had to be rebuked, repentance proclaimed, and the leaders warned of the fearful responsibility they had in watching over Israel. "The soul that sinneth, it shall die" (18: 4, 18), he thundered in his warning. False prophets or pastors are equally condemned (22:23-30). Watchmen are warned that the blood of Israel will be on their hands if they do not cry out against their sins (33:1-6); He proclaimed himself such a watchman of Israel (33: 7-19).

For a short while after landing in Babylon, Israel was a stiff-necked, hardhearted people, still rebellious and stubborn. It required many years in the "furnace of affliction" to soften them. In fact, many of the older, rebellious and sin-calloused set had to die before reform began. The ministry of Ezekiel was largely to this hardened, older group, and for this reason much of his ministry was necessarily rugged; it sounded of judgment. This was the basis of much that he said to the then-current generation.

Many of his prophecies, however, were intended to encourage and inspire. They pointed to another day, beyond which the old generation could not hope to live, and promised regathering to the homeland (36:21-24).

Also running through his prophecies, especially the latter part, is a Messianic strain which looked to the faraway future fulfillment. Like Isaiah, he views the covenant in blessed fulfillment and rejoices on seeing this day in his prophetic visions (40-48). The new Temple and the glories of the Messiah's kingdom occupy much of his closing scenes. All this was given to Israel as the "sure word of prophecy," the evidence of God's love for His erring people, His plan for their restoration, and their place in the world picture in coming days. Once he is understood, Ezekiel is full of encouragement for his age. His purpose, then, was to make Israel see the reason for their temporary punishment, that they might be restored to God's favor and become a powerful instrument in His hands for the bringing in of universal righteousness.

TIME

The book itself makes clear that his ministry was during the early part of the period of captivity. This period lasted for seventy years, 606-536 B.C. Along with ten thousand better-class exiles, young Ezekiel was carried to Babylon by

Emperor Nebuchadnezzar in 597 B.C. He seems to have received his prophetic call about five years later when he was thirty years of age. His ministry lasted for twenty-two years — 592-570 B.C. His written prophecies were doubtless recorded during this time, or shortly afterward. As there were several years between some of his visions (1, 3, 38, 40-48), these portions may well have been penned as they were received. In this way, the book originally could have been written progressively and finally finished in its present form by Ezekiel in his last days.

AUTHORSHIP

From the earliest times this book has been assigned to the prophet Ezekiel and has been so received by the Jews and the Christian church. It is filled with personal references and data which establish this beyond doubt.

Ezekiel was of the priestly line and may have been a priest himself, as his accurate knowledge of the sacrificial system seems to indicate. He may have been a pupil of Jeremiah, who was considerably older than he. One tradition has named him as the son of Jeremiah, but for this there is no historical foundation. Ezekiel preached among the captives that which Jeremiah was preaching in Jerusalem. Until it happened, he proclaimed with unswerving certainty the fall of Jerusalem (4-24). He then turned his attention to the fate of nations about Palestine, and those in the ancient world (25-32). In the remaining chapters his message concerns the final, glorious future state of Israel (33-48).

In Babylon Ezekiel lived by the River Chebar (1:1), probably a huge ship canal connecting the Euphrates and Tigris Rivers. This place was some two hundred miles north of Babylon. Daniel had been in Babylon — the city itself — some nine years when Ezekiel arrived; he had already become quite well established in his work. Possibly Daniel and Ezekiel met many times.

Ezekiel's wife died suddenly during the siege of Jerusalem, which for the next three years was used as a symbol of God's disappointment with Israel's lack of mourning over their sins (24:15-27).

Tradition has assigned to the region in which Ezekiel lived both the home of Noah and the site of the Garden of Eden. This may be why he makes reference to both in his ministry (14:14, 20; 28:13; 31:8, 9, 16, 18; 36:35).

Some of Ezekiel's ministry was accompanied by outstanding action. In this sense he may be called the "prophet of pantomime." He successfully used illustrated sermons in the following manner: He once remained speechless for a considerable length of time (3:26; 24:27; 33:22). He also lay on his side in one position for over a year, probably arising only for food and other necessities, and then eating only loathsome food (4:15). The passages explain what these actions symbolized to Israel.

More than any other prophet, he received his messages in visions. His book is one of the most difficult in the Bible to understand fully. It was probably better understood by the ancient Jews than now; however, there is a tradition that the Jews never understood it fully, either. A certain story tells of an ancient rabbi who promised to explain it fully, whereupon the council allocated to him three hundred barrels of oil for his lamp so that he could write. They supposed he would never finish the task, which he did not, as the story concludes. There are certain keys to this study, however, which make the book much more understandable than

this story would lead us to believe. The book is written in highly *symbolic language*. When he tells us, for example, that he was transported to Jerusalem, it does not necessarily mean that he *visited* Jerusalem, but merely that he was there in his vision, much as we may be somewhere in our dreams. The scope of this work will not allow lengthy explanations, but it is suggested that a good Bible commentary be used in studying this book.

One of the most sublime characterizations of God in the Bible is found in Ezekiel's vision of Him in the opening part of the book. This symbolism is difficult to understand. But then, no one can fully understand God. However, such descriptions do help the mind to appreciate the glory and majesty by which He surrounds Himself. Ezekiel and The Revelation, as well as Daniel, have something in common in their symbolic language.

Ezekiel was highly cultured, well trained, and possibly, next to Isaiah, one of the most sublime writers of the Old Testament. He was of noble birth and high character. His entire ministry bears out his high character. His ministry was to the captives alone, although his prophecies certainly had a profound effect upon all Israel long after his day. Of his last days and death, almost nothing is known. He probably finished his life and was buried among his people in Babylon, where he so faithfully ministered.

Two possible outlines of this book may be made — the first one in two parts:

I. First Part: call of the prophet, his vision of God, the fall of Jerusalem, and Israel's final restoration, 1-39

II. Second Part: final fulfillment of the Abrahamic *covenant* in future glory, 40-48

A second outline may be:

I. The prophetic call, visions of God, and warnings to Israel, 1-24
II. Dooms against Israel's neighboring, evil nations, 25-32
III. Sermons and visions of the future restoration and glory of Israel, 33-48

The second section, especially chapters 40-48, compares very favorably with Isaiah 40-66. Chapter 37 in the first part may foreshadow how Israel came to statehood (1948) and is yet to grow after centuries of being "dead", so far as national status is concerned.

A most glorious future time is predicted (47:1-2), which should be an inspiration to every Christian believer. It reminds one of other salvation passages (Isa. 12: 3; John 7:37-39; Rev. 22:17).

GREAT THINGS IN EZEKIEL

There are no *outstanding stories* in Ezekiel, but there are several *great truths* to note:

1. Ezekiel's call and vision of God (1: 1-28) show two things: first, that God always manifests Himself to those who seek to know His will, though by various

THE SITE OF EZEKIEL'S VISIONS. *The Moslem village of Kifl, in Iraq, is thought to be the site where Ezekiel saw the visions of chapter one. The river of Chebar, then a small stream or canal, no longer exists. The Shrine of Prophet Ezekiel stands beside a Moslem minaret.*

Courtesy, Matson Photo Service

THE ISHTAR GATE. *This dragon appeared on a wall of the massive Ishtar Gate which gave entrance to Nebuchadnezzar's Babylon, which he built in honor of the heathen god Marduk.*

means to different people. God has no set way to manifest Himself. Second, although His people were under sore *chastisement,* God did not forget them. Even though God must sometimes chastise His people, His love for them never changes. He works always for their ultimate salvation and blessing.

2. Ezekiel was stern, but still a man with the "shepherd's heart." His peculiar way of illustrating truth was much more difficult for him than for those witnessing it. In his actions of speechlessness (3: 26; 24:27) and lying on his side (4:1-8), he identified himself with his people in the strongest way he knew, to impress them with God's message to them.

3. The prophet listed three outstanding sins of a prosperous nation: pride, fulness of bread, and idleness (16:49),

although in captivity, Israel still maintained these evils. These three things can ruin youth more quickly than almost anything else. *Pride* leads to rebellion against God. *Fulness of bread* represents softness and self-indulgence which may lead to immorality and all sorts of vices. *Idleness* provides the mind with the convenience to be filled with unwholesome thinking and the opportunity for every kind of evil action. Nothing is better for youth than a proper humility, the necessity of being frugal, and constant occupation in worthwhile work and wholesome activities. It is the safest way to character development and usefulness in any age of life, and certainly, in youth.

4. Personal responsibility for sin is announced in the words, "The soul that sinneth, it shall die" (18:4, 29). Some blame parents for an ugly temper or bad disposition, but no one other than the person himself is responsible for his condition. Dispositional traits may be hereditary, but they can be corrected if a person will

try. God's grace is always sufficient. Everyone is responsible to God for his own sins.

5. Ezekiel denounced false prophets and teachers (22:23-31). His description of Israel's state reminds one of modern times. Jeremiah and Ezekiel had preached repentance; the false prophets had proclaimed an easy way and persecuted these rugged prophets for their stand. But in the end, these men were right, and the false "softies" wrong, as they always are.

6. The call for an intercessor (22:30) is an important truth. In God's work, one of the greatest needs of all time is prayer intercessors. Abraham, Moses, Elijah, Isaiah, Jeremiah, and Ezekiel are classic examples in the Old Testament.

Prayer is the most important single act of worship of which one is capable. *Intercessory prayer* — waiting upon God in seasons of earnest prayer, at considerable lengths, for specific things — is one of the greatest needs of the church today. Because God found no intercessor (22:31), destruction followed. This is admittedly a difficult thing to explain, but it appears in the Bible in a number of places that God spared people and nations only because someone prayed and interceded for His mercy. Lot was spared from Sodom by Abraham's prayer (Gen. 19), Israel from destruction by Moses' intercession (Num. 14:11-21), and Jerusalem from destruction by Sennacherib by Israel's and Hezekiah's prayers (Isa. 37:1-7, 34-36). Many other incidents could be noted. Decide in youth to become a *prayer intercessor*. It is one of the greatest works one can do for God's cause.

7. Under the parable of the King of Tyrus, Ezekiel portrays what many Bible scholars believe to be the fall of Lucifer, who became Satan, or the Devil, as he is more often called in the New Testament (28:11-19). A similar account of the same event is given by Isaiah (Isa. 14:4-23) under the symbolism of the king of Babylon. Isaiah refers to the person as *Lucifer* (Isa. 14:12). The name Lucifer means "light-bearer" and is supposed to refer to the chief archangel of God, who became the Devil, or Satan, by his rebellion against God and his determination to take God's place (Isa. 14:12-15). God was forced to cast him out of heaven and disassociate him from Himself forever because of his wickedness and rebellion. Jesus evidently referred to this event when he said, "I beheld Satan as lightning fall from heaven" (Luke 10:18).

We seem to have here a case of *prophecy in reverse*. Here is a revelation of something which must have occurred even before the creation of man. No earthly king could possibly fit the descriptions of Isaiah and Ezekiel in these two passages. Only a being such as Satan can fill the descriptions. It seems to be a revelation to these two men of the beginning of evil in the universe. It would be well to pursue this study with the aid of a good commentary. By using a reference Bible or a Bible with a concordance, one can find under the subjects of Satan and the Devil much more information in the Scriptures about the matter.

It will be noted that three main sins are seen at the root of Lucifer's fall: *pride, self-will,* and *selfishness.* Read the two passages carefully for these truths. These are the *basic sins* from which all others spring, of whatever type or nature they may be. Pride, for instance, may be manifested in many and varying forms, all of which find expression in some forms of self-will and selfishness. Almost every sin imaginable is expressed

in some form of *selfishness*. A serious
study of this subject will prove this dreadful fact. Until by the Holy Spirit mankind sees itself under God's powerful
searchlight of conviction for sin, it is far
more wicked than it is willing to admit.

8. Just as Ezekiel was made a "watchman" over Israel (33:7), so Christians
become watchmen over the souls of all
they influence. At the dawn of man's
history wicked Cain cried out, "Am I my
brother's keeper?" (Gen. 4:9). The only
answer echoing through all the centuries
since then has been a solemn *yes*! We
are responsible to God for all men whom
we influence, just as the law will hold
guilty anyone who *consents* to a crime
and stands by while it is done, without
protesting it. He is an *accomplice,* and
he must accept his share of the guilt.
One can sin by *default* as well as by
direct transgression. It is our solemn responsibility to try to get all men to desist
from their evil and turn to God.

9. The parable of the Valley of Dry
Bones is a picture of Israel's restoration
to Palestine, to God's favor, and to national life. It may also serve as an illustration of the conversion of a sinner from
being "dead in trespasses and sins (Eph.
2:1) to "newness of life in Christ" as a
new convert.

The book closes with a refreshing description of the heavenly Temple and
scenes of the coming Messianic glory to
be experienced under the reign of Christ
the Messiah (40-48). It breathes the atmosphere of the last days and is a final
summation of the future blessedness of
the righteous.

Memory Verse

*"And I sought for a man among them,
that should make up the hedge and stand in
the gap before me for the land, that I should
not destroy it: but I found none"* (22:30).

Daniel

Daniel means "God is my judge." The
book bears the name of its author. Although when taken to Babylon his name
was changed by his captors, he never
used his Babylonian name in the book.

TO WHOM

Probably the Jewish captives in Babylon were most immediately in mind in
the writing, but naturally there would
have been an appeal to all Jews scattered
everywhere. The matters in this book are
of great meaning to the Jews of those
times, as well as those of later times. The
book also has a universal appeal, as much
of it has to do with Christ and His kingdom.

PURPOSE

Daniel had probably been in Babylon
for about three years — sufficient time to
learn the customs, language, and some
general knowledge of the empire — when
the first great demand was made upon
him. He was called upon to interpret a
difficult dream which King Nebuchadnezzar had, for which he could find no
solution. By the inspiration of God, Daniel was able to give the correct interpretation. For this he was set on his way
to the high places of honor and responsibility which he occupied for many years.

Israel had been completely idolatrous
in her last days before captivity. Most
of the seventy years of captivity had been
spent in learning the one supreme lesson
that the gods of the heathen did not

count for anything and that it was folly to worship them. This seems to have been one of the main lessons God intended to teach them in Babylon.

He accomplished this by allowing to develop in Babylon many situations in which all the force, wisdom, authority, and power of the heathen gods were brought to bear and prove them to be utterly futile and useless. In each such instance, the God of Heaven and Earth, as God is often referred to in Daniel, came into the picture through Daniel or some of his fellow helpers and proved Himself equal to every emergency. In every case, it was shown that the true God had power, might, wisdom, and ability to *solve every problem,* while the gods of the heathen *could not solve one of these problems!* Note, for instance, Daniel's interpretation of Nebuchadnezzar's dreams (2:1-49; 4:4-27), something which all the wise men could not do. Or, how God saved the three young men from the fiery furnace (3:8-30), which no other gods could have done. Or, how when Daniel was cast into the lion's den (6), God delivered him.

These were mighty lessons, both to Babylonians and Jews, that God ruled in the affairs of men and that idols counted for nothing. While the Babylonian and Persian kings did not totally forsake idolatry, except perhaps Nebuchadnezzar, they did give place to God as the chief and supreme Being over all other gods and powers in the universe. This they did not hesitate to publish in decrees which went all over the empire (5:29, 30).

Daniel is both a history of these mighty events and a continuation of even more astounding prophecies concerning future events, which only the true God could have revealed to man. The truth of the latter prophecies is expected to be believed against the rich historical background of the profound miracles and mighty deeds of power wrought by the true God whom Daniel sets forth.

Daniel's purpose, then, in writing his book may be seen as follows: first, to set forth a correct and true account of the various miraculous ways in which God manifested Himself and proved His mighty power among His people in Babylon. This mighty movement had forever discredited and disgraced *polytheism* — the worship of many gods, and showed that heathen gods had no power, that it was folly to trust in or worship them. This established the Scriptural teaching which the prophets of all ages had thundered at the Israelites: "Hear, O Israel, the Lord our God is one Lord," who was to be loved, worshiped, and revered with all man's powers (Deut. 6:5, 6). It defended the Biblical position of monotheism — the fact of and the worship of one true God.

Perhaps it is well to state here that the Hebrew word for God used in the Deuteronomy reference above is *Elohim.* The ending *im* indicates plurality in the original, as with cherub*im,* and seraph*im.* God, it must be understood, *exists* in one glorious being, but *subsists* in *three persons* — Father, Son, and Holy Spirit. This is not merely three aspects of God — this would be only "modalism". There is but one God, one Being, but He subsists in three distinct personalities, Father, Son, and Spirit, each of equal substance, power, majesty, glory, and eternity. This is the profound mystery of the Trinity, in which all sincere Christians believe. This mystery *cannot be explained,* for it is beyond the understanding of the human mind. But then, again, if *man* could *understand God,* he would be greater

Courtesy, Steuben Glass

than God, for only the greater can understand the lesser. So it should not bother us that we cannot understand this mystery. In fact, there is very little in life that we do *fully understand,* but we do not reject something because we cannot understand it. Certainly, we should not expect to understand fully the nature of God, although He has revealed to us much about His moral and spiritual qualities.

In the second place, Daniel may have wished to set forth the fact that not only did the heathen gods have no power, but that in reality they did not exist. The ideas of other gods were merely fictitious fancies, superstitions held by the heathen in their ignorance. Their power and value had been totally disproved and contradicted; now the future step was to banish any belief in them whatsoever. This he does, not by condemning them in so many words, but by showing the heathen that there is neither power nor ability in any of their prophets or ministers, such as the soothsayers and magicians. This in turn would convince the Jewish people of the utter folly and stupidity of worshiping or fearing them in any sense. If this were included in his purpose, he succeeded well, for it is historically well known that after restoration from Babylon to Palestine, Israel *never again worshiped* idols nor *practiced any form of idolatry.* They were forever afterward *pure monotheists.* They are to this day!

Third, doubtless the main purpose of this work was to set forth in the prophetic

sense God's dealings with Israel. Its historical section had well established the power, glory, and majesty of God. Now, the purpose is to show God's plans for the future of Israel and something of the future of world government. You see, for many years Daniel had occupied a very high position in the Babylonian and Persian governments, possibly similar to that of a secretary of state in the United States or a prime minister in England. He, therefore, thought much in terms of governments and their relationships to people and to God. His latter visions had to do almost entirely with future world governmental powers, from his day forward to the time of Christ, then onward toward the end of the Christian age. He purposed, then, to give in this book the revelations which God had given him for the Jewish people — and all other peoples, for the book is universal in its basic appeal, especially in the latter part. This would provide a sort of prophetic guide, a kind of outline of future events. The Book of Daniel has been more successful in this particular type of prophecy than any other book of the Bible except The Revelation. Daniel, however, had to do largely with events prior to Christ's ascension, with only a brief forecast as to the things still in the future today.

TIME

The events of the book occurred during the Babylonian captivity, 605-536 B.C. Much of the book sets its own historical timetable by such references as those to Nebuchadnezzar, Belshazzar, and Darius the Mede.

Daniel had been in Babylon sometime before the burning of Jerusalem in 568 B.C. and the bringing of the last captives to Babylon. The book itself contains no date as to when it was written. It is

---

←

DANIEL IN THE LION'S DEN. *This engraved crystal stele shows Daniel in supplication to God.*

clear, however, that the events making up the book occurred over a period of some time. It will be noted, though, that there is no *progressive chronology* in Daniel. For example, Belshazzar's tragic end is described in chapter 5, while in chapter 8 Daniel is talking about a vision which he had during the third year of Belshazzar's reign. This will be explained later. The reference to the instruction to Daniel to go and stand in his lot (12:13) may indicate that he was a very old man when he finished his prophetic work. It is thought that his book was written in its final form just before the close of the captivity, possibly not long before his death.

AUTHORSHIP

That Daniel is the author of this book has been received both by the Jews and the Christian church throughout the centuries.

That Daniel lived in Babylon and did his great work at this time is historically well known from the Scripture references to him. His piety and dependability are established by Ezekiel's classification of him with Noah and Job (Ezek. 14:14, 20). There may have been a proverb about his wisdom in use then, to which Ezekiel refers (Ezek. 28:3). His historic character is established by the fact that Ezekiel and Daniel were both living in Babylon, not too far apart, at the same time. The Book of Daniel was placed upon the earliest lists of the Old Testament canon, proving it was received by the Jews as God's Word. The supreme authority rests upon the fact that Christ without hesitation quoted from Daniel as from a true and inspired book (Matt. 24:15).

Daniel was written originally in two different languages — Hebrew and Ara-

maic — Aramaic being the language of the Babylonians, and Hebrew that of the Jews. Some have wondered why this may have been, but the simplest explanation is that in the original, in all sections where Daniel *spoke* to Babylonians or *reported* what Babylonians *said,* he used their language. In other sections he used the Hebrew. This is merely a way of absolute accuracy, both in speaking and reporting, and it should only tend to make the prophet more deeply appreciated for his accuracy in both. In other words, he reported in writing just what he did and said in action. This seems sufficient reason to offer, for the English reader is not aware of this difference anyway.

Daniel is divided into two sections — historical and prophetical. The early part of the book (through chapter 6), is historical; the rest, prophetical. This explains *why* events which historically occurred during the first part are listed in the latter part. For instance, the fall of Belshazzar and the transfer of the Babylonian kingdom is listed in the historical section (5:1-31), while two of Daniel's visions are stated to have occurred during the first and third years of Belshazzar's reign (7:1; 8:1). This simply means that the major historical events were cataloged in sequence, then the *prophetical* section placed after the historical. This was evidently done so there would be no historical inserts into the prophetical portion except a mere mention of the *time* of the visions. Otherwise, there would be a "break" right in the midst of the prophetical section to place in this or that historical occurrence, disturbing the pattern of the prophetical section of the book.

This in no way detracts from the value or lessens the historical truth of the book,

Courtesy, The British Museum

TABLET OF THE BABYLONIAN CHRON-
ICLES. *The discovery of these chronicles
has enabled archaeologists to establish
dates for Biblical episodes.*

nor does it disturb the idea of its divine inspiration. It is simply this writer's style.

Another thing of interest is that we are here introduced to a new style of writing in the Old Testament. This is especially true in the latter part of Daniel, from the seventh chapter on. This is what is called *apocalyptic* writing. The term refers to "visions" of future events, usually associated with some form of *symbolism*. The other most important such book as this is The Revelation. You will notice in Daniel that sometimes animals are taken to represent rulers (8:5-12, 21-26). Daniel also contains other symbolisms.

The various historical accounts here related were probably kept by Daniel as they occurred. When the visions were finally all completed, his whole work was produced in one book as we now have it, and given to the people of God in his day. Copies of it were naturally carried to Jerusalem by the returning captives, where they were placed in the hands of the scribes, along with other books such as Ezekiel, Jeremiah, and others which were held in trust by those who kept the Sacred Books of Scripture.

A brief outline of this book is as follows:

I. Historical section, dealing with important events in Babylon, 1-6
II. Prophetical section, revealing future world government outlines, and the coming and work of Christ, 7-12

The last section is almost entirely occupied with what in Scripture has come to be known as "the times of the Gentiles" (Luke 21:24) and the kingdom of Christ. With the aid of reference books a study of this section is most rewarding.

As in the other great prophets, the Messianic strain occurs in Daniel, too. This will be seen toward the close of the book in an outstanding way. The *covenant* of God with His people is being expanded here again to show its more complete fulfillment. Note the reference to the actual name "Messiah" (9:26) and the mention of the "covenant" (9:27). This first refers to Christ's death (9:26). It then in the last verses leaps on over to the punishment of those who will reject Him. Back in the historical section there is reference to this Messianic progression in Nebuchadnezzar's dream. The "stone" cut out of the mountain side, which increased until it destroyed all kingdoms and replaced them, is explained as the kingdom of God which will at last prevail over all others (2:34-35, 44-45).

BABYLON IN THE SIXTH CENTURY B.C. *This painting by Maurice Mardin indicates the vastness of Nebuchadnezzar's Babylon. In the foreground is the Ishtar Gate.*

DANIEL, THE MAN

Daniel was of the royal seed of David. Taken to Babylon when very young, he soon was found to be a brilliant young man and was soon in the favor of the king's ministers, and upon the interpretation of his dreams of the king himself. He soon mastered the Babylonian customs and language, but without compromising with its evil; he became a very learned person who bore much governmental responsibility. The proverb, "Thou art wiser than Daniel" (Ezek. 28:3), indicates that even while still in his prime, he was widely known for his wisdom and learning.

References to him and traditions about him in ancient Oriental literature attest his popularity and his historical character as well. One tradition says that he taught two Persian kings the knowledge of the true God. It is believed by some that the Zoroaster of the ancient Persian religion was only a fictitious character, drawn from the image of Daniel. Some Asiatics went so far as to hold that Daniel was the original inventor of geometry. These traditions have no historical foundations, but they do serve to attest his wide popularity in the land of his life and work. Josephus, ancient Jewish historian, claimed that Daniel was well skilled in architecture and that he master-minded the building of the famous tower of Susa in Persia, where the Persian kings were enshrined.

Daniel was a man of strong character from his youth up. He was uncompromising in his loyalty to truth. He could rebuke a king as well as inspire his comrades (5:17-31). He probably lived to be an old man, and in the absence of any worthy tradition to the contrary, he likely remained in Babylon and was buried among his people.

GREAT THINGS IN DANIEL

Outstanding stories may be listed as follows:

1. A great resolve, 1:1-17
2. Trusting God in a crisis, 2:14-49
3. Courage without compromise, 3:1-30
4. A king condemned to insanity, 4:1-37
5. Belshazzar's warning and doom, 5:5-31
6. Faithfulness of Daniel in life's supreme test, 6:1-24

Great truths may be pointed out from these stories and other passages from Daniel:

1. Daniel and his three friends (1:5) made up their minds that they would not submit to the king's order to eat meats which were prohibited by their Jewish teachings and religious conscience. Daniel, who seemed to be the leader, purposed in his heart (1:8) to honor God and trust Him for the outcome. The others followed his advice. The outcome of keeping their religious convictions gave them a decided advantage over others who had no such convictions (1:20).

Youth today should remember that God will honor those who honor Him. But one should not do the right thing merely for reward, but because it is *right!* God wishes us to be loyal to truth for truth's sake, not merely for certain rewards. If young folks will shun every thing which is evil, no matter what the immediate cost, it will pay in the long run of life. Just as God prospered Daniel, so He gives grace and wisdom to those who stand up for Him. He may not always choose to prosper them financially or socially. Some of earth's greatest men have suffered much for their religious convictions of Christian duty, but they still came out ahead of those who compromised their convictions.

2. In his rage, Nebuchadnezzar was ready to have all the "wise men" of Babylon executed because they would not interpret his strange dream. They had no key to it. Securing execution's stay, Daniel and his three friends sought divine aid in prayer (2:16-18), and God gave him the revelation of the dream. Nebuchadnezzar was greatly impressed by the interpretation and spared the wise men.

Apparently, God was using the king as a medium through which to work, in order to accomplish His purpose with His people and also to give the world His message of salvation. Had Daniel had this vision himself, the Babylonian Empire would have had no revelation of the greatness and majesty of God, nor would it have known anything of His workings with His people. As it was, the truth about God was spread abroad over the whole realm.

How important it was that Daniel should be in such close touch with God that God could use him in such a signal way. Daniel was a "key" person in God's dealings with His people and with the Babylonian Empire. God needs His key men in all times. Every young person should seek to so live that should God need him in His service, he would be ready for such service.

3. The story of the three Hebrew children, as they are often called, who refused to bow down to the golden image which the king had set up, is a story of true courage which would not be compromised for personal safety or advantage (3:13-28). Note especially in verses 17, 18, and 19 that God was able to deliver them, "but if not, be it known unto thee, O king, that we will not serve thy gods, nor worship the golden image which thou hast set up."

Here was courageous action. Whatever the cost, they would not compromise the worship of the Lord God with that of idolatry. What a scene! Three young Hebrews, standing up in the face of the earth's mightiest emperor, with life and death in his hands, telling him his "second chance" scheme was useless; they had no intention of "bowing" to the king's demands. It is evident that these young men were prepared to accept death in the event God did not choose to deliver them.

This is the kind of true, heroic courage needed in this day. To remain faithful is to save the cause of Christ and to save one's own soul. Whether the pressure comes from high authority or from socially interested friends, refuse to give over to evil.

4. In the divine providence, it seemed necessary for God to permit King Nebuchadnezzar to lose his sanity and become almost a monster for seven years in order to bring him to his knees in repentance and proper recognition of the true God (4:23-25). "Seven times" here means seven years. Most likely in his hallucinations of insanity, he considered himself to be a beast of some kind and

so acted accordingly. In those days little was known of how to treat the insane, and many times they wandered in the woods and fields much like animals. The wild, insane man of Gadara is a good example of this (Mark 5:1-15).

Today this seems to us like a cruel treatment, but even so, it was perhaps the most merciful thing God could have allowed to happen to Nebuchadnezzar. It was by this that he was brought to know God and honor him, as he so freely admits (4:36, 37). It must be remembered that to us things may look cruel, harsh, or even unjust, but we cannot see as God does what is best for people. Even today there seem to be manifestations of the wisdom of God in allowing certain people to suffer and be deprived of much in life. Other things seem so hard to us. Behind all this is the tender, loving hand of God, who is working out His purpose in those lives. Remember that Jesus said it is better to be blind, lame, and halt here, than lose the soul in hell hereafter (Matt. 18:7-14).

5. God's punishment for sin is revealed in the wickedness and doom of Belshazzar (5:1-30). This brilliant young king knew much better than he was doing, and when Daniel came to read to him the strange handwriting upon the wall, he reminded him of this (5:21-23). Had Belshazzar taken the counsel of the king's chronicles and the royal decree (3:28, 29), and doubtless as well as the gentle advice of his mother, and possibly Daniel himself, how different would his place in history, and indeed, in eternity, have been! But alas, like so many other strong-headed young people, he wished to "paddle his own canoe" and run his own affairs! Read carefully this chapter and see to what a sad end he brought himself. Youth should take counsel from

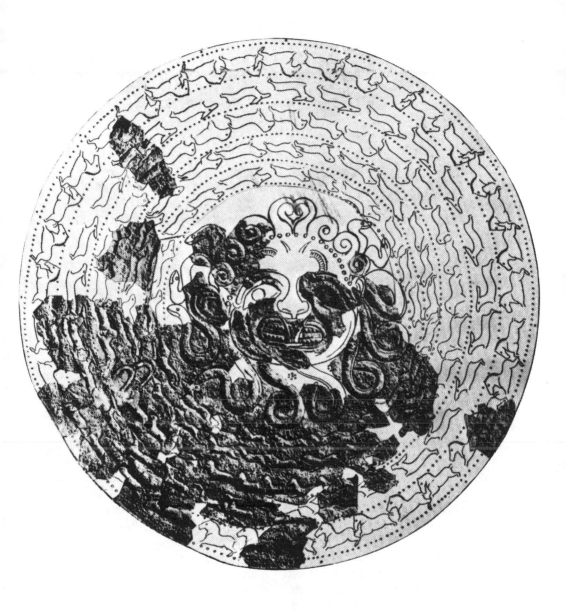

GREEK SHIELD. *This shield was found at Carchemish, a ruined city on the west bank of the Euphrates River, in present-day Turkey. Nebuchadnezzar hired Greek soldiers to fight for him. He defeated the Egyptian Necho at Carchemish in 605 B.C., putting an end to Egyptian power in Asia.*

this story and refrain from every form of evil.

Belshazzar was very young for his position. We know now from secular history that his father was away from Babylon at this time and that during his absence Belshazzar was reigning as a regent king in his father's stead. It has been estimated that he probably was about thirty-two years of age at his death.

6. Daniel's political enemies teamed up on him to destroy him. They knew of no other way to get at him, except in some matter of his religion (6:5). He was a spotless, upright, and remarkable man, but evidently they despised him and plotted his downfall and ruin. Read how they planned this scheme (6:1-9). But Daniel had been in tight spots before, and he knew where to go for help. He had seen his own life and the lives of others saved by prayer (2:16-18).

When Daniel knew of the decree to put him in the lion's den if he prayed to his God during the next thirty days, he did not shrink nor compromise his religious convictions. Had he been a modern-day Christian, he might have "reasoned" that it would be wiser to "be cautious" than to risk the possibility of survival in the den of lions! Ah, that is just it — too often our *caution* has been our ruin in Christian experience and practice! But Daniel opened his room window and prayed to God "as he did afore time" (6:10). He did not go to any extreme and put on a special demonstration for the fellows, as some religious people have done in their extreme zeal. No, he simply acted normally, just as always.

Naturally, the political enemies reported his praying to the king, who was very sorry, and tried with all his might

to save Daniel, whom he admired. But Daniel had broken the royal decree and the king found no legal way to save him from the lion's den. The king did encourage him, however, at the last moment to trust in his God, who could deliver him; he then spent a restless night, worrying over him (6:11-18). His worries were ended the next morning when Daniel shouted triumphantly from the lion's den, "My God hath sent his angel, and shut the lions' mouths, that they have not hurt me" (6:22). Then the other fellows had plenty to worry about for a short time; the lions took care of the rest of the work (6:24).

Behind all these great experiences there was one supreme purpose on the part of God: the working out of His plan for mankind's salvation and the progressive unfolding of His covenant, leading at last to its glorious fulfillment in Christ. Every story in this book has as its final end result, not only God's glory as the incident occurred, but His ultimate purpose for mankind through Jesus Christ.

The second section of Daniel is quite thoroughly apocalyptic in nature, and we shall not attempt here to draw any further lessons from this book.

This closes the section of the major prophets. As far as prophets go, we have been sitting at the feet of the greatest men God produced in Old Testament times.

Memory Verses

"But Daniel purposed in his heart that he would not defile himself with the portion of the king's meat, nor with the wine which he drank" (1:8).

"And they that be wise shall shine as the brightness of the firmament: and they that turn many to righteousness as the stars for ever and ever" (12:3).

The Minor Prophets

THE MINOR PROPHETS

This section, representing the minor prophets — twelve in all — deals with some of the most important times during the kingdom age and the latter period of Jewish history.

The minor prophets really begin with Jonah (790-749 B.C.) and Amos (760 B.C. and later) and close with Malachi, who lived around 430 B.C. Although the section opens with Hosea, he probably flourished about 750-725 B.C., somewhat later than Amos. We shall present these prophets as listed in the Bible rather than chronologically.

The term *minor* prophets designates those who wrote *less* extensively than the major prophets. It is generally supposed that the major prophets held a greater place of influence than did the minor prophets. The work of the latter, however, in their day was of great importance to Israel and the future history of redemption. While their written works are far smaller, their ministry of preaching was probably very extensive.

Hosea

The name Hosea means salvation. His prophetic ministry was an attempt to see Israel delivered from sin and brought back to proper relationship with God.

TO WHOM

The book was addressed largely to the Northern Kingdom of Israel, in which the prophet lived and worked. It was God's Word, however, to all Israel. Occasional references to Judah, the Southern Kingdom, are found in it.

It has a message for all men today and should be read in this light.

PURPOSE

Hosea's main purpose seems to have been to awaken Israel from her sinful condition and bring her back to God.

Like Ezekiel, Hosea's life was one of symbolism as well as prophetic ministry. He used his adulterous wife (1:2) as a symbol of Israel's forsaking God and worshiping idols. Her fondness for luxury drove her away from him (2:5), but in great love for her, he brought her back (3:1-2). These occurrences are used to tell Israel how God will forgive their spiritual adultery and take them back if they will only return to Him.

His children, likewise, became symbols of his message. The first one he named Jezreel (1:4, 5), representing God's punishment of Ahab and his wife for their evil at Jezreel. This name suggested to Israel's king and people that God would punish them for their sins. The second child was named Lo-ruhamah (1:6), meaning "No more mercy" for Israel. The name, Lo-ammi (1:9) meant "No longer my people." He then repeats the two names without the *Lo* — "not" — (2:1), predicting a time when Israel would again be God's people. But he further plays on the word to show that other nations would one day be called God's people (1:10). Paul quotes this passage in support of the Gentiles coming into the Christian church (Rom. 9:25).

Hosea makes clear his purpose is to warn and bring Israel back to God, if possible, but if not, to announce to them God's intention to punish them, to dispossess them finally, and to replace them with another people who love and obey Him.

TIME

Hosea ministered during the last forty years of the Northern Kingdom — around 760 B.C. He began his ministry when Jeroboam II was at his height as king.

Hosea was a younger contemporary of Amos and somewhat older than Isaiah and Micah. As a boy, he may have known the prophet Jonah, who had flourished somewhat earlier.

AUTHORSHIP

The authorship of this book has been ascribed to Hosea from the most ancient times. The internal evidence also points to this fact.

Little is known of his personal life, aside from what is given in his book. It is likely he was of the tribe of Reuben and lived near Samaria.

At what age he entered the ministry we are not told. There is a conjecture, based upon his statement in chapter 1:1, that he may have lived around ninety years. The reigns of these kings would cover about that long a period.

His lonely, tearful, and solitary life must have made a moving appeal to the people. But Israel as a whole rejected his ministry.

His writing is often abrupt, not free-flowing in style as Isaiah's, although his imagery and allegories are sometimes sharp and powerful. Some believe the book does not represent his publicly delivered discourses, but rather a briefer summation of what he taught in short, abrupt terms. This would have served

as a reminder to the people of his fuller ministry.

Hosea is highly regarded by New Testament writers and quoted many times (Matt. 9:13; 12:7; Luke 23:30; Rev. 6:16).

He is thought to have died shortly before the first invasion of Israel by the Assyrian king. He was spared the further heartache of seeing his prophecy being fulfilled.

The book may be outlined briefly in two sections:

I. Sins and laxities which pave the way for judgment, 1-3
II. Threats and denunciations, mingled with pleas to repent; prophecies of future glory for Israel, 4-14

GREAT THINGS IN HOSEA

Aside from Hosea's references to his wife, there are no *outstanding stories*. However, there are a number of *great truths* worthy of special mention.

Ephraim, the largest and most central tribe of the Northern Kingdom, became the symbol used by Hosea for the whole Kingdom (4:17). He characterizes the sins and weaknesses of Israel, and sometimes Judah, under this symbolic name. These same things may be applied to life today as a check on how one is living his Christian experience and life.

1. Your "goodness is as the early cloud, and the early dew" (6:4). There is no stability. Repentance, if at all, is very brief — then back to old sins.

2. "Ephraim, he hath mixed himself among the people . . . a cake not turned" (7:8). Ephraim — Israel — was willing to lose his identity to become popular. How many are like this today! Popularity, especially among young folk, is desired at any cost. The unturned cake

represents lack of proper "baking." Most difficulties of Christians can be traced to internal conditions — *half-baked* Christians (Rev. 3:15-16).

3. "Their root is dried up, they shall bear no fruit" (9:16). The tree ceases to bear because the roots are dead. Israel's difficulties sprang from spiritual decline, and deadness toward God. Unless the Christian is "rooted and grounded in Christ Jesus," there can be no spiritual life.

4. "Ephraim feedeth on wind" (12:1). Here Hosea likens reliance upon Assyria and Egypt to feeding on the wind. A "wind-sucking" horse used to get so bloated by this habit that he was useless for work. "Talk" is some people's greatest contribution to any worthy project. They are useless "wind-suckers"!

5. When Israel was youthful, he "spake trembling" and was exalted, but when he "offended in Baal, he died" (13:1). In national youth Israel honored God, but when he added Baal worship to the wicked calf worship at Bethel, he sank to hopeless depths. Backsliders not reclaimed early seem to add "sins to sin" until their cases become abominable. Beware!

Hosea mourns for Israel, tottering upon the brink of national disaster — Assyrian captivity. With this sign upon his lips, he closes his book.

There are certain Messianic passages in Hosea which clearly point to the future bliss of the Redeemer's kingdom and the fulfillment of the old covenant. Out of Israel shall come another people for the Lord (1:10-11; 2:23), and in that far-off day, Israel shall be gathered again, and return to God (3:4-5; 14:4-9).

Memory Verse
"Ephraim is joined to idols: let him alone" (4:17).

Joel

The name Joel means "Jehovah is God" and suggests the prophet's constant attention in the book to the fact that Jehovah is the God whom Judah should worship.

TO WHOM

The work was directed to the Southern Kingdom, Judah, as its first readers. He may have prophesied after the Ten Tribes of Israel were carried to Assyria, but his message was for all Israel and for all men. Its universal appeal is seen in the promise of the Holy Spirit's outpouring upon "all flesh" (2:28-32), which Peter quotes in this light (Acts 2:16-21). The last part of the book also deals with world events and is therefore universal in application.

PURPOSE

He undoubtedly intended to stir Judah to consciousness of her state and need. Some think his reference to the plague of locusts (1:4—2:11) indicates a natural plague occurring in his time, which he used to illustrate the destroying consequences of an invasion by the Chaldeans. Others believe it is merely symbolical, but portraying what an invading army of Babylon would be like.

The purpose was to turn Judah back to God. He wished them to repent and turn from sin, and thus escape judgment. A further purpose was to point out God's future plans for Israel and their final restoration.

Joel

TIME

Tradition assigns Joel to the period of Hosea, a possible contemporary. Nothing is known of how long he prophesied or when he may have written his book. It was likely produced near the close of his ministry as a summation of his preaching. Some place him as early as 830 B.C.; others as late as 750 B.C. His ministry certainly fell within this period, and he may have been among the earliest of the prophets of Judah.

AUTHORSHIP

The prophet Joel was, beyond doubt, the author of the book bearing his name. The fact that he has been quoted by others only credits him all the more as the writer of this book. Rather than having quoted others, as some have said, Joel *has been quoted.*

One of the best Scriptural evidences of his authorship of this book is Peter's quotation of his prophecy under the inspiration of the Holy Spirit on the day of Pentecost with actual credit to Joel (Acts 2:16-21). It is thought that Amos, living immediately following his times, quotes him (Amos 1:2 — a citation of Joel 3:16). Also, compare Amos 9:13 with Joel 3:18; Amos 7:3 with Joel 2:13. Isaiah 13:6 is a verbatim quotation of Joel 1:15, even using the same original Hebrew word for God — *"Shaddai"* — Almighty (Isa. 13:13, Joel 3:15, 16).

As one among the oldest Hebrew prophets, Joel enjoyed a great reputation among the prophets who followed him. His work is thus established without question.

Joel tells us nothing of himself or his days, but tradition assigns him as being born in the tribe of Reuben, not far from Jerusalem. Jerusalem and vicinity was probably his field of ministry. Much

JOEL. *This engraving depicts Joel preaching repentance to the people of Judah.*

of his book centers about that city and concerns the priests, Levites, and sacrifices (1:9, 13; 2:9, 15, 23; 3:1-8). Nothing is known of how long he lived or where he died and was buried. He evidently lived to enjoy a rather long ministry.

The book may be outlined briefly as follows:

I. Warnings, reproofs, and chastisements, 1-2:18

II. Promises of future blessings and mercies of God, 2:19-3:21

GREAT THINGS IN JOEL

No *outstanding stories* grace this book; several *great truths* are seen:

1. The scourge of locusts was used by Joel to point up God's chastisement of Israel for their sins (1-2). God often uses troubles, sicknesses, and sorrows which He permits as means of chastisement to draw His people nearer to Him and to awaken and save sinners.

2. The promised outpouring of the Holy Spirit upon the future Christian church (2:28-32) is one of the highlights of the book. Joel proclaimed that God would visit His people again, this time with a spiritual revival which would bring a turning to God. This was fulfilled at Pentecost, as Peter recognized in his sermon (Acts 2:14-40).

The church today has no greater need than the refilling with the Holy Spirit. Christian youth should make the Spirit-filled life their goal in Christian living.

3. There is a strong Messianic message running through Joel. His prophecy points to the judgment of the nations (3:1-12) and the battle of God against the forces of wickedness in the valley of Jehoshaphat (3:9-12). He speaks of God uttering His voice from Jerusalem and the "heavens and the earth being shaken" (3:14-16).

The latter part of Joel seems to be a prophetic picture of the Christian age

THE PROPHECY OF JOEL. *This pencil rendering of a mural depicts the two aspects of Joel's prophecy. The panel on the left portrays God's wrath and judgment: the invasion of the locusts and the destruction of crops and homes. The panel on the right depicts the Lord's compassion, the restoration, and the pouring out of the Spirit: a new world in close communion with God.*

Courtesy, John Knight

and its closing scenes. The Gospel of Christ, the true fulfillment of the Messianic covenant and its far-reaching claims in the final stages of the world's end is set forth in outline.

Joel saw through the distant vistas to the glory of the redeemed Israel that shall yet one day through God's grace in Christ, tread the soil of Palestine.

Memory Verses

"And it shall come to pass afterwards, that I will pour out my Spirit upon all flesh; and your sons and your daughters shall prophesy, your old men shall dream dreams, and your young men see visions: and upon the servants and upon the handmaid in those days will I pour out my Spirit" (2:28, 29).

Amos

Amos means "carrier," or perhaps better, "heavy" or "burden." He bore the "burden of the Lord" against several countries of his day. The word "burden" really means "denunciation." As a prophet, his ministry was a *denunciation* against the sinfulness of those countries, and he pronounced God's judgments upon them.

TO WHOM

The heart of his message was directed against Israel, the wicked king Jeroboam II, and the idolatrous priest of Bethel, the calf-worship center of Israel. Israel had adopted the worship of the golden calf at Bethel after the division of the

kingdom. To this had been added the most abominable Baal-worship, or worship of the sun-god. For some two hundred years this wickedness had gone on and had now become so deeply rooted as to be almost impossible to destroy.

Amos appears to have gone to Bethel from his home in Judah to deliver his stern message. Even though rebuked by the king of Israel, he stood his ground, telling the king and the false prophet of Bethel that they would both die at the hands of enemy armies which would invade Israel and conquer it.

In its written form the message of Amos was directed to all as well as to Israel. In its relationship to the latter days of restored Israel and its place in the world, the latter end of the book has universal appeal.

TIME

The message of Amos seems to have been delivered at Bethel some thirty years before the fall of Israel. Josephus says the "earthquake" (1:1) occurred when Uzziah, king of Judah, was struck with leprosy (II Chron. 26:16-21), which took place in 751 B.C. This would be about the time of his prophecy at Bethel, although some think the prophecy at Bethel came as early as 760 B.C. His book, however, may have been written considerably later, probably in his more advanced years.

AUTHORSHIP

Amos has always been considered as the author of this book.

The birthplace of Amos is unknown. Some think it was Tekoa, in Judah; but he may have been born in Israel and merely moved to Tekoa after being driven out of Israel by King Jeroboam II.

He had been a herdsman, a farmer of

BETHEL. *These house walls are from the days of the judges at Bethel. Amos denounced Bethel and its priests for their idolatry.*

sorts, "a gatherer of sycamore fruit." Some link his herdsmanship with Tekoa as his original home, but this is by no means certain. He may have followed sheepherding at different times during his life.

His educational advantages were limited. Not having attended the "school of the prophets," he was not recognized as a prophet at first. His public ministry, however, soon won him the award of an accredited prophet.

His first commission appears to have been his message against Bethel. Arriving in Samaria, he hastened to give his message against the wicked idol worship. Almost immediately Jeroboam ordered him

to leave the country, but before going, he gave the false priest Amaziah his sentence of ruin.

Israel had sunk to an all-time low in the days of Amos. The land was filled with brazen idolatry and moral rottenness; it reeked with adultery, swearing, stealing, injustice, robbery, and murder. Amos did his best to turn the tide. He was joined later by Hosea, then a younger prophet, but neither of them could save the day.

As a boy, Amos possibly knew Jonah, who had preceded him. He also may have heard Elisha tell the exciting stories about Elijah. Joel may have been a contemporary of his. Amos may have referred to Joel's plague of locusts (4:9). Amos and Hosea probably compared notes on the messages God had given each for those times. Isaiah and Micah were just young fledgling prophets in the last days of Amos.

Tradition has it that Amos was wounded by Jeroboam's followers and was carried from Israel back to Tekoa. He is believed to have lived here for a considerable time, carrying on his ministry after his experiences at Bethel. As late as Jerome's day (fourth century A.D.), the tomb of Amos was shown to visitors at Tekoa.

The prophecy against Bethel, possibly his first work, is recorded in chapter 7. The book does not seem to proceed as

---

AMOS, GOD'S ANGRY MAN. *Amos spoke with freedom and conviction, condemning the sin of Israel. Because of his fearlessness his life was in danger.*

Courtesy, Cathedral Filmstrips

the events occurred, but was possibly placed in this form when written later in the prophet's life.

The Messianic message is present in this as in most prophetic books. Toward the last he shows how the "remnant" of the people will be saved and how God's purpose with Israel and the redemptive covenant will be carried out.

The favorite expression of Amos, "For three transgressions, and for four, saith the Lord," is used many times in the book.

It may be outlined as follows:
- I. The prophet's call and his denunciations of various nations, 1-2
- II. Three prophetic addresses concerning Israel's ingratitude, idolatry, wickedness, and fate; each beginning with "Hear ye." (3-6)
- III. The Bethel prophecy; visions; Israel's destruction, 7—9:10
- IV. The Messianic presentation, 9:11-15

GREAT THINGS IN AMOS

Excepting his experiences at Bethel, there are no *outstanding stories*. Note, however, the following *great truths*:

1. Amos thunders at Israel, "Can two walk together, except they be agreed?" (3:3). To "walk with God" requires a harmony with His divine nature by a right relationship to Him through grace. Israel would not go this way.

2. "Prepare to meet thy God" (4:12), he argued with them. This is said to be a military phrase. Summon your strength if you will do battle with God. But you cannot win; therefore, surrender to Him. You who will not serve God, prepare your defense and offer your reasons.

3. "Woe to them that are at ease in Zion" (6:1). He warns them not to put

confidence in natural defense when defeat and dangers are so apparent.

Millions today trust human defenses when they should trust Christ alone for security of soul.

Memory Verse

"Therefore thus will the Lord do unto thee, O Israel: and because I will do this unto thee, prepare to meet thy God, O Israel" (4:12).

Obadiah

Obadiah means "worshiper of Jehovah." He was a faithful and devout worshiper of God, working hard to defend the name of God and proclaim His message.

TO WHOM

This brief, fiery denunciation was delivered against the Edomites. The entire book is devoted to this theme, although it does contain hopeful sidelights for Judah. Without doubt, it was intended for the Edomites, but it was also directed to the Israelites and received by them as an inspired writing.

PURPOSE

It was intended to declare God's punishment and final annihilation of Edom. Besides their early unbrotherliness to Israel in the wilderness, the Edomites had taken part in four assaults against Jerusalem (Num. 20:14-21). These assults occurred in: 850-843 B.C. (II Chron. 21: 8, 16, 17); 803-775 B.C. (II Chron. 25: 11, 12, 23, 24); 741-726 B.C. (II Chron. 28:16-21); and 597-586 B.C. (II Chron. 36:11-21; Ps. 137:7).

Obadiah predicted that the Edomites would be "cut off forever," as "though they had not been" (vv. 10, 16, 18). His purpose was to drive home this prophecy so they might know of their impending doom. He also encouraged Judah by telling them that their God would prevail (vv. 17, 19, 21).

TIME

From internal evidence — reference to Judah's "destruction" (vv. 11, 12) — this book has generally assumed to have been written during the reign of Zedekiah, the last king of Judah, 597-586 B.C. Jerusalem was destroyed in 586 B.C.

AUTHORSHIP

The book is beyond doubt the work of the prophet Obadiah. The book — smallest in the Old Testament — is a complete unit, well tied together by its style, language, and purpose.

Of Obadiah very little is known. He probably had a larger spoken ministry but recorded only this piece against Edom. Jeremiah probably quotes him (Jer. 49). The passage in Jeremiah is broken, appearing at intervals, while the Obadiah passage is straightforward, as an original work.

Tradition assigns his burial to Samaria, where his tomb was shown as late as Jerome's time.

The book may be outlined as follows:

I.   Coming destruction of Edom and the causes therefor, vv. 1-16

II. Israel's salvation and final restoration, vv. 17-21

GREAT THINGS IN OBADIAH

Great truths here may be listed as follows:

1. The ago-old feud between Jacob and Esau came to its pitiable end in Edom's total destruction. Conquered by the Babylonians, whom they had helped against Jerusalem just four years after Jerusalem's destruction in 586 B.C., they never rose again to power. They were fully subdued by the Maccabeans in 126 B.C. and absorbed into the Jewish state. In 63 B.C., when the Romans conquered Palestine, the Herods — an Edomite family — were placed in control. This is why the Jews hated the Herods so fiercely. In A.D. 70, when Jerusalem was destroyed by the Romans, the last trace of the Edomites was forever wiped away as Obadiah had predicted.

2. Vengeance against unrelenting hate and' unforgiving attitudes comes sooner or later. The Edomites — descendants of Jacob's brother Esau — would never forgive the wrong Jacob did to their forefather. In the end they lost all. Forgiveness is the only road to survival and usefulness.

3. God expects us to respect the rights of others. Israel, on their way to Canaan through the wilderness, had certain rights. They asked respectfully and peacefully for the consideration of these rights. Edom turned them down cold and persecuted them. God then promised that He would remember Edom's evil and punish them for it.

4. No security nor refusal of man can stop the divine hand in time of vengeance or chastisement for one's evil deeds. The red city of Petra, high in the mountains of Edom, seemed impregnable, and it was so for centuries. The Edomites could raid others, retire there, and be unreachable. But not forever! Finally, like all others, they reaped what they had sown.

5. The great, final triumphant shout of the prophet, "And the kingdom shall be the Lord's" (v. 21), is the Messianic note of the book. The last part (vv. 17-21) builds up for this wondrous shout of victory. So the prophet closes his word with a note of eternal victory upon his lips.

Memory Verses

"The pride of thine heart hath deceived thee, thou that dwellest in the clefts of the rock, whose habitation is high; that saith in his heart, who shall bring me down to the ground? Though thou exalt thyself as the eagle, and though thou set thy nest among the stars, thence will I bring thee down, saith the Lord" (vv. 3, 4).

Jonah

Jonah means "dove." It may signify that by nature Jonah was a rather quiet, withdrawing man. This seems to come out in the narrative in the fact that he had said nothing to the sailors of the ship on which he embarked until forced by circumstances to explain his reason for being there (1:7-12). He also proved very moody when the gourd vine dried away, leaving him in the hot sunshine (4:6-9).

TO WHOM

The book was undoubtedly written for all Israel, although the prophecy of mercy was for Nineveh. Its inclusion in the sacred books leaves no doubt that it was considered to be for the Jewish people.

Much of the story, however, has universal appeal and may be exceptionally fine reading for our day. Its most interesting story furnishes much devotional food for thought and warning against disobedience to God.

PURPOSE

The purpose of the book may have been to correct a narrow, nationalistic outlook on the part of the Jews, the thought that salvation was for Israelites only. God could in this manner remind Israel that "whosoever shall call upon the name of the Lord shall be saved" (Rom. 10:13).

God's purpose with Israel had originally been to make them missionaries, carriers of the message of salvation to all people. They had become disobedient and selfish and had lost their mission by becoming idolatrous. God would remind them that wherever repentance was genuine, He would forgive and save.

TIME

Jonah lived during the reign of Jeroboam II, 790-749 B.C. (II Kings 14:25). He made his famous trip to Nineveh sometime during this period, probably the earlier part of it. He would have been younger then and more able to cope with the situations in the story.

AUTHORSHIP

There are two theories of authorship: Some think it was written by someone other than Jonah — a later theory; others contend Jonah himself could well have written the story.

Those who believe another person wrote it do so because it is in the third person; Jonah is nowhere mentioned as its author and Nineveh is referred to in the past tense (3:3).

Those contending for Jonah's authorship say that many works, ancient and modern, are written in the third person; that as the whole book is about Jonah, he need not have introduced himself as its author; and that observation shows that sometimes present-tense situations are placed in past-tense terms. They further argue that a patriotic Jewish writer would hardly have placed his nation and one of its great prophets in so bad a light so long time after his death. No other writer could have observed so well the inner thoughts and motives of the hero of the story and recorded them in detail. This is inner, personal history. Another person, describing Jonah as is done here, would leave the reader with less respect for him, but this would *not* be true of a personal account. The book

JONAH. *As a last resort Jonah was thrown overboard. The artist also pictures the great fish about to swallow him.*

leaves Jonah under God's reproof — a thing which another author would hardly do.

The story seems to portray Jonah's genuine repentance, confession, submission to God, and his willingness to obey God. This adds to the personal character of the narrative, making it seem more likely his own writing.

However, there has been considerable debate about the book as to whether it is a true historical story, an allegorical tale, fiction, or a prose poem. This has been almost entirely because of the nature of the "fish story" in the heart of the book. Unbelieving minds have tried to find some way around the "miraculous" part of this story. Certainly, nothing else than a true *miracle* would be required for this section to be truly historical.

From the most ancient times the Jews have accepted Jonah as a genuine historical narrative. It is told in simple, direct language and nowhere even hints at being a parable or an allegory. There are no moralizations or added teachings, as would be true if it were all allegory.

The most important "clincher" is that our Lord accepted it as a true story; He accepted Jonah as an historical person. He alludes to Jonah's three days and nights in the whale as an illustration of His own similar period in the grave (Matt. 12:39, 40). He accepts as historical Jonah's descriptions of Nineveh also (Matt. 12:41; Luke 11:29, 30).

It is, of course, possible that someone else, inspired by the Holy Spirit, *could* have written this account of Jonah, but it is hardly necessary. Jonah himself could have done it more successfully, and this is most likely the case.

Jonah was from Gath-hepher, a village in Galilee. He was a prophet of the

Courtesy, The British Museum

GATEWAY STONE FIGURE. *This figure stood at the gateway to the palace of Ashurpanipal, King of Assyria, 883-859 B.C.*

Northern Kingdom and was likely a statesman and outstanding patriot as well as a prophet. He apparently helped to recover certain Israelitish territory during the reign of Jeroboam II (II Kings 14:25), even though he protested his ungodliness.

Possibly the oldest of the writing prophets, he was one of the most dramatic and colorful of all. His book would not likely have been listed among the prophets except for its prophetic significance. Because of his remarkable book, he is one of the best known of all the Old Testament prophets. Far outreaching its immediate story, his book is rich in valuable material.

The book may be outlined as follows:

I.   Jonah's call to Nineveh and his flight from duty, 1

II. His penitent prayer and deliverance from the fish, 2

III. His preaching and Nineveh's repentance, 3

IV. His disappointment and bitterness, 4

There is no direct Messianic message in this book; and yet, the whole book is in someway devoted to the message that God loves all men and will forgive and save all who repent. In this manner it shows the breadth of God's redemptive covenant and its ultimate purpose. Christ used Jonah's experience in the fish's belly to represent His death and resurrection; and in this way the book carries a profound Messianic prototype and message (Matt. 12:39, 40). He represents Christ's resurrection and worldwide mission to save all men.

GREAT THINGS IN JONAH

Jonah presents one *outstanding story* with several high points of interest. It depicts many sidelights of personality and character and sets forth a number of *great truths.*

1. At first, Jonah refused God's call to go to Nineveh. Finding a ship going to Tarshish (possibly ancient *Tartessus* in Spain), he "paid the fare thereof, and went down" into the ship to flee from God (1:3). Soon his disobedience caught up with him, and being cast overboard, he really *went down* — into the sea and the fish's belly! God finds some place to stop those running from Him. Down, down, down, is the way that leads from God.

2. In the fish's belly Jonah met not only God, but *himself,* face to face. One is never so awakened as when he really sees himself in God's light. His repentance brought rescue. Had he not repented, would he have been *digested* instead of vomited up? When we *face ourselves* sincerely, we are ready to *face God* again; then real life begins.

3. Note that Jonah's second commission was in no way changed from the first — to preach to Nineveh (3:1, 2). Postponement of duty only brings lost opportunities and sorrow — not relief (if

still possible to one) from the commission. Oh, the heartbreak and trouble saved in immediate obedience!

4. Jonah may have landed on the beach near Joppa and had to start from here again on his Nineveh mission. It was here, eight hundred years later, that Peter received his commission to preach to Gentiles. Did he remember *Jonah* and not back down?

5. In His mercy to Nineveh, God's mercy is seen to be universal. Jonah's message of his miraculous rescue story to the Ninevites, maybe with accompanying persons to back it up, must have had profound influence upon Nineveh. He may have been most impressive, since he was from a nation that Assyria, whose capital was Nineveh, had begun to plunder. Perhaps this act — kindness for cruelty — produced genuine repentance in Nineveh.

6. God's personal compassion for Jonah is seen in the preparation of the gourd. If His displeasure with Jonah's attitude when the gourd withered seems unworthy of God, remember He feeds the sparrows and notes even their death (Matt. 10:29).

7. The word "whale" (Matt. 12:40) is an unfortunate translation of "great fish" (1:17). Some think it may have been one of the huge "white shark" varieties of the Mediterranean Sea. Anyhow, the original verse, "Now the Lord had prepared a great fish to swallow up Jonah," amply cares for that problem. Besides, it is well known that there are sea monsters fully capable of swallowing men; in fact, some men have been swallowed and have survived. But the miraculous part of this story is the time period and Jonah's consciousness while inside the fish. Possibly this miracle added greatly to the effectiveness of Jonah's preaching.

8. Jonah's intense national loyalty made it very difficult to preach repentance to a nation already set to *destroy his own.* God would teach us that we must often swallow our pride and do what duty calls us to do. Often we do not understand what God is doing, but we should obey, knowing that later it will be made plain.

Jonah stands as a solemn warning against disobedience to God.

Memory Verses

"And the word of the Lord came unto Jonah the second time, saying, Arise, go unto Nineveh, that great city, and preach unto it the preaching that I bid thee" (3:1, 2).

Micah

Micah means "Who is like unto Jehovah?" As his name suggests, Micah was certainly a God-exalting prophet.

TO WHOM

This book, unlike most others, is addressed to both Israel and Judah. Jerusalem and Samaria were the capitals of the two nations; each represents a nation in Micah's scathing denunciations. It will be noted, too, that both are included, although less emphatically, in the prophecies of future glory. Here all Israel has more emphasis, as there was to be a restoration of the divided nation into one glorious people.

PURPOSE

Micah's apparent purpose was to bring both nations to repentance and so avert disaster, if possible. He served notice that if they did not repent, their calamity would be certain.

Finally, he encouraged the faithful among them to look to the future for ultimate deliverance from oppression. He rebuked the rich for oppressing the poor and encouraged the poor to look to God for justice. To encourage social justice was one of his great aims. His references to the coming, glorious Messianic kingdom are all worked into the other prophecies.

TIME

Micah prophesied during the reigns of Jotham, Ahaz, and Hezekiah — kings of Judah around 757-698 B.C. His spoken ministry was doubtless far larger than his written prophecies, which are the summation of his total ministry. He possibly prophesied as long as fifty years. His book was probably composed near the end of his ministry. He was a contemporary of Isaiah and possibly knew Hosea in that prophet's old age.

AUTHORSHIP

He was undoubtedly the author of this book. Little is known of his origin, which, like Amos, may have been very lowly. He seems not to have kept company with the elite as did Isaiah. He is sometimes called "the prophet of the poor" because of his defense of them. Though living in Judah, he ministered to both Judah and Israel, He may have traveled about, much as a modern evangelist does.

His reputation was high among the Jews, for in defense of Jeremiah he is quoted by the elders of the land (Jer. 26:18), thereby saving Jeremiah's life.

The style of his writing is rough, like a peasant writer of his times. It portrays quick temperament and brisk change from one subject to another and from one person to another. Sometimes he is bold, stern, severe; at other times he drops into sorrowful, loving tones. Little attention is paid to formal rules of composition; yet, many passages reach sublime heights.

Micah's prophecies shine with the Messianic message interwoven into the total pattern of the book.

The book may be outlined as follows:

   I. A denunciation of the oppression of the poor and the leading of false prophets, 1-3
   II. The Messianic scope of Christ's coming kingdom, 4-5
   III. God's controversy with His people, 6-7

GREAT THINGS IN MICAH

Outstanding stories are absent, but one may still see several *great truths*:

1. God defends the poor (2:1-3) and will punish the oppressors who exact their tribute and their possessions.

2. Micah alone proclaims the actual *place* of the Savior's birth (5:2). "Bethlehem" is named as the place from which the "ruler" whose goings forth are to be "everlasting" shall come. Only the birth of Christ could be meant here. Even the Jewish people before Christ's coming recognized this as the birthplace of the coming Messiah (Matt. 2:1-6.) This is an interesting passage and in this connection should be read just now, showing how prophecy was fulfilled at Christ's birth.

3. God's requirements of man are set forth by Micah in simple, clear terms

Courtesy, Cathedral Filmstrips

MICAH, "PROPHET OF THE COMMON MAN." *The style of Micah is simple; it is rugged but still elegant. He was very plain-spoken in rebuke of sin.*

(6:6-8). "To do justly, and to love mercy, and walk humbly with thy God" is far more than natural man's good-neighbor policy of religion will ever bring. No one can keep this admonition without a heart renewed in God's grace. Certainly no man can "walk humbly with God" and remain a proud, self-righteous, unregenerated sinner. About this passage there is much talk by those who never go deeply into vital religion, as though one could simply adopt this policy and be a fine, God-pleasing, good fellow. Only those whose sins are forgiven and whose hearts are made pure by Christ can "walk humbly with God" — the part without which the rest of the passage is impossible. Often sin-blinded, conceited moralists *think* they are fulfilling this demand, but one glimpse of their true selves in Christ's light will forever convince them otherwise.

4. Micah has been looked upon as one of the foremost of the Old Testament

prophets who worked for and promoted social justice and practical righteousness. This is attainable only in the light of the above conditions of heart.

Micah may well be called the prophet of practical religion.

Memory Verse

"He hath showed thee, O man, what is good; and what doth the Lord require of thee, but to do justly, and to love mercy, and to walk humbly with thy God" (6:8).

Nahum

In the Hebrew original, Nahum means "comforter." Certainly Nahum comforted God's people with promises of blessing, but he flayed the wicked without mercy.

TO WHOM

It was most certainly directed to Nineveh, for the whole book concerns its final destruction. By some it has been called "Nineveh's Death Song."

As it also contains comfort for God's people, it was also intended for the Jewish people, who held the book as a sacred, inspired book of God.

PURPOSE

The purpose is clear — to predict the ultimate destruction of Nineveh, capital of the Assyrian empire. Whether the prophet hoped for its repentance again, as in Jonah's days some 150 years before, is not clear. It seems to have been a doom sentence.

Its second purpose was to comfort the Jewish people and assure them of final triumph and deliverance; the captor of the ten tribes was at last being punished.

TIME

Thebes (called *No* in the KJV; *No-amon* in the RSV) had fallen in 663 B.C. (3:8-10). Nahum represents Nineveh as nearing its doom. It finally was destroyed in 607 B.C. But as it is pictured in this book — in the swing of its glory — it may be supposed that Nahum prophesied shortly before its fall. The date has been placed as about 630 B.C., just before the Cythian invasion began in 626 B.C. Nahum, then, may have ministered between 663 and 607 B.C. His book was likely written about the time of his prophecy, around 630 B.C.

AUTHORSHIP

Nahum's authorship of this book is unquestioned. At the time of this prophecy, Nineveh and Assyria were at the peak of their prosperity. It would have been impossible for a native Jewish prophet, uninspired, to have predicted so accurately just what happened in so short a time thereafter. The best political observer would hardly have guessed its tragic end.

Nahum was born in Judah, possibly at Elkosh, near Capernaum. The word Capernaum actually means "village of Nahum." He could have been a resident, or even the founder, of Capernaum. There is said to have been an Elkosh on the Tigris River, twenty miles north of Nineveh. Some think Nahum could have been among the Israelite captives taken there, but this is uncertain.

In the original the book is actually a poem. Chapter 1 is a psalm in alphabetical form, setting forth the majesty

and power of God and His mercy and justice in dealing with mankind.

Nineveh, the subject of the book, was uppermost in the prophet's mind. He has no personal grudge, but he pours out his soul in warning of coming doom. The main part of the city was then about thirty miles long and ten miles wide, protected by huge walls and supplied with water by the Tigris. From the fact that Jonah recognized 120,000 babies (not knowing the right hand from the left — Jonah 4:11), it is thought to have had a population of about one million.

Aside from the promises of Israel's restoration, there is no specific Messianic message in Nahum.

It may be outlined as follows:
I. God's majesty and power, mercy and justice, 1
II. Nineveh's destruction and the reasons for it, 2-3

GREAT THINGS IN NAHUM

There are no *outstanding stories* but several *great truths*:

1. The fact that Nahum comes with a message of doom 150 years after God sent Jonah with a message of mercy reveals God's way of dealing with mankind. He offers plenteous mercy. If this is rejected — after all means fail — justice must come.

ASHURPANIPAL. *Assyria reached its height under Ashurpanipal. His palace and temples at Nineveh had some of the finest of ancient sculpture. In this relief the king is seen hunting lions. Nahum prophesied shortly before its fall.*

2. God is "slow to anger" (1:3) but will not keep on offering mercy forever, only to have it rejected. Finally, to their eternal undoing, He will give up both men and nations if they continue to reject Him.

3. Nineveh's frightful destruction again declares the eternal principle of a law so often seen in the Old Testament: "Whatsoever a man soweth, that shall he also reap" (Gal. 6:7).

4. Some think the prophetic picture of the modern automobile may be seen in this book (2:3, 4), where some type of "horseless carriage" may be referred to by Nahum. Interpreters of this passage generally explain its meaning as having to do with the street battles of Nineveh, the water canals at night reflecting lights of fires like "torches."

5. Judah's hope is not forgotten, and there shines the Messianic promise of final triumph in the prophet's stern declarations against Nineveh (1:15).

Those who fear and serve the Lord

have nothing to fear from the destruction of the wicked.

Memory Verse

"Behold upon the mountains the feet of him that bringeth good tidings, that publisheth peace! O Judah, keep thy solemn feasts, perform thy vows: for the wicked shall no more pass through thee; he is utterly cut off" (1:15).

Habakkuk

Habakkuk means "one who embraces," which Jerome thought may be taken to represent one who wrestles with God in prayer, as did Jacob. His prayer (3:2) reminds us that he must have been a praying man.

TO WHOM

Judah seems to have been in the prophet's eye as the people to whom his message was directed. He probably ministered to Judah at large. His message also has meaning for the church today.

PURPOSE

Habakkuk apparently attempted to awaken Judah to her spiritual needs and warn her of impending doom by the Babylonians. Thinking they had little to fear, Judah seems to have grown more wicked after the fall of Assyria. He warns them to the contrary. Babylon stood ready to carry them away as Assyria did Israel.

TIME

This prophecy possibly belongs to the time between 625 B.C. and 606 B.C. The Chaldeans (Babylonians) were coming westward (1:6) but had not yet reached Judah (3:16). So the date may be as late as 607 B.C. The book was probably written sometime near the delivery of the final prophecies. Habakkuk may have ministered from around 625 B.C. until the captivity in 606 B.C.

AUTHORSHIP

The book itself gives every evidence of the prophet's authorship; it has been so received through the centuries.

Little is known about Habakkuk himself; he states only that he was a prophet (1:1). Some think he may have been of the tribe of Simeon. Tradition says he fled to Egypt when Nebuchadnezzar captured Jerusalem, but that he later returned to Judah, where he died. His tomb is said to have been shown in ancient times in the hill country of Judah, but this is not historically certain.

GREAT THINGS IN HABAKKUK

There are no *outstanding stories.* Several *great truths* are found:

1. Five woes are pronounced: (1) for increasing that which is not one's own (2:6); (2) against "him that coveteth" (2:9); (3) against him that "buildeth a town with blood" (2:12); (4) against "him that giveth his neighbor drink" (2:15); and (5) against all idolaters (2:19).

Directed largely against Babylon, these woes also served to warn Judah of God's displeasure for such things. And they likewise warn us today.

2. The height of the Messianic message of this book is seen in the pronouncement of that golden day when "the just

shall live by his faith" (2:4). He speaks of the vision which was to come, doubtless referring to the coming Savior, by whose faith we are to live.

3. Possibly the keynote of the whole book is the prophet's prayer (3:2). Judah faced destruction unless "revival" would save them. The church today needs revival more than any other thing.

4. A gem of perfect faith in Habakkuk's statement of truth (3:17-19). Read it carefully. Although all natural resources fail, he shouts, "Yet, will I rejoice in the Lord, I will joy in the God of my salvation." Here is the heart of practical religion.

Memory Verse

"O Lord, I have heard thy speech, and was afraid: O Lord, revive thy work in the midst of the years, in the midst of the years make known; in wrath remember mercy" (3:2).

Courtesy, Charles F. Pfeiffer

THE HABBAKUK COMMENTARY. *One of the Dead Sea Scrolls is a commentary on the Book of Habbakuk.*

36

Zephaniah

The name Zephaniah means "the Lord hath hid," or perhaps "whom Jehovah hides, or shelters." From the nature of his judgment message, he would need God's sheltering.

TO WHOM

The book has a two-fold audience: the Jews of his day, whom Zephaniah reminds are ripe for judgment, and "all nations" which will certainly come into God's judgment for their disobedience.

Upon this basis the book makes a universal appeal.

PURPOSE

Like his audience, his purpose is twofold. Israel must be warned and awakened, but so must all nations. The Gentile world is told that God will "assemble all nations to judgment."

TIME

Since Assyria and Nineveh had not yet fallen and Josiah's reforms had not yet begun, in which Zephaniah played so great a part, it is safe to say his main ministry was from about 640-625 B.C. His book was doubtless written toward the end of this period.

AUTHORSHIP

Zephaniah's authorship of this book has been accepted since ancient times. Little is known about him except that which is stated in the book. From his reference to Hizkiah, a possible descendant of Hezekiah (1:1), it is thought he in turn may have been a descendant of the good King Hezekiah. Apparently he was born in Judea, but where is not known.

Though not as rough as some, his writing shows little in the way of formal training. How long he ministered is not known, probably several years in the reign of the good King Josiah of Judah.

In the original, the book is couched in stern, rugged language; it is one of the most stern pictures of judgment in the Old Testament. There are passages of brighter prospect and hope, however, toward the end.

From the nature of the book it appears the prophet produced several addresses at various times, which were later collected into book form.

ASHURPANIPAL AND HIS QUEEN. *A royal feast was held after each military conquest. This relief sculpture was found in the ruins of the palace at Nineveh.*

Courtesy, The British Museum

It may be outlined as follows:

I. The impending day of wrath for Judah, 1:1—2:3
II. A day of wrath awaiting all nations, 2:4—3:8
III. The coming of a "pure language", 3:9-20

The closing portion of the book (3:9-20) is the Messianic section; it glows with the bright prospects of Israel's restoration, not only from the captivity which was yet in the future, but to the favor of God in the end time.

The reference to a "pure language" may very well be to Christ's Gospel message, by which all nations would come to understand the truth of God in an easy, direct, well-understood, universal message. This description best fits the Gospel message.

GREAT THINGS IN ZEPHANIAH

No *outstanding stories* are listed, but several *great truths* do stand out:

1. The book seems to be a complete unity, but it is divided into appropriate subjects. This first chapter is believed to

be the section from which came the Latin hymn of medieval times, *Dies Irae,* "Day of Wrath," written by an associate of St. Francis of Assisi. Zephaniah is considered the Old Testament classic pronouncement of the judgment of God.

2. Chapter 2 shines more brightly with hope. Here the prophet urges repentance: "Seek ye the Lord, all ye meek of the earth. . . ." (2:3). He adds that there will be mercy. Then, as now, God will have mercy upon those who will repent and turn to Him.

3. The last chapter furnishes the most hopeful picture for Israel and the world. Here the broad outlines for world conditions and hopes will fit no nation, and therefore must refer to some glorious end-time fulfillment.

4. Perhaps the single great truth presented may be summed up this way: God will by His own methods and the obedience of His people awaken and save all who will repent, but His final judgment will be poured out unrelentingly upon those who reject His mercy and continue in their sins.

Memory Verse
"The Lord thy God in the midst of thee is mighty; he will save, he will rejoice over thee with joy he will rest in his love, he will joy over thee with singing" (3:17).

Haggai

The name of this prophet means "festive" and doubtless refers to rejoicing of some kind. As a prophet of the early restoration period, he represents the joy and gladness with which Judah returned to the native land.

TO WHOM

The message of Haggai was to restored Israel, particularly the Jews at Jerusalem. He is sent to them with a message to get the leaders and people into action on the restoration program, especially that of the Temple.

PURPOSE

The entire purpose of this message seems to have been to stir up the people, inspire new zeal, and restore confidence. Haggai intended to make the leaders conscious of their responsibility to rebuild God's house — the Temple.

TIME

Haggai's work was accomplished about 520 B.C. or shortly afterward. His ministry was evidently short but very important and at that time, quite powerful. He may have prophesied over considerable time, but his main message, that contained in the book, was likely of brief duration.

AUTHORSHIP

There can be little question that the prophet Haggai was the author of this book. We know nothing of his parentage nor from what part of Judah he came. From the fact that he seems to have seen the "glory of the former house" of the Lord, (or Temple), some think he may have been carried away to Babylon as a child and that he later returned as an old man. This is not conclusive proof, for he could have known of the former Temple, even though he was born in Babylon, which some believe more likely.

THE RUINS OF BABYLON TODAY. *Excavations by archaeologists indicate the greatness of Babylon at the height of her power. Traces of streets and walls are observable.*

Like others of the preaching prophets, he likely collected his messages into book form near the close of his ministry. Of his death and burial we have no record.

One may use the following outline:

I. Beginning of work on the Temple, 1:1-5

II. Prediction of the future glory of God's house, 2:1-23

GREAT THINGS IN HAGGAI

No *outstanding stories,* but some *great truths* are presented in this book:

1. Haggai is a story-prophecy type of presentation. He was called to stir up the people to this great need of rebuilding the Temple. He accuses the people of being more interested in their own houses than in God's house, and he condemns them for this (1:4-10). Too often the Lord's work suffers by neglect of those who should promote it.

2. About one month after the scathing, condemning sermons, he began to see action. This time he counters with a word of comfort and encouragement, telling how God will fill the house with His glory. Encouragement always comes to those who do their duty.

3. He finally points Israel to the future restoration and glory which is to come to them through obedience to God.

Haggai is an ultra-practical man; he shows how God will reward His faithful ones and also how He will punish the wicked.

In the closing portion he presents a strong Messianic portrayal of God's dealings with all men through the coming Redeemer, the Lord Jesus Christ (2:21-23).

Memory Verse

"Thus saith the Lord of hosts; consider your ways" (7:1).

Zechariah

The name of this book means "Jehovah has remembered." It is a better way of spelling Zachariah, a rather prominent name in Israelitish history. This name suggests that God's mercy has been returned to Israel in their restoration to Palestine from Babylonian captivity.

TO WHOM

His message was to restored Israel and, of course, to all Israel. After the restoration of Judah from captivity, there is no more a divided Israel. From there onward the nation is thought of as one again. This message also may have significant meaning for us today as well. Especially the last part of the book is highly spiritualized and has a universal appeal to all God's people everywhere.

PURPOSE

There seems to be a twofold purpose in this book: The early part of the book appeals to Israel in particular, especially the Jerusalem Jews and their leaders. Zechariah's immediate purpose was to encourage the Jews and inspire them to finish rebuilding the Temple and to resume regular worship. The last part of the book contains a note of universal appeal and encouragement to the people of God. This section of the book is highly Messianic in its presentation and concepts. There one can clearly see the prophecies concerning Christ.

TIME

There seem to have been two periods of Zechariah's ministry. The earlier part of the book notes conditions which were contemporaneous with Haggai's ministry. The latter part apparently occurred sometime later. Zechariah began his ministry some two months after Haggai began preaching. While Haggai's ministry lasted around four months, Zechariah's ministry in connection with the Temple lasted about two full years, probably from 520-518 B.C.

AUTHORSHIP

The author of this book is thought to have been Zechariah, the grandson of Iddo (Neh. 12:4, 16). He has been confused with a Zechariah who lived in Isaiah's time, and also with the father of John the Baptist, but he stands alone, related to neither. He was likely born in Babylon, probably of the priestly line; this was of considerable advantage to his ministry to the Jewish leaders and priests.

Aside from notes in his book, little is known of his life. The first period of his ministry may have lasted from about 520-518 B.C. This was likely followed by a lull at least as far as his *writing* ministry is concerned. The latter part of the book may have been written several years after the first part. The book appears to be divided into two distinct sections, as seen in the following outline:

I.   Introduction, exhortations, and early visions, 1-6

II. Exhortations concerning the nature of true worship, 7-8

III. The future of Israel and the church, 9-14

Zechariah is the largest of the minor prophets and in some ways the most difficult to understand. The latter part of the book, especially chapters 9-14, is highly spiritualized, and the symbolisms are not always clear to our present day understanding. While Haggai dealt with the *material* and present-day aspects of the Temple building, Zechariah presented the *spiritual* aspects, along with a futuristic, prophetic view of its fuller meaning for both Jews and Christians of the church age to come.

The last section (9-14) is one of the most remarkable Messianic passages of the Old Testament. It is very descriptive of many things about Christ and His

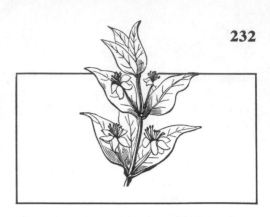

work. It is also more like Isaiah than any other Old Testament section of Scripture. Scholars believe this section was written much later than the first part (1-8) and under very different circumstances. It shows that restored Israel had not prospered as they had hoped; she was still a vassal nation under tribute, and though strangers had flocked to Jerusalem to learn of the Jewish religion, the Temple had not prospered by their gifts. The Jewish people were discouraged, and the prophet tries to encourage them. These things and the nature of the Messianic message of the last section of the book account for the difference seen in the two sections, rather than the supposition that two different persons wrote the two different sections, as some have contended.

MYRTLE TREE. *Eight symbolic night visions are described in the first part of Zechariah. The first is that of the Heavenly Couriers" in a myrtle forest. The myrtle tree is native to Mediterranean regions. It has shiny aromatic leaves and white or pink flowers.*

GREAT THINGS IN ZECHARIAH

No *outstanding stories* but certain *great truths* characterize this book:

1. Note that the "visions" are *symbolical* rather than historical in meaning. This will serve as a "key" to understanding them.

2. Section one is an illustration of God's way of encouraging His people in times of need. At times everyone needs encouragement to accomplish his best for the Lord.

3. Note the following outstanding passages which are prophecies about Christ; read them carefully in your own Bible:

(a) The triumphal entry of Christ into Jerusalem on Palm Sunday is made almost as plain here as in the gospel story of it five centuries later (9:9-10).

(b) Judas' betrayal of Christ for "thirty pieces of silver" is also vivid (11:12, 13).

(c) The piercing of Christ's side on the cross and the mourning at the cross are made as plain as a picture of it (12:10).

(d) The shedding of Christ's blood to make way for cleansing — the "fountain opened to the house of David . . . for sin and for the uncleanness" — is foretold (13:1).

(e) The "scars" or "wounds" in Christ's hands and side are referred to (13:6).

(f) Christ's arrest and the scattering of His followers is seen (13:7).

(g) The personal return of Christ in glory is also depicted, which, though still in the future, is as fully expected as any other prophecy (14:4).

These are the classic Messianic passages that should be memorized by every person.

4. Zechariah encourages Zerubbabel by saying, "Not by might, nor by power, but by my Spirit, saith the Lord of hosts" (4:6). How much this truth is needed in our day! Christians are to rely upon the Spirit of God for their aid and not upon their own power, social prestige, or some other means of success in Christian

work. One of life's greatest lessons for youth is to learn to rely absolutely upon the Holy Spirit for aid and guidance, using under His direction all the powers of training, courage, intellect, and will that God has given to accomplish His will in life.

5. "For who hath despised the day of small things?" (4:10). This question carries with it the suggestion that not all successful accomplishments have been launched with great fanfare. Some of the most useful and successful workers of God have begun in obscurity. Because they honored God, they have come to bless untold thousands. Small beginnings in one's own life are not indications of failure, but rather of heroic courage to carry on, despite the odds and the difficulties one meets.

This book has many other practical truths for our day.

Memory Verse

"In that day there shall be a fountain opened to the house of David and to the inhabitants of Jerusalem for sin and for uncleanness" (13:1).

Malachi

This name means "The Messenger of Jehovah." It carries the thought that this prophet brought a message from Jehovah to His people. He is the last of the Old Testament prophets and is thus the con-

necting link between Old Testament prophecy and New Testament fulfillment in historical reality.

TO WHOM

His message was intended for all Israel, but it also has a certain universal appeal which makes it very applicable to Christians today.

PURPOSE

The apparent purpose was to set before Israel a picture of her ingratitude in the manner in which she was living as a nation. One can see that Malachi desired to produce repentance in the heart-life of Israel and a return to true righteousness.

Certain portions of the message having reference to the priesthood and the tithes of the people could apply to the ministry and the church of our times. God's purposes in all His Word are to reveal Himself, to draw men to Himself, and to bless and make all men a blessing.

TIME

Scholars have long assigned to Malachi the honor of being the last Old Testament prophet. He is thought to have lived and given his message contemporaneously with Ezra and Nehemiah — around 450-420 B.C.

AUTHORSHIP

As to his origin, we know little of Malachi. He is assumed to have come from somewhere in Judah, since he prophesied around Jerusalem, where he later wrote his famous book. Of his last days and burial, tradition has left no certain word.

While some have suggested that his name may be merely symbolical and that possibly Ezra wrote the message of the book, there is no foundation for this. It is much more certain that Malachi himself penned this message.

Israel, discouraged in her weakness, had settled down in sins to which she had become wedded to await deliverance from the looked-for Messiah. Malachi assured them that He would come but that His coming would mean judgment to them.

His book sounds a strong Messianic note in its very closing portion.

One may use the following outline:

I. God's contempt for formality, 1
II. Rebuke for heathen intermarriages and carelessness, 2
III. Rebuke for unfaithfulness to God in various ways, 3
IV. The coming Day of the Lord, 4

Much of Malachi's ministry was of the nature of teaching with questions and answers. It is hardly too much to suppose that as he thundered his rebukes at the people they taunted him with questions which he in return answered just as did Jesus four centuries later.

GREAT THINGS IN MALACHI

No *outstanding stories* but a number of *great truths* claim attention here:

1. Malachi describes the ideal priest (2:5-7), who would correspond to the ideal pastor today. It should be read carefully by all young people thinking of the ministry. Every Christian worker should accept this rule of life.

2. The Messianic promise (3:1-3) reveals Christ's purpose in the lives of His followers. He wishes to refine the silver and purify the dross from life so that each one may serve Him with a pure heart and an upright life.

3. The dialogue of chapter 3:7-12 sets

forth man's financial obligations to God. Tithing — giving ten percent of one's income to the Lord's work — was practiced by Abraham (Gen. 14:18-20) and was adopted by Jacob in his famous covenant with God at Bethel as part of his religious life (Gen. 28:10-22). It was a religious custom long before Moses included it in the religious system of laws given to him by God. There are instances of ancient peoples who did not offer sacrifices, but of none that did not pay tithes.

Whatever one's feelings about the system as a Christian duty, it is the best, most equal, and most reasonable financial system ever devised for the support of God's work. And everyone who has ever whole-heartedly adopted it has been happy with it and has generally felt that God prospered him, just as He promised Malachi so long ago He would (3:10, 11). Young people will do well to accept this as the best basis of support for God's work and start practicing it, not as religious compulsion, but as a sacred honor and privilege.

4. The Old Testament opens with man in the Garden, free from sin and happy in his Creator's love, but it closes with fallen man, miserable and unhappy. It opens with man in a paradise and closes with him under a *curse* (4:6).

In this manner God would remind us that the only safe place is in His will.

Memory Verses

"Behold, I will send you Elijah the prophet before the coming of that great and dreadful day of the Lord: and he shall turn the heart of the fathers to the children, and the heart of the children to their fathers, lest I come and smite the earth with a curse" (4: 5, 6).

Between
the Testaments

BETWEEN THE TESTAMENTS

There is a gap of about four hundred years between the close of the Old Testament prophecies and the opening of New Testament times. Only brief outlines will be presented to acquaint the reader with what happened in this period with respect to the Jewish nation.

Malachi, last Old Testament prophet, seems to have been outlived by Nehemiah, the last God-appointed governor of the Jewish people. Nehemiah probably performed his last public acts as a leader around 409 B.C., soon after which he died at near seventy years of age.

About 408 B.C. the Samaritans built their famous temple on Mount Gerizim. Many Jews who would not separate from their heathen spouses and return to the pure way of the worship of Jehovah moved into Samaria. The temple there became a center of worship which was to continue for many centuries. This caused a division between the strict, orthodox Jews and the less conservative ones, resulting in a tension between them, which in time made them like two separate peoples. John refers to this in his gospel in chapter 4:9: "For the Jews have no dealings with the Samaritans." The Samaritans accepted the Pentateuch — the first five books of the Bible — but held that the rest of the Old Testament was not important to them. There are a few of the descendants of the Samaritans left in Palestine today.

At the close of Old Testament times, Judea — or the land of Palestine, for which Judea had come to stand — was a Persian province. The Persian political power lasted for about one hundred years longer, until about 330 B.C. Very little is known about Jewish history during this period. The Persian rule was mild and quite tolerant of the Jewish people.

Around the middle of the fourth century B.C. a new world power emerged. Philip of Macedon brought the Greek city-states together and began to weld them into a powerful military force. Greece had long been a cultural center among the nations of the Mediterranean. For well over a century its language and customs had made themselves felt among surrounding nations. Now with the combination of the several city-states under a powerful leader, Greece became a formidable power.

In 336 B.C., Alexander, Philip's son, took command of the Greek forces upon the death of his father. He was barely twenty years old but soon showed that his training had not been in vain. Very early he displayed skill as a military leader. In a short time his campaigns made him famous all over that part of the world. Like a meteor, Alexander's forces swept over Egypt, Syria, Assyria, Babylon, and Persia. By 331 B.C. the whole of the then-known world lay at his feet. He showed extra kindness to the Jews, spared Jerusalem, and even offered immunities to the Jews at Alexandria, Egypt.

Wherever the victorious armies of Alexander the Great went, they established Greek cities; the Greek language and Greek culture flourished. These cities became the centers of a new civilization known as *Hellenic* culture. The brilliant career of Alexander the Great came to an end in 323 B.C. when he died after a short stay at ancient Babylon, which he intended to make his capital; but the influence of his military campaigns and his establishment of Greek cities and their culture are felt in the world to this day.

After Alexander's death, his empire was carved into four parts by his four

leading generals. Palestine was first under Syrian rulers; it then passed under the Ptolemies, kings who ruled Egypt, under whom it remained until 198 B.C. About this time Antiochus the Great reconquered Palestine and it went back under Syrian rule. Palestine had enjoyed considerable freedom during the reign of the Egyptian kings, but fared less fortunately under Syrian kings. About 175-164 B.C., Antiochus Epiphanes, ruler of Syria and the bitter enemy of the Jewish people, determined to exterminate them if possible. He plundered Jerusalem in 168 B.C., defiled the Temple — even offering a hog upon the Temple altar to defile it — and erected an altar to Jupiter in the Temple area. He prohibited Temple worship, destroyed all copies of the Scriptures which could be found, and sold thousands of Jews into slavery. He punished others with every conceivable form of torture to get them to renounce their religion. This led to the Maccabean Revolt, which became known as one of the most heroic feats in history.

THE PERIOD OF INDEPENDENCE

The period from 167-63 B.C. has been called the Period of Independence, or sometimes the Maccabean Period.

The Maccabean Revolt was led by five warlike brothers and their father who became disgusted with Antiochus Epiphanes and his atrocious deeds. The father soon perished in the fighting, whereupon his son Judas took over the leadership.

←

MOUNT GERIZIM. *The Samaritans built their famous temple on this mountain about four hundred years before Christ was born. It was destroyed in 129 B.C. Jesus made reference to this mountain when conversing with the woman of Samaria. Sychar is in the foreground.*

A GREEK SOLDIER. *The Greek language and culture was spread through Greek conquests.*

Judas Maccabeus was one of the most brilliant and successful Jewish leaders. Against almost impossible odds, he won victory after victory over the Syrian forces. He wrested Jerusalem from Syrian hands, purified and re-dedicated the Temple, and restored the worship of the Lord. This great victory was celebrated by a Feast of Dedication, which has continued on the Jewish calendar for all time since.

The Maccabean leadership lasted until about 63 B.C. During this time the Jewish nation again became very strong and prospered in many ways.

THE ROMAN PERIOD

In 63 B.C. Palestine was conquered by the Romans under Pompey. Antipater, an Idumean and a descendant of Esau, was appointed governor of Judea. He was followed by his son Herod the Great, who ruled the country from about 37-4 B.C.

To secure the favor of the Jews, Herod rebuilt the Temple at Jerusalem in magnificent splendor, but he was a heartless, brutal ruler. He is best known in the New Testament as the king who was ruling when Jesus was born, he who ordered the slaying of all the babies around Bethlehem (Matt. 2:1-23). This presents a fair picture of his cruelty.

Possibly it should be stated here that due to a mistake in calculations when the calendar of the Christian era was formed, the date of the birth of Christ was missed by four years. It was set four years *in advance* of the actual time it occurred. This error was not discovered in the Gregorian calendar for many years. To have changed it would have been an almost impossible task. So scholars decided simply to refer to the birth of Christ as occurring in 4 B.C. To say Christ was born four years Before Christ (as B.C. means) sounds quite ridiculous, but it is the simplest way out of a rather serious historical mistake. This should always be kept in mind when dealing with the dates of this period.

OTHER THINGS OF INTEREST

During this period from Malachi to Christ, several other things of considerable interest to the Bible student took place.

Formation of the Old Testament canon. We have seen that the word "canon" means a measuring stick or rod, a standard by which a thing is measured or judged. Applied to the Old Testament, this simply means the selection of all the sacred writings of that period which gave evidence of meeting a certain standard. This standard was that of *divine inspiration*. Books which gave evidence of their divine inspiration to those who were responsible for their selection were included in the complete list of such books. The writings which did not give

such evidence were left out of this list. Books from the Pentateuch onward which gave evidence of inspiration by God were kept by the people and held as sacred. They may have been kept in the Tabernacle, and later, in the Temple.

Copies were made for the people as needs arose. During the Babylonian captivity these sacred books were preserved by the people. After the return from captivity, it is most likely that Ezra, the great scribe and man of God, gathered these books together in one collection. It may be too much to say that Ezra decided this canon and so listed the books in it. Rather, he collected the books which through the centuries of Old Testament times had always been received by the people as God's inspired Word to His people, and he placed them in a collection which was accepted as the Word of God.

This collection never seems to have been questioned by the ancient Jews, nor by the Lord Jesus Himself, nor any of His apostles. From it they all quote freely, as from the Word of God.

The thirty-nine books of the Old Testament compose this sacred canon. Another evidence that this is the whole of the canon is the fact that in the New Testament there are no quotations from any *other books* — with the exception of a possible single one in Jude, which some believe may have been from the Apocryphal book of Enoch (Jude 14, 15). This passage could refer to a prophecy of Noah, never before recorded until Jude by divine inspiration listed it. Christians in general have received these thirty-nine books as the complete revelation of God in Old Testament times.

The Apocryphal Books. During this period various writers produced four-

Courtesy, Trans World Airlines

teen other books which have claimed in varying degrees to have been inspired. Written by Jews, they have some historical value, but they were never accepted by the devout Jews themselves as being inspired by God, or as part of their sacred Scriptures.

The authorship of most of these books is uncertain and in many instances they have inconsistencies and inaccurate statements. They lack that pure, sublime atmosphere which marks all the other books of the Old Testament; they do not have the same high sense of spiritual mission in them as do the others.

These books were never recognized by the early church leaders as inspired, though at times they may have been quoted from by some. They were unfortunately included in an early Latin version or translation of the Bible (second century A.D.) and were carried over from this into the Latin Vulgate Version. This was because the translation was made, *not* from the Old Testament Hebrew Bible, but from the Greek Septuagint Version, to which these Apocryphal books had been added. They were

THE APPIAN WAY. *The roads built by the Romans helped to spread the Gospel throughout the world. The Appian Way was built in 312 B.C. and is still in existence today. The total length of this "Queen of Roads" was more than 350 miles. It was the chief highway from Rome to Greece and the East.*

thus accepted by certain parts of the church until the Reformation. The Protestant church leaders, following the true Old Testament Hebrew manuscripts, did not include them in their translations of the Bible. On the contrary, Roman Catholics, at the Council of Trent, A.D. 1546, included them as part of the Scriptures, and they are now included in the Catholic version of the Bible, the Douay Version.

The Septuagint Version. Outside of the formation of the canon, possibly the other greatest accomplishment of the Old Testament period from Malachi to Christ was the production of the Septuagint Version. This translation of the Old Testament Hebrew Scriptures into Greek was made at Alexandria, Egypt. Tradition says this translation was made at the request of Ptolemy Philadelphus about 285-247 B.C.

It is said that seventy learned Jews who were well versed in linguistics, knowing both Hebrew and Greek well, were brought from Jerusalem. They first translated the Pentateuch into Greek, then followed with the whole of the Old Testament. It was called the "Septuagint," referring to the seventy scholars who undertook the work. As Greek was the common language of the world at this time, it became the Bible of the common people. Apparently Jesus, as well as His apostles, used it, setting approval upon it as a translation of God's Word for the common people.

Probably no other source was responsible for such a widespread knowledge of the Old Testament Scriptures and Jewish history in general as this version of the Bible. It was read far and wide across the civilized lands where Greek culture had spread. Jewish synagogues sprang up wherever the Jewish people went, and there the Word of God was also made known. In this manner the knowledge of God was spread widely in the world, thus preparing for the coming of the Savior.

Greek Culture and Roman Roads. These two factors brought the ancient world much closer together than it was in the days of the Persian Empire, for example. The Greek city-states were evolving slowly from about 1,000 B.C. David wrote his Psalms in Palestine about the time Homer, the blind Greek poet, sang his famous poems around the ancient city of Troy. The Hellenic States arose about 775-500 B.C. and became famous for their democratic way of life. Following the Persian Wars, 501-331 B.C., the Greek war machine set out on its march to world victory, scattering Greek culture and language as it went.

Outside the influence of the Bible and Christianity, possibly no other influence has been so powerful or so lasting in the world as that of the Greek culture and language. Greek thought of such persons as Socrates, Plato, Aristotle, and others has molded civilization's thinking for more than twenty centuries. It was said in Roman times that the Romans subdued the Greeks politically, but that Greece conquered Rome, intellectually. Often the Greek slave in the Roman household was intellectually the Roman's master.

With the rise of the Roman empire there came an era of road building such as the world had never witnessed. The Persians had done something in this direction and the Greeks had developed "trails" where they went. But it was left for Rome to promote road building in a substantial way. Rome also developed world waterways and made great ships for such voyages as were necessary to conquer trade. She found the remotest parts of the then-known world and pressed her land emissaries and sea-going ships into them.

All these things were a marvelous help in preparing the way for the spread of the Christian religion. A universal mode of expression in the Greek language was now accompanied by roads and waterways to the ends of the earth — both means of communication by which the Christian missionaries could carry their world-wide message of salvation to all men. It might well be said that God was using the nations of those times to prepare the way for the spread of the Gospel. It was certainly no accident that these things came just before the "fulness of time" (Gal. 4:4) for Christ's coming.

THE NEW TESTAMENT

THE NEW TESTAMENT

The same general pattern will be followed in introducing the books of the New Testament as was followed in the Old Testament. Historical matters regarding these books will not be as involved as those of the Old Testament books, but they will be given proper consideration just the same.

The *great stories* and parables of the four gospels and Acts and the *great truths* they teach will be treated similarly. With the epistles, however, a somewhat different approach will be necessary, since there are really no *great stories* in these. Wherever there are stories behind the exhortations, these will be listed. *Great truths* will be listed in brief fashion as part of the work.

Please note the following items of general interest, which are very important to everyone who hopes to understand the New Testament. These should be learned well, for they will be appearing many times in the New Testament:

1. The term *New Testament* is much more meaningful than first appears. The word testament is not used now as it once was and so is not well understood. It actually means a *covenant* or a *legal document* in which two or more people make certain *promises* to each other, usually bound with an oath which they take to keep these promises. The Old Testament, then, represents God's *covenant* or promises to His people. It was "sealed" or attested to by sprinkling the "blood" of animals used in the sacrifices over the copy of the first five books (Pentateuch) when Moses had completed them. This symbol was extended to the whole Old Testament, although

the later books were not sprinkled with blood. In this manner God revealed to ancient Israel that He would keep His promises to them as surely as the old law had been sprinkled with sacrificial blood.

The New Testament represents God's new *covenant* with man. Jesus introduced this at His last supper with His disciples. "This is my blood of the new testament, which is shed for many for the remission of sins" (Matt. 26:28), He told them, speaking of His own blood which was to be shed on the cross. Christ intended this Lord's Supper to be a testimonial to His redemptive work, and so it is now each time it is observed (I Cor. 11:20-34).

The New Testament, or the new covenant of God through Christ with man, was His promise of salvation for all who believe, His work of redemption at the cross and in the resurrection. However, the New Testament, as we think of it, embraces also all those parts of it which relate in any way to matters of salvation, embracing the whole twenty-seven books of it. This is why it is called the New Testament.

Just as the Old Testament was sealed by blood, so is the New Testament, not by sprinkling Christ's blood upon the book, but by His blood being shed to make redemption possible. Without shedding of blood there is no remission of man's sins (Heb. 9:22). We are saved by the "precious blood of Christ" (I Peter 1:19), the "blood of the covenant" which Christ made with man (Heb. 10:29; 13:20), and so the church was "purchased with his blood" (Acts 20:28). It is said of Christ that we "have redemption through his blood" (Eph. 1:7; Col. 1:14).

When thinking of the New Testament,

always remember that it is God's new covenant with man, made through Christ, by which He guarantees to save all men who come to and fully trust in Jesus Christ.

2. The word *gospel* is also of peculiar interest as we study the New Testament. It is a new word, not found in the Old Testament. It comes to us from two sources — from the original Greek, in which the New Testament books were first written, and from the old Anglo-Saxon, the old parent English language.

The Greek word originally used meant *good news* or *glad tidings*. From it came our words "evangel," "evangelist," and the proper name, "Evangeline." These are almost *transliterations* of the original into English.

In the older English language, before our modern translations — before the King James Version was made — this word occurred as *god-spell*. Literally, it meant good mystery, doctrine, or secret, something hidden which was being brought out. The mystery of redemption which had been hidden, was now being brought out for all men to know about; it made known to men the good news of God's provisions for His creatures.

The four gospels have been called the four most important books ever written. They tell in simple, yet sublime language the most wonderful story ever told — the life, work, death, and resurrection of Jesus Christ.

"Why *four* gospels? Would not one have been sufficient?" it is asked. Yes, one could have been sufficient, but God seemed to present this story in a little wider range. Evidently many attempts were made by uninspired men to write a gospel or life of Christ (Luke 1:1), but only four were chosen by the Lord to render the account.

In those days the literary world was fast coming alive with great writers. Such men as Cicero, Virgil, Horace, Seneca, Livy, Plutarch, and Pliny were filling the minds of men with their writings. The times demanded that the life and works of Christ be given to the world in book form. The Holy Spirit directed these men to write the story of Christ in their own inimitable way, yet so guided by the Spirit as to be without error. They present us with four different views of Christ, all true views of His person, His life, and His redemptive works.

The gospels are followed by a historical statement of how the church began — Acts — and the various epistles, giving doctrinal and practical guidance for the Christians of all time to come and showing the operation of the church, its mission, and its work.

3. The New Testament may be divided into four sections: the gospels and Acts, the Pauline epistles, the general

SYMBOLS OF HOLY COMMUNION. *The grapes and chalice portray one of the elements, and the wheat the other. Jesus used bread to represent his body and wine to represent his blood.*

epistles, and the Revelation. These divisions will be followed in introducing the New Testament.

This brings us to some important groups of people of which a word should be said:

4. *The scribes,* often referred to in the gospels, were copyists of the Old Testament Scriptures, a calling of very early origin in Old Testament times, which gave them high esteem. They were to study and interpret the Scriptures as well as copy them. They were sometimes called "lawyers" because of their acquaintance with the law and the prophets. Sometimes decisions of great scribes, such as Ezra, had become a sort of oral "tradition."

5. *The Pharisees* were a sect believed to have originated in the third century B.C. before the Maccabean Wars. They arose as a reactionary movement against the prevailing Greek culture, opposing the "Hellenizing" of the Jews, that is, becoming like the Greeks of the times. Their purpose was to turn the people back to God and to preserve the national integrity and a spirit of patriotism among the people. They had later developed into self-righteous, hypocritical formalists, as seen in Christ's times.

6. *The Sadducees,* arising about the same time as the Pharisees, were guided by secular interest and were favorable to adoption of the Hellenic culture. They took no part in the Maccabean struggle

for independence, preferring to drift along with the tide of the times. Although they were a priestly clique, they were avowedly irreligious, yet they were some of the "religious" officials of their nation. They were only a relatively small group, but they were wealthy and influential, and to a large extent they controlled the Sanhedrin, despite their rationalistic worldly-mindedness. They did not believe in the immortality of the human soul, nor in angels or spirits, and likely not in the existence of even Satan himself.

7. *The Herodians* were a political party in Christ's times who favored the rule of King Herod, but they were of little power or influence. Reference is made to them in the gospels, but not often.

One should become well acquainted with these various groups so that when references are made to them he will know their positions and be able to place them properly.

8. *The Sanhedrin* was the governing body of the Jewish nation in the time of Christ. It may have originated as early as the third century B.C. It dealt largely with religious matters, as may be seen from the trial and crucifixion of Christ. This power was permitted it by the ruling powers who governed Palestine from time to time.

This body of the Sanhedrin consisted of about seventy members, largely priests, with a number of Sadducean nobles, a few Pharisees, and a sprinkling of scribes and elders. The high priest presided over it. The division of this body into several groups of leaders is seen in Paul's experience with them. When he cried in their midst that he was a *Pharisee*, it so upset and divided them into bicker-ing groups that a great argument followed (Acts 23:6-10). On this occasion he took advantage of their doctrinal divisions to divert their attention from him, thereby saving his life. He formerly may have been a member of this body.

9. The New Testament opens with a political situation much like that which existed in the time of Malachi. The Jews were under a different ruling power — Rome now — but were still a vassal state, paying tribute to a foreign power and groaning under the burden of it. This is why King Herod was hated by the common people. He was a sort of half-breed Jew who had become the puppet ruler of the Romans. Herod the Great was reigning when Christ was born and was the grandfather of the Herod who was ruling at the time of Christ's crucifixion.

Among the common people there was a hunger for spiritual things, but the leaders were largely formalists who had little concern for anything spiritual as long as they held positions of honor and power. This is seen in Christ's scathing rebukes of them in Matthew 23 and elsewhere. In their spiritual blindness, they did not recognize Christ as the true Messiah and Savior sent from God. Rather, they considered Him as a crazy fanatic and rejected and crucified Him as an imposter.

The New Testament opens with a man of God challenging Israel with his message, just as Malachi had prophesied (Mal. 4:5-6). The last of the prophets and the first Gospel herald, John the Baptist, preached repentance, calling the people back to God. His voice sounded like the prophets of old, but he heralded a new and wonderful day — the coming of the Lord Jesus Christ Himself.

The Gospels

Matthew

The name of this gospel bears the name of its writer, although his name is not listed in the book. It is thought to have meant "gift of Jehovah."

TO WHOM

The writer does not state in his preface for whom this book was written. Because of its general content, its many references to the Jewish people and Jewish things, scholars believe it was written principally for the Jewish Christians. There are, however, several references in the book to Gentile circumstances and events, for instance, the visit of the Magi, or Wise Men (2:1-12). This event has been thought of as being prophetic of the Gentiles coming into the church.

The writer also lists the healing of a Gentile (8:5) and records Jesus' warning to the Jews that Gentiles will be included in His kingdom, from which Jews will by disobedience be excluded (8:11; 21:43). The Great Commission certainly includes Gentiles in the "all nations" to which it refers (28:18-20).

The book may have been written, then, primarily with the Jewish Christians in mind, but with the Gentile converts also in view. This idea may be sustained from the fact that Matthew is the most Jewish of the four gospels. Jesus is presented as the Jewish Messiah who has come to fulfill all promises to the Jews; His ancestry is traced from Abraham to David; over sixty references are made to the Old Testament, in fulfillment of which Christ had come. Matthew is the only gospel in which the "church" is mentioned by name. It possibly refers both to the universal church (16:18) and to the local congregation (18:17). This reference may also be taken to represent the double role of writing for both Jewish and Gentile Christians.

PURPOSE

Relative to the purpose of this gospel, please note the following things:

First, the writer apparently intended to establish the position of Jesus as the Messiah, the promised One of God. In an attempt to convince readers of the Messianic mission of Christ, the book abounds in references to the Old Testament.

Matthew presents Christ as the Son of David (1:1; 21:9) and therefore, the rightful "King of the Jews" (2:2; 27:37). He reports that Jesus often called Himself the "Son of Man," qualifying Himself as the Heavenly Being of the various revelations concerning Him in Old Testament prophecies; thus He also announced Himself as the Son of God (16:16), accepting the homage of the disciples at this time. As Israel's Messianic King, he said He offered Himself to the Jews, but they rejected Him.

Second, the growing church in the world was demanding an authentic *life of Christ*. This gospel was seen to be a necessity. It was necessary to explain to the masses of Jewish and Gentile converts the reasons for Christ's rejection by the Jews, to establish His true Messiahship; to state His teachings, and to give the church a divinely-inspired record of these things. The church had to face a scorning world, and they needed the background of their beliefs stated in clear, lucid form so they could present their arguments more successfully.

Third, the church was faced with the necessity of knowing what to do concerning many ethical questions regarding retaliation in persecution, taking of oaths, divorce, the treatment of offending persons within the church itself, the relation of the Christians to the ancient Jewish law and ceremonies, and other ethical matters. The followers of Christ also needed devotional guidance in worship to be able to show wherein lay the difference between this new church and the older Jewish religion. The production of the *life and works of Christ,* with an appropriate background of His divine and human relationships to God and to man, was therefore a real necessity.

God met this pressing need by inspiring not only Matthew, but the other three writers also, to give the world the story of Jesus in the gospels. This message was to be for all time and to all men; and therefore, under divine inspiration, the Holy Spirit aided the writers to select and give from the life of Christ that which was most important to all men, their salvation and instruction in the Christian way. This, then, seems to have been the purpose of the gospels. Matthew's specific purpose may have been a bit more narrow: to provide the people of his times, especially the Jewish Christians, with these needs. Beyond doubt the ultimate purpose was a universal readership.

TIME

The exact time of the writing of Matthew's gospel is not known. It certainly was not the *first* book of the New Testament to be written, even though placed first in its present order. Nor is it known where it was written. Some think it may have been written at Antioch in Syria. It was not likely written before A.D. 50; some think it may have been as late as in the sixties A.D. A likely date for its writing would be A.D. 60.

AUTHORSHIP

The church has always credited this gospel to Matthew the publican, one of Christ's twelve apostles. No arguments to the contrary have ever been proved.

Possibly the oldest authority on Matthew's authorship comes from Papias, an early Church Father who lived around A.D. 130. He makes reference to Matthew as the author of the "sayings of Christ." This supposedly referred to Matthew's Gospel.

Some believe that Matthew first may have composed the "Discourses of Christ," such as the Sermon on the Mount (5-7), His parables, and His words in chapter 24. Then, using the discourses as the "heart" and the historical parts as the "framework," he may have written the whole story, as we now have his gospel.

Matthew would have had excellent preparation for writing his gospel. As recorded, he was an eyewitness to much of it. Peter, who had witnessed even more of Christ's life, was still living when Matthew wrote his gospel and could have furnished helpful information if needed.

In those early times much valuable literature, history, and tradition was passed along by *oral* report. People stored things in memory much better than now, for this was the main way of keeping it. Matthew would naturally have remembered many important things. He could have discussed the earlier details, such as Christ's virgin birth and the coming of the Magi, with Christ's mother, who lived for some fifteen years after the ascension of Christ.

By these facts alone one can see how much help Matthew would have had in making a correct gospel story of Christ. But beyond this, it must always be remembered that the Bible writers were *inspired* by the Holy Spirit, who helped them to record all things correctly. Jesus promised the disciples that when the Holy Spirit came He would "bring all things to your remembrance, whatsoever I have said unto you" (John 14:26).

Matthew may have first written his gospel in the Aramaic language — the popular form of the Hebrew language in Palestine in Christ's time — and later translated it into Greek, or he may have written only the discourses in Aramaic and then later composed the entire gospel in Greek. This latter supposition may have been the case, since his Greek gospel does not seem to have been a translation but an original writing.

This would be only reasonable, since his purpose was first to reach his own Jewish Christian people, then ultimately the whole world, with his message.

RUINS OF A JEWISH SYNAGOGUE. *Archaeologists agree that these ruins of a Jewish synagogue in Capernaum are from the second or third century A.D. It is possible that these ruins rest upon the remains of the synagogue in which Jesus taught.*

Matthew's gospel is not as sharp, rugged, and brief as Mark's, nor as smooth as Luke's; it is midway between in style. It is seen here that in inspiring the writers the Lord did not *dictate* to them the words but allowed their own personalities and training to play their part in their presentation of the Gospel story. They were so guided in their writing by the Holy Spirit as to present the truth without error, although many different facets of it are seen in the four separate presentations.

Matthew's gospel possibly had been placed first in the New Testament for the following reasons:

1. It is the most Jewish of the four gospels and therefore closest to the Old Testament. It perhaps draws more references from the Old Testament than any of the others. Coming fresh from reading the Old Testament, Matthew's gospel would be the most natural to read first.

2. It contains more of the teachings of Christ in His discourses than any other gospel. It therefore affords a better foundation in the principles which underlie the Christian religion and should be read first.

3. It shows more largely Christ's relation to the Jewish people than any of the others and therefore is best suited to be placed first in introducing the Christian story.

4. It declares Christ's "kingdom of heaven" teaching to the Jewish people and gives them the first opportunity to receive His Messianic message and become part of that kingdom.

Many scholars believe that Matthew's gospel was the first gospel to be written, thereby claiming first place among the others. Other scholars believe that Mark was the first gospel to be written. Among the gospels, Matthew is certainly one of

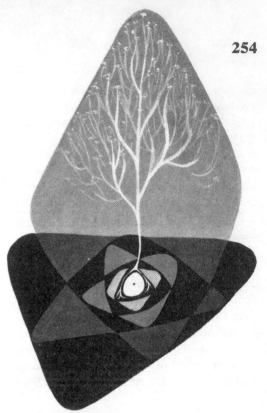

Courtesy, The National Union of Christian Schools, from HYMNS FOR YOUTH © 1966

THE MUSTARD SEED. *This symbolic portrayal of the Parable of the Mustard Seed indicates the growth of the Kingdom of Heaven.*

the most complete stories of Christ's life and work. For these reasons, those who formed the New Testament canon evidently felt it should have first place among the gospels.

There are certain things peculiar to Matthew, those not found in the other gospels. For instance, the term "kingdom of heaven" is used thirty-three times, while the phrase "kingdom of God" occurs only six times. Twelve of Jesus' parables begin with the "kingdom of heaven" reference. Jesus is referred to as a King, and His future relationship to the children of God is often spoken of in terms of the kingdom of heaven. Among the gospel writers, Matthew alone uses this expression.

Matthew also records in the various discourses the fullest account of the *ethical* teachings of Jesus.

This gospel may be divided roughly into two major sections — the historical framework and the discourses. Note carefully in the *outline* how this is done, for these are not in sequence, or straight order, but in a sort of patchwork manner. A more detailed study of Christ's life may be made by taking each major event as listed in I, and then placing the appropriate discourse listed under II, with it. Matthew has grouped them all together in his story, but the historical framework and the discourses are not at all in sequential order here, as they are in the *outline*.

A brief outline may be the following:
I.   Historical framework, 1-4; 8-12; 14-23; 26-28
II. The Discourses, or teachings, 5-7; 13; 24-25

GREAT THINGS IN MATTHEW

Outstanding stories may be listed as follows:
1. Christ's virgin conception by Mary, 1:18-25
2. The birth of Christ and the visit of the Magi, or Wise Men, 2:1-12
3. The flight to Egypt and Herod's slaying of the infants, 2:13-17
4. The coming of John the Baptist and the baptism of Jesus, 3:1-17
5. The temptation in the wilderness, 4:1-11
6. Entry of Jesus into His ministry; His calls to the disciples, 4:17-25
7. Opposition of the Pharisees, 12:1-30
8. The rich young ruler and the price of discipleship, 19:16-27
9. Christ's triumphal entry into Jerusalem, 21:1-46

10. Jewish rejection of their King, 26:1-75
11. Judas and the great betrayal, 26:14-16; 27:3-10
12. The Last Supper and the new Lord's Supper, 26:17-30
13. Gethsemane and the great agony, 26:36-46
14. Arrest, betrayal, and trial of Christ, 26:47-75
15. Crucifixion and burial, 27
16. Resurrection, appearances, and the Great Commission, 28

Since the Discourses quite largely speak for themselves, we shall be content to state some of the *great truths* pointed up by the *outstanding stories* in the life of our Lord:

1. The virgin conception of Christ — the story of how He was conceived by the power of the Holy Spirit coming upon Mary and creating in her the embryo of the body of Christ, without a human father — is a demonstration of God's power, wisdom, and love in providing redemption for mankind. It cannot be fully *explained* because it remains one of the divine mysteries of the Bible. It must be accepted by faith, without trying to reason it out. The basis for this fact of the virgin birth, however, is this: In order that Christ may be the Sinless Sacrifice for our sins and as a Savior satisfy the demands of divine justice, He had to be both human and divine, and yet, He had to be sinless. Sin is imputed to Adam and through the paternal side of the race it is legally descended to all men and women. Had Christ had a human father, His humanity would have been tainted with this original sin. It was necessary that He be born of a virgin, without a human father, that He might be a sinless human being. Since He was born of the woman, he was totally human; yet, as a

Frankincense and Myrrh Trees. *The Wisemen brought gifts of "gold, frankincense, and myrrh." The milky-white liquid from the frankincense tree (left) was used in many religious rites. The trees are native to Arabia, India, and China. The myrrh tree (right) secretes a substance which was used in a variety of ways: as an ingredient in oil for anointing, as perfume, and as an embalming ingredient. The tree grew in Arabia.*

---

virgin-born child, He was sinless. But He was also the Son of God. He had always been the Son of God from all eternity; now He also becomes the Son of Man, yet the two natures, human and divine, are so blended into one as to make Him only *one personality*. He did not become two beings — God *and* man. To say this is never correct; rather, He became the *God-man,* a divine-human Being with all the qualities of the two natures gloriously and perfectly blended into one person and being. He is, then, as theologians say, the "theanthropic" Being — the God-man. Only in this way could He become mankind's Savior.

2. The story of the birth of Christ is one of the greatest stories ever told. In this way God showed His love for mankind (John 3:16). All have sinned (Rom. 3:23), and only in Christ is there hope for salvation, for He came to "save his people from their sins" (1:21).

Some think the coming of the Magi, or Wise Men, from the East, speaks of the fact that the Gentiles, who are scattered over all the earth, were to be brought together in Christ. Christ's coming would bring all men to know about the true God, and by the spreading of His Gospel, some from all peoples of the earth would come to Christ. Today there are Christians all over the world.

3. In the flight of Joseph and Mary to Egypt with Jesus to protect Him, there may be the hint that God expects His children to use the providences of God in their care. God could have protected Christ in Palestine as well as in Egypt; but He chose this way instead. To protect and forward His work among men, God often uses ways and means that are not miraculous.

The slaying of the innocent babies by Herod illustrates to what lengths sinful man will go to carry out his selfish purposes. It also points up the fact that the innocent have always suffered because of the sinfulness of man. This seems unavoidable in the present world.

4. John the Baptist's coming shows how God fulfills His promises right on time. The last promise of the Old Testament was that God would send the prophet Elijah to turn the people back to God, just before the Messiah came (Mal. 4:5, 6). Jesus recognized this promise as being fulfilled in the ministry of John, who came in the Spirit and power of Elijah (11:7-14).

God is never late, never early; He is always on time. We may think He seems late or early, but He does things by divine accuracy, not by human time.

In the baptism of Jesus we have another fulfillment of God's law and order. Though Christ was the eternal Son of God, He kept God's laws and ordinances just as He expects us to keep them. Christ perfectly fulfilled these Old Testament demands of law and ordinances, freeing us from them. They are no part of our salvation. His keeping of these does not free us from keeping the *moral* laws of God as stated in the Ten Commandments. The ceremonial laws of the Old Testament were fulfilled in Christ, but not the *moral* laws.

Christ's strict adherence to His Father's will in obeying those laws and ordinances is an example for us. God wants His children to obey the laws of Christ, which He laid down for us, as carefully as the Savior obeyed His Father's rules for Him. Christ said, "A new commandment I give unto you, that ye love one another; as I have loved you, that ye also love one another" (John 13:34). We are to keep Christ's commands as He

kept His Father's commandments (John 15:10).

5. Christ's temptation and how He overcame it reveal His humanity. God cannot be tempted; therefore, Christ was tempted in the flesh and endured it for our sakes, that He might be a "merciful high priest" to us. For the Word says, ". . . but [he] was in all points tempted like as we are, yet without sin" (Heb. 4:15). And again, "For in that he himself hath suffered being tempted, he is able to succor them that are tempted" (Heb. 2:18).

The temptation of Jesus was a stern reality; it was not merely a play of Satan for Him which He shunted off as though it had not happened. To take this position would be to make it a farce and rob it of the spiritual force which it certainly carried in His life. It was not a light thing at all.

One encouraging thing about this temptation is that Christ used the same sources of power and help which all God's children may use. He quoted the Scriptures to Satan and rebuffed him with God's Word. Christ was also filled with the Spirit at His baptism — not as a cleansing, for He ". . . did no sin, neither was guile found in His mouth" (I Peter 2:22). This baptism of the Spirit was to strengthen His humanity and anoint Him for His work. Just as Christ in the power of the Spirit withstood Satan and used God's Word to rebuff him, so may we. God has sent His Holy Spirit into the world so that all men who believe in Christ may have this blessed comfort and strength to guide, teach, protect, and anoint them for resisting temptation and living the Christ-like life, empowering them for service to Christ.

6. Just as Christ called disciples to follow Him and work with Him in spread-

ing the Gospel, so He still calls workers today. He once told His disciples, "Pray ye therefore the Lord of the harvest, that he will send forth laborers into his harvest" (9:38). As was true in His day, so it is now: "The harvest truly is plenteous, but the laborers are few" (9:37).

Young people should keep their hearts open to the Lord's voice as He speaks to them through His Word, through His Spirit, in His providence, and through His church. If there is a call for service to Him, consider it the highest honor to accept such a call.

A *disciple* was known as a "learner." All who start to follow Jesus are learners. With Christ we are always in His schools: the schools of prayer, of obedience, of suffering, of following, and of service.

7. Christ's ministry was popularly received wherever He went in His first days of ministering. Great multitudes thronged to hear Him. His wonderful healings attracted wide attention and brought people in great numbers to seek His aid. His other miracles, such as feeding the multitudes, also lent popularity to His ministry. Even the Pharisees and other leaders in many instances attended His ministry without complaint. But as He began to press the claims of the kingdom of God and of personal righteousness upon them, the leaders became infuriated and turned against Him. Had He offered them an easy way to heaven, political freedom, and a land of plenty here and now; had He catered to their whims, and put them in the foreground of His vanguard, then all would have been well. But if it meant that *they* must change their way of life, lay down their old prejudice, suffer themselves to take a lower place, and accept His kingdom with humiliation and lowliness, this was a different story.

He had pressed home upon them His claims of the ability to forgive sins, His power over disease, and even death, and His right to their acceptance of Him as their Messiah. His claims and manifestations would have led them to accept Him as Messiah, had they not been blinded to the nature of His approach. But when His claims upon the leaders began to demand a turning from the old ways and an acceptance of His new kingdom way of life, they "balked" and refused to follow Him any further. There began to grow a sense of rejection of Him.

This came to a very rude, open case in the story told in chapter 12:22-37. Following the healing of a demon-possessed, blind, and dumb person, the Pharisees began to question by what power or authority He did His miracles. To say He did these miracles by the power of God would put them into the position of having to accept Him as God's Servant, the true Messiah. This they were not willing to do. In their spiritual blindness they had not been *willing* to accept Him. Now they were more doggedly determined not to do so because of public sentiment toward Him.

Whatever the cause, they attributed His work of casting out "devils" — literally, *demons,* from the original Greek — to the power of Beelzebub. The word *Beelzebub* was used by them to refer to Satan himself. In reality there is but one Devil or Satan; the original Greek always has the word "demons," whereas the English has the word *devils,* in the plural form. These doubtless refer to the fallen angels which fell with Lucifer when he by disobedience fell from his position as an archangel and became the Devil he is today. See Luke 10:18; Isa. 14:12-23; Ezek. 28:11-23; Rev. 12:3-11. The pas-

ROMAN THEATER IN CAESAREA. *Herod the Great built the city of Caesarea as a showplace for Roman culture. One of its attractions was this huge amphitheater.*

sages in Isaiah and Ezekiel must be understood to refer to this fall of Satan, as no earthly king could have filled the description given there.

Christ pointed out to them the terrible sin of attributing His works to Satan and warned against the "blasphemy against the Holy Ghost" (12:31-37). It is possible that with their light as leaders, they may have committed this sin and so sealed their eternal doom. If they did this, they became unforgivable and in this state would have become all the more determined to destroy Christ. This may

be the only light in which we can understand *why* they would have labored so long and hard to bring Christ to crucifixion and so remove Him from their midst.

Here is a fearful lesson of the danger of rejecting the light which God shows us regarding our spiritual needs. Sin is progressive and will lead one downward into more and more forms of disobedience. Everyone should carefully read this warning concerning the possibility of what rejecting Christ may bring a person to do.

8. The story of the rich young man who was a ruler — possibly a synagogue ruler of his community — and his coming to the Master shows that there is a *price,* as it were, to be paid for discipleship of Christ. Jesus Himself taught that men should count the cost and that there should be no turning back once one started to follow Him (Luke 9:62; 14:25-33).

This young man wanted all the *benefits* of Christ's salvation, but he did not wish to make the sacrifice of denying himself selfish pleasures. Many people would have Christ's gracious protection and offer of eternal life if they could still have their sinful ways of indulgences and selfish living. But if it is going to cut across their pathway to fame, fortune, or other selfish interests, they want nothing of it, at least for *now*. They would like to have Christ come to their rescue at the end of a life lived selfishly and for pleasure and gain, and then take them to heaven. But it is well to remember Christ's words that without willingness to bear the cross in life, one is unfit for true discipleship here or in eternal bliss hereafter.

The Christian Way is so important that Christ demands one's all to enter it. It is so revolutionary that once one enters it truly and fully, he will not desire the sinful pleasures of life. He will be fully satisfied and so taken up with this new way of life there will be no room for the old way.

9. Christ's triumphal entry into Jerusalem fulfilled an ancient prophecy (Zech. 9:9). This simple and unceremonious act was doubtless another attempt upon the Savior's part to help the Jewish people to see the fulfillment of their long-awaited prophecies. Even in the midst of this lowly portrayal of Himself as their King, who had come to redeem them, His heart throbbed with the knowledge of their rebellion and rejection of Him.

Here is a lesson that tells us that God sometimes comes to us disguised in the simplest of ways to test our willingness to obey Him. Maybe the very humble person upon whom so little depends is the one whom God would use to test our obedience. It is quite easy to be kind to someone of importance, but to show the same unselfish kindness toward a person of little concern is sometimes a different thing. And yet, we must remember that we are made in the image of God and that the "brother of low degree" has human feelings, needs of friendship, and kindly interest as well as the more important person. Christ taught this mighty lesson: "Inasmuch as ye have done it unto one of the least of these my brethren, ye have done it unto me" (25:40).

The Jewish leaders rejected this Scriptural sign of their Messiah's coming and proceeded with their plans for His destruction. They had overlooked this because their eyes were blinded by rejected light. Once a *pattern of sinning* has been set in a human life, it is so easy to follow it, but very hard to break away. Only by the mighty grace of God changing the life can one ever break away from such a pattern of sinning once it is deeply entrenched in the life.

10. In the final rejection of the Christ, when the Jews rejected their King, one sees the final culmination of sin. Even with the most soul-searching questions the Savior could ask and the urgency of Pilate that He be spared, nothing availed now. The course was set, and they intended to carry it through.

Perhaps nowhere in Scripture do we see the *savagery of sin* in such a way as in the trial of Christ and the demand for the death penalty for him. One cannot read this intensely dramatic story without feeling the shame of Christ's treatment, His innocence, the dilemma of Pilate, the seathing hatred of the leaders against Him, and the utter futility of all attempts to gain justice for Him. Yet, here was earth's most religious court; here, if anywhere under heaven, man should have had the opportunity to have justice. These were God's professed people. They had received every mercy themselves, and now they were put to the test as to whether they would show mercy or demand that even innocence itself be subjected to the mercilessness of their whim.

Here, then, is sin at its blackest, its deepest dye and most dangerous blindness. Its ignorance, too, is not absent, for the apostle Paul said years afterward that Israel's leaders had not the "wisdom of God." ". . . Had they known it, they would not have crucified the Lord of glory" (I Cor. 2:8). But ignorance is no excuse for sin; both knowledge and light had been rejected, and as a result, sin culminated in mankind's most dastardly deed — the crucifixion of Christ.

Just in this same way, each individual sinner brings himself to the darkest sins of his life. The light of God in one's conscience, the laws of the land, the Bible, and the Christian message cannot be rejected without the most serious consequences. Everyone should take heed to let the light of Christ shine into his heart and save himself from the heartaches and sorrows which sin always brings in the end.

11. The story of Judas' betrayal of Christ is another dark picture of individual rejection of Christ and the result of unchecked sin in a life. Judas started out along with the others and had every opportunity they had for making good in life. He heard the same messages of Christ, saw the same miracles, and was evidently aware of the same personal, tender care for him which the Savior manifested for all His disciples.

Judas did not make the best of his opportunities as did the others. He did not deal personally with his own needs and face up to them. Doubtless, his intentions at first had been as good as those of Peter, James, or John. But he did not carry them through. When the real test came, Judas went down because he failed to deal with the matter of personal sin as it arose in his own life.

The Old Testament prophecies had foretold that someone would betray Christ, but it was nowhere stated that *Judas* should be that one. He was under no necessity of disobedience. God could never put anyone under the necessity of disobedience and then hold him responsible for his act. Judas was an actor upon the stage of life whose actions were free and voluntary; he chose to betray Christ because he had not dealt with the matter of need in his own heart.

Is not this the picture of everyone who ever betrays the Savior? There are no circumstances which we can blame, no conditions we may lay the responsibility upon, and no one else whom we may charge with our disobedience and downfall. We must accept the personal responsibility for our every action.

Judas, by allowing Satan to take the rule in his life forever disgraced his name and became for all time to come the symbol of treachery and fraud.

Let every young person think seriously of the consequences of his own acts regarding his relationship to Christ. We

can never unload our responsibility to Christ upon another; we must shoulder it and face Christ and the world with the consequences.

12. Hardly had Judas gotten out of the room when Christ instituted one of the most precious of all the Christian sacraments — the Lord's Supper. This tender story shows Christ's care for His followers. It reminded the disciples of the Passover long ago in Egypt, when the blood of the lamb placed over the door of the home saved all the firstborn of the Israelites. It was right after they had celebrated this last Passover that Christ introduced the new Lord's Supper.

The simple elements of bread and wine were introduced as the symbols of His broken body and shed blood which was shed for the redemption of man. It was His last meal with them before Calvary. Wherever Christianity goes, this simple ceremony also goes as the constant reminder to worshipers of Christ's death for them. (See I Cor. 11:23-34 for Paul's explanation of the Lord's Supper.)

13. Christ's prayer in Gethsemane was the greatest prayer battle ever waged. It was no ordinary prayer. Here Christ fought alone the battle of the ages. His most trusted friends were a stone's throw away, but asleep! His soul went to the bitterest depths of agony to which a soul can go. So great was His mental anguish that ". . . his sweat was as it were great drops of blood falling down to the ground" (Luke 22:44). Never did anyone suffer such anguish of soul and spirit as He, as He carried the load of the world's sin that night!

No one else will ever carry so great a burden nor endure such anguish in prayer as He did. There are times, however, when the true Christian may know great burden and anguish of soul in prayer. This has been true across the centuries. Sometimes when one is dealing with God in prayer about the needs of his own personal soul, there may be anguish of spirit. Or, when he prays for the salvation of relatives or loved ones, such anguish may accompany prayer. During supreme crises in life, when great decisions which affect one for a life time are being made, or when one is praying for the successful carrying out of God's work, anguish and burden of soul may be present.

Such times are in keeping with normal Christian life. It is then that one is partaking of Christ's "sufferings." Christians should welcome the burden of prayer for Christ's cause just as He did for man's salvation.

14. The sufferings of Christ which surround Calvary reveal that His sufferings were unavoidable if men were to be saved. We have salvation through His sufferings, through His shed blood, and through His resurrection power. Christ never once tried to evade Calvary. The Gethsemane prayer was not an attempt to *avoid* the cross, but a request for strength to *carry* it. He never once tried to prove His innocence, and even when another was compelled to carry His cross (Luke 23:26), it was others who forced him to do so, not Christ.

A good lesson seen in Christ's sufferings is that every Christian must also assume his full share of crossbearing for Christ. Jesus taught that crossbearing would be part of His way of life for His followers.

←

"THE PRINCE OF PEACE." *Sculptor Moissaye Marans took his title from Isaiah 9:6, ". . . and his name shall be called The Prince of Peace." This sculpture now stands in the Church Center of the United Nations.*

Courtesy, Moissaye Marans

Courtesy, Charles F. Pfeiffer

THE VIA DOLOROSA. *Pilgrims to Jerusalem frequently commemorate the events leading to Christ's crucifixion by walking this narrow roadway called the Via Dolorosa, the Way of Sorrows. It now leads to the Church of the Holy Sepulchre.*

Each one must bear his own cross; none may shun it, and no one may bear it for another (16:24, 25; Mark 8:34-36; Luke 9:23, 24). No one but a Christian can bear the persecutions and mockings for Christ.

Another outstanding lesson from Christ's trial and crucifixion is that Christians may not always expect to receive fair and impartial treatment from the world. Courts of justice, held by impartially minded men, are appreciated. Here one may generally receive justice. But in everyday grinds of life, rubbing shoulders with all sorts of people, one may expect to endure the annoyances of injustice, false accusations, and ridicule.

Christ's silence when wrongfully accused is a powerful lesson for His followers. In persecutions and misunderstandings, we should commit our souls to Him and follow His example, who, ". . . when he was reviled, reviled not again; when he suffered, he threatened not; but committed himself to him that judgeth righteously" (I Peter 2:23). This is admittedly a courageous stand to take, and only by God's grace can one take it. But if we follow Christ our example, there will be grace sufficient for every need.

15. The crucifixion of Christ is perhaps the best known story in the world. It has been used in many forms to illustrate suffering unjustly and vicariously. We are all acquainted with the very central truth of redemption which Calvary's story brings to us. It was Christ's death there which made atonement for mankind's sins and made human redemption possible.

Every Scripture of the Suffering Messiah in the Old Testament was fulfilled either at Calvary or in the events immediately preceding and following it. Calvary and Christ's death are central to our redemption. This the apostles proclaimed by mouth and pen all over the world. Together with the Resurrection, it is the central theme of their writings in the New Testament.

Just as there could be no resurrection until there had been the crucifixion of the Savior, so there can be no radiant Christian life until the believer has accepted Christ and had the results of Calvary applied to his life. Belief in historical Christianity may enlighten the head, but it can never warm the heart with the love of God. Only when one is "justified by faith" can he have "peace

with God through our Lord Jesus Christ"
and have the "love of God shed abroad"
in his heart (Rom. 5:1-5). It is faith in
God's finished work through Christ at
Calvary which brings men into the relationship of "peace with God."

16. The resurrection of Christ, His appearances to His disciples; the Great
Commission to go and preach this Gospel
throughout the world, and His ascension
into heaven to the right hand of God climax the "greatest story ever told." Without the Resurrection the rest of the story
would be incomplete.

The apostles placed the resurrection of
Christ at the apex of their message. It
was the crowning miracle of all miracles,
the acme of all evidence. This was
God's *confirmation* of the life, ministry,
and death of Christ as being His way to
provide salvation for mankind. The Resurrection was the final test and witness of
God to Christ's atoning work. It was the
foundation upon which the Christian
church would be built. This the New
Testament constantly affirms, and even
more so as it develops the historical and
doctrinal aspects of the Gospel.

With this note Matthew closes, giving
Christ's Great Commission to go into all
the world with this message of Christ.
Matthew has been called "the greatest
book ever written," and is possibly one
of the most widely read of all the New
Testament books.

Memory Verses

*"Come unto me all ye that labor and are
heavy laden, and I will give you rest"* (11:
28).

*"Go ye therefore, and teach all nations,
baptizing them in the name of the Father,
and of the Son, and of the Holy Ghost:
Teaching them to observe all things, whatsoever I have commanded you: and lo, I
am with you alway, even unto the end of
the world"* (28:19, 20).

Mark

This gospel bears the name of its author
as part of its title. The name Mark is
supposed to have been derived from the
Latin "Marcus," which means "hammer"
— a strong hammer, able to crush the
flinty rock. It is thought by some that
this was quite fitting for Mark, as he is
supposed to have been a very forceful,
impulsive, and direct speaker and writer
like Peter his "father in Christ." The
complete John Mark represents his full
connection with both the Jewish people
and the Gentile world. John was his
original Hebrew name and Mark his sur-
name.

As his history progresses in Acts and
the epistles, the name John gradually dis-
appears and Mark takes its place. This
may have been due to Mark's ministry
more and more in the Gentile sections
of the church.

TO WHOM

It is generally thought that Mark wrote
more largely for Gentile Christians, particularly the *Romans*. One tradition says
his gospel was written at Rome, for the
Roman church, which was composed of
both Jews and Gentiles, with a possible
Gentile predominance.

Several things indicate that Mark had
Gentile readers in mind when he wrote:

1. His *explanations* of things which
Jews would have naturally understood
— such as references to the River Jordan,
the fasting by John and the disciples of

the Pharisees, and the "time of figs," which every Pharisee would have known by the season — are typical references which indicate that his readers were not acquainted with Jewish customs and life and the geography of Palestine.

2. The graphic, short, and speedy way in which he presents his Gospel story would also benefit the alert and progressive Roman mind of the times. Nothing is slower or more meditative than the Jewish mind tended to be, but on the contrary, the narrative moves along with terseness and speed. The writer uses short, descriptive words and terms and keeps the story moving with rapidity. He uses such words as "straightway," "immediately," and "forthwith" over forty times, or half the times they are used in the New Testament. By contrast, Luke employs such terms only eight times.

The general tenor of his whole gospel seems to be aimed at catching the attention of the busy common reader. He makes no use of stilted theological explanations as John does; nor does he present mystic materials; but he goes straight to the heart of the story in simple fashion. Beyond doubt, he had in mind the common masses and their need of the Gospel in its most elemental form. He packs into the short limits of his gospel more of the *deeds* of our Lord and far less of His discourses; nevertheless, he gets sufficient of His teachings in to convince his readers of the sublimity of his Savior's words as well as the superiority of His life and actions.

PURPOSE

The purpose of Mark's gospel is quite evident from what has been said already. We should note, however, that he probably had in mind the need of the Gentile world for a complete, concise statement of our Lord's life and works. Probably, if tradition is correct, he intended first of all to leave for the church at Rome a copy of this gospel. There had doubtless been other attempts to make such a record, even at this early date, which had proved faulty and unsatisfactory. The oral reports of our Lord's life and ministry would, by passing through so many reporters, however sincere, in time become somewhat inaccurate. This gospel, then, would provide an official statement of Christ's ministry, words, and works, upon which the church could rely as being totally correct and fully dependable.

By the time of this writing Mark had gained stature among the apostles of our Lord. His gospel would unquestionably carry sufficient weight with the church to be accepted as an official document for future reference for all time to come.

Then, too, he probably had in mind the further necessity of providing all men outside the church a record of the life and ministry of Christ. The early followers of Christ were in deadly earnest to win all men to Him. For this purpose they preached, labored, and witnessed continually. It is certainly very probable, therefore, that Mark had in mind the outside world in his writing. For this reason he is very descriptive of events and definite about times and places. He gives very careful explanations of matters which may not have been understood by an outside person not acquainted with the church and its message. This makes his gospel all the more valuable to the world today.

TIME

Some have believed that Mark's gospel was the earliest to be written; others, however, believe that Matthew's gospel was the first. There is no reason to suppose that either Matthew or Luke would have needed to work out their gospels from Mark's original, as some believe.

There is a possibility that this gospel may have been written in the late fifties, as some maintain. It seems wise from what scholars have said, however, to accept some year around A.D. 60 as the probable date. The exact date is not of great importance as long as the genuine authorship is established.

Tradition has almost universally held that the writing occurred at Rome, but there is no historical evidence of this. The fact that there appears to be a number of "Latinisms" in the Gospel of Mark favors the tradition that it may have been composed at Rome. Some have argued for an original Latin composition, but it is generally agreed that it was originally written in Greek. This would

in no way prohibit the use of words which had distinct Latin colorings.

AUTHORSHIP

From the most ancient times the church has always accepted the second gospel as the writing of John Mark. There is little or no reference to the writer in this gospel itself. It is thought by some that reference to the young man who fled "naked" from the scene of the Lord's arrest was a reference by the writer to himself, but this is not certain (14:51, 52). Fortunately, however, the testimony

---

GALILEAN FISHERMEN. *Mark tells us that as Jesus walked by the Sea of Galilee, "he saw Simon and Andrew his brother casting a net into the sea. Fishermen still cast their nets into the sea of Galilee.*

of early Christians has very well established his identity so that there is little doubt that John Mark was its author. Papias (around A.D. 60-150) refers to this gospel as having been the work of "Mark, the disciple and interpreter of Peter."

John Mark is first seen in the New Testament in Mark 14:51, 52, if the above reference to him as the "young man" fleeing from our Lord's scene of arrest be a correct assumption. Evidently at this time he was not yet a disciple of Christ, and so does not list himself as such. He was the son of a certain woman named Mary, who was a prominent woman among the disciples and probably a lady of wealth (Acts 12:12). He traveled with Paul and Barnabas from Jerusalem to Antioch (Acts 12:25) and was with them part of the way on their first missionary journey (Acts 13:5). Under possible discouragement, he returned, leaving them at Pamphylia (v. 13). For this reason Paul objected to taking him on a second missionary tour. The contention over this was so strong that Barnabas and Paul split up their party (Acts 15:36-41), Paul taking Silas, and Barnabas choosing Mark, each going separate ways.

Several years later, however, Mark seems to have reestablished himself with the apostles. We find him with Peter at "Babylon" (I Peter 5:13), which some think refers to Rome. He is here referred to by Peter as "Marcus my son," possibly referring to his having been converted as a result of Peter's labors with him. Whatever differences there may have been between him and Paul, they were likely only matters of Mark's immaturity when he was desirous of going on the second missionary trip. These were reconciled, for during Paul's imprisonment at Rome he asks that Mark be sent to him, saying, "for he is profitable to me

for the ministry" (II Tim. 4:11). It is well known that Mark was a nephew of Barnabas, and it would be natural that he would defend Mark, despite his failure at Pamphylia (Col. 4:10). From this last reference and from Philemon 24 it will be seen that Mark was with Paul in Rome when the apostle sent greetings from him also to other brethren in Christ.

Further historical proof that Mark wrote this gospel may be seen from the fact that Eusebius, the most celebrated early church historian, reports Clement of Alexandria and Origen, early Church Fathers (around A.D. 150-220; 185-254, respectively), both connected this gospel with Mark and Peter.

While it has been accepted from the most early times as the work of Mark, there has been a difference of opinion as to whether Mark wrote the gospel entirely upon his own or whether he wrote it as Peter dictated it to him. From the earliest times it has been believed that Mark not only may have witnessed many of the occurrences of what he wrote, but that he was also influenced greatly by his relationship with the apostle Peter.

There are many marks of Peter in this gospel. It is quick in movement, impetuous, and to the point. It plays *down* the good traits in Peter and tends to magnify the less noble ones. Its descriptions are often somewhat in accord with Peter's language elsewhere, as in his Pentecost sermon or his epistles.

Whether Peter dictated it or it is entirely Mark's composition we have no way to know. It is quite sure, however, that Mark was greatly influenced by Peter's interpretation of the Gospel in his many sermons and that the gospel of Mark's recording, however he did it, has the stamp of Peter upon it.

Augustine appears to have been the

first early writer to maintain that Matthew's gospel preceded Mark's and that Mark *abridged* Matthew's gospel, producing a reduced form of it instead of an *originally* written gospel. But there is little foundation for this conjecture; it has never been given much serious consideration. The main thing to remember is that this gospel was inspired by the Holy Spirit, however its human recording may have occurred.

Mark appears to have been an evangelist working along with Peter and Paul, especially during the last days of these two great men. It is traditionally accepted that he died in Alexandria, Egypt, in the eighth year of the Roman Emperor Nero — the same Emperor who put Paul to death in Rome.

The book of Mark does not have an outstanding framework of Christ's life as do Matthew and Luke. He comes quickly to the beginning of His ministry, passing over the virgin birth and the earlier facts which the other two relate. This may be due to his Roman audience of readers, who would not be as interested in these things as would either the Hebrews or the Greeks, those for whom the other two were written. Mark has very limited reports of the discourses of Christ. However, he is exceptionally heavy on the miracles, recording eighteen of the thirty-five miracles of our Lord. Of the some seventy parables and parabolic statements, he lists but eighteen, balancing the amount of miracles recorded. The Book of Mark may be outlined in the following manner:

I. Beginning of the Gospel and preparation for Christ's ministry, 1:1-13
II. The great Galilean ministry of Christ, 1:14—7:23
III. Events from the retirement to the Triumphal Entry, 7:24—10:52
IV. Events from the Triumphal Entry to the anointing in Simon's house, 11-13
V. The Passion narrative, 14-16

GREAT THINGS IN MARK

Mark includes the following *outstanding stories*:

1. The calling of Levi, 2:13-17
2. The stilling of the storm, 4:35-41
3. Healing of a demoniac, 5:1-20
4. Healing of Jairus' daughter and the sick woman, 5:21-13
5. Feeding of the five thousand, 6:30-44
6. Honoring of the Syrophenician woman's faith, 7:24-30
7. The great confession and the teaching about the cross, 8:27-38
8. The Transfiguration, 9:1-13
9. The boy with seizures, 9:14-29
10. Teachings about divorce, 10:1-12
11. The rich young ruler, 10:17-31
12. A fig tree cursed, 11:12-14, 20-26
13. The Temple cleansed, 11:15-19
14. Caesar's tribute, 12:13-17
15. Christ anointed, 14:1-11
16. The rending of the Temple veil, 15:37, 38

Special note: Such stories as Christ's betrayal, arrest, trial, and crucifixion, as well as the Last Supper and His resurrection appearances have not been noted here. This means they have been dealt with in Matthew's gospel or will be noted in one of the two remaining gospels. Mark records particular events which seem to have select lessons for us; these have been chosen to illustrate the following *great truths* evident in Mark's gospel:

1. In the call of Levi (a Jewish man who had become a Roman tax collector and so disgraced himself in the eyes of

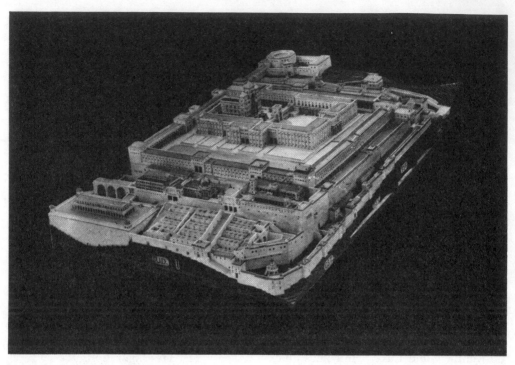

THE HERODIAN TEMPLE. *Herod recon-structed the Jewish Temple on a grand style. Work began in 20 B.C. and ended in A.D. 64, just six years before it was destroyed. This model was constructed by Conrad Shick.*

Jewish society) we see the Savior's love for and insight into the needs and use-fulness of man. Christ saw in Levi (who became Matthew, author of the first gos-pel) a wonderful worker for His king-dom. Though discredited by the Jews, he was called by Christ to accept His personal salvation, become a disciple, and later take part in the work of His kingdom.

Christ knows no racial, social, reli-gious, educational, or other boundaries. He chooses all men from all walks of life and grades of society to be saved and work for Him.

2. When the disciples were at their wit's end in the storm-tossed boat, they were alarmed to see Jesus asleep. When they awoke Him, He stilled the storm with a few calm words, and the disciples marveled. His rebuke for their unbelief must have surprised them, but they should have realized that Christ would not allow the boat to sink; He was in it and had as much at stake as they did, so why should they worry? How often we are like those disciples in life's situa-tions. We should remember that as Christians, Christ is in the situation *with us,* and He will allow nothing to happen to us outside His will.

3. The demoniac who lived untamed among the tombs may represent a per-son whose sinful life has become uncon-querable. Sometimes persons with bad habits desire to break away from them

but find they have practiced them so long that they have no power to "break" them. When this man was reached by Christ, his case was solved: his mind was healed and his body was restored. How beautiful to see him sitting at the feet of Jesus, "clothed in his right mind" (5:15).

When people come to Christ and become followers of Him, they always find themselves in a happy state of contentment. They sit at Christ's feet in adoration, clothed with humility and inward goodness, and spiritually in their right minds.

The sad sequel to this story is how the people of that country desired Jesus to leave them alone; they preferred their unharmed hogs to having their neighbors well again! This is a horrible indictment, but it is still true today. Men in certain industries which are ruinous to both man's bodies and souls, desire their wealth and prestige from such nefarious things more than the wellbeing of their fellowmen.

But note what happened to this man. He witnessed everywhere in his country "how great things Jesus had done for him" (5:20). Young people should take courage from this man's witnessing and tell what Christ has done for them everywhere they have opportunity.

4. In this gospel the first instance of a dead person raised to life is that of Jairus' daughter. As soon as she was alive, Christ ordered that she be fed. Christ's coming into anyone's heart represents a newness of life; he has been raised from being dead in "trespasses and sins" (Eph. 2:1) and should immediately begin to feed upon the Word of God and have the fellowship of God's people.

How great was the faith of that woman sick for twelve years, who wanted only to touch Christ's garment to be made whole! And her faith was rewarded by complete healing. It is not how much praying or doing of this and that which brings results. It is often the simple act of believing. Christ would in this way teach us that the power is not in *us,* but in Him; and yet, the *possibilities* of that power being manifested lies in us, for if we do not believe, there will be no results.

5. One of the great miracles of Christ was the feeding of the five thousand. It seems so simple how Christ broke the loaves and fishes and how the great crowd ate and were satisfied. But there are some other things which we should not overlook. First, someone willingly furnished the five loaves and two fishes with which the Master started (6:38-41). In each case where Jesus fed multitudes miraculously, *someone* held the key of the original amount of food. Do you suppose it is safe to say, had they refused to give to Christ all they had, in each case, the great crowds would have gone away hungry? Once it was a "little lad" who had the original food. He held the key; his unselfishness unlocked the mighty resources of the miraculous power of Christ.

Did it ever occur to you that *you* may hold the key to some most remarkable life-situation and that if *you* will give your all to Christ, He may with your gifts, talents, or even your meager sum of offering, do miracles? Every great man or woman who has been used of God in His work one day offered the Savior his "all." From this humble beginning, God made that person to grow until his ministry in some way touched the world. Could this not be said of the author of this very gospel? Had John Mark kept "running away" from the

Savior as at the scene of the arrest, this gospel would never have had Mark as its name! Every young person should think this over seriously and decide to give his *all* to Christ.

Again the disciples became Christ's helpers, for they passed the food out to the people. Christ is still today dependent upon His helpers to pass His Word along to the hungry world. He needs thousands more workers all over the world to help Him get His Word out to the millions of needy people everywhere. How about becoming a volunteer for His service?

Finally, the people had to "accept" the food to receive benefit. They could have said, "My, this food is so strangely multiplied, I fear there is something wrong with it!" Had they refused, they would have gone away hungry. We, too, must accept Christ's "bread of life" for our souls or we will go away eternally hungry.

6. Perhaps one of the most remarkable incidents of faith in Christ was that of the Syrophenician woman. Christ seemed to push her away at first, as if to try her to the limit. But she refused to be discouraged. When He told her that the children were to be fed, not the "dogs," she reminded Him that dogs ate the "crumbs" from the master's table. (Gentiles were sometimes called "dogs" by the Jews.) Then her faith was honored, her persistence commended, and her daughter healed.

Christ would teach us here a lesson of humility, of dauntless courage, and yet, of accepting our station in life with that supreme confidence in God which makes triumph out of even seeming defeat. There is no situation in life where there is not help for us from Christ, if we are but patient and humble, and yet, having faith in our prayers.

7. In Peter's great confession of the Sonship and deity of Christ, we have the heart of the Christian message. Without this there would be no truly "good news" in the Gospel story. Around this central truth every fiber of the Gospel is woven. From the story of the birth of Christ, to the miracles, the final confession of the disciples, the vicarious suffering, and miraculous resurrection of Christ, this truth of Christ being the Son of God is foremost.

Christ reminded Peter, ". . . flesh and blood hath not revealed it unto thee, but my Father which is in heaven" (Matt. 16:17). This truth is never truly taught by mankind alone. Although it is certainly taught *historically,* and all who are ever to know it more deeply must believe it historically, yet, in true reality it is only when Christ has come into the heart by faith that one knows for a certainty that He is the Savior.

Upon this confession and its eternal truth the whole Christian church is founded. It is this fundamental faith which makes Christianity alive and vigorous, a different religion from all others. All other religions point to *dead* founders and leaders. Christianity alone can point to an eternally living Founder, Lord, and Savior, with whom its followers hold personal communion through prayer and faith.

Hardly had this confession been made when the cross loomed high on the horizon. The disciples could *not* believe that such a One as Christ could ever die.

SITE OF THE TOWER OF ANTONIA. *This site in Jerusalem was the location of the Tower of Antonia, the Roman headquarters in New Testament Times.*

This shows their misunderstanding of His mission. He bore the cross for us that we may not have to bear the wrath of God.

8. Among the most thrilling stories of the gospels is the "Transfiguration." With the three faithful inner-circle disciples — Peter, James, and John — on the mountain, Christ was transfigured in glory before them. Moses and Elijah appeared there with Him, talking over the plans for His great redemptive work at Calvary. Such glory baffled the disciples, and they could not understand what was going on, but were aware of a great and wonderful blessing. Peter even desired to stay there always.

This marvelous scene was in preparation for Christ's work at the cross. All that transpired we are not told. But there is this suggestion, as to the experience itself: Christ's transfiguration allowed His inward glory of Sonship to shine forth outwardly for a little while. The word "transfigured" is from *metamorphosis,* a Greek word now used in geology. It means a complete *change* in a thing. The word occurs only in the gospels, in Romans 12:2 (in English rendered "transformed"), and in II Corinthians 3:18 (rendered "changed").

Geologists tell us that sometimes the *metamorphosis* caused by heat, pressure, or other things may so completely *change* a bedrock that its present state does not show any indication as to what it originally was. This may illustrate the fact that Christ's redemptive power, working in a man's life, can change, transfigure, transform, and so work in him that his life will be completely *changed* from the old sinful life to a new life altogether in Christ! (II Cor. 5:17).

9. The boy with seizures — some type of convulsions — who could not be cured

Courtesy, The National Union of Christian Schools, from HYMNS FOR YOUTH © 1966

NET AND FISH. *The net and fish have become symbols of the work of Christ as Fisher of Men. He also commissioned his disciples to become fishers of men. Christ also likened the kingdom of heaven to "a net that was cast into the sea, and gathered of every kind."*

by the disciples of Christ was awaiting His return from the Mount of Transfiguration. From every mountain peak of glorious communion with God, we must always return to some valley of supreme testing.

Jesus explained to the disciples that they could not heal the boy because they lacked faith. Some cases, He explained, required "prayer and fasting." In other words, some work which we are called upon to do for God demands more than human strength and wisdom. We must have divine strength and wisdom.

Let this be a lesson to us: To do God's work we must not go in the strength of mere human wisdom, but in His strength. "The arm of flesh will fail you, ye dare not trust your own" is very true. For it is ". . . not by power, nor by might, but by my Spirit, saith the Lord of hosts" (Zech. 4:6) that we are to do God's work.

10. Jesus, referring to Moses' permissive ruling, was emphatic about the rea-

son for divorce. This, Christ explained, was not God's original plan, but was permitted because of the sinfulness of the human heart. He reminded them that this was a temporary arrangement and that He was now giving them the only reason for which divorce could be granted.

Mark's quotation here (10:2-12) is very brief. A much fuller statement may be seen in Matthew's accounts (Matt. 5:31, 32; 19:3-12). Here it is explained that from the Christian standpoint "fornication" is the only reason for which the divorce may be lawfully had. One should consult a good Bible commentary for further explanations. It may be said here that "fornication" appears to be more than the mere act of adultery once committed; it perhaps refers to a *perpetual state* of illicit sexual conduct, destroying all moral foundations for the two to remain together.

Young people should *never* marry if there is any thought that perhaps the marriage may not last. Divorce should *never* be in mind in any marriage.

11. The story of the rich young ruler reminds us again that far too many people are not fully willing to give themselves and their all to the Lord. Christ will not accept a half-hearted devotion. We either go all the way with Him or go our own way — without Him. This may seem stern, but it is the only way. No one can really do his best giving loyalty to two different causes. The human heart was not made for *divided loyalties!*

12. In the story of the fig tree which Jesus cursed, He would teach His disciples of God's displeasure with religious fruitlessness. The fig tree had long been a type of the Jewish nation, which the disciples doubtless understood. Its fruit-

lessness, even in the early spring, was justifiable cause for its fatal dispatch. For while the main season of figs had not arrived, there were generally early figs on the trees of this area. His stern lesson may have been meant to teach us that fruitlessness is inexcusable, whenever it may be in evidence, even in youth!

We know this is in keeping with His teaching that the vines which did not bear were pruned away and cast into the fire (John 15:6). It was a solemn warning to His disciples, both of God's displeasure with the Jewish nation for its rejection of Christ and of His wrath which would soon fall upon the nation; they, too, must "have faith in God" (11: 22), not fruitless, but fruit-bearing (John 15:16).

Fruit has a twofold purpose: to be eaten and to reproduce its kind. Christians are likewise useful in God's work, and they should win others to Christ. Christians should possess the "fruit of the Spirit" (Gal. 5:22, 23; Rom. 14:17) and bring others to Christ.

13. Because of their sinful blindness, the Jewish leaders had allowed greed and covetousness to cause them to overcharge the worshipers in the temple for their sacrifice animals and fowls. These were necessary, and under the law; Christ did not condemn the use of the sacrifices, but He scathed them for having made the place a "den of thieves" — stealing from the people by overcharging. We are told that they required a special "temple shekel" with which to buy these sacrifices. The evil was in the fact that in order to get the temple money, they were charged a far higher rate of exchange than was lawful or right. In this way they were robbed by a form of extortion. It was this wickedness against which the Savior cried out.

Some people have condemned all selling of the Bible and Christian literature in connection with religious services of any kind because of a misunderstanding of this passage. It was not so much the sale of the sacrifice animals which the Savior condemned in the temple area, but the "money changers," with their extortion and taking advantage of others.

We must be careful not to allow one extreme for goodness to push us into a narrowness in some other extreme which would hinder the progress of God's work.

14. Christ's answer about paying tribute to Caesar was one of His most clever

Courtesy, The British Museum

COIN OF HEROD THE GREAT. *Roman coins were in common use during Jesus' day.*

replies to His critics. His enemies tried to implicate Him in a political situation which would give them leverage against Him, but His answer completely silenced and confounded them.

Christ's answer was all-inclusive and sublime: "Render to Caesar the things that are Caesar's, and to God the things that are God's" (12:17). To us this may sound trite; but those who first heard it recognized its supreme wisdom. As has been well said, Christ knew that when men had rendered to God the things which were His, there would be *little left for Caesar!*

15. Christ's anointing in Simon's house was a symbolic approach to His last mighty redemptive act at Calvary. This Christ recognized. Note the following things about this event:

a. It was accompanied by deep and reverent devotion. This little-known Mary, whoever she was, poured upon the Savior a rich token of devotion. The ointment, highly perfumed, was worth about sixty dollars in modern money. It speaks to us of a deeply felt desire to show appreciation and love for Him.

b. Total devotion to Christ is always expensive, but the returns in deep soul-satisfaction and eternal reward are far beyond its cost.

c. This became a memorial act which has been told wherever the Gospel has gone. In her unselfish act of devotion, this woman gained immortal renown (Matt. 26:13).

d. Selfless devotion to Christ is always noticed by others, and in time properly rewarded, though unexpected on the part of the one rendering it.

e. By contrast, the complaint by Judas shows his own selfishness and meanness. His "excuse" that this may have been used for the poor was a sham on his part, as John informs us. He merely wanted some more money in the treasury that he might be able to steal a little more (John 12:6).

f. Complete devotion to Christ is always met with opposition and cries of "fanaticism," "foolishness," and "over-emphasis on religion" by those who have no understanding of real Christianity. One must not be discouraged by such accusations but remain firm in his devotion.

16. The rending of the Temple veil when Christ expired on the cross was God's way of showing Israel that He had

now finished the work of the law, along with its sacrificial system. He had instituted His Son as the High Priest of salvation forever, and the old system was to be done away with. It had served its day. A new and better way was now being ushered in. Man was no longer to look to animal sacrifices for atonement but to Christ, the atoning Savior, and His finished work on Calvary.

This veil was a huge curtain which hung in the Temple before the Holy of Holies, where only the high priest went once a year for the annual sacrifice of atonement. When this veil was rent, it indicated that all men could now come to Christ freely, without the aid of any priest. Christianity is the religion with the priesthood of all believers.

The act of rending this veil also meant that there was no longer a "middle wall of partition" between the Jews and the Gentiles. In Christ all men were to be equal; all were to have the same privi-

THE SEA OF GALILEE. *This lake in the northern part of the Jordan Valley is twelve and one-half miles long and seven and one-half miles wide. It is variously known as the Sea of Galilee or Chinnereth, or Lake Tiberias. Many of the miracles of Jesus were performed on the shores of the Sea of Galilee, or on the lake itself.*

leges and relationships, without discrimination.

God would in this way teach us that all men are our racial brothers. We must have respect and love for all peoples. All peoples the world over should have the opportunities of the Gospel of Christ and its benefits.

Memory Verses

"And he said unto them, Go ye into all the world and preach the gospel to every creature. He that believeth and is baptized shall be saved; but he that believeth not shall be damned" (16:15, 16).

Luke

The third gospel bears the name of its famous author, although Luke did not place his name personally within the framework of the introduction, as did his great companion worker, Paul, in his epistles.

This gospel is the largest of them all. Some of Luke's chapters are unusually long (1, 22, and 24, for instance).

TO WHOM

In the very opening words the writer tells us that he had prepared his gospel for "the most excellent Theophilus," who may have been a special friend of his. That Theophilus was a Greek is beyond question; his name indicates this. He may have been a high Roman official who by oral means had heard the Gospel. Luke now intends to give him all the major facts of it in properly written form.

Theophilus may have been a convert to Christianity whom Luke had won and who needed full instructions about Christ. Although Theophilus *may* have been a misinformed official, whom Luke desired to set right about Gospel matters, the very atmosphere of Luke's address to him makes it more probable that he was a brother in Christ. The reference to his title, "most excellent Theophilus," certainly indicates that he held a high position of some kind.

There is also the possibility that this gentleman may have been a wealthy person who had offered to sponsor the special edition of Luke's gospel, so that it could be produced in several copies for the many churches of an area. The name Theophilus means "friend of God," and perhaps in an extraordinary sense he was a friend of God in helping the Gospel cause along.

Whoever Theophilus was, it should be kept in mind that this gospel was most likely prepared with the entire Greek world in mind.

PURPOSE

The writer not only intended to give his friend a correct account, but doubtless his intended purpose was much broader. There was the need of the written Gospel in the great areas of the Greek-speaking churches of those times. Most of them certainly needed the Gospel in their own native tongue. These churches may have had the benefit of the accounts of Matthew and Mark, but Luke must have felt impelled by a desire to give a more *detailed* account of the life and works of Christ.

He also may have had in mind a higher class of readership than was being reached by the former gospels. His treatise is certainly the acme of precision with respect to historical certainty. His preface says he had made sure of these things, doubtless doing much research to establish the historical truth of his narrative. Addressing Theophilus as an official of the Roman world would naturally give it much more prestige with many of the better educated classes. We know that already during the last days of Paul converts were already being made in Caesar's household. Christianity had reached some of the elite of Rome, and multitudes of the higher educated Greeks were doubtless within its fold in the second half of the first century.

Then, too, it would only be natural that an evangelist such as Luke would have desired to win the outside multitudes to Christ. His gospel was doubtless intended to reach and convince the unconverted among the educated as well as the more general public of the Greek world.

The pitch of his evangelistic fervor can be seen in many of his stories, such as the Prodigal Son, the Rich Young Ruler, the Pharisee's and the Publican's prayers at the Temple, and the story of the Two Thieves, one of whom turned to Christ on the Cross. His burning desire to reach the unsaved with the Gospel message may have prompted him to write much of it in terms of *how* to find salvation, as in the cases of the Prodigal Son and Zacchaeus. Perhaps, too, the warnings against turning away from it, as in the case of the wealthy farmer (12) and the rich man (16), may be part of this same plot.

TIME

It seems likely that it was not written before most of Luke's travels with Paul. It has been suggested that he may have

SHEPHERDS' FIELD. *"And there were in the same country shepherds abiding in the field, keeping watch over their flock by night" (Luke 2:8). This photo shows the "Shepherds' Field," with Bethlehem in the background.*

written it while staying with Paul at Caesarea. If so, this would correspond to about A.D. 56-58. It may be possible that it was not published until later; however, there is no certainty of this. We may suppose the date to be around A.D. 56-58. It was certainly written and published sometime before the book of Acts (Acts 1:1).

AUTHORSHIP

Almost universal and uncontradicted tradition has linked the authorship of Acts with Luke. His mention of a "former treatise" (Acts 1:1) is held by almost every scholar to refer to the Gospel of Luke. There was a well-known intimacy between Paul and Luke, as may be seen in Acts and in several of Paul's epistles. It will be noted in Acts 16:10 that he includes himself in the apostle's company, saying ". . . we endeavored to go into Macedonia. . . ." Also in Acts 20:5 and 21:18, and onward to the end of the book, the writer lists himself as with Paul.

Luke was not an eyewitness to Christ's life and teachings but was rather a second-generation Christian. He received his information from others, as he plainly tells us in the opening preface (1:1-4). There is no doubt that he was greatly influenced by Paul's ministry. Paul received much of his information from the apostles of our Lord and also by divine revelation (Gal. 1:11-24). Some ancients held the opinion that the Gospel of Luke was actually dictated by Paul and written and published by Luke. This opinion, however, has never been held widely nor with great credit in the church, but it serves to show how close these two workers were known to have been.

Eusebius, the earliest of all church historians, refers to Luke as the author of two divinely inspired books, and Jerome refers to Luke as the author of the Gospel of Luke.

Another internal evidence of Luke's authorship arises out of the Scripture reference to him as "Luke, the beloved physician" (Col. 4:14). Almost all ancient church tradition accepted this as a reference to the writer of the third gospel. Another remarkable thing about this reference is that research scholars have found in this gospel a considerable number of original Greek words — the gospel was written in Greek originally — which are definitely *medical terms*. These are technical words which none but a trained physician would have thought of using. Often these words are found in the common run of the gospel narrative, *not* just where a healing or other incident calling for them occurs. They are such words as a physician would naturally employ out of habit. This applies also to the Book of Acts, which has always been accepted as written by Luke. This small circumstance goes far to credit this gospel to Luke.

Ancient tradition assigns this gospel to Luke. There is no other authorship to which it has ever been assigned. This should be sufficient evidence of his authorship.

Just who Luke was is not fully established. Some claim him to have been a Jew and an early convert to Christianity; others, however, from his name, culture, and style of writing, believe he was a Gentile. Eusebius claimed he was a native of Antioch and a physician by profession. Those believing him to have been a Jew think this is established by Paul's reference to him along with other Jews — listing him with Epaphras and Demas, rather than the former three, who were most likely Gentiles (Col. 4:10, 11,

14). These latter were "of the circumcision" — Jews. Some believe him to have been one of the Lord's seventy disciples (Luke 10:1-20). He is the only gospel writer to mention this commission. It is thought he may have been related to Paul. In keeping with this opinion, a number of ancient and very learned men thought he may have been one of the two disciples who met Christ after the resurrection on the Emmaus way (24:13-35). One of these is named Cleopas; the other is unnamed, which, if Luke, he modestly omits naming himself in his account of it.

If this opinion is true, then Luke would have been an eye-witness of much that he wrote; but, of course, not of the earlier events of the birth of Christ and His early years. Further, this position may be buttressed by Luke's reference in chapter 1:3 to ". . . having had perfect understanding of all things *from the very first.* . . ."

His being a native of Antioch would not necessarily pose a problem, as he was not "one of the twelve apostles." He could very easily have been a well-trained physician in his early days, have been visiting in Palestine as a Jewish person, and have become so interested in Christ as to become one of His numerous disciples. His Greek education was no exception, for many Jews of that age were completely Hellenized as far as education and culture were concerned.

Whatever his native home or race, the most important thing was his relation to Christ as His Savior. In this capacity he early desired to be of service to Him and found the richest rewards and immortal fame in his association with Paul and others of his company, as well as the early church leaders in general.

He was a close companion of Paul. He is called the "beloved physician,"

probably often attending Paul as his personal physician (Col. 4:14). He is listed by Paul as his fellow-laborer (Philemon 24). He accompanied Paul on various occasions as may be seen from Acts 16: 8-40; 20; 27; and 28 by his use of the "we" and "us." He was with him during much of his imprisonment at Rome. (Acts 28; also II Tim. 4:11, which appears to be the last apostolic mention of Luke.)

There is a tradition that after Paul's martyrdom at Rome Luke went into Italy and Macedonia and preached there, finally meeting with martyrdom in Greece. But this is not historically certain.

Regarding chronology, or the time sequence, there are several differences in the Gospels of Matthew and Luke. It was once thought that Luke may have borrowed much from Matthew's gospel, since Luke's was later and he admits much research (1:1-4). This, however, is not likely. He certainly was aware of Matthew's gospel and doubtless had read it, but Luke's is an original story, written under the inspiration of the Holy Spirit.

Matthew's account is quite well timed in historical sequence, listing things more or less as they occurred. On the contrary, Luke is interested more in *classification* of things than in their continuous sequence. He seems to want an orderly classification of materials, so he groups things in this way. This may be seen in the *outline,* where five distinct classifications are listed.

This plan of classification of materials for public presentation seems to have been followed by some ancient historians. Luke wants to present a convincing *total picture* of Christ, rather than a more sequentially connected story of Him. He was writing for the more logically trained Greek mind, rather than the more com-

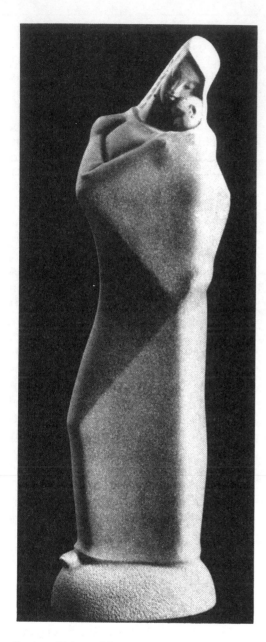

Courtesy, Moissaye Marans

MADONNA AND CHILD. *Mary and the Baby Jesus have been the subjects of artists throughout the centuries. This contemporary sculpture was executed by Moissaye Marans.*

mon mind of the average Roman or the religious mind of the Jew, which Mark and Matthew sought to impress. For this reason he follows the classification plan in presenting his gospel.

Luke's gospel may be outlined as follows:

I. The events surrounding Christ's birth, 1:1—2:40
II. Christ's infancy and youthful days, 2:41-52
III. Introduction to the genealogy of Christ, 3
IV. Total Galilean ministry of Christ; work and miracles, 4:1—9:50
V. Christ's remaining ministry and redemptive work, 9:51—24:53

GREAT THINGS IN LUKE

The following may be considered the *outstanding stories* in Luke:

1. Zacharias' loss of speech, 1:5-25
2. Jesus in the temple, 2:39-52
3. Jesus and a sinful woman, 7:36-60
4. The story of the seventy, 10:1-24
5. The Good Samaritan, 10:25-37
6. Sitting at the feet of Jesus, 10:38-42
7. A rich man's foolish choice, 12:13-21
8. The story of the Prodigal Son, 15:11-32
9. The rich man and Lazarus, 16:19-31
10. The healing of the ten lepers, 17:11-19
11. The widow and the unjust judge, 18:1-8
12. The Pharisee and the Publican, 18:9-14
13. Christ and Zacchaeus, 19:1-10
14. Peter and his sad denial, 22:31-34, 54-62

15. The salvation of a penitent thief, 23:39-43

16. Heart-burn on the Emmaus road, 24:13-35

17. The last promise, 24:49

Luke contains many *great truths*:

1. While Zacharias was serving his course as priest and was in the Temple burning incense, as his duties required, the angel Gabriel appeared to him and announced that he and his wife Elizabeth would have a son who would introduce the coming Messiah. Zacharias could not believe this to be possible, as they were both old; he requested a sign. The angel told him he would be unable to speak until the son was born.

When the son was born, relatives wanted to give him a family name, but his mother insisted on "John," the name which Gabriel had told Zacharias to call him. When they asked Zacharias, he wrote, "His name is John." Immediately his tongue was loosed and he praised God. People were filled with wonder at this; they knew God had visited Israel again.

Zacharias' *doubt sealed his mouth*. How very often the doubts of professing Christians have also sealed their lips and stopped their testimony for Christ. But, if like Zacharias, one is willing to speak out in faith and obedience, his mouth will be opened again and he will find himself praising the Lord. Had Zacharias *not* written "John," in obedience to the angel's word, he may never have spoke again. Obedience brings witnessing, with joy.

2. The story of Christ lost in the Temple by His parents for three days is always interesting to youth. Jesus was so lost in His Father's house and about His Father's business, He may scarcely have been aware that the family had left for

Courtesy, Cathedral Filmstrips

MARY AND JOSEPH. *This photo from a dramatization of the presentation in the Temple show the typical dress of the day. Joseph and Mary traveled to Jerusalem with Jesus.*

ROAD FROM NAZARETH. *Nazareth is located about midway between the Sea of Galilee and the Mediterranean, in the hill country north of the Esdraelon Plain, which can be seen in this photo. Notice the road which leads to Nazareth.*

home. The parents, on the other hand, were so taken up with the kinsfolk and temporal things, they had hardly missed Him.

How easy it is to become so preoccupied with secular things — work, recreation, school, friends, job, money, etc., — that one goes on for days sometimes without the true manifestation of Christ's presence in devotions. One is often too apt to take spiritual things for granted, just as those parents did in this case.

Jesus' first recorded words are, "Wist ye not that I must be about my Father's business?" (2:29). This should be every young person's highest aim in life — to be always about the Father's business, serving Christ.

3. When a very sinful woman — possibly a prostitute — heard that Jesus was near, she wanted to see Him. She was convicted of her sin and manifested her sorrow for it by washing His feet with tears and wiping them with her hair. This act of penitence brought compassion to Christ's heart and He forgave her.

Jesus taught Simon, His host, the supreme lesson that they who are forgiven *much* also love *much,* and vice versa. No matter how great the sins of one's life, Christ can forgive them all. All He demands is repentance and faith. Some believe this woman was the Mary Magdalene of Scripture fame, who was last at the cross and first at the tomb. Others regard her as another person. She is referred to by some as a possible "prostitute," while others take the words "sinful woman," from the Greek, to mean simply, "heathen woman." Whoever and whatever she was, her story shows the love and power of Christ to lift the lowly and exalt them with forgiveness to a place in His kingdom.

4. The seventy disciples sent out by Jesus to evangelize in the cities of Israel and proclaim His kingdom represent one of the most extensive and intensive propaganda campaigns ever launched in religious work up to that time. The main purpose of this drive was to spread the good news of the kingdom of God in ". . . every city and place, whither he himself would come" (10:1). They were to heal the sick and proclaim, "The kingdom of God is come nigh unto you" (v. 9).

This evidently was done that the people should have prior knowledge of Christ's coming and be prepared to hear and receive His message when He came. "Propaganda" here does not mean evil falsehood and half-truth, as it is now so often used, but rather advanced advertising, preparing the people for the great message of salvation.

This illustrates Christ's attempt by every suitable means to win all men to Himself. In our day the church would be wise to follow this method more fully. Some of the most successful campaigns of soul-winning in modern times have followed this method of advance preparation.

5. The story of the Good Samaritan is one of the most dramatic and touching of human interest stories. Here the Savior showed just *who* every man's neighbor really is. Our neighbor may not always be the person next door. Anyone within the reach of our ability to help and minister to is our neighbor.

It is so easy to pass by the needy, as the priest and Levite did in this case.

But Christ's way is to stop, to help however one can and to show the spirit of mercy, sympathy and love to anyone in need. One should learn early in life that it does not pay to be in such a hurry that we have no time to help others. This is selfishness!

6. The story of Mary and Martha has a good lesson for us today. Jesus did not condemn Martha nor request Mary to leave her worshipful position. He merely pointed out Martha's greatest problem. She was "troubled about many things." In the original this means that she was *distracted* by the many *things dividing* her mind or *attention,* and so her spirit was thrown into *turmoil.* She was unduly upset.

Martha is not to be condemned; nor did Christ mean this, for she was then preparing the meal for Him and His disciples — a good and necessary work. Perhaps the meaning is simply, "Martha, do not go to so much trouble for us; serve a very plain meal, and let us give our attention to the things which are of more importance — the things of the kingdom of God."

How often do God's people become far more concerned with earthly things than necessary. One can lose his soul while attending to perfectly right and good things, yet neglecting the more important spiritual matters of life. This lesson we should all learn well.

7. The parable of the rich man who planned to retire with his fortune and give himself to worldly pleasures for the rest of his life illustrates several truths:

First, he did not reckon with life's uncertainties. He made no plans for the unexpected. This is folly in anyone's planning.

Second, he had no thought of *others.* There are no less than ten references to *self* in this passage and not one to anyone else. He was utterly selfish in his whole outlook on life.

Third, he made no preparations for the spiritual welfare of his life. Nothing is said about his relationship to God or His kingdom. His plans were utterly materialistic in every way.

Fourth, he did not consider God in all his plans. No reference is made to God's will or plans in all his future life. To leave God out of the plans for one's life is about as wise as to try building a house *without a foundation!*

Fifth, his judgment was terrible. It came swiftly — "This night." And it was costly — "thy soul shall be required of thee." What an awful cost to lose one's soul in the pursuit of sinful pleasures. Finally, Christ called him a "fool" — meaning one who uses no moral sense.

It is well to note that there is not *one thing* which he planned to do which was in itself sinful. His sin lay in his utter selfishness and leaving God out of his life entirely. It is another illustration of the fearfully deadening effects of a *materialistic concept* or *outlook* upon this life! "Man shall not live by bread alone," said Christ, "but by every word that proceedeth out of the mouth of God" (Matt. 4:4).

8. The story of the "Prodigal Son" is one of the most tender illustrations in the gospels of God's great compassion for the lost sinner. This wayward boy, once he discovered his terrible mistake, came penitently home to his father and was joyously received.

Every person who has gone into sin has strayed from the Father's house and needs to come back in the spirit of repentance and humility. The plight of the human race is here pictured. The one boy had sinned publicly and scandalous-

ly, while the other had remained dutifully at home. But the bad attitude of the moralist was as much in need of correction and forgiveness as that of the wayward one.

The ring on the lad's finger, sealing the father's forgiveness, and the fatted-calf dinner, showing the joy of reunion, both speak to us of God's love in forgiving and restoring the sinner and making him joyful with the peace of assurance of forgiveness.

9. The story of Lazarus and the rich man presents another of the contrasts of life. The very fact that Lazarus was near the wealthy man's home speaks of his tolerance, moral goodness, and willingness to help the poor. There were many beggars in Christ's time. One could not feed them all. There is nothing spoken against this man's life.

But beyond the line of worlds there is a terrible difference in the situations of these two persons. Lazarus resting in bliss, and the rich man in torment tell us there had been something wrong with the rich man's relationship to God in this life. *Materially* he had done well by himself but *spiritually* he had failed miserably in life. What a supreme lesson to all young people to make sure the spiritual interests of life are not sacrificed for the material!

It has been conjectured that the three rich men of Luke's gospel may be the same man in different situations of life. If so, then he is first seen coming earnest-

THE BELLS OF THE CHURCH OF THE HOLY SEPULCHRE. *This church supposedly stands on the site of the burial place of Jesus. From this vantage point one looks over the rooftops of Jerusalem to the Mount of Olives. The Dome of the Rock, a Muslim shrine, is visible in the right foreground.*

ly to Christ as a "young" man, but sadly turning away. Later he is pictured as the "rich fool," so suddenly taken away in the midst of his prosperity and finally pictured as a lost soul, forever too late to undo his sadly mistaken past. There is no evidence for this theory; it is only *conjecture*. But in these three phases of these men's lives, whether they were one or three different persons, there is the picture of the *progressiveness* of sin and its consequences.

Some believe this was an actual story from life; others, that it was only a parable. Whatever the case, it must be remembered that a parable is meant to teach a deeper truth of which it is but the shadow. This means that the sad state of affairs into which the rich man came is fully as dreadful in reality as the story makes it to be.

10. The story of the ten cleansed lepers, only *one* of which returned to give Christ thanks, illustrates one of man's greatest weaknesses — *ingratitude*. Next to *selfishness,* of which it is doubtless a part, ingratitude is one of mankind's supreme sins.

Probably *selfishness* in all its forms is man's greatest sin. There is hardly a sin known to man but what *selfishness* is at its root. This evil turned a beautiful archangel into the very Devil himself. Every form of immorality, murder, thievery, and crime has selfishness at its base.

These nine ingrates were only acting out the parts of their native characters when they went heedlessly on, enjoying their restored health without so much as returning to say a brief "thank you" to Christ for healing them.

How can one be so ungrateful? Simply by acting in keeping with his basically sinful, selfish nature. A man once plunged into the water and rescued a drowning young man, saving his life. This young man walked away from the scene and spent his entire life without ever as much as thanking the man who saved him — a modern illustration of this very thing Christ faced.

11. One morning the unjust judge must have said, "Who is that knocking on my door?"

"It's that widow, your honor, who has been coming day after day," his servant replied.

Gruffly he said, "Admit her!" Once in his office, she told her story. Though he was hard-hearted and ruthless in many respects, he granted her request so that she would not harass him by her "continual coming." He saw that this lady *meant business* and would not be politely put off in her request.

In effect, Christ said, "If this wicked judge will grant a poor widow's request because she keeps coming back, will not God hear the prayers of His saints who cry day and night to Him?" If a mere sinful man can be moved by the constant cries of another human being, how much *more* will God's great love be moved into action by the cries of His devoted children?

This story teaches one major lesson — the glorious privilege of *intercessory prayer* and God's willingness to hear and answer such prayer. One of the church's greatest needs today is for more people who will become *intercessors* in prayer. An intercessor is one who prays for another and is usually thought of as one who continues to pray despite discouragements, until his prayers are answered. Young people should decide early in life to become *intercessors*.

12. Christ illustrated the *nature* of true prayer by the story about the Pharisee and the publican. The Pharisee's

prayer was prayed mostly for his own pleasure. It consisted largely of self-congratulations, reminding God of his moral goodness and legal correctness. No mention is made of God's great mercy or of his need for forgiveness or cleansing. Nothing is said about the needs of others.

The publican, on the other hand, did not so much as lift up his head. His sense of need was overwhelming. He did not present himself as a model for future generations. He smote his breast in deep grief for his sins and prayed for mercy. He did not blame others for his plight nor defame the nearby Pharisee for his harsh and unkind remarks. His was a personal prayer filled with deep realization of need and desire for help: "God, be merciful to me a sinner."

This short prayer has in it many of the characteristics of true prayer. It is filled with humility, confession of need; it is accompanied by the spirit of contrition. It is a good sample of every sinner's prayer for forgiveness. Furthermore, all true prayer must be accompanied by humility, renunciation of any known thing displeasing to God, and willingness to obey God. It must express faith in His goodness and mercy.

13. The story of Zacchaeus' conversion to Christ is told by Luke alone. A little man, he knew he must get above the crowds to see the Savior. He was likely quite as much surprised as anyone when the Lord asked him to "come down" from the tree, but immediately he complied and joyfully received the Savior.

This is a case of sudden conversion to Christ. Some have felt that there is a necessary waiting period of serious mental reflection upon the matter of accepting Christ. It was not so with Zacchaeus. He evidently made his decision rather quickly. But there was genuine sincerity in it. That day Christ went to his home and defended him against the quibblers and hecklers. Christ said, "This day is salvation come to this house" (19:9). Evidently Zacchaeus had been brought into a saving relationship with Christ.

It is not so much how long one seeks to become a Christian that counts, but how sincere and how much in earnest he is as he comes to Christ. Paul apparently had an instant conversion (Acts 9:3-6), but it was a very successful one. Others likewise have experienced very sudden changes in their lives in turning to Christ. Some have attended the preaching of the Gospel with no thought of becoming Christians, but before the service was finished they had found the Savior and remained steadfast Christians for life.

14. One of the most touching stories of the gospels is Peter's denial of Christ and his bitter tears soon afterward. Possibly Christ had no more sincere, determined, whole-hearted follower than Peter. Peter made his blunders, his zeal often going beyond his knowledge, but he had a heart of gold. His determination to follow Christ to death was sincere; but he found himself lacking in grace and courage to go through with it when facing the possibility of death.

There have been many followers of Christ whose weaknesses have been their worst enemies. Christ knew Peter's weakness as well as his strength. He warned him that Satan had desired to sift him as wheat, but He encouraged him by pointing out that when he came back again, after his sad denial, he could then "strengthen the brethren." It may have been this word of encouragement which Peter needed most in his dark and bitter hour of regret after denying Christ.

Despite his temporary backsliding, Peter came back to Christ and became one of the greatest of the apostles. It was a time of great rejoicing for Peter when Christ accepted him back on the shore of Galilee and gave him the commission of his life's work. Read the story about it (John 21:1-19).

The story of Peter's failure shows how a great man failed sadly, but by God's grace was restored and did a mighty work for God. It should be an encouragement to everyone who has not been successful in his first attempt to serve the Lord. Just as Christ restored Peter and then used him for a great work, so God will restore and use those who will come back to Him with sorrowing hearts as Peter did, even though they have failed at first.

THE LITHOSTROTOS. *This pavement of the Court of Antonia, known as the Lithostrotos, may have been the place of Pilate's judgment. The huge paving stones are of the Herodian era.*

15. The thief on the cross who turned to Christ in repentance and found salvation at the last hour of his life shows the greatness of God's mercy. Sometimes those who are not willing to be Christians use this to bolster their hopes of a late conversion. But this is very risky business. It is trusting too much upon living longer than one may and of having time at last to repent. One may die suddenly, without an opportunity to pray.

The thief accepted what was perhaps his *first* opportunity to see Christ and be saved, whereas those who put off salvation may become hardened by sin and *never* repent and be saved. He accepted his first opportunity, while those who love their sins and wish to continue in their evil ways have turned down many chances to be saved.

God's time is not later, but *now*. "Come now, and let us reason together" (Isa. 1:18), He says. "Behold, now is the accepted time; behold, now is the day of salvation" (II Cor. 6:2). God never tells

anyone to put off salvation until later. He always says, "*Come now, and be saved.*"

Christ is willing to save all who will come to Him, under whatever circumstances they may come. But those who turn Him away from their hearts in life when all is well may find it very hard to pray and find His grace in an hour of extreme pain or suffering, or when senses are dulled by powerful medicine, as many are at the closing hours of life. The only sensible thing to do is to attend to one's personal salvation now, in youth, while you have everything in your favor. God needs your *life* in His service here, not just your soul in heaven after you have *wasted your life* serving the devil! This is the way to avoid the sorrow and heartache of possible failure at last.

16. The disciples on the way to Emmaus did not recognize Christ until they asked the blessing before the meal. When He vanished from them, they returned to Jerusalem at once to tell their story.

"Did not our hearts burn within us while he talked with us by the way . . .?" (24:32). What blessed heart-burn this was! Their quickened memories recalled His explanations of Old Testament Scriptures about Himself. They could hardly go fast enough to get this message back to their brethren.

Christ desires to walk and talk with His followers in the various ways of life. Life can become a most beautiful and glorious thing when Christ walks with us, imparting blessing and meaning to it.

17. In the parting words of Jesus to the disciples, recorded by Luke, a most gracious promise is coupled with an exhortation. The disciples were to go to Jerusalem and await the fulfillment of the promise of the coming of the Holy Spirit.

This exhortation to "tarry" for the

CARVINGS ON THE LITHOSTROTOS. *The "king's game," played with dice, occupied the time of the Roman soldiers stationed in the Antonia.*

Holy Spirit's coming was *never repeated* in the New Testament. This exhortation was in keeping with the Old Testament prophecy of Joel (Joel 2:28, 29). Whether Christ told them that this outpouring would come at Pentecost is not known. It is certain that the disciples recognized this great feast of the Jews as a time when God might manifest Himself in some new way; but how they may not have known. They were told to tarry until this fullness of the Spirit came to them. It may have been left this way to test their faith and obedience.

Christ was seen of "above five hundred brethren" (I Cor. 15:6) during His days on earth before His ascension. But there were only 120 who were present when the Holy Spirit came to them at Pentecost! Where were the other 380? Did they not know of this exhortation? Was it not given in connection with His ascension? Had they so soon forgotten?

The Holy Spirit is now in the world administering the things of God and Christ to the believer. None now need to *tarry* for His incoming. Simply open up the heart and let Him come in. He longs to come in fullness and make Christ more fully known to every believing heart.

The church's greatest need today is for the fullness of the Holy Spirit in the lives and work of Christ's followers. None who read the New Testament carefully can doubt this. Young people should open their hearts to Him and give their lives in service to Christ.

The church needs a host of Spirit-filled laymen who will serve Christ and exalt Him in their daily lives as well as offer service to His cause in the church.

Luke's gospel, written in beautiful, smooth-flowing style, with its touches of the writer's cultural background, has been called "the most beautiful book ever written." It is the *longest* book in the New Testament.

Memory Verses

"For the Son of man is come to seek and to save that which was lost" (19:10).

"And behold, I send the promise of my Father upon you: but tarry ye in the city of Jerusalem, until ye be endued with power from on high" (24:49).

John

The fourth gospel carries the name of its author, John, one of the two apostles whom Jesus called "sons of thunder" (Mark 3:17). He is often referred to as "John the beloved," whom one thinks of as quiet and even tempered, but as the young man pictured in the gospels, he was a far cry from this.

TO WHOM

Since early times it has been believed that John wrote his gospel primarily for Christians in general. The very nature of his gospel, so very different from the other three, seems to suggest this. It has been called the "spiritual gospel" because of its emphasis upon the spiritual nature of Christ's work and mission, and upon His eternal Sonship. John, more than any other of the gospels, presents Christ as the Son of God.

It is apparent that Matthew wrote largely for the Jews, presenting Christ

Courtesy, George A. Turner

as the Messiah-King; Mark, for the Romans, presenting Him as the Conquering Servant; Luke, for the Greeks, picturing Him as the Son of man, the Perfect man, to capture the Greek mind. John supremely presents Christ as the Son of God and Savior, to be glorified by all Christians, Jewish and Gentile, universally. For this purpose he chose the universal language of his times — Greek — in which to present his work.

PURPOSE

The purpose of John, then, must have been rather extensive, since his gospel was the last to be written and he undertook to express so much in it.

First, John endeavored to give the young church a comprehensive view of the life and work of Christ relative to His ministry and redemptive mission. In this light he endeavors to convince his readers at once of Christ as the eter-

THE GOLDEN GATE. *This view of the Golden Gate is from inside the Old City section of Jerusalem.*

nal Son of God. This thought is paramount in his whole gospel.

John's gospel opens with a description of Christ with the Father in eternity, before creation. He shows Christ to be the eternal Son of God and deals with His birth merely by saying that the "Word was made flesh, and dwelt among us, (and we beheld his glory, the glory as of the only begotten of the Father,) full of grace and truth" (1:14). He does not deal with the details of the human birth of Jesus, since Matthew and Luke had done this. John shows the correct relationship of God and Christ as Father and Son, and also His relationship to man, as the Son of man. This he does largely by his explanation of the divine relationships in eternity before time and

THE MOUNT OF OLIVES. *The Church of All Nations now stands on the slopes of the Mount of Olives.*

by Christ's revelation of God to man. He traces the evidences of this relationship throughout the gospel, climaxing with the appeal for faith in this statement: "These things are written, that ye might believe that Jesus is the Christ, the Son of God; and that believing ye might have life through his name" (20: 31). In chapter 21 he seems to add the last words of convincing proof of what he has just said.

Second, he wrote to reach both the Jews and the Gentiles in the church, as well as the unconverted in both fields.

It will be noticed that he has included many things which would appeal to the Jews, to convince them of the truth of his argument. The stories of the wedding in Cana, of Nicodemus' visit to Christ, of His burial by a wealthy Jew (Joseph, also a believer), and of the appearance to the disciples bear this out. His reference to the Greeks who came to seek Christ (12:20-23) was probably intended to show their interest in Him, even during His ministry. Perhaps his most universal appeal is the listing of Christ's own words to Nicodemus. It seems easy to forget that Christ was still talking to Nicodemus when He spoke these sublime and universal words: "*For God so loved the world, that he gave his only begotten Son, that whosoever believeth in him should not perish, but have everlasting life*" (3:16). What more universal appeal could there ever be made than this? Just below this John added: "For God sent not his Son into the world to condemn the world; but that the world through him might be saved" (3:17).

John strove to make his gospel appeal to all men everywhere and for all time to come. The universality of his appeal has never been doubted by any serious minded person.

Third, it is possible that John also had another purpose in mind when he wrote. He was last of all the apostles to write any part of the New Testament; therefore, his words were the final words. All the other apostles of our Lord were dead a considerable time before John passed on. He may have wished to place upon the sacred records the finishing note of the deity of Christ and His saving mission among men.

As John lived until about the close of the first century, he also witnessed another new phase of the youthful Christian church. He saw it somewhat leave its apostolic age and merge into its new position as a world organization. Along with this came another change which grieved him. This may be noted in his message to the churches in the Revelation, where the lukewarmness of the church is deplored by Christ in His rebuke to the churches.

Along with this newer generation of Christians there arose certain "heresies" which had to be combatted. "Heresy" is any teaching which is contrary to the *true* doctrines of the church. Some think John first wrote his gospel, and later the epistles, in an effort to correct and batter down certain heresies which were creeping into the church.

A group of people known in church history as *Gnostics* (pronounced *nostics*) was rising. This group rejected the eternal Sonship of Christ and taught that He "became" the Son of God at His baptism, when the Holy Spirit descended upon Him. He was not virgin-born, they said, but was born as anyone else.

His divine relationship to God as Son was *begun* in *time*. This, of course, made Christ a mere man raised to divine relationship by a super-natural act, and therefore not truly God, as the apostles and Christ Himself had taught.

Some believe that it was against this group of *unbelievers* in the deity of Christ, who yet professed to follow Him, that John wrote much of his gospel. It is certainly apparent that he intended to convince all readers of Christ's eternal Sonship to God, and of His essential deity as a result of this relationship. He also presents Him at the same time as truly man. Had he used the most correct theological formula ever formed to express this relationship, he would have referred to Him as the *God-man*.

Whether or not John had the Gnostics as a body in mind, he was certainly aware of the evil of this very type of unbelief which was creeping in among the people of God. From the most early Christian times the church has been plagued by some who have held these and other heretical doctrines concerning the Sonship of Christ and the relationship of the Holy Spirit to Christ and to God. John did more in his gospel to correct the wrong teachings and give the correct views about these matters than any other gospel writer. Could it be that God left John here so long that he could see the beginnings of some of the greatest evils which have beset the Christian faith, and give the church a foundation in doctrine which cannot be shaken? It is entirely possible that this is true.

TIME

There have been differences of opinion as to when this gospel was written. Some have contended for a date as early as A.D. 65; others as late as A.D. 97. The most probable date, however, seems to place its writing about A.D. 86.

In all probability it was written at Ephesus, where the apostle John made his home during the last years of his life.

AUTHORSHIP

From the most ancient times the church has received the Gospel of John as written by the "disciple whom Jesus loved," later to become known as "John the beloved."

The writer does not identify himself until he comes to the end of his gospel (21:20, 24), where he states simply that he is the "disciple whom Jesus loved" (13:23; 20:2), which identifies him at once as the apostle John.

What we know of John most authentically is found in the New Testament. He was the son of Zebedee (Matt. 4:21), and Salome (Matt. 27:56; Mark 15:40), who seems to have been the sister of Jesus' mother (19:25). If so, then John was Jesus' cousin, which may account for his being Christ's most intimate apostle — the only one of whom it is said that he "leaned on Jesus' breast."

John was a fisherman in Galilee, a man of some means who had hired servants (Mark 1:16-20); he also seems to have owned a home in Jerusalem (19: 27). He was the youngest of all the apostles, probably being younger than Christ by several years. Some believe him to have been about twenty-five at the time of the crucifixion. He seems to have been personally acquainted with the high priest (18:15, 16), which may suggest that he was a man of some social standing and wealth.

He was a disciple of John the Baptist (1:35, 40), and was not hard to convince that he should become a follower of Jesus after His baptism. If John were related to Jesus by the above relationship, then he was also linked to John the Baptist by some relationship. In this case, he most certainly would have been told all the intricate matters concerning both the birth of John the Baptist and Christ. It is little wonder, then, that when John the Baptist appeared in the wilderness, heralding his gospel of repentance, he was ready to follow Christ. Christ recognized the Baptist's divine mission, and equally, when John the Baptist announced Christ as "the Lamb of God, which taketh away the sin of the world" (1:29), it was easy for John to become one of His first five disciples (1:35-38).

There was a mixed population in Galilee in John's days. It is quite possible that John, being of the wealthier class, often may have been in contact with the Hellenistic (Greek) cultural influences of the times. His thinking and writing are definitely colored by Greek thought, and he was, no doubt, considerably influenced by Greek culture in his early days.

In the last half of our Lord's ministry, John, with Peter and James, became a member of the special inner circle of Jesus' most trusted disciples. These three apostles accompanied Christ on His most important occasions: the Transfiguration (Matt. 17:1-8), at Gethsemane (Mark 14:32-41), and at the preparation of the Last Supper (Luke 22:8). Of the twelve disciples, Peter and John alone accompanied Him to the judgment hall of Pilate, but only John followed Him to the cross (19:26). Peter and John were the first of His apostles to be at the tomb after His resurrection (20:3-4).

Peter and John became the leaders of the early church and were often found together (Acts 3:1, 11; 4:13; 8:14).

THE SEA OF GALILEE. *Fishermen mend their nets on the shore of the Sea of Galilee. Mount Hermon (Mount of Transfiguration) is visible on the opposite shore.*

Gradually, Paul came into the church's leadership picture and overshadowed John in the latter part of Acts. From a human standpoint, the church's success was due largely to the preaching of Peter, the missionary zeal of Paul, and the theological foundation of John.

John was not always the smooth, lovable person pictured in the minds of many. At first he was boisterous and sometimes vehement. Note his forbidding the stranger to use Christ's name in his work (Mark 9:39) and his wishing to call fire down upon the Samaritans (Luke 9:54). But this disposition was brought under control and sweetened by Christ's love in his heart. His writings later are filled with love. Yet, upon occasion, he could be sharp, even unto the end, as his epistles show. (I John 4:20; III John 10).

There is an old tradition that the beloved disciple was in the public bath when he learned that Cerinthus, a heretical teacher of the times, was also in the place. He at once ran from the place, not wishing to be associated with Cerinthus in the place, lest it fall down upon them! This is without foundation, but serves to illustrate how John's disposition was looked upon in early times. He had a holy hatred of all evil.

John's dependability was illustrated by his closeness to Christ and in the fact that Jesus, among His last acts before His death, committed His mother to John's life-time care (19:25-27). It is said that Mary lived with John for some fifteen years after Christ's death.

John seems to have left Jerusalem before the persecutions and to have gone to Ephesus, where he is thought to have served for a long time as bishop of the Ephesian church. Tradition, as expressed by early Church Fathers, says he was taken to Rome by the emperor Domitian during his persecution of the Christians and immersed in a caldron of boiling oil, but escaped unhurt. He was then banished to Patmos, where he saw the visions of the Revelation. Soon after Domitian's death he was recalled by the emperor Nerva. He returned to Ephesus the next year, being about ninety years of age. Some claim that John lived to be about one hundred. He is reported by tradition to have been the only one of the apostles who died a natural death, although this tradition is not confirmed fully by historical evidence. Jerome reported that when John was so old and enfeebled that he could no longer preach an ordinary sermon, he was carried into the assembly, where his custom was to say in every meeting, *"My dear children, love one another!"*

There are several things peculiar to John's gospel. First, he does not give the attention to the historical framework which the others do. His major was more in the *doctrinal* and *spiritual* sides of the Gospel, since the other three writers had well covered other aspects.

Again, he majors upon the *witnesses* to Christ's deity, of which there are a number: (1) the witness of John the Baptist (1:19-34), (2) Christ's own witness to His deity to the woman of Samaria (4:1-42), (3) the witness to the Gentile official (4:46-54), (4) the witness to the public (12:44, 50), and (5) Christ's witness of His deity to His disciples (13-

17). Besides these, there are the witness of God to Christ's Sonship, that of the disciples to the miracles He wrought, and that of His resurrection. The last chapter of the book is a detailed account of Christ's post-resurrection appearances, which attest His deity.

The key words of John's gospel are the words "witness" and "believe." Along with these are three other related words: *love, light, know.* The word *believe* alone occurs ninety-eight times. Witnessing is one of the most powerful thoughts in this gospel. All these great words are in some way made to serve this central idea.

John gives more of Jesus' discourse on the Holy Spirit than any other gospel writer. This again demonstrates his display of the spiritual, doctrinal, and practical side of the gospel.

John also uses more symbolism for Christ than any other gospel writer. He is introduced as the "Lamb" of God (1:29, 36). John gives Jesus' presentations of Himself under symbols. These discourses are peculiar to John's gospel alone, not being reported by the other three. Jesus represents Himself as the "Bread of life" (6:22-65), the "Water of life" (7:37-39), the "Light of the world" (8:12), the "Good Shepherd" and the "Door" of the sheepfold (10:1-18), and the "True Vine," of which His followers are the branches (15:1-16). Just before this (14:6), Jesus cried, "I am the Way, the Truth and the Life: no man cometh unto the Father, but by me" (14:6). The Greek word, here rendered *way,* literally means *the road.* Christ is the pathway to God; besides Him, there is no

THE POOL OF SILOAM. *Still in existence today, the Pool of Siloam was the place to which Jesus directed the man who was blind from birth.*

other way. The early church often used the term *way* to signify the Christian life. It was not unusual to ask in those days, "Are there any of the Way here?" See Acts 9:2.

All these symbols are highly significant of spiritual values, as one can readily see. They speak of John's intense desire to make all see Christ as God's solution to man's spiritual problems and needs. He was to become Sight to the blind, Bread to the hungry, Water to the thirsty, a Door to the lost, a Shepherd to the redeemed, a Vine of sustenance to the new believer, and the very Way to God Himself. All these symbols pointed to man's needs and God's supply of these through Christ.

This book has been called the "most important literary production ever composed." This may well be said to be one of the most *important* books ever written.

A *brief outline* may be as follows:

  I. The prologue; Christ pre-incarnate, 1:1-18
 II. The witness of the Gospel, 1:19—6:71
III. Christ and the Jewish people, 7-12
 IV. Christ and His disciples, 13-17
  V. The Passion and death, 18-19
 VI. The Resurrection, 20
VII. The epilogue, 21

GREAT THINGS IN JOHN

Outstanding stories in John are:

1. Peter's introduction to Christ, 1:40-42
2. Christ's first miracle at Cana, 2:1-11
3. Nicodemus' visit to Jesus, 3:1-21
4. Jesus and the woman of Samaria, 4:1-38
5. The adulterous woman, 8:1-11

6. The resurrection of Lazarus from the dead, 11:1-54
7. Jesus and the Greeks, 12:20-43
8. Christ's comfort to His followers, 14:1-31
9. The High Priestly Prayer, 17:1-26
10. A meeting which was disturbed, 20:19-23
11. A doubter satisfied, 20:24-29
12. Commission of Peter 21:15-19

Several great truths may be pointed out:

1. Andrew found his brother Simon and brought him to Christ. Christ named him *Peter,* meaning "a stone." Peter's flinty side more often than not showed itself in his earlier days. But he was made of genuine "stuff" and always came back with a bound. He was one of Christ's best workers.

Andrew, later an apostle of the Lord Himself, is little known today. He wrote no book of the New Testament and is not listed among the "great" of those early days, although tradition does assign him a place among the early missionaries and a martyr's death. But his one great success may have been the winning of Peter to Christ. Here is one of the great lessons in personal soul-winning. Like the unknown man who won the great evangelist D. L. Moody to Christ, Andrew's reward will be great indeed.

Possibly no other life, that of Paul excepted, has had such a profound influence upon the course of human history wherever Christianity has gone as Peter's. And yet, he was won to Christ by a brother who had concern for him and whose greatest deed was perhaps this one act of devotion.

2. Some believe that the bridegroom at the marriage of Cana, in Galilee, where Jesus performed His first miracle, was the

young apostle John himself. This tradition has no historical support, but if it *were* so, this must have been a most blessed occasion in the life of John. However this may have been, we do know that Christ's presence and His contribution by the miracle indicate His sanction upon the marriage. Doubtless He had great joy in helping the embarrassed bridegroom out of his dilemma.

Christ is still the Friend of youth. He is pleased to share both their joys and sorrows, as of old when He blessed the babies and said, "Suffer the little children to come unto me, and forbid them not: for of such is the kingdom of God" (Mark 10:14). Young people should remember Christ's interest in them in every time of need, sorrow, or joy.

3. The visit of Nicodemus to Jesus shows the hunger in the true Jewish heart for the truth respecting Christ's mission. Nicodemus asked for and received the great truth of the kingdom of God, namely, that it is a spiritual kingdom and that men can only enter it by a spiritual rebirth. Their hearts and minds must be changed to conform with God's ideal of life. This happens when the Spirit of God works this change in a person's heart by repentance and faith.

Jesus explained to Nicodemus how God had provided this. Jesus was still speaking to Nicodemus when He stated that most beautiful of all Scripture passages, John 3:16. Down through verse 21, Christ is explaining to Nicodemus the spiritual nature of the kingdom, stating sinful man's objections to it and why they object. Here in brief scope is the clearest lesson in the New Testament of God's provisions for man's salvation and *why* man rejects this provision. One should study it well.

4. John's record of Jesus and the woman at the well in Samaria shows Christ's utterly unselfish attitude toward all peoples. The Jews and Samaritans had no dealings, but Christ allowed this barrier of selfishness no place in His life. He was as interested in this woman, whose sinful life was very evident, as in the noblest woman in Judea!

Jesus explained to her how God had provided salvation for all, and that she was no exception. Here is one of the greatest addresses on personal evangelism ever delivered.

Christ offers the "water of life" as freely to the Samaritans as to the Jews. Here again, John scores high in his appeal for the universality of the Gospel of Christ. All men everywhere find an answer to their needs in this wonderful message of God's love and power. We as Christians are obligated to go ". . . into all the world, and preach the gospel to every creature" (Mark 16:15).

5. The woman taken in adultery was placed before Christ by the sinful Jewish leaders, who hoped thereby to ensnare Him. The Old Testament law required that any person who committed the sin of adultery was to be stoned to death. Knowing Christ's reputation for mercy and forgiveness, these evil leaders evidently thought if they could trap Him into forgiving this woman and releasing her from the death penalty, they would then be able to bring against Him the charge of breaking Moses' law — a very serious offense.

But note how cleverly Christ handled this case. He *knew their* sinful hearts. So, in ordering the execution according to the Mosaic law by saying, "Let him that is without sin cast the first stone . . .," He opened the way for two things: First, their guilt would be exposed publicly, for they could not comply with His request. Second, He would then be at liberty to deal with the woman according to the law of love and mercy; for Christ came not to enforce justice, but to bring mercy to mankind, through redemption.

The dumbfounded plotters looked at each other, bowed their heads and went out of the presence of Christ and the woman. Christ's words, "Neither do I condemn thee," must not be misunderstood to be a condoning of her sin. Rather He was saying, in the light of the Mosaic law, "Neither do I condemn thee to die; go, and sin no more." It has been thought by some that Christ wrote her pardon in the sand as He stooped over while her accusers were leaving. Here is justice met by mercy: sin condemned, but the sinner forgiven and spared. This is the work of Christ for all who are truly penitent.

6. Lazarus was one of Jesus' best friends among the common laymen. Yet, upon learning of his illness, He purposely stayed away until he had died (11:6). This was a great trial to the faith of Mary and Martha. They could not understand it, just as we often cannot understand what seems like the Lord's delays in answering some prayer of ours.

When Christ came, they told Him the story of his death and begged for His help. He asked to see the grave. When He saw it, John records His reaction in the *shortest verse* in the Bible: "Jesus wept" (11: 35). His great heart knew the deep pangs of human sorrow. He "groaned" with grief, yet all the while knowing what He would do. Here is one of the supreme mysteries of Christ, the God-man. As *man*, He wept with those weeping sisters and friends; as God, He called Lazarus forth from the grave!

Here is a choice lesson for us. Christ may sometimes seem to delay His coming in our times of distress and need, but He will always come in time. Though He is

PHYLACTERY. *These frontlets or phylacteries were strips of parchment on which were written passages of Scripture. They were placed either at the bend of the left arm or on the forehead. Pharisees wore them at all times and made them as conspicuous as possible.*

very and eternal God and knows no weaknesses as such, yet, in His glorified state, He is still capable of being "touched with the feelings of our infirmities" (Heb. 4: 15). Upon His own cross Christ cried, "My God, my God, why hast thou forsaken me?" (Matt. 27:46) in His own darkest hour. He will certainly never condemn His poor, heartbroken follower for crying out for help and understanding in *his* distress!

The resurrection of Lazarus from the dead provided a good demonstration of Christ's deity and power over death. Consequently, it made followers for Him (11: 45). But among His enemies it also produced opposition and determination to destroy Him (11:46-54). A demonstration of God's power is almost always accompanied with similar results. Those who believe are confirmed in their faith; unbelievers are made even more bitter and opposed.

7. When the Greeks who were at Jerusalem for the feast came to inquire of Christ about the way of life, He informed them that this eternal life could not come, except through His death and resurrection. The "corn of wheat" must first die; after

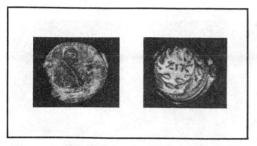

COINS OF PONTIUS PILATE. *As official Roman procurator of Judea, Pilate resided in Caesarea. His rule from A.D. 26-37 was marked by frequent conflict with the Jews. It was abruptly ended when he was summoned to Rome and replaced.*

it is buried in the soil, then life comes from its heart. He who will try to hold on to life — as the Greeks were likely to think of doing — for its pleasures and joys, will lose it in the end. Only he who *commits* his life fully to Christ, dying to the old *life* and ways and living anew, can hope to have real life, and eternal bliss.

Christ's prayer for divine assurance was immediately answered by the Father speaking to Him (12:27-29). This John records as a public witness to Christ's deity; and as it happened in connection with the visit of the Greeks, it is another testimony of the universal appeal of the Gospel.

8. John 14 contains some of the most tender words of comfort in the New Testament. There are the *promises* of the heavenly home (vv. 1-3); of Christ's coming again for His followers (v. 3); of answered prayer (v. 13); of the coming Comforter, which He said the Father would send (vv. 16-18); of the assurance that the Holy Spirit will work in the hearts of His followers, comforting, aiding, and strengthening them (vv. 26, 27); and of His peace which would be left with His followers always (v. 27).

Matters pertaining to the ministry of the Holy Spirit in the believer's life are also found in chapters 15 and 16 and should be studied by everyone. The greatest need of the church today is to accept and obey the ministry of the Holy Spirit in individual lives. Passages such as John 15:26, 27 and 16:7-15 should be read carefully with open heart, allowing their meaning to sink into the heart and mind.

The disciples were naturally saddened by Christ's announcement that He was going to return to heaven and they would have to carry on in His absence. He gave them these promises and this assurance of the work of the Holy Spirit for their comfort. The word *Comforter* may also mean teacher, as well as advocate, or one who helps, "a helper along side of another."

Christ wanted the apostles to understand that should He remain here, in His human state, He could minister only in one place at a time. But by ascending to heaven in His glorified state and sending the Holy Spirit back to execute His redemptive work, He could work all over the world. He explained that it was "expedient" — much better; it would help them along — if He returned to the Father. With this explanation, they became satisfied.

9. In the High Priestly Prayer — the real Lord's Prayer — Christ prayed for the following things: His reinstatement in the "glory" of His pre-earthly state (17: 1, 2); the sanctification of His disciples, that they may be "one" in the unity of the Spirit, that through their witness the world "may believe that thou hast sent me" (17: 3-23); and that His disciples may finally be with Him in His heavenly glory (17: 24). He also prayed for "all them also which shall believe on me through their word" (17:20). This includes all believers to the end of time.

Courtesy, Homer A. Kent, Jr.

TEMPLE MODEL. *This view of the Temple model in Jerusalem shows the Court of the Gentiles.*

It is comforting to know that Christ prayed then, and prays now, for everyone who believes in Him, and for the ungodly also, that they turn and repent.

10. As the night shades fell on that first Easter Sunday evening a small group of troubled and puzzled men met in a home in Jerusalem. Although it is not known for certain, it is possible that it may have been in the home of either John Mark or the beloved apostle John. Reports that some of the women had seen Him alive were circulating, but none of the apostles present there had seen Him. The men on the way to Emmaus had not yet returned with their story. Things looked very dark for the little group, and out of intense fear the doors were shut and bolted (20:19). There may have been a rumor of putting all the apostles

to death to stop this resurrection story.

Every heart must have trembled when there came a sudden, sharp rap upon the door. Finally, investigation proved it to be Cleopas and possibly Luke (Luke omitting his own name because of his writing the story). With boundless joy these two brethren told of walking and talking with a stranger who they found out was Christ and how He explained the Old Testament Scriptures to them. Everyone listened, spellbound.

Suddenly, without a door or window opening, there stood Jesus in their midst. Some were frightened; others doubtless panicked, but those who had so lately seen Him assured the rest that it was Christ. Immediately He dismissed their fears, telling them to touch Him and see, "for a spirit hath not flesh and bone, as ye see me have" (Luke 24:39). Then they knew He was risen from the dead. There were no more doubts; His presence was now a blessed reality.

Courtesy, George A. Turner

HERODIAN FAMILY TOMB IN JERUSALEM. *Note the rolling stone such as that which was placed at the entrance to Jesus' tomb.*

Christ brings assurance to His followers today, though in a way different from that of bodily appearance. The Holy Spirit gives God's children assurance through the Word and by His presence in the heart (Rom. 8:14-16; 10:8-13; I John 3:1-4).

11. Thomas was not present at the first meeting of Christ with the eleven apostles, and he must have felt a bit left out. Why had Christ passed him by? Could He not have appeared to him singly, as to Mary? What had he done to be left outside the circle? These or similar thoughts troubled him.

We could also ask *why* Thomas was absent from this Sunday evening meeting. Was it necessary? Was he uninformed of it? Did he fear the Jewish retaliation and stay away? No one will ever know. But he must have been in fellowship with them, for they told him of the appearance as soon as opportunity afforded. He was very much disturbed, and he refused to believe until he *saw* Christ for himself. Was he naturally skeptical by nature, as has been supposed? Was he hurt, and in this way manifested it? Did he feel a deep sense of grief? Could he not bring himself to accept the story of the others? Whatever the cause, he made an effort to be present the *next Sunday evening* when they met for worship. As the little group assembled, doubtless there were questions in their minds as to whether Christ would appear again, as He did the Sunday evening before. They had not long to question, for soon Jesus stood in their midst, just as before. He looked at Thomas, knowing full well his complaints, and He requested him to place his hand in His nail-pierced hands and spear-riven side and urged him to "be not faithless, but believing" (20:27).

Courtesy, Charles F. Pfeiffer

THE GARDEN TOMB. *This tomb in the Garden of Gethsemane is believed by some to be the tomb in which Joseph buried Jesus.*

Thomas' cry, "My Lord and my God" (20:28), is the triumphant shout of a faith fully convinced; it places him among the rest of the apostles as a first-rate witness to Christ. In this faith Thomas went to the "ends of the earth," going to far away India. There he established the Christian church, and this church still continues to this day, dating its beginning to the labors of the apostle Thomas. The Thomas Church of India has recently realized a new awakening and is growing stronger in the original faith of Thomas.

12. When Christ met the disciples on the shore of the Sea of Galilee, Peter was a bit backward, having denied Christ as he did. After the meal, Jesus talked to them as in other days. He asked Peter the famous three questions, testing out his loyalty. Just as Peter denied Christ three times, he now had to express his faith and love for Him three times. Each time Peter confessed his love, he came a bit closer to Christ. Then he received his commission, not to be the chief leader, the bishop or the pope, but simply to "feed my sheep" (21:16-17), a task distributed to all ministers of the gospel.

What a supreme lesson! Despite the fact that as a young believer one may stray away from the Lord under pressure and temptation, yet He stands ready to restore and commission one for great service when he truly returns to Christ, as did Peter.

Peter was told of his future privilege of suffering for Christ's sake (21:18, 19) and was rebuked almost in the same breath for his hastiness in inquiring into another's business. Christ was firm with him, though He had just commissioned him for high service. God likewise will be firm with all His children, chastising them when needed, even if they have hardly finished their greatest testimony or work in life.

John closes his gospel with his own personal witness to Christ and His works and by his statement that even the world could not contain the books if all Christ's words and works had been recorded (21:25). The God-fearing and Christ-exalting writers of the four gospels had chosen just the material God knew was fitting and necessary for mankind to have about Christ in order to be convinced of His Sonship to God and deity. This faith in His Sonship the apostle constantly affirms as necessary to personal salvation. At its close (21:24) John states again his main purpose for writing his gospel.

Memory Verses

"And many other signs truly did Jesus in the presence of His disciples, which are not written in this book: but these are written, that ye might believe that Jesus is the Christ, the Son of God; and that believing, ye might have life through his name" (20:30, 31).

The History
of the Early Church

Acts

This book has been called The Acts of the Apostles from early times. Some have said it should have been called "The Acts of the Spirit *through* the Apostles," since so much of its history has to do with the work of the Holy Spirit in the early believers in establishing the church. In reality, the work of the risen and ascended Lord Jesus Christ is carried forward through the Holy Spirit, which He promised to send, working with His followers in the progressive unfolding of this remarkable book. Many of the same things which Jesus did on earth — preaching, teaching, healing, casting out demons, bringing sinners to conversion — are seen here, only on a larger, more far-reaching scale. This fulfilled His promise, "He that believeth on me the works that I do shall he do also; and greater works than these shall he do . . ." (John 14:12). It was but the continuation of Christ's ministry in His followers.

TO WHOM

Acts evidently was written for the same person to whom Luke addressed his gospel (1:1), probably with a similar reason as stated in Luke 1:1-4.

Beyond doubt the writer had in mind a far larger reading audience than merely the "most excellent Theophilus" of Luke 1:3 and Acts 1:1, and his immediate friends. It has been held by some that this book may have been dedicated to

Theophilus, in this way giving it prestige in the mind of the reading public, by which it would gain a far wider reading. Or, it may have been written out of circumstances similar to those surrounding Luke's gospel, which is addressed to this same person. (See the notes on Luke under this same heading.)

PURPOSE

The purpose for producing this book may have been similar to that for which Luke was written. (See notes of the PURPOSE there). However, there also may have been an additional purpose for writing this book. He would wish to bring his readers up to date on what followed the death, resurrection, and ascension of the central figure of that gospel story. In doing this, though, he would be further able to set forth the primary objectives of Christ and something of how well they had been accomplished by the young church. In this phase of the purpose he may have been attempting to win converts to Christ and the cause of Christianity.

There seems to have been another purpose in his writing of Acts. As the church grew there was the necessity for a correct and trustworthy historical record of how it began and the most important highlights of its progress over the years of its initiation. There were also very important theological matters — such as the Jerusalem Council's decision not to require circumcision of Gentile converts as a requirement for church membership — which must be properly recorded.

The history of the establishment of the church in foreign lands and its progress along other lines also needed to be preserved. A properly recorded document of the leaders of the church and their decisions and activities would be of inestimable value in later times. These and perhaps other reasons underlay Luke's writing of Acts.

The *Pentateuch* (first five books of the Bible) show forth God the Father's glory in creation, law, and order; the gospels set forth Christ the Son's message to man and His redemptive work; Acts displays the glory and work of the Holy Spirit in His relationship to God, Christ, and the church. The Holy Spirit is the *executive* member of the Godhead. He *works out* the plan of redemption in men's lives by convicting them of sin, drawing them to Christ, regenerating them when they repent and believe upon Christ; His is a work of cleansing, comforting, teaching, and guiding them as they progress in the Christian way. In Acts one sees something of the Spirit's work for and with man in this relationship. This may be another purpose God had in inspiring Luke to write this remarkable book.

TIME

There has been much discussion by various authorities about the *time* during which this book was written. Some think it may have been written at Caesarea while Paul was imprisoned there (A.D. 59-61), with the finishing details added later at Rome. Others believe Rome was the probable place of writing and the date about A.D. 63. It may be well enough to suppose that parts of it were written at Caesarea, as Luke would have had ample time for it there while attending to Paul's affairs. He could also have secured materials for it from the church leaders at Jerusalem. It was likely finished at Rome about A.D. 63, some time before Paul's execution there, as it does not mention his death, which it most likely would have if he had died before its completion. Some scholars think it may not have been *pub-*

lished however, until as late as A.D. 70. Acts covers about the first thirty-four years of the church's history and activities in general.

AUTHORSHIP

From the earliest times Christian writers have attributed this book to Luke. His reference to a "former treatise" to Theophilus, his friend in Rome (1:1), indicates that the writer was the same person who wrote the book of Luke (Luke 1:1-4). No serious attempt has ever been made to assign this work to any other author, since its authorship has been credited to Luke with so much historical and traditional certainty.

Concerning Luke as a person and writer, please see the account under AUTHORSHIP in the introduction to Luke's gospel.

This book was originally written in Greek, as was the Gospel of Luke. There are places in the book which show marked signs of Paul's influence, if not his actual writing — such as his speeches, discourses and possibly chapters 17-18. These sections can be accounted for, however, as recordings of events by Luke in Paul's words and style. It could be that in Luke's absence, as in 17-18, Paul kept a record of events which was submitted to Luke for copying. This would do no damage to the authorship of the book.

The actual words of Peter's Pentecostal sermon, for instance, would have been heard by Luke himself. When Luke later wrote this book under the inspiration of the Holy Spirit, the Spirit could very well

DAMASCUS. *A scene on the "Street Called Straight." The Lord spoke to Ananias, "Rise and go to the street called Straight, and inquire in the house of Judas for a man of Tarsus named Saul."*

have given him these words from memory. Many other accounts, such as that of the Samaritan revival and the conversion of the eunuch of Ethiopia (8), could have been furnished by others. For example, Philip lived at Caesarea and could have informed Luke of these details while there. Luke may have been in Jerusalem for such famous events as the meeting of the early church council (15:6-29).

It is interesting to note that Luke wrote more of the New Testament than any other writer. He is by far the largest writer of all *historical* data of the New Testament.

Acts is largely a book in which the Holy Spirit is prominent. The disciples were to receive power from the Holy Spirit (1:8); they were said to have been "filled with the Holy Ghost" (2:4); the Holy Spirit spoke by the mouth of David (2:25-36). The new converts were to be baptized and receive the "gift of the Holy Ghost" (2:38, 39); the disciples were refreshed by another infilling with the Holy Spirit (4:31). Two persons were struck dead for lying to the Holy Ghost (5:1-11).

Peter and Stephen are said to have been "full of the Holy Ghost" (4:8; 6:5); the disciples and the Holy Spirit are said to be witnesses together of the Gospel, and the Holy Spirit is given to them that obey Him (5:32). Peter and John were sent to Samaria to pray that the Holy Ghost would be given to the new converts there (8:14-17).

The early disciples were multiplied, "walking in the comfort of the Holy Ghost" (9:31). God is said to have anointed Jesus with the Holy Ghost (10: 38), and the Holy Spirit was poured out upon Cornelius' household (10:44-48). Paul and Barnabas were separated unto the work of God by the Holy Spirit (13: 2) and were "sent forth by the Holy Ghost" (13:4). Peter declared to the general council at Jerusalem that the Holy Spirit had been given to Cornelius' household as a purifying agent of God, just as He had been to them at Pentecost (15: 7-9). The Spirit forbade Paul to preach in Bithynia (16:7), and Paul prayed for the Ephesian disciples, who then were filled with the Holy Spirit (19:1-6).

The Holy Ghost is said to have made the church leaders "overseers" of the church of God (20:28), and Paul warned the Roman Jews that the Holy Spirit had before spoken by Isaiah of their rejection of Christ (28:25-29).

These and other references show what a great place the ministry of the Holy Spirit holds throughout the Book of Acts. His ministry is peculiar to this book. Acts shows the infant church at work and the Spirit's ministry, fulfilling the Savior's promises to His followers. It also may serve as a pattern for the people of God, showing that God's Spirit must work within the church if anything of true spiritual value is to be accomplished by the church.

Acts may be briefly outlined as follows:

 I. Witnessing in Jerusalem, 1-7

 II. Witnessing in Judea and Samaria, 8-12

 III. Witnessing in the Gentile world, 13-28

There are two other main divisions which also may be used: Chapters 1-12 show Peter in the lead as the most prominent figure, while Chapters 13-28 present Paul as the most dominant char-

---

ANTIOCH-ON-THE-ORONTES. *Men were first called "Christians" in Antioch, one of the most magnificent cities under Roman rule in the Near East. A city in Turkey, it is called Antakya.*

acter. Grouping incidents in Acts around these two central figures is an interesting project. It has been well said that chapters 1-12 present the *home missions* effort of the church and chapters 13-28 show the church at work in *foreign missions*.

Acts is the most important historical book in the early church world. Without it we would know comparatively little about the church from about A.D. 29-53, the time when the first epistle of Paul was possibly written. We would learn far too little from the epistles alone. Therefore, Acts should be studied with great care.

GREAT THINGS IN ACTS

The *outstanding stories* in Acts are:
1. The election of Matthias, 1:15-26
2. Pentecost and its varied events, 2:1-47
3. The first healing, 3:1-18
4. The first imprisonment, 4:1-22
5. The failure of early communism, 4:34—5:11
6. Two liars struck dead, 5:1-11
7. Stephen's defense and martyrdom, 6:5—7:60
8. Revival in Samaria, 8:1-25
9. A foreigner converted, 8:26-40
10. The conversion of Saul, 9:1-22
11. Dorcas raised from death, 9:36-43
12. First Gentile received into the church, 10:1-48
13. Saul introduced to Antioch Christians, 11:25-30
14. Peter delivered from prison, 12:1-19
15. A proud monarch destroyed, 12:20-25
16. Paul and Barnabas commissioned for missionary activity, 13:1-3
17. Paul stoned at Lystra, 14:8-20
18. The great church council meeting, 15:6-31
19. Paul and Barnabas separate; Paul and Silas form party, 15:36-41
20. Entry of the Gospel into Europe; the Philippian jailer's conversion, 16:9-34
21. Paul's trip to Jerusalem and imprisonment at Caesarea, 21:15—26:32
22. Felix trembles; Agrippa is almost persuaded, 24:22—26:32
23. A veteran saved from shipwreck, 27:13-44
24. An honorable and active prisoner, 28:16-31

The following *great truths* are found in Acts:

1. The election of Matthias to take Judas' place as an apostle is the first church election in democratic form in the Christian church. It may have been a pattern, so far as the democratic form of congregational government is concerned. But one is forced to recognize that these brethren, by making the choice before being filled with the Spirit to guide them, evidently missed the Lord's choice. The Scriptures strongly imply that Paul became the twelfth apostle (I Cor. 9:1, 2; 15:8-10; II Cor. 11:5). These references indicate that Paul became the "last apostle," rather than Matthias.

This also points up how important it is that Christians be "led by the Spirit" (Rom. 8:14) in all such weighty matters (13:1-3).

2. *Pentecost* was a special feast of the Jews which occurred fifty days after the Passover, at which time Christ had been crucified. This was a most suitable day for the Holy Spirit's dispensational outpouring. It was the time of offering the firstfruits of the land to God, a time of great rejoicing, and of renewal — springtime. It was a time when great

throngs of people from over the then-known world would be in Jerusalem (2: 8-11). It fulfilled the old pattern of rejoicing over the firstfruits of the land by presenting to the nation and the world the firstfruits of the Christian church — its first three thousand converts being won on this day.

The descent of the Holy Spirit appears to have occurred about nine o'clock in the morning (2:14, 15), which was the very hour of the beginning of the morning sacrifices in the Temple. In this way it signified to all men that these sacrifices were no more necessary. Christ, "the Lamb of God," had come and had by His death "taken away the sin of the world" (John 1:29).

Peter's preaching shows with what power and demonstration of Spirit the Gospel now came. Peter, the Christ-denying disciple of only a few weeks before, had now been transformed into the fearless apostle of Christ. What else, except the Spirit's baptism and endowment with power (1:8) could possibly have made this great change in him? All Christians need the fullness of the Holy Spirit to make their personal lives and Christian work effective for Christ.

The great sense of conviction for sin which came at this time (2:37) and Peter's counsel, "Repent, and be baptized everyone of you in the name of Jesus Christ for the remission of sins, and ye shall receive the gift of the Holy Ghost" (2:38), indicate that Christ's promise about the Holy Spirit's work was fulfilled (John 16:7-12). This is still the Spirit's mission in the world, and will be as long as the church endures. It is encouraging to know that wherever the Gospel is preached in the Spirit as Peter did, the Holy Spirit will convict and draw men to Christ. Missionaries and others working with those who have had the least Gospel opportunities have found this so.

3. Early in the history of the Christian church, healing appeared in connection with its ministry. This was but a continuation of Christ's ministry of healing. The church in all ages has been the depository of help for men's bodies and minds as well as their spirits when it has been in its best spiritual condition. Healing should never be placed on a par with salvation in the church's work, but neither should it be rejected as having no place in its work.

4. Persecution has often been the lot of earnest Christians throughout the centuries. This first imprisonment of the apostles was but the forerunner of untold sufferings for Christ by the Christians of all times. After a later persecution, the apostles rejoiced that they were counted worthy to suffer for Christ (5:41). So should Christians rejoice today when suffering for Christ.

Christ taught His disciples to expect sufferings and perseuctions as part of their fare in living for Him (Matt. 5: 11, 12, 44; 13:21; Mark 4:17; John 15: 20). It is still so in many parts of the world today.

5. Early Christians tried to practice a type of communal life — everything belonging to one central authority, to be dispersed according to need. This method, though arising out of the best of intentions and administered by godly people, met with dismal failure. In its earliest experience it produced two vicious liars — Ananias and Sapphira (5: 1-11). It is, of course, only fair to say that the system simply brought out the disadvantage of the whole group rather than its advantage. Further, it is noted that the "widows" in the group later received unfair treatment (6:1). The

weaker and less important suffered in this system, despite the good intentions of its managers. Though this was immediately righted, it nonetheless did not finally work out.

Before too long Paul was taking collections for the "poor saints at Jerusalem" (I Cor. 16:1-8; Rom. 15:25-27, 30, 31). It is quite possible that this failure of the communal life at Jerusalem had rendered the saints there very poor and left many in destitute circumstances.

SAMARIA. *"Philip went down to the city of Samaria, and preached Christ unto them." Jacob's Well is located in the area shown in the center of the photo.*

While it is not known for certain that this was the case, it is not at all unlikely that the failure of this system did much to bring about the poverty-stricken conditions of the Jerusalem church. Paul's offerings from the newly established Gentile-Jewish churches show that there had been no such system attempted in them, or they would likely have been in the same conditions.

This should teach us that communal life in *no form* has ever worked successfully. It is contrary to every principle of economic soundness and social fair play. Wherever this system has been tried it has generally wound up with the few in charge of it enjoying the privileges and the masses suffering from it. It works no better in government than it did in

the church. The church abandoned it early as an unworkable system.

6. The danger of hypocrisy is seen in Ananias and Sapphira being struck dead for lying to God. Had they gotten by with their evil plotting the church would have been much more easily corrupted. Not all people who have lied to God have been struck dead, but this serves as a firm warning of the seriousness of this wickedness.

Lying in any form does not pay. It may *seem* to get one by temporarily, but it will lead to ruin at last. To attempt to lie to God is of all hypocrisies the most foolhardy! When in distress or sorrow, to promise God certain things if He will help one, and then afterwards to forget these promises, is a form of lying to God. Playing with lightning is not as serious as this!

7. Stephen, the first Christian martyr, was a very godly man. His rebuke of the religious leaders of his day (7) was too much for them, so they stoned him to death.

It is regrettable that many persecutions heaped upon some of the most godly persons across the Christian centuries have come from the cold-hearted and sinful within the professed pale of the church itself. Unbelieving Jews killed Stephen, but it has often been professed Christians who have persecuted the more devout ones among them. It is sad but true that the church has done herself great harm in the eyes of the world by this evil.

One must never allow persecutions in any form to hinder his progress in true Christian living.

8. The Samaritan revival (8), was the first introduction of the Gospel outside Judea, and it was an instant success. This was the beginning of the fulfillment of Christ's commission, "Go ye into all the world, and preach the gospel to every creature" (Luke 16:15). When at its best, the church has always been missionary in its efforts.

9. The African eunuch's conversion through Philip's preaching shows how simple faith in Christ, upon receiving the Word as true, brings peace with God through Christ (Rom. 5:1). There are no racial barriers in true Christianity.

10. Aside from Pentecost, perhaps the greatest story in Acts is that of Saul's conversion. Some modernists have suggested that he had a "sun stroke," but if so, it surely affected him strangely! It was different from any other sun stroke in history. Someone else suggested reverently that it was a *Son* stroke all right — the Son of God struck him down and brought him to his senses. It was a sudden but genuine conversion from which Saul never wavered.

To his everlasting credit, it can be said that Saul of Tarsus was a sincere man. When Christ revealed Himself to him, he did not go on dishonoring Him, but immediately repented when he saw his wrong; he turned to God. He considered the only reason he had received mercy at all was his "ignorance" in what he was doing before his conversion (26:13-18; I Tim. 1:12, 13).

How marvelous is the power of grace as seen in this incident. Saul the malicious persecutor is by God's grace through Christ transformed into Paul the mighty preacher. "Saul" is the Hebrew form of the apostles's name; "Paul" is the Greek form. Paul means "little," in reference to his size and stature.

This story reveals God's patience with sinners and His willingness to forgive; sudden conversions can become permanently successful; however great the sinner, God's grace is equal to the need. Paul often regretted his own sinful past and apparently felt that he was reaping what he had sown (I Tim. 1:15, 16). This story has served to encourage more wicked people to turn to God than possibly any other outside the gospels themselves.

11. Peter's prayer, after which Dorcas was raised from the dead, showed to all the power of Christ and brought many new converts to Christ. This was only following the pattern of Jesus in the gospels.

It certainly is possible today for the dead to be raised, if God wills it and one prays the prayer of faith; however, there seems to be no need for this today, since Christianity is well established and its power otherwise known. And yet, through prayer many have been saved from death, and some brought back from what seemed the very jaws of death. Prayer is powerful and should be held in great reverence.

12. Peter's visit to Cornelius' home, his preaching there, and his witnessing the baptism of the Spirit upon the devout, prayerful Cornelius and his house brought the pointed question, "Can any man forbid water, that these should not be baptized?" With this bold step the first Gentiles were admitted to membership in the Christian church. For them, baptism was the token of their acceptance, as it had been of the acceptance of a Gentile as a proselyte into the Jewish religion.

How marvelous was this transaction. It was not Peter who brought this about, but God. Cornelius' prayers were answered, and God showed him, as well as Peter, that Gentiles were to be included in the glorious Gospel benefits. This is an important part of the Gospel.

Had it not been for this great move we may still have been in heathen darkness and Christianity may never have become a success.

13. When Barnabas brought Saul (Paul) into the Antioch congregation, he perhaps knew that Paul, with his extraordinary talents and abilities, would soon take the lead and leave him as second in importance. But his love for Christ and the church superseded any personal ambition.

It is also safe to say that had it not been for Barnabas, who helped and strengthened Paul, both after his conversion and here, Paul may never have become the worker he was. Each person has his part to play in kingdom work and should do his bit, leaving the results with the Lord. Barnabas made a noble and lasting contribution to the church in this work.

14. Peter's deliverance from prison is another remarkable incident of the power of prayer. The amazing thing is that when Peter appeared at the prayer meeting scene, his fellow Christians did not believe it was truly him (12:13-17). Perhaps they had other opinions as to *how* he would be delivered.

God often surprises us with His answers to our prayers. Sometimes they come sooner than expected, sometimes much later, and often in a very different way. But however they may come, prayers prayed in the Spirit and in earnest receive their answers sometimes, somewhere.

Young people must guard against the idea that every prayer will be answered. Someone has well suggested that God answers every prayer, but He often answers many of them with a no! This is very true. It is important that we learn early to commit anything we pray about

to God and accept whatever answer He gives as best for us.

From this point onward in Acts, the work of Peter begins to fade in the story and that of Paul becomes more prominent, not that Peter faded out, but because the writer chose to present Paul's work more fully as he brought more and more of the Gentile world into the church.

15. The destruction of Herod by a horrible disease because he did not give God the glory for the position he held, but took honors of deity, reveals God's dealings with men outside the church. God has not abandoned the world to its

THE CONVERSION OF SAUL. *"And as he journeyed, he came near Damascus; and suddenly there shined round about him a light from heaven. . . ."*

fate just because we do not see His workings every day. Behind the scenes He still holds the reins and ultimately things will come out as He has planned them.

Let this be a warning that none take to himself honors which belong to God. Even the mildest praise of men should be given over to God as an honor which we have received because of God's mercies and grace to us.

16. Possibly the most important ordin-

PAUL DECLARING HIS ROMAN CITIZEN-
SHIP. *Upon declaration of his Roman
citizenship Paul was treated with much
greater respect by the Roman soldiers.*

---

ation and commission service ever held
was the one at Antioch, when Paul and
Barnabas were separated to the church's
missionary work. Not since the outpouring of the Spirit at Pentecost had there
been such a momentous and far-reaching
action taken by the church.

That day the brethren had not the
faintest notion of the eternal good being
done when they sent these men upon
their great mission. This was the first of
Paul's three famous missionary journeys
and the starting point of westward missions for all time to come. No other single
service has had so much results as this
one.

It is a solemn thing to set men apart
for God's service and lay hands upon
them in ordination or consecration to a
special task. This is one of the greatest

lessons in the New Testament, pointing
to the necessity for the Holy Spirit's leadings in selecting men for their work. Possibly the brethren who sent them out were
a bit doubtful about the success of the
endeavor, and especially about the "little fellow with the sore eyes" — Paul.
Barnabas they could trust, but Paul had
yet to prove himself. Never was a mission more highly successful than this one!
Their confidence was forever justified.

17. When Paul was stoned at Lystra
and left for dead, he saw visions of glory
which were too profound to repeat. II
Corinthians 12:1-5 doubtless refers to this
occasion at Lystra. From this stoning
onward, Paul seems to have suffered some
difficult affliction, from which God did
not choose to deliver him.

Sometimes crosses, afflictions, difficulties and physical handicaps are allowed
to come into the lives of Christians. Often one cannot understand *why* these
things are permitted. This is especially
true of younger Christians. The lesson

to remember is that God has His purposes for everything which He allows to come to His children. One must always remember Christ's words to Paul (II Cor. 12:9; Rom. 8:28). It would be well to memorize these.

18. One of the greatest meetings ever held in the early church was the council meeting at Jerusalem where the matter of requirements for the Gentile converts was settled. Had the strict traditional Jewish element prevailed in this meeting, those who required circumcision and keeping Jewish ceremonial laws, the Christian church would never have succeeded until this yoke was broken. As it was, the more spiritually-minded brethren, such as Peter, James, and Paul, ruled the meeting and brought to the council the true Gospel freedom which Christ meant to be taught. It was the overruling power and grace of the Holy Spirit, here again, which made this decision possible (15:28).

This lesson points up the fact that while there are certain rules of life necessary for Christians, too much legal bondage to regulations alone will greatly hinder the Gospel of Christ. ". . . The letter killeth, but the Spirit giveth life" (II Cor. 3:6), as Paul was to say much later. Love to God and one's fellowmen is the supreme test of Christianity (I John 4:20, 21).

Here again, one sees how very important it was that the Holy Spirit fill the hearts and rule the minds of those leaders who had to make such great decisions. It is also important that the Holy Spirit fill the hearts of all God's children, that they may obey His leadings today.

19. John Mark was a young man of considerable talent, but he had become discouraged; he left Paul and Barnabas at Pamphylia, going back to Jerusalem (13:13; 15:38). Barnabas wanted to take him on this second missionary journey, but Paul opposed this because of John Mark's earlier instability. He evidently feared something similar would occur again. However, Barnabas, Mark's uncle, was determined to take him along. After a rather strong debate, Paul and Barnabas decided to separate and form two parties. Paul chose Silas as his traveling companion, while Barnabas took Mark. (See further notes on this in the Gospel of Mark under AUTHORSHIP.)

This is a helpful lesson in human relationships. These brethren certainly did not agree. They discussed the matter, each contending for his own view. When they could not reach an agreeable decision, they separated, but evidently, without any unchristian attitudes or behavior. Neither of them is ever represented as having sinned or lost his Christian influence among the brethren. Maybe this division into two parties was best for the work in the long run. More was apparently accomplished in this way.

Christians should always be so filled with the Spirit that they can settle their human differences in a way becoming to Christians, as these brethren did. The best of Christians often disagree, but they need not have strife or hard feelings over it.

20. Paul's night vision, his determination to carry the Gospel into Europe, and the conversion of the Philippian jailor were events of outstanding historical significance. Had Paul gone farther into Asia instead of entering Europe, and the Gospel not come to Europe, the Western world could well have been in the same position as much of the unevangelized parts of the world today.

One can see again how very important it is that men be led by the Holy Spirit.

Paul had intended to go another direction, but he and his party were ". . . forbidden of the Holy Ghost . . . and the Spirit suffered them not" (16:6, 7) to do this. Being a man of deep piety and faith, Paul waited until the Holy Spirit directed his way (16:8-10). This waiting was not for long, but what mighty dividends it brought in kingdom building and the spread of the Gospel! One of the richest and deepest of the epistles — Philippians — was written by Paul to this church in later years. The church would have missed much had he not been obedient to the Holy Spirit in this matter.

It is likewise important that Christian leaders, and even young people whose lives are ahead of them, learn to obey the leadings of the Holy Spirit. One of the greatest needs of the church today is Spirit-filled, Spirit-led people.

21. It seems difficult to understand why Paul would go to Jerusalem, when it meant imprisonment for two years at Caesarea and final imprisonment at Rome. He was warned by the Holy Spirit that this would happen (20:22, 23; 21:10-14) He was fully conscious of what to expect, but it seems this was in some way a part of his ministry, as he saw it (20:24). His zeal and passion for the work carried him onward despite this prospect.

Perhaps in this way, the apostle ministered to more people than he ever could have reached otherwise. It seems that he went "above and beyond the call of duty," inasmuch as the Spirit had warned him what to expect and the saints urged him not to go. It was not stubbornness, but rather, an undying love for the cause of Christ which pressed him onward in this great conflict.

Let us look at it this way: There are many young people who may remain at home from the mission field and get to heaven. But by the undying devotion to Christ and the lost, in going to the field, they will greatly aid the church in its work and receive a far greater reward in heaven than if they had remained at home.

22. Two historical figures to whom Paul witnessed during his imprisonment were Felix and Agrippa. Both of these men were greatly moved by the ardent witness of the apostle and by the Holy Spirit, who evidently dealt with them. Upon the pages of Acts they stand as lone, solitary figures of men who rejected Christ.

Since these men made no contribution to the cause nor detracted from it, one may wonder why Luke decided to include them in this account. Except as they briefly touch Paul's life, they apparently have no place in the story.

Could it be that the writer decided to place their stories here to warn later readers of the deceitfulness of sin and its attendant hard-heartedness? These men were *officially* generous to Paul, but they, with cold-heartedness, rejected his Christian message and its Savior, but not without the visible effects of the Spirit's work upon them. "Felix trembled" and Agrippa was "almost" persuaded, but they never became Christians. Here is a warning to all not to take the sinful way of worldly living, for in the end it will prove the eternal snare to ever becoming a Christian.

23. One of the most dramatic human interest stories in Acts is that of the shipwreck of the boat on which Paul was being taken to Rome. Since he was only a "prisoner," his good advice was ignored (27:10, 11). But his stock in trade went up every day as the captain finally saw the folly of not listening to him.

After many days of dreadful suffering

PAUL BEFORE KING AGRIPPA. *Permission to speak was granted to Paul by King Agrippa. After Paul's eloquent defense,* King Agrippa said, *"Almost thou persuadest me to be a Christian."*

PAUL BEFORE FESTUS. *Festus re-investigated Paul's case and was satisfied that he was innocent, but he attempted to* please the Jews by suggesting that the apostle be tried at Jerusalem.

ST. PAUL'S BAY, MALTA. *Paul suffered shipwreck here on his journey to Rome. The islands are called St. Paul's Islands. On the larger island a statue has been erected to commemorate the event of Acts 27.*

by the crew, because of the distressing conditions, Paul came forward with a cheerful message. He had been encouraged, he said, by a visit from an angel. He informed them that none of the crew or passengers were to be lost. Note the inspiring words of the angel of God, which Paul relayed to the captain and crew: "Fear not, Paul . . . God hath given thee all that sail with thee" (27:24). Despite this, however, the hard-hearted Roman soldiers wanted to kill him and all the prisoners when they saw the ship was finally breaking up. How ungrateful sinful men can be.

A more sane centurion saved the day for Paul; on the island, his faith triumphed again and many were won to Christ. This must have been one prisoner the sailors did not understand. Christians are delightfully different from sin-hardened people, but they are often misunderstood, despite their kindness and love for others.

24. As a prisoner at Rome, Paul soon gained a reputation both as a preacher, a noble person, and an active Christian. Apparently, Luke was with him at Rome for a considerable portion of his first

imprisonment. Paul was kept busy preaching, counseling, and working for his Lord (28:30, 31).

It is certain that he wrote several of his epistles during this first imprisonment. This may have been the providential reason for his imprisonment. Had not John Bunyan been imprisoned for twelve years in Bedford Jail in England, the world may never have had *Pilgrim's Progress*. Paul's prison epistles are some of his richest contributions to the New Testament.

God does not always announce to His servants His purposes in allowing afflictions, sufferings, imprisonments, and the like to befall them. But He always has His reasons for allowing these to come.

At this point, near the end of Paul's first two years in prison at Rome, Luke lets the curtain fall upon the grand old apostle's life and work.

It is generally agreed that Paul was released from prison and made another visit to the churches in Greece and Asia Minor about A.D. 65-66. Following this he was again imprisoned at Rome. It was during this last imprisonment that he appears to have written the pastoral epistles — Titus, I and II Timothy. II Timothy was apparently penned just a short while before his execution at the Roman Emperor Nero's gruesome beheading block in Rome (II Tim. 4:6-11). Tradition says his death occurred about A.D. 67.

Luke did not choose to record the final ending of the story of the greatest of all the apostles. Rather, he leaves him at the peak of his activities during the first imprisonment. He appears to have been with him to the last (II Tim. 4:11), but perhaps he felt Paul's last letter to Timothy made the best ending. Probably, too, Luke's account was published just after he finished it, and he did not wish to add a postscript. Whatever the reason, Paul is seen in Acts at the apex of his work as the story closes in this most important book of early church history.

Acts closes the historical account of the New Testament. By this time — probably A.D. 63 or 64, when Acts was finished — the church was well on its way to becoming a world-wide organization. Its message had reached into Egypt, Africa, all of Asia Minor, well into Asia, into parts of Europe, and possibly into India. Acts does not tell the full story of its spread, but only records largely the work of Peter and Paul. But the Christian church was fast becoming a world missionary power which was to girdle the globe and bring millions into its fold.

Every person should become well acquainted with the content of this most important book.

Memory Verse

"But ye shall receive power, after that the Holy Ghost is come upon you: and ye shall be witnesses unto me both in Jerusalem, and in all Judaea, and in Samaria, and unto the uttermost parts of the earth" (1:8).

The Pauline Epistles

Romans

This epistle was so named because of its connection with the church at Rome. The name of Rome was then world-renowned, and anything carrying the name of Rome stood for universality in some sense.

TO WHOM

It is quite certain that the author had in mind the Christian church at Rome. His epistle was not necessarily addressed to the Romans, for the church there was very metropolitan, composed of both Jews and Gentiles, of free men and slaves. It had reached the wealthy as well as the poorer classes, and even some of "Caesar's household" were within its membership.

To all these various groups who had experienced God's grace the apostle wrote his classic letter, ". . . to the Jew first, and also to the Greek" (1:16). It also may be that he had in mind any unsaved who might read its message, for he makes a strong argument relative to sin and salvation (3:23; 6:22, 23).

PURPOSE

The purpose for writing this epistle is made plain, in part, at least. The writer wanted to gather some fruit for Christ among them, as he had done elsewhere; he also felt a certain sense of obligation to them, as he says, "I am debtor . . .to the Greeks . . . barbarians . . . wise . . .

unwise . . . so, as much as in me is, I am ready to preach the gospel to you that are at Rome also" (1:13-15).

At this writing, Paul had not yet been to Rome. This was to come for him some years later. In his epistle he gave them what has been called by some "The Gospel according to St. Paul." It is the most complete and fully explained presentation of the Gospel message he gives anywhere. His other epistles are much more like letters. The form of argument used is most likely similar to what he used in a series of messages preached to convince men of the truth of the Gospel.

His first aim, then, seems to have been to herald the Gospel of Christ and declare Him the Son of God with power to save men from sin (1:1-4). He doubtless also intended to convince any Jewish readers who had any doubts, that Christ was the Son of God. This is seen by his constant references to the Old Testament Scriptures which Christ fulfilled in His redemptive work and death.

The church at Rome was composed of both Jewish and Gentile believers. He proposes to show them how Christ is the end of the law to those who believe, and that no more ceremonial laws and special sacrifices are necessary, as in the Old Testament. Men are now saved by faith in Christ, God's Son, who has come to fulfill all Old Testament prophecies about Himself. He sets forth God's purpose in raising up the Jewish nation (3:1-31), but that men are saved by faith, not by works, as seen in Abraham's case (4: 1-25). This faith is revealed in Christ, God's Son, the fulfilment of God's promises to Abraham (5:1-21). While sin reigns in the hearts of all men, through Christ there is hope for freedom from sin (6:1—7:25), and in Christ there is glorious liberty from the power of sin for those who accept Christ and live for Him (8:1-39). This is the nature of his argument. In chapters 9-11 he shows how the Jews forfeited the Christian hope through rejection of Christ and how the Gentiles gained favor with God by accepting Christ; but he also shows that Israel will finally be restored when they return to Christ in faith at the end. Chapters 12-16 are used to show the application of the Christian faith to daily, practical Christian living.

His purpose is to show that in Christ all men find common meeting ground and that in Him there is the way to life and the power to live this good life.

TIME

Some think this epistle was probably written during Paul's last missionary journey, possibly while he was at Corinth. The year A.D. 56 would be the most probable date for it, the time just before his last trip to Jerusalem, where he was arrested and imprisoned at Caesarea.

THE PANTHEON. *This temple in the city of Rome was built by Agrippa in 27 B.C. and rebuilt later by Hadrian. It is still remarkably well preserved.*

AUTHORSHIP

From the most ancient times the authorship of this book has been credited to Paul. Numerous early writers either refer to, quote from, or list this book in such a way as to recognize its genuineness and accept it as being inspired of God.

Unlike many Scripture writers, Paul lists himself in the very opening verse of this epistle as its author, hastening soon thereafter to state his reasons for writing in an overall manner (1:1). He is quick to state his authority for writing, since the church at Rome knew him only by reputation (1:5-7). Following this, he reveals his deep concern, prays for them and states his plan to visit them, in order to impart to them spiritual benefits which he believed such a visit would bring (1: 8-15).

There cannot possibly be any question about the identity of this writer. There are far too many qualifying facts in his life, relating him to the Paul pictured in Acts and elsewhere in the New Testament, to be anyone other than the Saul of Tarsus converted on the Damascus road. His whole presentation in this book is in keeping with this Paul.

Born at Tarsus, in Cilicia, near Syria (Acts 21:39; Gal. 1:21), his name originally was Saul, the Hebrew form of the name. Later it was changed to Paul, which means "little" or "small." This, evidently, because he was small of stature. He received his theological education at Jerusalem under Gamaliel, the great Jewish teacher. His earlier education was likely in his home country and was beyond doubt considerably colored by Greek culture and philosophy. He spoke both Greek and Hebrew fluently, though all his epistles were originally written in Greek, the prevailing language of the Eastern world in his day.

Before his conversion, he was a strict Pharisee, zealously keeping the law and persecuting the Christians, as he believed them to be a heretical sect which should be destroyed as fast as possible (Phil. 3:3-6; I Tim. 1:15, 16). He felt he obtained mercy because he did this in ignorance.

The story of his conversion and entrance into the ministry (Acts 9:1-30; 11:25-30; 13:1-4; Gal. 1:11-24) is one of the most thrilling and challenging accounts of the New Testament church's history.

Apparently, Paul was never a very well man after his earlier years in the ministry, although a more wiry and enduring man we would have to search far to find. Possibly his stoning by Jewish fanatics at Lystra (Acts 14:19) greatly impaired him for life. He may have been partially blinded by the powerful light which shone about him at his conversion (Acts 9), although this is not certainly known. But likely his sight was again impaired by the incident at Lystra; and his face may have been badly mangled, leaving lasting scars. (Read carefully II Cor. 10:10; 12:1-10, noting especially v. 9, 10; also, Gal. 4:13-15; 6:17.)

Of the twenty-seven books of the New Testament, Paul wrote at least thirteen, possibly fourteen, if he wrote Hebrews, which some believe he did. Although Luke wrote more *words* of the New Testament than did Paul, yet in content and ideas, Paul is by far the most outstanding contributor. His profound arguments and doctrinal statements, his setting forth of ethical Christian practices and views, and the important information concerning Christian living certainly place him as one of the foremost New

Testament writers. The church owes more to Paul for its theological beliefs in concrete form than to any other writer. Paul and John were the major theologians of the New Testament, just as Luke was its chief historian.

Probably no other man, with the exception of Moses, has had so profound or lasting an influence for good upon the world as Paul. When reading his writings, remember you are sitting at the feet of one of the most brilliant minds, most devout souls, and mightiest of the apostles of Christ who ever lived.

In the Book of Romans Paul has left on record his strongest theological arguments, the nearest to a systematic theology in the New Testament. Paul's genius as a writer and thinker comes out at its best here. His best logic, philosophy of approach to the problem, and principles of interpretation are seen here as they relate to Christ and His redemptive work, the unfolding of the Old Testament Messianic prophecies. Here he plumbs the depths and reaches the heights of Christian doctrine. The doctrines of God, Christ, the Holy Spirit, man, sin, grace, faith, justification, regeneration, sanctification, atonement, death, resurrection, and future rewards and punishments are all dealt with in this brief compass in an astounding manner. It is little wonder that Coleridge called Romans "the most profound work in existence" and Martin Luther pronounced it "the chief work of the New Testament."

The Book of Romans may be briefly outlined as follows:

    I.   Doctrinal presentation, 1-8
    II. Dispensational presentation — Jews' present state, 9-11
    III. Devotional presentation—Christian qualities and requirements, 12-16

Special notes: Romans is the first of the "epistle" or "letters" of the New Testament. These books were originally composed like large *letters*. Some were sent to churches and some to individuals, as we shall see. But they were also inspired by the Holy Spirit, for they had a far larger mission than merely their first contact. Christ knew they were to become part of the New Testament. Peter refers to Paul's letters or epistles as "Scripture" (II Peter 3:16). They could be part of the promise of Christ: "I have yet many things to say unto you, but ye cannot bear them now" (John 16:12). These epistles have been preserved by the providence of God and the guidance of the Holy Spirit and made part of the message of God to all men for all times. Look up the meaning of the word epistle in a good dictionary.

Since there are no *outstanding stories* in the rest of the New Testament, this section will be dispensed with from here onward. We will present only the *great truths* in the remaining books of the Bible.

GREAT TRUTHS IN ROMANS

1. One of the first things Paul points out in Romans is that Christ is "declared to be the Son of God with power" (1:4). He builds the whole argument of this book upon that fact. Christ, the Son of God, is the foundation of his whole epistle and entire ministry. Around Him clusters every doctrine and every hope of the Christian church.

2. His next presentation is the *Gospel* (1:15-17). This "good news" — for so the word gospel means — is conditioned upon the "power of God" through Christ. For Paul, Christ *is* the Gospel. Without Him, there would be no "good news" for mankind.

Courtesy, Italian State Tourist Office

3. He then plunges into the next most important fact of his letter — the matter of *sin*. He paints a most dark and gloomy picture of man and his condition as a result of sin. He leaves no question as to man's moral condition and need of redemption in the argument which follows (1:18—2:29).

4. Moving a bit close to his point, he presents Jew and Gentile as alike — darkened and ruined by sin. None of the race has escaped, for "all have sinned and come short of the glory of God" (3:23), he explains. Jews could not, because of their covenant relationship to God, escape the consequences of sin (3:1-31).

5. He then comes even nearer to the Jewish heart by denying that salvation can be had by *works*. His argument here is that even Abraham was not justified by works, but by faith. Abraham had

THE COLOSSEUM. *This large amphitheater in Rome, which originally seated about fifty thousand spectators, was begun by Vespasian but completed by Titus in A.D. 80. Gladiators fought here, and according to tradition, Christians were thrown to beasts.*

faith long before the law had made possible the keeping or doing of it for salvation, or peace with God (4:1-25).

6. Paul introduces *justification,* or being made right with God, as coming through faith in Jesus Christ, God's Son (5:1-5). It is conditioned upon the blood of Christ and His atonement (5:6-19). The work wrought in the heart by the Spirit when one is justified is known as "regeneration." It is a starting of new life in Christ by the Holy Spirit (John 3:1-7).

7. Christ, rather than the law, is then presented as the answer to man's sin.

THE ARCH OF CONSTANTINE IN ROME. *Constantine, as Roman Emperor, issued the Edict of Milan in 331. It put a stop to the persecution of Christians and placed Christianity upon a footing of equality with other religions in the Roman Empire.*

Sin brings bondage, but Christ brings freedom (6:1-22). He climaxes this thought with the reminder that the "wages of sin is death; but the gift of God is eternal life through Jesus Christ our Lord" (6:23). The original word, here rendered "wages," may be thought of as "daily pay," as of a Roman soldier, for example. The daily pay of sin is death.

8. Still dealing with sin, the apostle points out the dual nature of man, that he can be conscious of the desire to do good and yet have within him evil which counteracts this desire at the same time (7:14-17).

There have been several arguments about this passage (7). One is that Paul here presented a picture of himself, in the first person, present tense, as he was before his conversion. It contends that this is a picture of the zealous, God-fearing Jew, striving to keep the law, but without grace. He is totally aware of the good which the law demands, but is unable to render it because of the bondage of sin in his life, which forbids him to do so. It is only as Christ, God's remedy for sin, comes into his life that he is able to shout triumphantly, "There is therefore now no condemnation to them who are in Christ Jesus . . ." (8:1).

Another theory is that Paul here portrays the state of a justified person, in whose heart Christ dwells by faith. But in this state there is still the "remains of sin"; the "carnal mind," which hinders the growth of God's grace, still dominates the person to a large extent. Many of the best scholars have held to this theory. Others have admitted that this *may be* the state of the justified Christian; but if so, it portrays the lower state of Christian life not that high state which is pictured in chapter 8.

9. Whatever state or condition Romans 7 describes, the goal of the Christian for daily living is set in chapter 8. None who are sincere can doubt this. Obedience to the carnal mind is warned against as bringing spiritual death (8: 6-8), and total obedience to Christ and the Holy Spirit is pointed out as the way of spiritual freedom and life (8:9-14).

The classic passage on the *witness of the Spirit* (8:16) should be memorized and made a heart-treasure by every young person. This is one of the high peaks of Romans. Christianity is a supernatural religion, and God is pleased to make Himself known by His Spirit's witness in the hearts of those who love Him.

10. One of the greatest passages of triumph in Christ is 8:32-39. Those who are wholly committed to Christ have every provision for their keeping. God's grace through Christ is sufficient for even the most difficult places in life.

11. The present state of the Jews in their unbelief and rejection of Christ is dealt with in chapters 9-11. Faith in Christ, confession of Christ, and witnessing of Him to others is stated as the condition of salvation (10:8-12). The Jewish people who refuse to do this have been rejected by God until the time when they turn to Christ as Savior.

As part of the parenthetic message of this dispensational passage about the Jews' rejection of Christ, Christian missions are urged as the only means of the world's salvation (10:13-17). None can shirk this duty and be pleasing to God. All cannot *go,* but all can pray and give

that the God-called ones may go with this message to all the lost.

12. This dispensational truth about the Jews is sandwiched between chapters 8 and 12 as a long parenthesis. To get the best connection of the continuing argument, one should really read the last verses of chapter 8, then go immediately to chapter 12, beginning with verse 1. Note the close connection of thought by doing this.

Paul here presents the most complete set of injunctions, or *demands,* for Christian living to be found in the New Testament in one section (12:9-21). The passage should be carefully studied, and memorized if possible. It is closely akin to I Corinthians 13; it pictures one of the highest and noblest plains of Spirit-filled Christian living. Only those totally committed to Christ (12:1, 2) and filled with His Spirit can hope to live upon this grand tableland of daily Christian living. This is not merely an ideal to strive for; it is the actual life of Christians at their best!

13. Matters of obedience to civil law, treatment of the weak brother in Christ, and equality of all believers in Christ occupy chapters 13-15. Special greetings and last words of information fill the final chapter.

This is Paul's second largest book, but it is by far his most important work. One should master the *plan* of this book and grasp its *content* as thoroughly as possible. This will provide one with a much better understanding of much that Paul writes in his following epistles, or letters.

Memory Verse

"I beseech you therefore, brethren, by the mercies of God, that ye present your bodies a living sacrifice, holy, acceptable unto God, which is your reasonable service. And be

not conformed to this world: but be ye transformed by the renewing of your mind, that ye may prove what is that good, and acceptable, and perfect, will of God" (12:1-2).

I Corinthians

This book was named for the people to whom it was written. The people who lived in this city were popularly known as Corinthians, and so the book has been called Corinthians from the most ancient times. It is the first of two epistles by this name.

TO WHOM

The book is addressed to "the church of God which is at Corinth . . ." (1:2). The apostle not only had in mind the elect and most devout, whom he calls "sanctified" and "saints,". but he also included a great number who were not so spiritually minded. This epistle was meant for general reading among all classes of the church and has its specific messages to various groups. It has rightly been called the "most diversified of all Paul's epistles." This is due to the large number and different types of persons with whom his letter deals.

The church at Corinth was composed of both Jews and Gentiles, for there were many Jews in the city. The recent banishment of Jews from Rome by the Emperor Claudius had caused many to flee to Corinth. Here is where Paul met Aquila and Priscilla, later to become Gospel co-workers (Acts 18:2). Jews had lived there for many years before; however, the population and the church there were both predominantly Gentile.

In writing this letter, then, Paul had in mind not only the several factions of the church, but also the different races, for there were numerous colors and racial segments in the church. His writing also embraced the worldly-minded, sophisticated Greek, as well as the more lowly common slave and free man; the devout, as well as the careless and carnal believer.

PURPOSE

Relative to the *purpose* of his writing, several things may be said.

1. He had been there previously, founding the church and becoming its first pastor. Now after some years he was informed that there had arisen certain very unwholesome situations in the church. These needed to be corrected. Doubtless, this was his first purpose in writing.

2. There seems to have been some prior correspondence between him and the church, probably the church leaders. In this there had been questions asked which he needed to answer (7:1). This required a reply, which formed part of this epistle.

3. Factions, corrupt morals, and certain bad practices in the common church services also needed his attention. He wrote to correct all these things which local church leaders had allowed to develop, those which were about to destroy the church there.

4. He proposed to unify the churches of Corinth into one working unit which would present a solid front to the world, one that could show what Christ's grace had done for them. It is quite evident

that the work of the church had spread over the general area and a number of smaller congregations had developed. There were no large meeting places in those days. Homes or some type of halls were generally used. Church buildings were not generally developed for worship purposes until some two hundred years later, after the great persecutions had somewhat subsided. The fact that there were several local congregations may have given rise to the divisions more easily, by which some claimed to be following Paul, some Peter, and some Apollos, as indicated in Paul's rebuke to them (1:12, 13).

Possibly something of the city of Corinth and its conditions should be noted to help in understanding the church's conditions and problems.

Corinth had originated several hundred years earlier; it was situated on the Isthmus of Corinth, which was about three miles wide. It was also the provincial capital of the Roman territory of Achaia. In Paul's time it had a population of some 400,000 and was a center of Greek culture, of Roman trade between East and West, and of world travel. It had a metropolitan population and was very wicked and immoral.

The city was governed democratically, and free assemblies, such as the Christian church, were permitted. Freedom of speech was common. It was a center of cults; immorality was practiced freely and was generally condoned rather than condemned. The wealth of the city made it a place of ease and pleasure, as well as giving opportunity for all kinds of sins to flourish.

Such standards of life and conduct would naturally contribute to various kinds of religious and moral problems, such as are seen in Paul's epistle to this church. For instance, bickering and loud talk by the women in the services could easily have arisen out of the freedom of assembly to which they were accustomed. Paul had to explain that order was to be maintained in the church services (14:33-35). The same would apply to the matter of speaking in several languages in a church service, possibly to show their ability to do so. This also had to be set in order (14:1-35).

The case of immoral conduct within the church (5:1-7) is another problem arising out of the laxity of morals in the city life in general. The matter of women's hair styling also arose out of the same condition (11:1-16). Immoral women wore no "covering" for their hair, but tended to overdress it to attract the attention of men. Men, on the other hand, who wore long hair, were generally thought of as sex perverts, so it was a "shame" for a man to wear his hair long (11:14). These conditions were local or at least confined to those times and that general area, but had to be dealt with.

In this same environment the manner in which the Lord's Supper was observed had been altered to where it was a large meal, during which the church people ate and drank to excess. It was necessary for the apostle to correct this abuse (11:20-34).

With this background one can see better how the problems with which Paul had to deal would have arisen.

TIME

As to the time this epistle was written, there has been some difference of opinion. It is now believed that it may have been written as early as A.D. 55. Paul had labored at Corinth about a year and one-half establishing the church there. He had moved on to Ephesus, where he established the church and ministered for about three years. It seems that he had received word of conditions in Corinth, possibly from a delegation sent to inform him. Apparently they had written him earlier and he had replied in a letter that has been lost (5:9). This letter, then, was written just before he left for Jerusalem, early in the spring, possibly to his largest church, and certainly, his most problematic one.

THE CORINTH CANAL. *Built in the late 1800's, this canal crosses the Isthmus of Corinth. The ancient city of Corinth is located on this isthmus.*

AUTHORSHIP

Paul designates himself as the author in his opening address (1:1-2). There has never been any serious attempt to dispute this claim. There are too many characteristics of the apostle in the writing to question Paul's authorship of it.

As founder of this church, who could possibly have had more concern for it than the apostle himself? Like a father correcting his children, he is here correcting his infant church, straightening out its *problems* — of which there were many — and setting it back on the right course.

There are two major sections of this epistle, as seen in the outline, each consisting of a chain of "problems" which Paul intended to correct. The *great*

truths in this book are largely clustered about these various problems and their solutions.

This epistle may be outlined as follows:

I. Things about which Paul had "heard" indirectly, 1-6

II. Things about which they had written him, 7-14

III. Explanation of resurrection and eternal life, 15

IV. The offering for the saints; personal matters, 16

GREAT TRUTHS IN I CORINTHIANS

1. Divisions which evidently had arisen (1-4) were caused by strong local leaders who were posing as followers of the different apostolic and general church leaders. They had emphasized one aspect of their lives to the neglect of other important truths, which naturally brought divisions. They had even become contentious and strife had developed.

Paul admonished that the *cross* should be the center of all true preaching. Christ, not His followers, is the supreme message of Christianity. Any time we look away from Christ to any leader, however great, we miss God's way of salvation. Divisions among God's people are hurtful and should be avoided. There is to be unity of belief and witness among Christians (1:10).

2. Immorality had come into the church in a most disgusting form (5: 1-2). Paul quickly summed up the situation, believing he had spotted the guilty party. He was cautious in his approach, but nevertheless, pounded heavily upon the local church leaders who would tolerate such wickedness.

Evidently the persons involved were rather prominent in the church. Possibly they had not been removed from any positions they may have held. The reference to the fact that this was unheard of among the Gentiles literally means that it was not *allowed,* or *condoned.* Such cases existed among the heathen, but were condemned by the best of heathen people.

Christianity cannot sanction *any form* of immorality. Sexual impurity is one of the common sins of youth in general, but it should be avoided; otherwise, this problem will grow worse with age, wrecking all hopes of happiness in marriage in later life.

3. Strife had arisen between certain members of the Corinthian churches, and they had gone to law against each other (6). Paul condemns this, reminding them that if the Christians will one day judge the earth, they certainly should be able to live peaceably together in this life. This is the pattern for Christians now and always. Christians can settle their differences without lawsuits against each other.

4. On matters of marriage Paul had some wholesome advice. He explained that during that particular time of persecution, one could serve the Lord more effectively if he remained single, as he himself was. He would not be hampered by having someone else to be responsible for, as married persons do. However, if a single person could not be content, he recommended that he should marry. It was better to marry, he said, than to "burn" —not in hell fire — but with burning passion, or unsatisfied sex desire (7:9).

Husbands and wives are to be considerate of each other and are not to withhold from each other the normal sexual relationships of married life (7: 3-5). In doing so, either one at fault may become a stumbling stone to the other, causing him to be tempted to marital unfaithfulness, because of his unsatisfied sexual desire. Failure to obey this advice has probably caused the breaking up of many marriages!

Christians who have unsaved companions are warned against leaving them, for in remaining with them, they may win them to Christ (7:12-16). Marriage is the only proper solution to a happy life for most people. Although single himself, the apostle realized this. Celibacy — or remaining single — as the happiest way of life has never proved successful nor practical for most Christians whether laymen or ministers.

5. If a person explained to a Christian in those days that the meat being served at any meal had been offered to an idol, to Jupiter, Venus, etc., the Christian was then to refrain from eating it, out of respect to the one telling him (10:28). Some people with a weak conscience felt that they were honoring the idol if they ate this meat; therefore, if a stronger Christian ate it, he might cause a weaker one to do wrong by following his example. In today's meaning, we should not do things which may cause anyone else to sin by following our example, though we do not see any harm in the thing we are doing.

In chapters 8-10, Paul explains that meat offered to idols is in no way damaged; the one eating it does not in reality worship the idol god to whom it may have been offered. It was a heathen custom to offer meat to idols and then sell it to those who wished to patronize that particular idol. Worshipers of Jupiter or Mars, for instance, would buy meat in the market place — like our large farm markets in the cities — which had been offered to Jupiter or Mars. In this way,

they felt they were associating themselves with this particular god. Paul explains that a true Christian believer who knows this does nothing to the meat, nor does it associate him in any way with this idol. But there were some younger Christians who still felt that to eat this meat was to worship this idol. So, Paul explains that for their sakes, older, stronger Christians should not eat such meat before them, lest they be turned away and tempted to again return to idol worship. This is what he means by saying that if it would be offensive, he would eat no more meat while the world stood, that is, no more meat which had been offered to idols, not that he would not eat *any* meat! (8:13).

The lesson for us today is that stronger Christians may be able to do certain things which to them are not evil. They understand fully what they are doing, and are doing nothing which to them would be wrong. But this liberty of theirs may cause some weaker Christian to start doing something which he is influenced to do, which will bring him into condemnation. Then, the older, stronger Christian should forego certain things which he may otherwise do, lest he cause the weaker one to stumble.

This whole section (8-10) really has to do with the stronger brother in Christ looking after the interests of the weaker and securing him against possibilities of falling into sin. We must suffer for the brethren that we may help to establish them in God's grace.

6. Women's dress (dealt with earlier

SACRED SPRING AT CORINTH. *Excavations of the ancient city of Corinth began in 1896. Archaeologists have discovered that the city dates back to the Neolithic period.*

in this chapter) and the Lord's Supper are next in line. Paul deals with them at length (11), giving advice.

The Lord's Supper is a memorial service of highest reverence, not a common meal, he explains. He rebukes their festive practices and states the twofold purpose — to remind us of Christ's sacrifice for us at Calvary and to point to our faith in His personal return (11:23-26).

Young Christians should never refrain from taking part in this because they feel unworthy. None of us are truly *worthy;* but if our hearts are set to serve the Lord and we are trying our best to follow Him, then we have no reason to worry. It is only those who know they are hypocrites and are not truly at heart serving the Lord who should fear the consequences of taking the Lord's Supper.

7. In discussing spiritual gifts and their relationship to Christian service (12-14), Paul lists nine gifts of the Spirit (12:8-10) which are vested in the church for the benefit of Christians. These are to be used by persons to whom they are given by the Holy Spirit. Their purpose is to unify the church. He uses the word "body" eighteen times (12:12-31) as a symbol of the Christian church, as Christ's body of believers on earth.

The order of Christian workers is also listed (12:28), showing how these match up with spiritual gifts. The Corinthians were great for *works,* but evidently, rather weak on deeper spiritual life. Paul points out that there must be spiritual life, unity of the Spirit, and fellowship to go along with works.

Young people are often very active for the Lord, but one should remember that much activity without the Spirit of Christ becomes a dead letter and spiritually avails nothing.

Perhaps the highest point of the en-

tire epistle, if not of all Paul's writing, is reached in the famous thirteenth chapter, where he describes *divine love.* The word charity used in the King James Version carried much more of the original thought some 350 years ago than it does now. One should always substitute the thought of *divine love* for the word charity when reading this chapter; he will then get a much clearer view of what is meant. Henry Drummond called love "The Greatest Thing in the World" in his book on this chapter. It is the highest point in Christian experience and practice. It is said that John Wesley read this chapter every day for many years. Everyone would do well to memorize it entirely.

The matter of speaking with other tongues, or languages (14) not understood in the public service, has also been dealt with earlier.

8. Possibly the greatest and most profound discussion of the Resurrection ever penned is presented by Paul. There had doubtless been a misunderstanding among the Corinthians; so he proceeds to clarify the matter, taking Christ's resurrection as his basis for the resurrection of the saints.

He deals with two major phases of the Resurrection: first, its *certainty* (15:1-34); second, its *nature* (15:35-58). Its certainty is based upon Christ's resurrection (vv. 1-11); he lists Christ's appearances, including His appearance to himself on the Damascus way.

The nature of the Resurrection he bases largely upon nature, but explains that it will be a far superior form in which glorified bodies will appear. The heart of the argument is in verses 42-45. Only the experience of it in the coming world of bliss can ever fully explain it to one.

This is the climactic goal of all Christian living. To miss this would be to miss everything Christianity means. It is the final purpose of all Christ's redemptive work.

9. The final problem Paul had to deal with concerned the "collection" for the poor saints at Jerusalem. He explained in a few words how this was to be cared for, but the matter was of sufficient importance to claim special attention.

The saints at Jerusalem were a major concern to him. With this special offering he had doubtless wanted to prove to the Jerusalem Christians the true and genuine Christianity of the Gentile churches.

Christian charity as seen in practice is here taught. It is too bad that most charity today has fallen into the hands of the community, the government, or other agencies, the church has too largely neglected it. Liberality in giving is a truly Christian concept. Young people should learn early the blessedness of giving.

Other *great truths* touched upon as the apostle tackled these nine problems are:

1. The blindness of unregenerate man to God (2:14). Spiritual or religious things are "foolishness" to him — they don't make sense to him. He sees no necessity for them.

2. The Christian's body as the temple of the Holy Spirit (6:19). He should not practice any habits or allow anything to be done with his body which would not be for the betterment of his Christian life. He is to treat it as the Lord's property (6:20). To keep this always in mind will help one to do the things which are right.

3. Christ's intention that ". . . they which preach the Gospel should live of the Gospel" (9:14). This means that every church should support its pastor, if possible, so that he may give full time to his ministry. Young people should learn the joy of giving to the church and its program. The church is worthy of our total support.

4. Paul said that he kept his body well disciplined, so that it did not cause him to disobey the laws of God. The words, "I keep under my body," literally mean "I beat my body, and bring it unto subjection." The original word here means to *beat,* as *to strike under the eye, beat black and blue.* The thought is *total discipline.* No one who does not discipline his body and its desires can live as a Christian. The body as such is not sinful; it is neither moral, nor immoral — it is amoral — non-moral. The body is only the instrument of the spirit and soul of a person. It does whatever the mind and will direct it to do. Sin is a matter of the spirit, but the body becomes involved when it is used to commit anything sinful.

For instance, the body may crave food, and this is no sin. To steal it becomes a sin. The body may have natural sex drives and urges; these are not in themselves sinful, any more than craving food is sinful. It is the satisfying of this desire in a wrong way that is sinful. It is clearly an act of the will which constitutes sin. Sin is not native desire; this is only biological hunger or urge. "Sin is the transgression of the law" (I John 3:4). "All unrighteousness is sin" (I John 5:17). Sin, then, is the willful transgression of a known law of God.

By God's grace, Christian people must so keep their bodies under control so as not to transgress God's laws willfully. This may seem very hard, or even impossible. But as Paul was promised by

Christ, God's grace will be sufficient (II Cor. 12:9).

5. Paul states one of the greatest truths of the Christian way (10:13) when he says that no temptation will overtake the believer that he cannot overcome by God's grace. God has made provisions for each Christian for grace which overcomes, "a way to escape" even the worst of temptations. This passage should be memorized by every Christian.

Memory Verse

"And now abideth faith, hope, charity, these three; but the greatest of these is charity" (13:13).

II Corinthians

This epistle, like I Corinthians, takes its name from the city of Corinth and the church to which it was written.

TO WHOM

It was written to the Corinthian Christians. For this section one should read the notes on I Corinthians, to gain a better background for this epistle. Much said there still applies to this writing.

PURPOSE

The *purpose* of this letter was possibly as follows:

1. It appears that his first epistle to the Corinthians had, after sometime of waiting, worked much of the desired effects which he sought, though not all. He wished to commend the church for

their response to his letter, so a part of this letter was commendatory (1:13, 14).

2. The first letter of Paul brought very great sorrow to many in the Corinthian Church and Paul wished to comfort those who sorrowed.

As the *offenders* of I Corinthians 5:1 had been severely dealt with and had evidently repented, but were still suffering, Paul did not wish his punishment to be too severe (2:1-10).

3. But perhaps one of his major purposes was to reestablish his position as an apostle of Christ among them (3:1-17). This reference is merely to pinpoint the start of his argument, for much of his argument on through to the end of the letter is based upon his apostolic authority. His first epistle had at first produced much of the desired effect, but there had arisen a Jewish party in the church who claimed to have "letters of commendation," possibly from some authority at Jerusalem who had denied Paul's apostleship and tried to discredit him among the church people (3:1). He at once proceeds to set this right by pointing out his divine mission, sufferings, and his concern for them; he climaxes this with his strong emphasis upon his apostleship (4-12). Note his special references to his apostleship (11:5-33 — especially 11:5; 12:1-13; 12:11).

4. A final purpose was to encourage the getting ready of the offering for the poor saints at Jerusalem, which had now been waiting for about a year (9).

TIME

Some believe it followed Paul's first epistle to the Corinthian church a few months afterward; others, that it was perhaps about a year later, when Paul was in Philippi the second time. The probable date was about the fall of A.D. 56, which allows the first letter to have been written sometime in A.D. 55.

AUTHORSHIP

There is no question but what the same writer penned both I and II Corinthians. All the connecting links of interest between the two lead to this conclusion, aside from the fact that its opening address claims Paul as its author.

For more information on the apostle Paul, see the notes in Romans under AUTHORSHIP.

I Corinthians was written from Ephesus to arouse the church at Corinth to its duty regarding matters of conduct and to answer certain important questions which they had asked the apostle. Timothy was sent to take the first epistle,

it is believed, and the report was not too favorable at first.

Some believe a letter taken by Titus followed this in quick succession, and that it has been lost and is not now known. This second letter, they think, is referred to by Paul's mention of coming "a third time" (13:1). But there is no proof of this. Again, some believe the apostle himself made a quick visit to Corinth from Ephesus, which is not recorded; this may be what is meant in chapter 13:1. It seems likely, however, that Titus was sent to Corinth to try to

THE APOLLO TEMPLE AND THE ACRO-CORINTHUS. *Ruins of the Acropolis of Corinth still remain on the top of this mountain. On its summit stood the temple of Aphrodite.*

straighten out matters. This visit was prolonged beyond the time the apostle had expected, and it is to Titus' return that he alludes in II Corinthians 7:5-6.

After having written the first epistle and sent Titus afterwards, Paul left Ephesus for Troas, but did not tarry long there. He was so distressed in spirit he could not bear it, so he went on to Macedonia (2:12-13). On this trip, and in Macedonia, Paul appears to have been sick from the exhaustion of his work and the burden of the way things had gone at Corinth, as the two references above show. But the coming of Titus and the good news from Corinth did more for him than all else that may have been done. From Titus' report it is clear that the Corinthian church had repented, and much was accomplished by the first epistle (7:7-9).

It was at this time that the second epistle was written. Timothy was apparently with him here at this time (1:1; Acts 20:4), as well as Titus who had just returned to him from Corinth.

Despite the fact that the Corinthian church had submitted to his rebukes and done much to clear the whole situation, there had developed a strong Jewish party in the church, which apparently tried to discredit Paul's apostleship. This letter was needed to correct this error and reestablish his authority (4-12; 11:5; 12:11).

Probably no other writing of Paul shows so truly his human nature and his heartaches in the work as this epistle. Here he bares his heart as in no other. To know Paul better, read this book carefully.

There are two ways this book may be outlined; the first is:

   I.   Defense of Paul's ministry, 1-7
  II. The collection for the saints, 8-9

 III. Vindication of Paul's character, 10-13

Another outline may be:
   I.   The preface, 1:1-7
  II. Narration concerning himself and his work, 1:8—7:16
 III. Narration concerning the collection, 8-9
 IV. Paul's defense against false apostles and false workers, 10-12
  V. Miscellaneous matters, 13

GREAT TRUTHS IN II CORINTHIANS

1. This book presents two very human aspects of Paul's life. He was stern when occasion demanded it (1:23, 24); but he was also very tenderhearted, full of compassion and sympathy (2:1-4).

The New Testament gives us no word picture of Paul. All that we can gain is from this epistle and other side glances. One second-century legend makes him a man of moderate height, curly hair, small crooked legs, blue eyes, knit eyebrows, a long nose, but full of grace and pity. Another tradition says he was a small man, stout, bowlegged, bald-headed, close-browed, with a prominent nose, but full of grace in appearance. No one knows just what he looked like; however, his Greek name, Paul, does mean small, and may suggest something of his features. After his conversion, it is reasonable to believe that from his persecutions, he suffered from a weakened body and possibly bad eyes (Gal. 4:15; 6:11). Apparently he had some type of infirmity which detracted from his appearance. (II Cor. 10:10; Gal. 4:13, 14).

God sometimes greatly uses those whose personal appearance and physical bodies are not as strong as others (I Cor. 1:27-29). One should give God all he has, to use as He wills, and leave the results with him.

Christians should be strong against all evil but treat everyone with kindness. This is not being a "sissy," but being a really mature, well-balanced, strong personality. We live in an age of hardness, but we must not allow it to dominate us, or we will lose some of the best things in life.

2. The Gospel has marvelous power through Christ to transform men's lives. This is well illustrated from the Greek word used for "changed" (3:18) — metamorphosed. (See the note on Matthew 17:2.) There is power in Christ's word to change people's lives completely.

3. The Gospel of Christ is not hidden to anyone except those who are blinded to it by sin (4:3-6). It is the work of Christians to witness of Christ and cause others to come to see this glorious light and be saved (4:5-6).

4. This treasure of the love of God we have in earthen vessels — meaning our bodies, our heart-life. Whatever may happen to us physically or socially, we can still have this grace in our hearts (4:7, 18).

This is to be done by renewing this blessed relationship to Christ day by day, looking always to Him. Life's trials are trifling compared to the eternal rewards (4:17, 18).

5. Life in Christ is all-inclusive, all-transforming, according to Paul (5:17). Old things of life which were sinful pass away when one comes into true fellowship with Christ. New things take their place. One is said to become a "new creature."

A good evidence of new life in Christ is the change which comes to one when he learns to know Christ.

6. Young Christians should think of themselves as "workers together" with Christ. They should endeavor to so live that their lives may not become an "offense" to anyone (6:1, 3). Nothing can take the place of a wholesome Christian life and influence. "Good work" will never outshine careless living.

7. Strong warning is given to believers not to "yoke" up with unbelievers. Illustrations of light and darkness, Christ and Satan, are used to show us this should never be (6:14-18).

Think for a moment: What *yoke* is stronger, or tighter, or for longer, than *marriage?*

How many times only heartbreak and sorrow for the Christian come from marriage with a non-Christian. Too often the non-Christian one wins. A good question to ask is: "Can two walk together, except they be agreed?" (Amos 3:3). No! It is never wise to go against God's plain warnings in His Word; one always loses when he does so.

8. Sufficient grace was offered to Paul by Christ when He did not choose to heal him of his infirmity (12:9). God always knows best for us. Sometimes Christians feel that God could answer and relieve them of this or that trouble. He *could*; but He does not always choose to do so, for our sake.

Christ saw that Paul would be of more service to Him in his afflicted state, and that it would be better for Paul, too, than for him to be well. Why some are committed to suffering when others, not half so useful, are allowed to go free and never pained, no one understands. But our commitment to Christ holds us to Him as did the faith of Paul, that if we cannot be made well, we will "glory in" our infirmity, that the "power of Christ" may rest upon us (12:8-10). "Many are the afflictions of the righteous: but the Lord delivereth him out of them all" (Ps. 34:19). But note: It did not say *when* the Lord would deliver them, nor *how*. For some it may not be until death. Think of all the great saints who were afflicted in the past, and take courage.

9. Self-examination (13:5) is a good thing for every Christian. The warehouse, the lumber yard, and the large department store all take regular inventories of their stocks.

Sometimes in the Christian's life, it pays to "count up one's assets and his liabilities." If he finds certain "liabilities" clinging to him, he should prune them off. If he finds he needs to add more to his "stock" of values, such as more patience, kindness, love, or other virtues, he should go to Christ for them.

This is a good book to read when feeling discouraged or tempted.

Memory Verse
"And he said unto me, My grace is sufficient for thee: for my strength is made perfect in weakness. Most gladly therefore will I gather glory in my infirmities, that the power of Christ may rest upon me" (12:9).

Galatians

The name of this book is taken from the churches to which it was written, which were located in the country then known as "Galatia," in central Asia Minor. About the third century B.C., a large number of Gauls settled in this country and gave their name to the country.

TO WHOM
The opening address says the epistle was sent "to the churches of Galatia." There is some difference of opinion as to whether this refers to the northern or southern part of the province of Galatia. Since Paul had preached and established churches in the southern area, at Antioch in Phrygia, Iconium, Lystra, and Derbe during his first missionary journey; it seems logical that this section of the country would have been the area to which the epistle was sent.

PURPOSE
There was a large concentration of Jewish population in this area. There had been some Jewish converts but apparently, many more Gentile converts. Later, Jewish teachers had come into the area, teaching the new Christians that they must accept the Jewish laws and ceremonies and follow these to be saved. This brought a controversy between the Jewish and Gentile Christians. This epistle was sent to the churches to correct this false teaching.

Galatians, then, was written to both Jewish and Gentile converts, pointing out that men are not saved by the works of the *law,* but by *faith in Christ.* Paul shows that even Abraham, the "father of the faithful," was saved by *faith,* long before the *law* was given (3:6-14). Keep in mind when reading this book that two groups are being addressed — Jew and Gentile. Some scholars believe the letter was addressed more largely to the Gentiles, as it describes the liberty they are to have in Christ. The Jewish element of the church, however, is not overlooked, for in his writing the apostle

Courtesy, Kelsey Museum of Archaeology

addresses himself time and again to those with Jewish background.

It is thought that Paul visited these churches again on his second missionary tour, about A.D. 52 or 53 (Acts 16:1-6). At this time he discovered some things which were not good (1:9; 5:21). Some evidently took offense at his plain speaking (4:16) and then became more inclined to listen to the false teachers who came after Paul had left.

When Paul heard what was happening in Galatia, he was probably in Corinth or Ephesus. He wrote at once to correct this false teaching. That was the main purpose of this letter.

These Jewish teachers — probably from Jerusalem, those who had accepted Christ but had also remained loyal to the law — were teaching the Gentile con-

ROMAN AQUEDUCT. *These ruins are located in Antioch of Pisidia. Paul probably preached in this area during his first missionary journey.*

verts that they must also keep the law. They insisted that they be *circumcised* as every Jewish boy had to be soon after birth. This was one of the main rites of the *ceremonial law* of the Jews. (Please look up in a good dictionary the word "circumcision," so as to understand this epistle better). Paul rejected this teaching entirely, saying that neither this rite nor any other *ceremonial* law was necessary to salvation (5:4). Paul did not infer that Christians are not to keep the moral law — the Ten Commandments —

THE TAURUS MOUNTAINS. *This mountain range dominates southern Asia Minor, now Turkey. The churches at Derbe, Lystra, and Iconium were located in this region.*

---

but only the laws of the ancient rites and sacrifices of the Old Testament. These foreshadowed Christ, and were done away with when Christ fulfilled them.

The second purpose of the letter was to establish his authority as an apostle, equal with any other apostle of Christ. Some think Peter may have preached the Gospel only to the Jews in this same region, before Paul reached the Gentiles on his missionary tour. Peter mentions "Galatia" in his first epistle to the Co-rinthians (1:1). It may be that Peter's Jewish converts were responsible for the Jewish teachers coming into the region and stirring up the trouble between them and the Gentile converts of Paul. Paul's authority would naturally have been belittled or denied by these teachers, while Peter was held up as the chief apostle. Paul had to correct this and assert his reasons for his own apostleship. Paul presents his apostolic credentials (1:11—2:15) with a very convincing argument, not that he cared for the honor so much; it was necessary to establish the *truth* of the *Gospel* he preached. Read carefully this historical section (1:11—2:15); then the reason for his writing it will be more clearly seen.

This bit of historical information is

placed early in the epistle to show the Jewish readers where Paul stood with respect to the apostles and his apostolic authority; He wanted to convince the Gentile readers that he had as much right to preach the Gospel of truth as did Peter or anyone else. Apparently he was successful in reestablishing his apostolic authority among the Galatian churches.

The final purpose of this book was to turn the tide against *Judaizers* in general. Judaizers in the early church were those false teachers who insisted on making all Gentile converts Jewish proselytes, becoming circumcised and keeping the Jewish ceremonial laws. Paul contended Christ meant no such thing and that His Gospel was to be universal, that men are saved by faith alone, without any reference to law. This stand the Jerusalem council finally affirmed (Acts 15), and it became the Gospel standard for all Christianity. Had the Judaizers succeeded, Christianity may have been wrecked; or if not, seriously hindered in becoming a worldwide religion. This was the battle ground of the book of Galatians.

TIME

As to the *time* at which this book was written, there is considerable difference of opinion. Some have placed it as early as A.D. 48, others as late as the spring of A.D. 58. Most scholars, however, have taken a more middle date, placing it probably about A.D. 55 or 56, which is likely the more probable date.

Some have maintained it was the first of Paul's epistles, but without too much success. The arguments in Galatians are definitely closely akin to those in Romans, while the heart-anguish is much like that of II Corinthians. It is now generally believed that Paul wrote Galatians from either Corinth or Ephesus, about A.D. 55 or 56, *after* the Corinthians letters, and *before* his epistle to the Romans.

AUTHORSHIP

From the most ancient times, the authorship of this book has been credited to Paul.

What has been said above about the apostle establishing his apostleship is truly Pauline. It corresponds to the same pattern used in II Corinthians. His last remarks at the close of the book, referring to his physical condition, and his personal signature are also further evidence of his authorship (6:11-16). In the midst of the heated battle, no one else could have written more fervently for the position of the book than Paul. Its every expression breathes the Pauline atmosphere. There can be no doubt of his authorship.

One may outline Galatians as follows:
  I.   Personal matters, 1-2
  II. Doctrinal presentation, 3-4
  III. Practical applications, 5-6
Another outline may be:
  I.   Defense of divine authority and Paul's apostleship, 1-2
  II. Salvation by faith in Christ alone, without the works of law, 3-4
  III. Christianity's rules applied to daily living, 5-6

As in Romans, "justification by faith" is the key to the entire book. It is one of the best of the apostolic *apologetics* — argument or presentation in defense of the faith.

GREAT TRUTHS IN GALATIANS

1. Paul's assurance that he preached the true Gospel was so great that even if an angel from heaven preached anything contrary, he pronounced a curse

upon him (1:6-9). This is the height of personal assurance. But if Paul needed and had divine assurance, so can Christians today be assured that the Gospel is true. The Holy Spirit gives assurance to those who fully trust in Christ (Rom. 8:16, 17; I John 3:1-3).

2. Paul tells of his conversion and call to the ministry (1:11-24). Note: (a) His zeal was great against Christ (1:13). (b) He was not converted by preaching but by divine conviction and Christ's revelation to him (1:12-17). (c) His conversion stood in the power of God (1:16). (d) His message of the Gospel was Christ-revealed (1:12). (e) The church accepted him as a true Gospel minister (1:22-24).

3. Paul's stand before the Jerusalem Council (Acts 15) saved the day for Christianity. God needs men like Paul, Luther, and Wesley, who in times of the church's greatest crisis, will not fear to stand up and be counted for the right. They are needed today in every quarter of the earth! Christianity was rescued from Judaism by Paul's remarkable stand. Paul was God's apostle to the Gentiles (2:8).

4. He stood up to Peter, who was much his superior in age and leadership, but who was in the wrong at the moment. It requires courage to do this, especially for one younger in the faith than another (2:11-16). One great need today is for young people who have settled Bible convictions and grace and courage enough to stand up for them wherever they are!

5. Crucifixion with Christ is the answer to true Christian victory in everyday life (2:20). This is more than simple identification *with* Christ; it is total commitment *to* Christ, with an utter faith for this commitment, day by day.

To "frustrate" (2:21) is to disturb. He did not disturb the pattern of this grace, but was in full accord with its workings in his heart. This is victory in Christ.

6. Christ is the center of faith and worship. To trust in anything else is vain. The Christian ceremonies and observances are good, such as baptism, the Lord's Supper, etc. But there is no salvation in any of these alone, any more than there was to the ancient Galatians in observing the Jewish ceremonial laws. One must be careful never to trust in any of these observances or good works for salvation; such a person may be deceived and thereby fail of the grace of God. This is the teaching of the heart of this epistle (3-4).

7. Galatians may be said in some sense to be a supreme warning against *backsliding,* or going back to the old life before conversion. Note the warnings in this passage (3:1-5). One is never so well established in his Christian experience but what falling away from it is possible (5:1-8).

8. Two kinds of "fruits" are shown (5:19-23). The first list (5:19-21) shows the unregenerate man's life from the heart standpoint. This is a revelation of his *inward* life, working out into daily living. The second list shows the fruit of the Spirit in the life of the devout Christian (5:22, 23). Compacted into these verses is the height of Christian victorious living and Paul's standard for a normal Christian. Verse 24 explains *how* this life is possible. Only the Holy Spirit can apply this truth to the open heart which sincerely commits all to Christ. Verses 25 and 26 give the rule for radiant Christian living.

9. Strong Christians are always to help restore the weaker ones who may stumble and fall into sin again (6:1-5).

The Greek word from which the English "overtaken in a fault" comes, means to be *seized upon quickly*; *surprised, taken suddenly before he is aware of it.* Someone used to say, "It means as if one stepped on a banana peel and slid down quickly!"

". . . Ye which are spiritual, restore such an one in the spirit of meekness; considering thyself, lest thou also be tempted" (6:1). None of us, however spiritual, are immune from the possibility of temptation and falling into sin. We have no right to treat with unkindness any fallen brother. Rather, we should do our best to get him back on his feet and into fellowship with Christ. But none need fall, for Christ has keeping power.

10. One of the great and inevitable laws of Scripture is that of *sowing and reaping* (6:7). We have seen this referred to many times throughout the Bible, especially in the sense that whatever *evil* things a person does, he will reap them again. Actually, the apostle is here using this law to illustrate this fact in regard to Christian *giving* (6:8-10). It is also true that if we sow sparingly in our fields, we will reap a small harvest; but if we plant plenty and cultivate well, we shall reap a good harvest. If we give cheerfully to Christ's cause with a pure motive to glorify God, we will be blessed bountifully with spiritual blessings.

But it is well to remember that this rule also works in regard to sinful deeds. There are many Bible passages which support this truth. Old sayings such as, "Chickens come home to roost," "The devil is to pay in the end," and "He's getting repaid for his meanness," illustrate how the public has reacted to this great law of *sowing and reaping*. The following lines of an old song also speak this truth:

"Every *deed* you perform is as *seed* to someone,

And the *influence* will never die;

So be careful each day, what you *do, what you say,*

For you'll *meet it again by and by.*"

Memory Verses

"Stand fast therefore in the liberty with which Christ hath made us free, and be not entangled again with the yoke of bondage" (5:1).

"Be not deceived; God is not mocked; for whatsoever a man soweth, that shall he also reap" (6:7).

Ephesians

The book is named for the people residing at Ephesus, particularly the Ephesian Christians.

TO WHOM

In our Bibles the letter is addressed to the saints at Ephesus (1:1). Ephesus was one of the chief cities of Asia in those days.

There has been a considerable amount of discussion as to just whom the epistle was originally written, since in some of the older Greek manuscripts the words "at Ephesus" are not found. This has given rise to the opinion among some that the apostle may have intended the epistle for the churches of Asia in general, as a circular letter.

Courtesy, H. Gokberg

THE GREAT THEATER OF EPHESUS. *The stage had three stories, and the amphitheater itself seated 24,500 people.*

Since Paul spent two or three years at Ephesus, it seems that he would have made some references to persons in that city had the epistle been intended locally. However, others contend, as it has been claimed from the most ancient times, that the letter may have been addressed to the Ephesians, yet intended to be circular in nature and to minister to other churches of that area as well. The Ephesian epistle we now have is thought by some to be referred to as the "epistle from Laodicea" (Col. 4:16). The epistle would naturally have been brought first to Ephesus; hence, the name of *Ephesians* would have finally become attached to it to distinguish it. However all this may have been, the important thing for us is that it is a genuinely true epistle, inspired by the Holy Spirit and highly valuable to us today.

PURPOSE

One of the chief purposes of this epistle seems to have been to produce a greater spirit of *unity* among these Christians. It may have been intended especially for the Gentiles of these churches. It endeavors to head off a split in the church, by which there would have developed Jewish and Gentile segments or branches of the church. The writer pleads for unity in Christ as the ideal of all Christians. (Note especially chapter 5:18-33, where the husband-wife relations are used to illustrate the unity needed in the church.) Some scholars feel this argues favorably for the circular idea of this epistle.

Paul saw keenly the grave danger of

an ultimate splitting apart of the Jewish and Gentile sections of the church. This he strove to avoid by every possible means. His major argument in this connection was that the body of Christ — the church — should be a *unit,* not two separate parts or bodies. This he drives home in his illustration of man and wife (5:25-33).

Some believe that Paul's gesture of love for the Jerusalem saints in taking a great love offering for them, from all the Gentile churches was based upon this motive. He wanted to prove to the Jerusalem church by this expression of love that the Gentile Christians loved and cared for them.

Finally, there seems to be no particular difficulty in the Ephesian church or churches to which the apostle directed his letter, beyond the basic purpose of unity as stated above. The letter contains many instructions for Christians in the higher way of spiritual living. It reveals that the great eternal purpose of God for His church was grounded in God's sovereign will. Perhaps more than any other epistle, this one lifts up the sovereignty of God.

TIME

Relative to the time at which this epistle was written, it is clearly one of Paul's "prison epistles," written while he was imprisoned at Rome. It is thought from references that this was one of three —Colossians and Philemon being the other two — written at once.

This epistle was taken to the Ephesian Christians by Tychicus (6:21); at the same time he took one to Philemon, as he accompanied Onesimus back home to Philemon. Since Paul's imprisonment at Rome was from about A.D. 59-61, it is likely that he wrote this epistle during this time — possibly A.D. 61, at Rome.

AUTHORSHIP

The Pauline authorship of this epistle was not doubted until the nineteenth century. This question was based upon the absence of references and personal greetings by the author to persons at Ephesus. Other scholars explained this as likely arising from the general *circular nature* of the epistle; they held that it argues nothing against its authorship.

Furthermore, the most ancient writers among the Church Fathers quote from this epistle more largely, it is reported, than any others as a special epistle to the Gentiles; they always credit Paul as its author. This gives it the highest validity from external evidence.

The matter of its being so nearly like Colossians in many expressions, and even sentences, can be accounted for by the fact that both these epistles were written about the same time. They were written under similar circumstances, possibly with much the same purpose in mind. They were sent to these churches by the same person (6:21; Col. 4:7-9), and it is only reasonable that they may sound somewhat alike. This tends to confirm the Pauline authorship rather than question it.

Like most of Paul's epistles, this book also has its doctrinal and practical sections, although certainly not as pronounced as Galatians or Romans, for example.

No one knows for certain who founded the Ephesian church. It may have been started by believing Jews returning from Jerusalem after Pentecost. Paul visited it on his second missionary journey (Acts 18:18-21). On his second visit he stayed and preached there for

DIANA. *Ephesians worshiped this goddess and erected an immense temple in her honor.*

about three years. He refers to this on his third missionary tour (Acts 20:31).

Ephesus was the heart of that region of Asia, and a great city in itself. It was a center of cult-worship, and much Greek philosophical thought flourished there.

In this epistle Paul reached the most sublime heights of his entire written ministry. It has been called the "divinest composition of man" and "the most heavenly work." In no other writings of his does he come so near to the very heavenlies themselves. Next in order of sublime language is Colossians.

Ephesians may be outlined as follows:
I.   Opening salutation, 1:1-2
II. Doctrinal presentation, 1:3—3:20
III. Practical aspects of religion, 4:1—6:20

GREAT TRUTHS IN EPHESIANS

1. God's eternal purpose for Christians is that they should lead lives of triumph in Christ (1:4). The Christian life is compared to a warfare, a race, and a steady walk, but in each case the Christian is to be the victor, not the one who is beaten.

2. Christians are "quickened" — made alive in Christ — by the power of the Holy Spirit (2:13). This new life is not something one puts on as he accepts a new creed, as a new suit of clothes. It is rather something which is wrought or worked in his heart by the Spirit of God, through faith in Christ, and by grace. Christians are not made; they are born (John 3:3, 7). They must "grow in grace, of course, but they cannot grow *into* grace.

3. The word workmanship (2:10), is from a Greek word which means "poem." It could be said, "We are his *poems. . . .*" A poem is a beautiful thing. It is the expression of its author. It is one of the highest forms of artistic expression. It is an extraordinary way of expressing something. It may be said that in some sense, Christians are God's expressions of His love and grace. We should strive to be true copies of the original, so far as we can, and expres-

sions of the Author which will be a credit to His work.

4. Ministers, missionaries, and Christian workers are of God's *making,* rather than of their own decisons alone (3:7). Does it not seem that God is a better judge of whom to *call* to this work than we? Such an important calling should only be entered into with a sense that it is God's calling. God-called workers will usually succeed, other things being equal; man-called ministers are never likely to be very successful nor deeply serious in their work.

5. God's ability to answer prayers, to care for and protect His children, and to meet every emergency of life is beautifully set forth in the apostle's benediction (3:20, 21). It is inspiring to know that one may depend upon God for every need when his life is completely committed to God.

6. Paul emphasized unity of spiritual life, but diversity of gifts for the Christian Church (4:1-16). One Lord — Jesus Christ; one faith — saving faith in Him; one baptism — the Christian baptism, was his motto. Yet, there are many different types of gifts from the Holy Spirit, given to various members of the body of Christ — the church.

7. The way to victorious Christian living is shown (4:20-32) with instructions as to how to achieve it. There are things to "put off" and things to "put on" in successful Christian living.

8. God's ideal for Christian living is a life as God's child, fully Spirit-possessed and Spirit-directed (5:18-21). This is the ultimate in Christain living. Every young Christian should make this his goal.

9. The most beautiful picture of the Christian husband-wife relationship in the New Testament is given (5:22-33).

This is used to illustrate the relationship between Christ and His church. This is a most beautiful relationship in which all members love and care for each other, with no friction, backbiting, and the like. This is only possible when the church is a body of Spirit-filled believers.

Young people thinking of marriage should read this passage most thoughtfully and solemnly. This is the acme of marriage relationship and happiness.

10. Children and young people are to obey their parents, even though they feel quite "grown up" (6:1). Failure to do so will certainly produce sorrow later

"THE WHOLE ARMOR OF GOD." *This symbol is a combination of the elements listed by Paul in Ephesians 6:13-17. The sword is ornamented with the Chi Rho, monogram of Christ.*

in life, especially when the parents are God-fearing people.

In the case of godless parents who insist that children disobey God, the rule is perfectly clear — Christian children are to obey their parents *"in the Lord."* In other words, Christ first demands obedience to His commands. If one cannot obey his parents *and* the Lord, the choice is plain — one should obey God (see Acts 5:29).

The final admonition should ever ring in the ears of us all: "Finally, my brethren, be strong in the Lord, and in the power of his might" (6:10). Let this ever be the motto of all Christians.

Ephesians is beyond doubt *one of the brightest gems* of the New Testament and one of the most precious pieces of devotional literature in existence.

Memory Verse
"And be not drunk with wine, wherein is excess; but be filled with the Spirit" (5:18).

Philippians

This book takes its name from the fact that it was written to the church at Philippi, which was founded by Paul in the midst of persecution. This church continued to flourish on into the second century A.D.

TO WHOM
There can be little doubt that this epistle was intended for the church in the city of Philippi, located in Macedonia.

This was one of the least troublesome of all the churches to which Paul wrote letters, or epistles. It was filled with goodness and love; it held a keen interest in Paul, its beloved founder. It will be noted that Paul has no special admonitions to this church as a whole, because there were apparently no real difficulties in the church.

PURPOSE
There seems to have been a fourfold purpose for this epistle: First, he writes them in gratitude for their thoughtfulness of him in sending a love offering to him while imprisoned at Rome (4:10, 15). He wanted to be courteous and send them a message of thankfulness for this kindness.

Second, it may be that he also wished to thank them for their kindness to him in general. Before this time he had received funds for his Gospel work (5:15, 16).

Third, he wished to spiritually share with them something of his state of mind. He seems to have written just before he thought he might be called upon to die the martyr's death, or else would be set free from prison (2:17-24). He wished to report to them of his affairs.

Finally, he wished to recommend that two ladies of the church be fully reconciled to each other (4:2), and to warn the Philippians against those who would tempt them to return to Judaism (3:2-4). He also pled for unity of purpose and work within the church by all of its members (3:15-17).

TIME
In regard to the time at which this epistle was written, there is general agreement that it was during the very last part of Paul's imprisonment at Rome.

It was probably written about the latter part of A.D. 61.

AUTHORSHIP

From the most ancient times there has never been any serious doubt that Paul wrote this epistle. It has been called the most personal and most affectionate of all his epistles. Many personal references make his authorship all the more certain.

Paul had founded this church at Philippi during his second missionary journey (Acts 16:1-34), about A.D. 51. It is believed by some that Luke, author of the Gospel of Luke and Acts, who was with Paul at this time, was pastor of this church for the first several years. His ministry may have been one reason for the unspotted character of this church.

Philippi was a very ancient city noted for its gold mines. It was named for Philip II of Macedonia in the fourth century B.C. It was the site of the famous battle in which Brutus and Cassius were defeated, when the Roman Republic fell and the Roman Empire was born, 42 B.C.

This is one of the most letter-like of the epistles, being filled with so many personal mentions and solicitations. Paul thanks the church for its generous love offering, sent to him at Rome. Epaphroditus had evidently risked his life in bringing this offering to the aging apostle. This church had stood by him with gifts for his work more than any other of his churches. They had sent him offerings when he was at Thessalonica (4:16) and also at Corinth (II Cor. 11:9), as well as this last one to him in Rome.

Some have believed that since Timothy was then with Paul in Rome (1:1), and sent greetings, he may have been the person who wrote this letter as dictated by Paul. It is well known that Paul's letters were written by persons who served as his secretaries, as he was too nearly blind to write them himself. However, the subscription at the end of the letter places the name of Epaphroditus as the secretary. Timothy was with Paul when the church was founded, and he may have accompanied him on one or more of his visits there afterward. There is little doubt that Epaphroditus took the letter to Philippi (2:25-30). Some think he was of the Philippian church at that time. Paul planned to send Timothy, either with Epaphroditus or a little later (2:19-23). At this time he was also hopeful that he would be acquitted and could return to visit them (2:24). It is believed that he was released from prison and did revisit them and their churches (I Tim. 1:3).

No mention of Paul's apostleship is made in this letter, for there had been no dispute of it as there had been by the Judaizers at Corinth. This is a family-type letter, with tender solicitudes, an outpouring of affections, and deep concern for personal happiness and success of the church. (Read especially 1:1-11; 2:1, 12-17; 3:1; 4:1; 4:8-23.)

No book of the New Testaments shows the joyful and triumphant side of Paul's life more than does this book. Romans and Galatians show his theology; the Corinthian letters reveal his fight for order and recognition of apostleship, together with his heartbreak and the sorrowful side of his life. Ephesians presents the heavenly atmosphere, without too much personal memoranda, while Philippians pictures the happy soldier, though in prison, extremely contented and at rest (4:11-14).

PHILIPPI. *Philip II of Macedon enlarged an earlier settlement called Krenides and then named it for himself. In 42 B.C. Antony and Octavian defeated Brutus and Cassius in the Battle of Philippi. It then became a Roman colony. Paul established a Christian church there.*

This epistle may be outlined as follows:

I. Personal greetings, 1:1-11
II. Personal considerations, 1:12-26
III. Tender exhortations, 1:27—2:18
IV. Personal hopes, 2:19-30
V. More exhortations on Christian living, 3:1 — 4:9
VI. Personal thanksgiving, 4:10-20
VII. The final salutations of friends; the benediction, 4:21-23

GREAT TRUTHS IN PHILIPPIANS

1. The sweetness of Christian fellowship and the abounding love of Christ in Christians' hearts is the theme of Paul's introduction (1:3-11). This is the highest point of Christian fellowship, and it is reached by the road of personal prayer.

2. Paul wishes success for the Gospel under any circumstances (1:18). Christians should look for the ultimate good results in the labors of all men for Christ, and not worry about the present outcome.

3. Singleness of motive is beautifully set forth in Paul's willingness to be with Christ or to remain on earth (1:21-26). This is the result of *total commitment* to Christ. Only persons who are wholly committed to Christ can have such an attitude toward life and death.

4. The ultimate goal of all Christian living is set forth in these powerful words: "Let this mind be in you, which was also in Christ Jesus" (2:5). This is one of the most profound passages in the New Testament (2:5-9). If possible, study it thoroughly with a commentary on the Bible. It shows the price Christ paid for our redemption.

To have the *mind of Christ,* one must be born again and have His Spirit in the heart, directing life and its motives and drives. It may be well to ask, What was "the mind of Christ" about obedience to God? Love for His brethren? Doing God's will? Living unselfishly? Other things? Then, by God's grace, one should try to follow that pattern which His life set for us as an example (Peter 2:21-24; I John 3:1-3).

5. Christians are to trust only Christ

for salvation — not good works or any other thing. Paul had most excellent qualifications for God's approval, if any human merit could avail anything (3: 2-11). If Paul's good life and works were not enough to recommend him to God, without Christ, neither are anyone else's. It is only in Christ that we have salvation. Good works are a *result* of one's love for God, not the cause of it.

6. The heart of Christian life and experience is found in *fellowship with Christ.* Paul rejoiced that this was his greatest glory; it provided his grandest hope (3:10-13). This is one of the high peaks of the apostle's Christian testimony. There are several things one may expect in fellowship with Christ: First, one must *know Him.* We never have *fellowship* with anyone until we know the person. The better we know one, the deeper and sweeter the fellowship. This is also true with Christians and their relationship to Christ.

Second, it was in the "power of his resurrection" that Paul knew Christ. His faith was established in this great *historical* truth, and it became the certainty of his Christian experience. Here modernism breaks down. In denying the true, historical resurrection of Christ, it robs Christianity of all its power to save men.

Paul also includes the "fellowship of his sufferings." Spiritually-minded Christians often "suffer with Christ" in His sufferings over the wayward Christians, over the sinful people whom he loves and wants to save, and over other needs of the church. Young Christians should have a deep concern about these spiritual matters. This is the real Christian way.

Finally, there is the fellowship of "being made conformable unto His death."

This is a step further than many Christians have gone. To identify one's self with Christ's death, as a possible martyr for Christ, means to become a living witness for Him. The word martyr is from a Greek word which means "witness." A true witness is a martyr, and a true martyr is a witness.

This affirmation of identity with Christ also speaks of the believer's commitment to Christ, totally and finally, as if unto death. Is this a great and unexpected thing of a Christian? Indeed not. Does not each couple in marriage pledge themselves to each other "until death do us part"? Is the Christian's commitment anything less than this commitment of human love? Hardly so!

7. Forgetting the past and reaching for the future mark of God's approval in Christ was the apostle's motto for life (3:13, 14). He exhorts all others to follow this pattern. If we are otherwise minded, God will reveal this to us. He will help us to keep in this good way of victory.

8. "Euodias and Syntyche, get together, and stop quibbling about small matters," the apostle is saying (4:2). Christian fellowship cannot be broken without dreadful results. Christians must *not* hold grudges, retaliate, and refuse to fellowship with each other. This is wrong (Matt. 5:21-24; 6:14, 15; I Cor. 6:1-2 ; Gal. 6:1-5; I John 2:8-11; 3:10-17).

Young people should always cultivate love for other Christians, of whatever faith. If one is not a true spiritual Christian, this fact will soon become known. One cannot have fellowship with dishonest, deceitful, and hypocritical persons who may call themselves Christians. But one must make sure, first, that he does not misunderstand the motives of

Courtesy, Charles F. Pfeiffer

NEAPOLIS. *The Turkish city of Kavalla is the Biblical Neapolis. It was the seaport for Philippi. Paul first entered Europe at this point.*

another before branding him as false.

9. "Think on these things" (4:8). Here is a beautiful list of Christian *thinking materials*. This list is so ample that it may be applied in some form to everything about which Christians should think.

The *mind* is one of the most important aspects of one's being. Whoever *wins the mind* wins the soul. This is why Satan has always fought so hard to win the battle of the mind. And this is why God has said so much about the importance of the mind in the Bible. Take a concordance and look up references on the mind, on thinking, and on thought, and it will amaze you.

Youth is the time to set the course of pure, wholesome, noble, and right thinking. Never allow evil thoughts to take over, even for a moment. John Wesley once observed, relative to evil thoughts, "We cannot keep the birds from flying over our heads, but we can keep them from building nests in our hair!" Remember, as a person "thinketh in his heart, so is he" (Prov. 23:7). We cannot keep thoughts about evil things from coming to our minds, but we can keep them from lodging in our hearts and leading us to do evil things.

10. Contentment of mind is a great blessing. Paul said he had "learned" this secret (4:11), and it was possibly one of his greatest lifelong lessons. Again, he said, "Godliness with contentment is great gain" (I Tim. 6:6, 8).

Christians have more to be content

with and less to worry about than any people on earth. Why, then, make all the fuss about small matters?

11. Possibly the greatest secret of the Christian life was stated by the apostle in these wonderful words: "I can do all things through Christ which strengtheneth me" (4:13). Here is the acme of Christian victory, the summit of Christian experience, made possible "through Christ." Think all that can be counted into these two little words *"all things"!* Can you think of *anything* which is a Christian's duty that you *cannot* do *through Christ?* There is no cause for defeat in the Christian life except our own failure to take the *strength* from Christ by which to do the "all things" which life may require of us.

12. The supply of "all needs" from the bounty of God's riches through Jesus Christ is one of the most comforting promises of the Bible (4:19). Every Christian should memorize it and make it a part of his program of faith in God. "All your needs" is all-inclusive. Whatever your *needs* — not merely your desires or wishes — but needs, as God knows them, are awaiting fulfillment in Christ Jesus.

Among the letters of Paul, Philippians is one of the finest books for personal enrichment. Here is a storehouse of wondrous passages from which to draw spiritual help in every time of need and trial. Anyone will do well to memorize many of these.

Memory Verses

"Brethren, I count not myself to have apprehended: but this one thing I do, forgetting those things which are behind, and reaching forth unto those things which are before, I press toward the mark for the prize of the high calling of God in Christ Jesus" (3:13, 14).

Colossians

This book was so named because of its connection with the people of the city of Colossae, a city in Phrygia. At Pentecost some Jews from this country were present.

TO WHOM

This letter was written to the Christian church located at Colossae and the saints which may have been in the near vicinity of it. It is a companion letter to Ephesians and Philemon, having been written about the same time and probably brought to Colossae by Tychicus and Onesimus, who brought the Ephesian letter to that church (4:7-9).

PURPOSE

The purpose of its writing seems to be set forth in the epistle itself. The necessity of the letter grew out of certain *doctrinal* difficulties which had developed within the church. There may have been some admixture of Greek, Jewish, and Oriental religions which had developed into a serious "heresy" — false doctrine.

Before their conversion to Christianity, the Colossians evidently had been worshipers of angels (2:18). There had developed a sort of "higher thought" cult, which Paul refers to as "philosophy and vain deceit" (2:8). The Colossians had fallen into this vanity of philosophical worship, reverencing and possibly praying to angels, trying in this way to make their religion more agreeable to the pagan mind.

Evidently these "angels" were thought of as *intermediaries,* or "go-betweens" between God and man. In this sense they probably placed them in the position which Christ should have had in their worship. They were also being tempted toward Judaism. Strict observance by Jewish rituals is doubtless referred to by Paul (2:16, 21). All this false worship and strong ritualistic matter was being worked out as part of the Gospel of Christ. Christ was becoming secondary in their worship system.

The main purpose of the epistle, therefore, was to assert the Godhood and all-sufficiency of Jesus Christ as Redeemer, Lord, and Savior. They must see that man needs no one to go between him and God, except Jesus Christ. In personal prayer we come directly to God through Christ. No other person is needed to intercede for the Christian in any sense whatsoever.

TIME

This book was written about the same time as the other "prison epistles," while Paul was imprisoned the first time at Rome. It seems that Epaphras, possibly the current pastor at Colossae (1:7), had come to Rome and may have been imprisoned there with Paul (Philemon 23). He reported the church's condition to Paul, who was just then writing to the Ephesians and to Philemon about Onesimus. Tychicus and Onesimus were going near Colossae to deliver the Ephesian letter (Eph. 6:1), so Paul decided to write to the Colossians to correct this grievous error of false worship among them (4:7-9). Very likely he wrote this letter just before they left, as Timothy was still with him when this was written

(1:1); Timothy was to accompany them on his way to visit the church at Philippi. So this epistle was likely written sometime late in A.D. 61 and taken to Colossae by Tychicus and Onesimus on their way to Ephesus and Philemon's home.

AUTHORSHIP

There can be little doubt that Paul wrote this epistle. It has a number of similarities to Ephesians and is in the same warm, spiritual atmosphere as that book and Philippians.

There is some difference of opinion as to whether Paul had ever visited Colossae. Some see in the letter evidence that he had; others think he had not, because of his reference to those who had "not seen my face in the flesh" (2:1). This, it is argued, is not sufficient proof, as it could refer to new members who had joined since his visit there. References to his work in Phrygia (Acts 16:6) and that of a later time, "strengthening the churches" of this area (Acts 18:23), lend some strength to the possibility that Paul had visited this church.

As the "apostle to the Gentiles," this church naturally came under Paul's jurisdiction — or leadership — care — and he felt responsible for its welfare. This church may have been composed of a mixture of both Jews and Gentiles, as many early churches were, with a possible predominance of Gentiles. This may be the reason for the strange mixture of false doctrines in the church.

The main burden of this epistle seems to be the proof of the deity of Christ and His eternal Sonship of God (1:12-20; 2:2, 3; 2:18, 19; 3:1-4; 3:15-17; 4:1-4).

PAUL IN PRISON. *Several of Paul's epistles were written while he was imprisoned in Rome.*

As one reads this book, he will do well to pick out the titles used for Christ. Note such terms as the "Image of the invisible God," "Firstborn of the creation," "All things created through him," "He is before all things," "In him all things consist [hold together]," "Head of the church," "The beginning," "The firstborn from the dead," "In him all fulness dwells," "Through him all things are reconciled," "Christ in you the hope of glory," "In him are all the treasures of wisdom and knowledge," "In him dwells all the fulness of the Godhead bodily," "In him ye are made full," "The head of all principality and power," and "Firstborn of all creation," not meaning that Christ was *created,* but that as God's eternal Son, He is the heir to all creation.

Notice that "thrones, dominions, principalities, and powers" are attributed to Christ (1:16). This shows that He has the *power*s of deity, as these ascriptions would otherwise never have been given to Him.

In the light of these statements, there can be little doubt that Paul's primary purpose was to establish the doctrine of the eternal Sonship of Christ, — His essential deity, and therefore, His supreme Saviorhood of mankind.

This book may be outlined as follows:
I. Personal greetings, 1:1-12
II. Doctrinal statements, 1:13—2:3
III. Polemics, or the arguments and proofs for doctrines, 2:4—3:4
IV. Practical applications of Christianity, 3:5—4:6
V. Personal matters, 4:7-18

GREAT TRUTHS IN COLOSSIANS
1. Faith, love, and hope (1:4, 5) are mentioned as key words of the book, and are the trio of graces so often in the New Testament associated with Christian experience. One will find them recurring in various ways in this book. When writing to the Corinthians, Paul listed this trio as the highest of the graces, with love being the most important (I Cor. 13:13).

Every Christian should strive to cultivate these in his heart by means of prayer, Bible reading, and service to Christ by serving others.

2. Paul rejoiced for deliverance from sin and "translation" into the kingdom of Christ (1:10). Born-again Christians (John 3:3, 5, 7; I Peter 2:2) have been taken up out of Satan's kingdom and transplanted into Christ's kingdom in a spiritual sense. It is as real an experience to become a Christian, spiritually, as to physically transplant a tree or shrub.

3. Christians are to "seek" the things of God and endeavor to live in an atmosphere of obedience and service to Christ (3:1). This certainly echoes the words of Christ: "Seek ye first the kingdom of God . . ." (Matt. 6:33). Too many Christians are lost to the cause of Christ and true usefulness by seeking to become wealthy, successful, or to get to the top in their jobs or professions at the expense of their loyalty to Christ.

4. Christians are to set their affections on spiritual things rather than on earthly pleasures, possessions, friendships, and associations (3:2). True commitment to Christ, total dedication to His cause is the true goal of all spiritually minded Christians. This does not apply merely to ministers, missionaries, or Christian workers. It should be the goal of every Christian. There is no better time to start in this direction than in youth!

5. The security of the believer in Christ is a wonderful thing. He is "hid with Christ in God" (3:3). He is de-

clared to be *dead* to his old sinful life and selfish ways of living. His life is now made new in Christ Jesus (II Cor. 5:17), and he is protected by God's great love and power. This is a spiritual relationship, but it is nonetheless real to the believer.

6. Following his statement of being hidden with Christ in God (3:5-25), Paul proceeds to set forth the *life* of the real Christian. The social, moral, and ethical standards for Christians are listed (3:5-11). The relationship of believers to one another (3:12-17), of wives and husbands to each other (3:18, 19), and of parents and children (3:20, 21) is stressed. Relationships of employer and employee are also given (3:22-25).

Christian conduct is one of the most important themes of the New Testament. Our conduct as Christians either shows our relationship to Christ to be vital and real, or betrays it to be very shallow and weak, or broken.

7. The "how" of victorious Christian living is set forth by the apostle (3:16, 17). Only as we "let the word of Christ dwell" in our lives richly can we hope to live the truly vital Christian way. This is not merely *memorizing* the Word of God, but allowing its counsel and guidance to control and direct the motives and activities of life.

This wonderful book exalts Christ as the genuine Christian always should. He should have first place in every Christian life.

Memory Verses

"If ye be risen with Christ, seek those things which are above, where Christ sitteth on the right hand of God. Set your affection on things above, not on things on the earth. For ye are dead, and your life is hid with Christ in God" (3:1-3).

I Thessalonians

This letter bears the name of the people to whom it was written. The ancient city of Thessalonica, in Greece, is the present site of the modern city of Salonika.

TO WHOM

There is no question but that it was directed to the Christian church at Thessalonica. This church apparently was founded by Paul on his second missionary journey (Acts 17:1-9).

It is believed that three classes of people made up this church: (1) a few Jews, (2) a number of Gentile converts to the Jewish religion, who, when they heard the Gospel, accepted it as the true way of God, and (3) a large group of heathen who turned "from idols to serve the living and true God" (1:9), as noted by Luke at the time of its founding (Acts 17:4).

That this church was largely made up of Gentile converts may be seen from the following: The Jews of Thessalonica persecuted Paul viciously. In this epistle he mentions little that in any way would refer to Jews or Jewish conditions. His references to circumstances which pertain to persons new to the religion of the true God make this book outstanding.

PURPOSE

Paul and his workers had gone to Thessalonica and after a few weeks they had founded the church. Because of bitter persecution Paul had been forced to leave, going over to Berea, some fifty miles away. The Jews followed him there, stirring up such a storm of persecution that he fled to Athens. Here Timothy and Silas overtook him. Being so burdened for his new converts at Thessalonica, he sent Timothy back to minister to them and help them to get established in the Christian way.

When Timothy returned, he found that Paul had gone to Corinth, where he overtook him. Upon hearing of the good news from Thessalonica, but also that some were confused about the preaching he had done, he immediately wrote this letter.

The major purpose of this letter seems to have been twofold: (1) He wanted to encourage and comfort these new converts in living for Christ. (2) They had misunderstood Paul's preaching about the second coming of Christ and feared that those who had died had missed this glorious event. He set them right about this, as seen especially in the latter part of chapter 4.

TIME

Some scholars believe that this missive was the first of Paul's epistles to be written. In fact, some have maintained that it was the *first* book of the New Testament to be written. This is questioned by others, but without doubt it was among the earliest. When Timothy returned from ministering to the Thessalonians and reported the conditions at Thessalonica to Paul at Corinth, the apostle immediately wrote this epistle, about A.D. 50 or 51.

AUTHORSHIP

There can be little question of the Pauline authorship of this book. Its very content beams with this indication. Its opening statement ascribes it to Paul, with Timothy possibly doing the writing as Paul dictated it (1:1).

The personal references throughout the epistle strongly leave their imprint upon it. This is especially true of the first three chapters. Paul shows the personal concern of anyone who has won someone else to the Lord.

This letter is much like a pastoral letter, just a heart-to-heart talk to his converts. It is a bit difficult to outline. It is not a treatise, like Romans or Galatians, but more personal communication.

It may be divided into two parts:
I.   Personal matters, concerning the writer and his friends, 1-3
II. Doctrinal and practical matters, 4-5

GREAT TRUTHS IN I THESSALONIANS

1. The Christians in Thessalonica had turned from idols to serve God (1:9). One of the great curses of all older civilizations has been their idol worship.

In our modern culture people no longer worship idols of wood and stone. They now devote themselves to such idols as money, greed, lust, and pleasure — to securing wealth and power at any cost. Such activity is just as sinful as ancient idol worship.

2. Paul was able to witness to them that his conduct had been blameless among them (2:10). This is important in the life of every believer when he is among others with whom he labors. We can never have a more effective influence for Christ than that which our lives will back up in daily living.

3. The highest goal toward which the Christian moves is that of complete dedication to Christ. This makes for final

establishment in Christ by which he is enabled to live the victorious life. Out of this comes the readiness for Christ's return or any call He gives (3:13). When a Christian has reached this state of experience, he is prepared to be of valuable service to Christ.

4. Paul explains to the Thessalonians about the coming of Christ and the relationship of the "dead in Christ" (4:13-18). One should study this passage with care, that he may know what to expect at Christ's return for His saints.

5. The warning that Christ's return may be like a "thief in the night" should cause one to be prepared at all times. If one lives a life of readiness for Christ's return, he will be most useful for service to Him in life.

6. Paul's exhortation to "comfort the feebleminded" (5:14) is taken from the Greek, meaning "comfort the *little-souled*" people. It is unfortunate that there are many Christians who are very "little-souled" people! They have made little progress since they started. Every Christian should have as his goal that of becoming the strongest possible Christian.

7. Paul lists a most gracious catalog of "do's" and "don'ts" for Christians (5:23, 24). This standard of conduct is made possible in the Christian's life when he becomes a full partaker of the Spirit-filled life. The apostle's benediction blessing, which he prays that the Thessalonians may have (5:23, 24), will bring power to live this life.

Memory Verses

"And the Lord make you to increase and abound in love one toward another, and toward all men, even as we do toward you: To the end he may stablish your hearts unblameable in holiness before God, even our Father, at the coming of our Lord Jesus Christ with all his saints" (3:12, 13).

II Thessalonians

This epistle, like the preceding one, was named for the people to whom it was written.

TO WHOM

The church at Thessalonica may have grown sufficiently so that there were more congregations than one, for this second letter is addressed to the "church of the Thessalonians," meaning the main body of the church as such.

PURPOSE

The purpose of this epistle seems to have been twofold: (1) From his first letter to the Thessalonians there had arisen a misunderstanding about the Second Coming, or the return of Christ to take the church to heaven. They had interpreted his words (I Thess. 4:13-18) to mean that the coming of Christ was just at hand. Therefore, a number of the church people had stopped work and apparently were waiting around for the glorious event to occur. In this state they had developed into busybodies and the church was suffering because of this condition (3:11).

The apostle meant to correct this error in their thinking about the coming of Christ. Paul has been accused here of changing his thinking about Christ's coming, but this is unjust accusation. He merely added to the sum of what he had said, explaining that the coming of Christ

ATHENS TODAY. *Athens is still a thriving city. Paul fled to Athens from Thessalonica and Berea after being persecuted by the Jews.*

---

would not occur until after there had come a great apostasy, or falling away of the Christians into false doctrines (2:1-12). He assures them that this had not come, and that it would not come immediately.

(2) He had to deal with the situation which had arisen out of this misunderstanding. He ordered the dilatory people to return to work so there would be no confusion and tale bearing among them (3:6-12).

TIME

There is little doubt that this epistle followed the first one within a few months. It was likely written from Corinth in A.D. 51, possibly with Timothy assisting Paul as his secretary (1:1).

AUTHORSHIP

Unquestionably, Paul wrote this epistle. It is a companion book to the former one, and without it, would be incomplete. His authorship has never been successfully challenged.

Thessalonica was a thriving city of some 200,000 people in Paul's time. It was largely a heathen city, with only a relatively small Jewish population. The "devout Greeks" referred to (Acts 17:4), likely were Greeks who had been converted to the Jewish religion — "proselytes," as they were called. Many of these finally believed the Gospel and were converted to Christianity, forming perhaps a large part of the new church there, together with numbers of heathen converts. The Jewish membership appears to have been a small minority of the church.

This great city was on the main East-West Highway from Rome to the East, a military highway. The city was on the Aegean Sea, and as such afforded another outlet and inflow of commerce and travel.

In Paul's time it was the leading city of Macedonia.

The church here had been founded more or less in haste, and there were many things which it needed that Paul could not provide, being driven away so soon by persecution. This second letter was another heartthrob for his young church. It is an attempt to set right, as much as possible, the doctrines and practices of the young Christians there. It breathes the very atmosphere of Paul's heart-cry for his converts, as well as his parental-like rebukes and admonitions to those who needed such attention. The whole letter is filled with so many Pauline references and admonitions that one cannot doubt his authorship.

Like the former one, this epistle is so personal, it is difficult to outline it in any analytical style. It is a personal letter, written to correct an unfortunate misunderstanding of the doctrine of the return of Christ and certain abuses which had arisen because of this misunderstanding.

This epistle may be divided into four parts:

I. Salutation and faithfulness in affliction, 1:1-12
II. Corrections about the Second Coming of Christ, 2
III. Admonitions to believers, 3:1-16
IV. Closing remarks, 3:17, 18

GREAT TRUTHS IN II THESSALONIANS

1. The revelation of Christ at the final end of this world order will be one of "vengeance" upon the wicked as well as reward for the righteous (1:7-10). Here one cannot go into all the phases of the doctrine of Christ's return. Each interested person should seek further information upon this great subject. Here it is sufficient to say there will be a fearful visitation of divine justice upon the wicked at that time. Christians should always live with this return of Christ in view and be ready to give an account to their Lord when He comes (1:11-12).

2. The "falling away" (2:3) probably refers to the dreadful apostasy — a denial of the central truths of Christianity, such as the Virgin Birth of Christ, His miracles, His vicarious atonement, and His literal resurrection.

This movement has gained considerable strength in the last century, even within the church at certain points. Anyone who denies that Christ is the eternal Son of God, equal with the Father in power, glory, and majesty, is an *unbeliever* in every sense of that word. This is what the apostle John is speaking of when he refers to the antichrist and the spirit of antichrist (Read carefully I John 2:21-24; 4:1-6). Everyone must be careful *what* he believes. It is very important that he should "know and believe the truth" as it is in Christ.

3. The "mystery of iniquity" (2:7) and the results produced by the rebellion of those who will not accept the truth should prove a warning for all. One needs to seek the fuller explanations in a good Bible commentary. Here let it be said that if we keep our hearts open to Christ, we will never be condemned with the rebellious, unbelieving wicked!

4. Laziness, idleness, loafing, and the general gang spirit are soundly condemned by the apostle as no part of Christian life. Christians are to be industrious; they are to work for their living, avoid tale-bearing, be orderly, and act becoming to the Christian life and doctrine (3:7-12). Young people should learn early that to be usefully employed is best at all times. "An idle mind is the devil's workshop," said wise old Benjamin

Franklin. Another has well said, "Satan finds some mischief still, for idle hands to do."

Work-dodging and general time-killing processes should not be part of the lives of Christian people! No sensible person should wish to indulge in these.

Memory Verses

"Now our Lord Jesus Christ himself, and God, even our Father, which hath loved us, and hath given us everlasting consolation and good hope through grace, comfort your hearts, and establish you in every good word and work" (2:16, 17).

I Timothy

Timothy is the English form of the Greek *Timotheus*. The name originally meant "honoring God."

TO WHOM

There is no question that this epistle was written to the Timothy who is spoken of in Acts and the epistles as Paul's co-worker in the Gospel, his traveling companion on many occasions.

Timothy was a native of Lystra (Acts 16:1), the son of a devout Jewish lady who had married a Greek. His father is not named in the New Testament, perhaps either because he was dead or was never converted to Christianity, and therefore, not connected with its history in any way.

Eunice, Timothy's mother, and Lois, his grandmother, were godly women and had brought young Timothy up in this faith (II Tim. 1:5).

Possibly Timothy had been converted to Christ during Paul's first visit to Lystra (Acts 14:6), for he calls him his "son in the faith" (1:2). On Paul's second visit to Lystra (Acts 16:1-3) he found Timothy a very outstanding young Christian and decided to take him on as a co-worker in the Gospel work. This choice seems to have been indicated to Paul by the Lord 1:18). Evidently, he was ordained by the elders at Lystra and by Paul (4:14; II Tim. 1:6). This was not likely two ordinations, but one ordination in which both the elders and Paul took part. Paul likely had a leading part, placing his hands upon him in ordination, as he was to be his constant co-worker.

Timothy immediately became Paul's traveling companion, co-worker, and possibly his private secretary. He worked with him most all of Paul's remaining life, being absent from him only when sent on missions by the apostle, or when circumstances were beyond his control.

Timothy got his first taste of Gospel missionary work at Philippi, soon after his induction into the party. It is thought he escaped imprisonment there because of his youthfulness or his inferior position in the party.

From Philippi the party went to Thessalonica, where Paul was soon forced to leave because of persecution. He left Timothy in charge. Rushing on to Berea, Paul again was soon forced out by persecution. He went to Athens in Greece and from there he sent for Timothy (Acts 17:14, 15). Later he sent him back to Thessalonica to look after the church there (I Thess. 3:1-2). Upon Timothy's return he found that Paul had gone to Corinth (Acts 18:5; I Thess. 3:6) and

THE MARBLE STREET IN EPHESUS. *When the church at Ephesus experienced difficulties, Paul sent Timothy to take charge of affairs there.*

there he joined Paul in writing the Thessalonian letters (I Thess. 1:1; II Thess. 1:1). Possibly he served as secretary to Paul while these letters were dictated.

Later Paul sent Timothy to Ephesus to attend to certain matters in the churches there (I Cor. 4:17). After this Timothy again joined Paul in Macedonia, where he assisted in writing II Corinthians (1:1; Acts 19:22). He went part of the way with Paul on his last journey to Jerusalem, to take the great offering, but it is not known whether he went all the way. He is not mentioned during Paul's two-year imprisonment at Caesarea, so he probably was engaged in some missionary activity for the apostle. He joined Paul again at Rome during his first imprisonment and assisted in writing Philippians (Phil. 1:1; 2:19-22), Colossians (Col. 1:1), and Philemon (Philemon 1).

During his last imprisonment, Paul

urged him to come to Rome immediately (II Tim. 4:9), but whether he arrived before Paul's execution is not known. It seems Timothy and Luke were Paul's most constant travel companions, and were with him on many of his most wonderful occasions and in some of his saddest hours.

Apparently, Paul had sent Timothy to Ephesus to straighten out affairs there about the time this epistle was written.

Assuming that Timothy joined Paul at about eighteen years of age, in A.D. 51 — a pure assumption — he would have been in his early thirties at the time this epistle was written. The Greeks considered one still in youth until forty years of age. So Paul's admonition, "Let no man despise thy youth" (4:12), would certainly not have been out of keeping with his age. Evidently Timothy was not a strong, robust man but suffered somewhat (5:23). He is said to have been timid and retiring, but he was a faithful worker. Some believe that he was placed in charge of the church at Ephesus, where he remained until his death. The Ephesian church had many congregations, over which Timothy presided as a kind of general leader. He is thought to have suffered martyrdom under Emperors Nerva or Domitian. His ministry, if this is true, may well have been paralleled by that of the apostle John, who is known to have lived and ministered there in his older years.

PURPOSE

The purpose of this epistle seems clear from the circumstances surrounding it. First, the apostle having left Timothy at Ephesus to correct certain evils and set the church in order (1:3-4), evidently felt he needed this advice, counsel, and instruction. In reading the book one can see that Paul has given him complete pastoral instructions, as well as leadership instructions for one given the supervision of several churches.

In those days there were no large church buildings in which to gather — not for some two hundred years after Paul's days did these arise. Therefore, there were many different groups of believers in any city where there was a large church. This necessitated several pastors, deacons, elders, and leaders. Possibly the word "bishop" then signified no more than a local pastor of a congregation. The purpose of the apostle, therefore, in writing to Timothy, was to give him complete instructions of *how* to organize, supervise, and carry on this great work as the over-shepherd of the church there. He also listed specific rules and guiding principles for Christian conduct, qualifications for church officers, and the like.

Second, it is likely that the apostle realized that his earthly work was drawing to a close and therefore he must prepare others to take his place of leadership among the churches. His *written* instructions would be much more permanent than his oral advice and counsel, so he wrote these out for his son in the Gospel. These two major things appear to have been the main reasons for this letter.

TIME

Concerning the time at which this epistle was written, there has been considerable discussion. Many have thought the reference to Timothy's order to remain in Ephesus (1:3-4) was given while Paul was in Macedonia, just after his visit to Ephesus. Their reason: In Acts there is no mention of Paul's going from Ephesus to Macedonia; it is mentioned *once*, the time at which he wrote to him. This would be about A.D. 56. But this cannot be the date for this epistle for the following reasons:

1. Timothy was not in Ephesus at this time; he had gone on into Macedonia at Paul's orders (Acts 19:22).

2. Paul speaks of his intention to visit Timothy soon (3:14). Immediately after having left Ephesus, he had no plans to revisit it "soon." His plans were very different (II Cor. 1:16; 11:4).

3. The errors which Timothy was to combat in Ephesus did not arise until well after the time of this first visit (Acts 20:29, 30). References in both I and II Timothy make it sure that these two books were written closer together than this will allow.

So, we must conclude that there had been a visit of Paul to Ephesus at a later date. It seems that *after* Paul's release from his first imprisonment in Rome, he with Timothy, revisited many of the missionary churches. Seeing that the conditions at Ephesus demanded a firm hand, he left Timothy in charge of affairs there.

Moving on into other sections of the work, Paul felt that Timothy needed written instruction and advice. Also, Paul did not know when he himself might be taken from the field, as he was in constant danger, and he was growing older. So, he wrote his first epistle to Timothy during this final missionary tour, *before* his last imprisonment in Rome.

The best information assigns this time of freedom to about A.D. 63-67. No one knows just *where* the apostle was when he wrote this epistle. Some think he was at Nicopolis, others, at Laodicea, in Phrygia, but no one knows for certain It was most likely written between A.D. 64 and 65.

AUTHORSHIP

From the most ancient times the two epistles to Timothy have been accepted

THE ERECTHEUM. *This building stood on the acropolis of Athens. It was one of the finest examples of Greek architecture.*

by the church as written by Paul. Only a brief comparison of the contents of these two books with Paul's other writings will show many striking similarities in the language.

The reference to Timothy as "my son" (1:2), his constant care for Timothy, and his thoughtfulness of his every need, such as his care for his bodily needs (5:23), all speak of Paul's authorship.

The relationship of Paul and Timothy through the years had been a very tender and affectionate one — as father and son. This attitude is maintained by Paul until the very end (6:20; II Tim. 4:9-22).

This particular epistle may be considered as nearly as any could be, the young people's book of the New Testament. Its many personal instructions to Timothy, although he was a Gospel minister, are very fitting to youth in all ages. Young people will find its last chapters especially very helpful for advice and counsel in the Christian life and conduct. It is one of youth's finest lessons in Christian ethics.

It may be outlined as follows:

I. Opening greetings, 1:1-2
II. The Ephesian situation, 1:3-17
III. Paul's charge to Timothy for the church, 1:18 —3:16
IV. Personal instructions to Timothy, 4:1—6:21

GREAT TRUTHS IN I TIMOTHY

1. That "Christ Jesus came into the world to save sinners" (1:15) was one of Paul's most fervent cries. He considered himself the very chief of sinners. He had persecuted the Christian Church, but he saw the light of Christ (1:15, 16; Acts 9). Now he knew the freedom from sin which Christ's power brings to those who repent and turn to Him. We should always seek to exalt Christ in every witness we give for Him, as did Paul. It is Christ who saves us, not our good works.

2. Paul exalts Christ as the only "mediator between God and men" (2:5). No other earthly person or system is needed to bring men to God. Christ is the great High Priest of the redeemed, and there is no necessity for anyone else to intercede for us. Christ is our Intercessor; we need no priest, no minister, and no other saint to *intercede* for us. To add such is to dishonor Christ and grieve God. Certainly Paul himself requested the prayers of others, and we should do likewise; but this is far different from having another intercede mediatorially for one.

3. Modesty of dress and becoming conduct was the apostle's exhortation to Christian women (2:9-10). Immodesty of womanhood and the impurity which so largely follows has often been the forerunner of the downfall of civilizations from the most ancient times. Christian young ladies ought always so to dress as to give no *justifiable* occasion for the unbecoming remarks of ungodly men.

4. Church and Sunday school officers should read with deepest concern the whole of chapter 3. Here is the Scriptural standard for the officers of the church. Young people should read this passage with care and prepare to accept these solemn duties in the church when they are old enough to be chosen for such positions.

5. "Let no man despise thy youth" is advice which can still be given to all young people today (4:12). This is perhaps the highest point of Paul's personal exhortation to Timothy. Although given him as a pattern, it is equally as good for all youth as it was for Timothy. This

admonition should be heeded simply by living a life that is above reproach in every aspect and by being a useful person, always ready to be of service.

Along with this was the positive phase of this exhortation: *"Be thou an example of the believers."* This was a pretty strong statement of requirement. Yet, if Christ fills the heart and life of youth, will they not live exemplary lives? Please check the points on which youth should set the Christian example: in *word, conversation* (behavior), *charity,* (love), *spirit* (attitude), *faith,* and *purity.*

6. Paul urged Timothy to "give attention to reading" (4:13). Mental laziness is a disgrace to any individual. Sam P. Jones, outstanding evangelist of the last century, once said, "Ignorance is an heterogeneous compound which neither God nor man can use."

John Wesley observed, "A reading people will be a growing people." By the same token, people who do not read may be expected to shrivel up and die, mentally. Young people should regularly read God's Word and also good wholesome Christian literature. Otherwise, they become religious dwarfs, whose lives accomplish little or nothing for Christ.

7. Older people are to be treated with the utmost respect and care (5:1, 2).

8. Be not a "partaker of other men's sins: keep thyself pure" (5:22). This is not only good advice for Timothy, but for all young people. It is so easy to be drawn into someone else's misdeeds if one does not watch. One should be ever alert to see that he never takes part in anything which is not right. Too often young people are dragged into some evil scheme by older people because they are not on their guard. Moral, social,

and religious purity of life and habit pay well in the end.

9. *Money* is not the most important thing in life. Paul warned that "The love of money is the root of all evil" (6:10). Too often young people see *money* as the answer to every problem of life. Really, it is the answer to very few of life's problems, and it possibly *creates* more than it solves.

Money should be the last thing young people worry about. The correct approach to life is first to let Christ come into the heart and to be totally committed to Him. Then, secure the best education possible. One of the best methods of securing an education is to *work for it!* Decide to whom you can give the most of yourself and your talent, without regard to personal income. Then dive into it as though money were no part of life.

Never allow money to be a controlling factor in any decision which will influence your life of service to God and humanity! Happiness does not come through money, but through peace of mind and contentment in the service rendered to others. Always remember these two rules; in them you can find complete, supreme happiness in life.

10. "Fight the good fight of faith, lay hold on eternal life" (6:12). The Christian life was sometimes likened to a warfare by Paul. Nothing in life which is valuable comes without some effort. The Christian life is no exception. There are battles against evil to be fought, stands against wrong to be taken, and real enemies to be met and defeated.

Satan will see to it that the young Christian is met with every form of temptation and trial he can muster against him. One of his best instruments in this battle for the soul is *discourage-*

ment. One who is really discouraged is half whipped. Satan knows this and tries in every way to get one to say, in effect, "There's no use; I might as well give up now!" Not so; this is the wrong attitude! The correct attitude is, "Though all things seem to be against me and everything seems to go wrong, I'm *not quitting,* now, or *ever!*" Satan cannot match a courage such as this.

11. Riches or extra wealth can often prove a snare (6:17-19). If you are blessed with plenty, make up your mind to use your share of this wealth to the best possible advantage for Christ's cause.

PAUL AND TIMOTHY. *Paul greets Timothy as he arrives in Rome.*

Courtesy, Religious Films Limited

There have been many wealthy people who used their money for Christ's cause and did great good with it. It is not money *itself* that is evil, but "the *love* of money." To set no special prize upon money, but to use it for God's glory, is indeed the only proper attitude toward wealth. It is not so much the *amount* of money one has which counts, but the way in which it is held and used. If one has wealth, God will hold him responsible for how it is used. "The earth is the Lord's, and the fulness thereof," and in the end all one has belongs to God. "For we brought nothing into this world, and it is certain we can carry nothing out" (6:7).

Read this book often and thoughtfully for the best of Christian counsel.

Memory Verse
"Let no man despise thy youth, but be thou an example of the believers, in word, in conversation, in charity, in spirit, in faith, in purity" (4:12).

II Timothy

This epistle, like the former, received its name from the person to whom it is addressed. Timothy was one of the most outstanding young men of the early Christian church.

TO WHOM
Beyond question this letter follows the former one and was intended for Paul's son in the faith, the Timothy mentioned in Acts and the epistles many times. For further information, see the notes under this same heading in the prior chapter.

PURPOSE
This is one of the most personal of all Paul's epistles, except perhaps Philemon. He wrote it near the end of his life, and he probably had two or three things in mind:

1. To encourage and admonish Timothy to be faithful to Christ during the terrible persecution which had just broken out upon the Christians of the western area of the church.

2. To place him in command as his successor in the general leadership of the Gentile churches in particular (2:1-19). To this end he gives him more pastoral advice and administrative counsel in this epistle.

3. To give Timothy his last words of testimony concerning the validity of the Christian faith and its strength in the hour of death, and finally, to request his presence in Rome as soon as he could come. Paul knew that his "departure" was "at hand" (4:6), and he wanted Timothy, if possible, to be nearby when it came, much as a father would like his son near him at death.

TIME
This epistle was written, it is generally agreed, just before the apostle's martyrdom at Rome.

Through the centuries the Christian church has generally accepted the fact that Paul was twice at Rome and was twice imprisoned there. Of the fact that he was in prison when this epistle was written there can be no mistake (1:8; 2:9). There is abundant proof that Timothy was *with* him during his former imprisonment, as we have seen from his association in writing several of the epistles. So this epistle could *not* have been written then.

During that former imprisonment he had liberty (Acts 28:30, 31), while this time he was held in bonds (2:9).

The traditional date the church has held for Paul's execution is June, A.D. 66. This may not be certain, as some have thought the date to be as late as A.D. 67. It is safe to say, however, that this epistle was written only a short time before Paul's death (4:6-9). The apostle certainly had received the sentence of death, or was very sure of this fate, when he wrote this letter. So far as is known, this is his last writing.

AUTHORSHIP

That Paul penned this epistle there can be no doubt. The atmosphere of every portion breathes the spirit of Paul. For further comment see the notes on this subject in the preceding chapter.

PAUL'S MARTYRDOM

Christianity had made great headway in the Roman Empire up to this time. Thousands of Christians could be found everywhere, though most of them were admittedly of the more common class.

Nero, then emperor of Rome, though a fanatical ruler, was nevertheless a great builder. He evidently wished to rebuild certain parts of Rome to beautify it. But to do this, much of the city needed to be removed. To accomplish this he fell upon the hideous plan of "burning" much of the city. It is now generally believed that he either personally set these fires, or had it done by his henchmen. Then, tradition says, while great sections of the city burned,

this brute played his violin with glee! But somebody had to be found upon whom to lay this blame.

When suspicions pointed toward Nero, he found a ready scapegoat in the Christians of the city and surrounding areas. No less a person than the Roman historian Tacitus is the source of this information. To cover up his vile deed, Nero ordered a mass persecution of these Christians, accusing them of burning the city.

Since Paul was the most outstanding leader among them in the West, it would be logical to have made a big show by arresting and executing him. It is thought that he may have been arrested at Troas, in Asia Minor (4:13).

Taken to Rome, the center of the imperial persecution, he was immediately tried, condemned, and imprisoned. Apparently he had no defense attorney at this time, everyone being afraid to risk the fury of Nero, lest he also be accused and arrested (4:16). Verse 18 is not so much an expectation of temporal deliverance from Nero as final deliverance by Christ, in a triumphant death and translation into the heavenly kingdom.

Humanly speaking, this is a sad and gloomy picture (4:9-17). Forsaken by friends, imprisoned innocently, convicted of a crime of which he was not guilty, and sentenced to death, he faced this ultimate fate almost alone — "only Luke is with me" (4:11). But verse 18 is the final shout of triumph.

PAUL AND LUKE. *Imprisoned in Rome, Paul dictates one of his epistles to Luke. During Paul's second imprisonment, he was not allowed the measure of freedom he experienced during his first imprisonment.*

Thus came to its end one of the most beautiful, unselfish, and sacrifical lives ever lived since Jesus Christ went to Calvary! It may have seemed to many of that day that the grand old apostle died in defeat, that he had fought for a lost cause. But not so! As the ancients said, "The blood of the martyrs became the *seed* of the church." Soon everywhere the church sprang up again, more alive than ever. It rose to triumph over all; it became the most powerful force in the world for good and righteousness; it remains such to this day.

In that far-off day, men named their sons Nero, and possibly would not have disgraced even their dogs with a Christian name. But oh, how the tables have turned! *Today,* men name their *sons Paul,* and their *dogs* Nero!

This epistle may be divided into four parts:

   I.   Personal salutation, 1:1-2
   II.   Instructions for pastoral care, 1: 3-17
   III.   Paul's farewell admonitions and last testimony, 4:1-18
   IV.   Final greetings and benediction, 4:19-22

GREAT TRUTHS IN II TIMOTHY

1. One of the finest of these passages is Paul's *great committal* (1:12). Every young Christian should memorize this famous passage. But more: Each one should follow his example, in total committal to Christ. Not until one is fully committed to Christ and filled with His Spirit is he really ready for the highest service to God in the Christian life.

2. Timothy was admonished to "be strong in the grace that is in Christ Jesus" (2:1). No one admires a *weakling* who is forever giving excuses for not being what he should be. Some young people need to trade in the *shoestring* which they are using for a moral backbone and get a real *spine!* God loves a positive character for good, but He must despise a dilly-dallying weakling (Rev. 3:16). Take a stand for Christ; He will give you grace (Rom. 5:1, 2).

3. To encourage one to "endure hardness as a good soldier of Jesus Christ" (2:3) is good counsel to all youth today. The Christian life is not the way of the sickly "sissy" but the way of red-blooded, courageous young people who have something to offer life.

Always remember that *Christianity is not merely a religion of getting*; rather, *it is primarily a religion of giving!* Jesus Christ gave His all for us; so did many of the early church leaders, and so have men and women all through its history. Youth today must be prepared to do no less.

4. Paul's admonition to Timothy to *study* to show himself "approved unto God, a workman that needeth not to be ashamed" (2:15) certainly has a place among Christian youth today. There is no excuse for ignorance about spiritual things when there is an abundance of good, wholesome Christian literature everywhere. (Please see the comment on I Tim. 4:13.)

Everyone needs to master the great Bible doctrines and be prepared to defend them as need arises. It may be well to remember that Martin Luther was relatively young when he launched the Reformation and that John Calvin was only twenty-six when he took up the battle cry of the Reformation. Young people who are trained and who are mentally and spiritually alert are needed everywhere today.

5. The admonition, "Let everyone that nameth the name of Christ depart from

iniquity" (2:19), is most certainly as important to every young Christian today as to Timothy. One cannot serve the Lord Jesus Christ and at the same time play with the foulness of sin. "No man can serve two masters," Jesus warned (Matt. 6:24).

To see young Christians who give a testimony to Christ's saving grace indulging in smutty, suggestive jokes, unguarded conversations, and conduct not becoming to their profession is indeed grievous. Christ must certainly be disappointed in such, and the Holy Spirit grieves. Christians should not "grieve the Spirit" (Eph. 4:30). The Christian should keep his witness for Christ as bright as he can. His failure to do so hurts the cause of Christ far worse than the criticisms of non-Christians.

6. The sins of the last days are cataloged by Paul (3:1-7), who warns that everyone should avoid these by all means. Reading this passage is like reading the current daily news. These are evil times, and we must stay close to Christ and shun these evil ways; otherwise we may find ourselves partaking of them.

7. The great inspiration passage of the Bible (4:16) should be memorized by everyone. It reveals how God inspired the writers of the Bible. The words, "given by inspiration of God," in this verse come from the Greek original, meaning *"God-breathed."* God breathed His Word into the hearts and minds of the Bible writers; He directed and supervised them in its writing so that, although using their own personal mannerisms in expressing it, they stated it without error. It is fully trustworthy for our salvation, and all things revealed therein are true. The Bible does not merely *contain* the Word of God; *it is* the Word of God!

8. What is perhaps the grandest and most profound dying testimony ever recorded in Christian history is found in this epistle (4:6-8). Possibly written in the old Mamertine prison in Rome, where it is believed Paul spent his last days, this last witness of his to Christ's power to keep is filled with most profound words. How it glows with the brilliance of eternal triumph and rings with the clarity of perfect assurance. It sounds as if the apostle may be expecting the executioner's call at any moment. But above and beyond this, one seems to sense his listening for the announcing herald of the angelic host which is to convey his ransomed spirit into paradise, and for the voice of the Son of God, welcoming him, "Well done, thou good and faithful servant; enter thou into the joys of thy Lord!" One is struck with a sense of the heavenly as he lingers to read again this great dying testimony.

To Paul, the executioner's block was close to the heavenly home. Christians need not fear death; it is but the gateway for them into eternal life.

Paul was beheaded at the Emperor Nero's command, sometime in A.D. 66 or 67, but his beautiful life and influence have far outlasted the Roman Empire, and it will never die.

Memory Verses

"For I am now ready to be offered, and the time of my departure is at hand. I have fought a good fight, I have finished my course, I have kept the faith: henceforth there is laid up for me a crown of righteousness, which the Lord, the righteous judge, shall give me at that day; and not to me only, but to all them also that love his appearing" (4:6-8).

Titus

This epistle takes its name from the person to whom it was written. Titus was one of Paul's co-workers.

TO WHOM

There can be little question but that the person to whom this letter was written was the same Titus who was associated with Paul in his work on various occasions.

Titus was a youthful co-worker of Paul's, although he does not seem to have been such a constant *travel* companion as was Timothy. This may account for the rather strange fact that though he attained a very prominent position, he is not mentioned in the Book of Acts!

Titus was a Greek, probably a heathen at his conversion. He accompanied Paul to Jerusalem, but Paul steadfastly refused to have him circumcised (Gal. 2: 3-5). He was one of Paul's own converts (1:4).

Considerably later he is seen with Paul at Ephesus, and Paul sends him to Corinth to straighten out the disorders there and prepare for the great offering for the saints at Jerusalem (II Cor. 6:8, 10).

The words, "for this cause left I thee in Crete" (1:5), in this epistle possibly indicate that Paul had been there with him, leaving him in charge of the churches there, those formed as a result of the apostle's ministry. After this ministry he was to leave the churches in the hands of others and rejoin the apostle in Nicopolis, in western Greece (3:12).

The last mention of Titus tells us he had gone from Rome to Dalmatia, probably on the last assignment of Paul, his dear imprisoned friend (II Tim. 4:10). He possibly had rejoined Paul; he may have been with him upon his arrest and accompanied him to Rome. Tradition says that he became bishop of Crete, where he remained until his death in old age, but there is no historical certainty of this.

PURPOSE

It is quite clear that this was both a personal epistle and a pastoral letter. Evidently Titus had accompanied Paul on his evangelizing mission to Crete and was now being left in charge to complete the task of organizing and setting the churches in order. The main purpose of this epistle seems to be to give advice, counsel, final instruction, and admonition to Titus, both as a personal son in Christ and as a Gospel minister and administrator.

For this reason it will be found that it is very similar to I Timothy.

TIME

It is generally accepted as the next to the last of Paul's epistles, II Timothy being the final one.

By the fact that he directed Titus to join him at Nicopolis, in Macedonia, it is likely that he wrote this epistle to Titus while he was there. This would mean that he likely wrote it only a short time before his final arrest and imprisonment at Rome, soon after writing his first epistle to Timothy, who was then in Ephesus. It may have been written about A.D. 65.

A ROMAN SOLDIER. *The New Testament events must be seen in the light of the Roman Empire. Roman soldiers were found in many parts of the world.*

AUTHORSHIP

Paul's authorship of this epistle is unquestioned by the best of authorities. He asserts this in the opening words (1: 1), and the general tenor of the writing is quite Pauline throughout.

As the next to the last of his epistles, much of the tender care of a personal friend and older worker for his junior companion-in-labors is seen throughout this letter.

Evidently Titus was not as closely associated with Paul as was Timothy, but apparently he was a more stable personality and a strong man. Nothing is said of his physical condition, as was the case when writing to Timothy. Possibly he was the better of the two when it came to handling difficult matters. Note that Paul sent him to Corinth to handle difficult matters there and gave him a tough assignment in Crete. He may have been Paul's best "trouble-shooter" among his co-workers.

CRETE

The island of Crete, southeast of Greece, on the border of the Aegean and Mediterranean Seas, was a large and prosperous island in Paul's days. There were upwards of one hundred cities on it. The apostle and his co-workers (3: 13) had founded churches in a number of these cities (1:5). These needed pastoral care, and apparently Titus was better qualified for this task than any other person whom Paul could leave in charge.

The work in Crete was likely done by Paul between his release from his first imprisonment in Rome and his last imprisonment there. Apparently he also had visited much of his former mission territory again on this tour, just before his last arrest, possibly at Troas.

Some think the original work in Crete may have been started by the Cretans who were at Jerusalem on the day of Pentecost (Acts 2:11). That there were Jews there, and some who tried to hinder the work by teaching that Christians should also observe the Jewish ceremonial laws, is clear from Paul's words to Titus (1:13, 14). To combat this doctrine and place strong, dependable pastoral leaders in charge was part of Titus' mission there.

In those early days there were no colleges and seminaries for training ministers; the young pastors had to be trained under the leadership and teaching of older, experienced men. Paul trained such men as Timothy and Titus, who in turn were to train others for the ministry (II Tim. 2:2).

This letter may be briefly outlined as follows:

I. Opening salutation to Titus, 1:1-4
II. Pastoral instructions, 1:5—3:11
III. Closing greetings and benediction, 3:12-15

GREAT TRUTHS IN TITUS

1. The "hope of eternal life" is the greatest blessing of the Gospel of Christ (1:2). It is based upon the promise of God who cannot fail to keep His promise.

2. Each reader should give special notice to the qualifications for Christians who are to be leaders in the church (1:6-10). It is important that all Christians conduct themselves so as to make worthy examples for others.

3. One cannot rise any higher than his heart-life, nor will he sink any lower. This means that we finally act out in life what we are in heart (1:15).

4. Paul sets forth Christian social standards for young men and women (2:4-8), urging that Titus be a "pattern," as he had told Timothy to be an "example." Christianity can rise no higher than the standards of conduct practiced by its followers. It is, therefore, of the utmost importance that Christians "adorn the doctrine of God" by consistent Christian living which will glorify the Savior.

5. "Sound speech" (2:8), free from profanity, vulgarity, and suggestive remarks which cause evil thoughts, is expected of all Christians. Conversations bordering upon indecency, and revealing low, unwholesome thoughts, have no place among Christians. One's *daily speech* reveals what he *is at heart* (Matt. 12:33-37).

6. The power of the Gospel in one's life produces the proper Christian conduct (2:11, 12). When one serves his country in the armed forces, as a congressman, or as an ambassador to a foreign country, everyone expects him to *act like a soldier or statesman.* Just so, when one is a Christian, he should *act like a Christian!*

7. Paul states God's purpose in salvation and Christian experience (2:13, 14) and explains that Christ came to save men from sin and to give them grace to serve God acceptably in daily life. Religion which does not give one this grace has not gone deep enough in Christian life.

8. Evil speaking is one of the greatest causes of trouble among the best of people. It is possibly one of the worst common evils among men. Christians are to "speak evil of no man" (3:2). Everyone should establish the rule never to speak evil of anyone and to avoid saying unkind things to anyone. One should ask himself, "If I were in *his place* and he were in *my place,* what would I want him to do?" Then, act accordingly. Oh, how much pain and sorrow of heart would be avoided if only all people lived by this rule!

Memory Verses

"For the grace of God that bringeth salvation hath appeared to all men, teaching us that, denying ungodliness and worldly lusts, we should live soberly, righteously, and godly, in this present world; Looking for that blessed hope, and the glorious appearing of the great God and our Saviour Jesus Christ; Who gave himself for us, that he might redeem us from all iniquity, and purify unto himself a peculiar people, zealous of good works" 2:11-14).

Philemon

This little book bears the name of one of Paul's personal friends.

TO WHOM

This letter was sent to Philemon, a former co-worker of Paul's, including his household, with special greetings to the church which met in his home.

Philemon, who lived at Colossae, was a well-to-do man, owning slaves — possibly a man of prominence in his area. He had been converted under Paul's ministry (v. 19). Paul likely visited Colossae, which was not too far away, during his three-year stay at Ephesus (Acts 19).

Probably Apphia was Philemon's wife, and Archippus, their son. He held some place of responsibility in the Colossian church (Col. 4:17).

PURPOSE

The purpose of this short letter was Paul's desire to aid Onesimus, the runaway slave of Philemon, in getting matters fixed up with his master. It appears that a few years after Paul had been there, while he was at Rome during his first imprisonment, Onesimus had run away from Philemon and gone to Rome. Rome was a good place to hide. It afforded many opportunities. After some time, Onesimus evidently heard of Paul being there. Either out of desire to see him — for he likely had become acquainted with him when Paul ministered at Colossae — or from conviction for his wrong doing, Onesimus came to see Paul.

Paul won him to Christ, and he, in turn, began to minister to Paul as a private helper in whatever way he could.

Paul realized he must send Onesimus home to Philemon soon, but he was not sure how he would be received. In those days many people owned slaves, and the slave was the property of his master. He could do as he wished with him. There was no law protecting slaves. In this light, Paul wrote to Philemon, pointing out that since Onesimus had been converted to Christ, he had become not only a valuable slave, returning home to correct his wrong, but indeed, a brother in Christ. He hoped that this new relationship of Onesimus to his master would cause Philemon to deal kindly with Onesimus, even possibly to set him free — though he did not *ask* this.

Paul makes a most tactful plea for Onesimus, his son in the Gospel (vv. 9-17), even offering to pay whatever Onesimus owed him. (vv. 18, 19).

TIME

It seems quite clear that this letter must have been written during Paul's first Roman imprisonment, possibly about the time Colossians and Ephesians were written. Some think it was Paul's first epistle while in prison.

Evidently, Paul wrote this epistle just as he was arranging to send epistles to the Colossian and Ephesian churches. Tychicus apparently agreed to accompany Onesimus back to Colossae, taking the Colossian and Ephesian churches. This was probably about A.D. 61.

AUTHORSHIP

From the most ancient times, the Pauline authorship of this letter has never been questioned. Neither the ancient heretics, who hammered away at

PAUL AND ONESIMUS. *The Epistle of Paul to Philemon is the letter sent with Onesimus as he returned to his master, Philemon.*

many of the books, nor modern critics have ever denied the authorship of this book.

Just *why* such a book, which is entirely personal and offers no special advice and counsel to the church, should be included in the sacred canon has puzzled some. But there is a place for such a work, for by its very nature it teaches much about the social side of the Gospel.

The New Testament writers did not legislate against slavery, for instance. To do so would have been to *create* a problem which the early church could not have solved. But the message of love, forgiveness, and the equality of all men in Christ was a death-dealing blow to this institution. Once slave masters became Christians, as multitudes did, they became conscious of their moral obligations to slaves. Even the Gospel must change certain social orders — slowly, rather than by upheaval.

As it is a personal letter, no outline is offered for this book. Unlike the personal letters to Timothy and Titus, which were pastoral, this does not contain any instructions for the church at large.

GREAT TRUTHS IN PHILEMON

1. Redemption relates all men in Christ. Paul, the apostle, Philemon, the slave owner, and Onesimus, the slave, all become brothers in Christ through redeeming grace. Although it does not

change their social status, Christian experience makes the rich and poor, educated and ignorant, those in high positions and those of lowly employment all "one in Christ."

2. Christian grace often obligates the greater to the lesser. Paul, to whom Philemon owed everything, still obligates himself to Philemon (vv. 8-14). In turn, Paul reminds Philemon that though he is the owner of Onesimus, yet, he is to receive him now not as a servant only, but as a brother beloved (vv. 15, 16).

3. Love goes far beyond bare necessity; it *gives* and goes as far as it can to aid another. Paul simply could have sent Onesimus home to take the consequences. But he went beyond this. He wrote a letter, pleading for mercy for him. Moreover, he offered to pay Onesimus' bill (v. 18). Christians should always be ready to go the extra mile and give the cloak needed by another, as the Savior taught (Matt. 6:40, 41). True Christian love delights in doing for others, that they may be blessed thereby.

Memory Verses
"I beseech thee for my son Onesimus, whom I have begotten in my bonds . . . that thou shouldest receive him for ever; Not now as a servant, but above a servant, a brother beloved, specially to me, but how much more unto thee, both in the flesh and in the Lord" (vv. 10, 15, 16).

Hebrews

Evidently, this book is so named because it was addressed to the entire Jewish section of the Christian church.

TO WHOM
There is no declaration in the opening chapter as to whom is addressed, as there is almost every other one of the epistles. The general tenor of the message, however, makes it quite clear that it was written to Jewish Christians.

From the most ancient times and the best sources of the early Church Fathers, it was believed to have been originally written for the Christian Jews of Jerusalem, and perhaps Palestine in general. Some believed that it was intended finally for all the Jews scattered over the world. Its message declares that Christianity has taken the place of the old Jewish sacrifices and rituals, and that it was the true outgrowth of the promises of God to send the Messiah, which was Christ, the Lord.

PURPOSE
Its purpose may have been two- or threefold:

1. Some think that as the Christian Jews at Jerusalem continued to worship in the Temple and offer the sacrifices, even after accepting Christ, they needed this explanation to prepare them for what was ahead of them. It was evident that Rome sooner or later would deprive them of this privilege. Many of these Christian Jews, expecting Jerusalem to develop into the world center of a coming messianic kingdom, would have an awful shock when Jerusalem was destroyed and the temple sacrifices done away with completely. They, therefore, needed this preparation.

2. It was needed to explain that since Christ, the Lamb of God, had *fulfilled* all the Old Testament rites and ceremonies, these were no longer necessary.

This epistle, more than any other, shows the purposes of these old symbols and their meanings. Now, in Christ, they are all fulfilled, so they should no longer be used. Christ had come and brought the *real* factors of redemption; therefore, we no longer need the *types* and *shadows*. When we have the brilliant light of the sun, we no longer need a candle.

3. The Christians living in Jerusalem and Palestine, where the temple sacrifices and the full course of the old way of Judaism was still in force, would be in most danger of going back to Judaism and rejecting Christ as the only Savior. It was intended to *warn* them of the *danger* in going back to Judaism (6:1-9; 10:26-31). These two passages refer not to ordinary backsliding, or sinning, but to *apostasy* — the complete rejection of Jesus Christ as the Savior and divine Lord of mankind. Hebrews was written to show the superiority of Christ to the old Jewish system and the all-sufficiency of His atoning work for salvation.

TIME

Regarding the time of the writing of this book, there has generally been complete agreement: 1. It must have been written *before* the fall of Jerusalem, A.D. 70, when the Temple was destroyed and all sacrifices ceased. Had this event taken place before the writing, the writer would most certainly have mentioned it as part of his argument. 2. The language of Hebrews 8:4 and 10:1, 11 shows that the temple sacrifices were most certainly still in practice at the writing. The best date for its writing, then, has been placed about A.D. 66.

AUTHORSHIP

The probable authorship of this book has caused more discussion and various opinions than any other New Testament book. There is no statement in the book itself, and the appendage in some of the Bibles which says that Paul wrote it is merely based upon tradition. Let us trace this tradition briefly.

The eastern section of the church, now known as the Greek Orthodox Church, accepted the Pauline authorship of this epistle from as far back as can be traced. But for the first four hundred years the western section, with headquarters at Rome, did not.

Among the early Church Fathers who favored Paul as its author were Eusebius (early church historian), Clement of Alexandria, Origen (who thought Paul may *possibly* have been its author) and Augustine. Finally, at the Council of Carthage, A.D. 397, it was accepted by the western church as Pauline. It had been considered so by the Roman Catholic Church ever since.

On the other hand, Clement, bishop of Rome in early times, often quoted Hebrews, but never attributed it to Paul. Tertullian called it "the epistle of Barnabas." Luther thought Apollos, one of the most eloquent preachers of Paul's time (Acts 18:24; 19:1; I Cor. 1:12, 3:4 wrote it. John Calvin assigned it to one of the disciples of the apostles, but denied that Paul could have written it.

The theory for the Pauline authorship has been strong for centuries. It is said that since Paul was not popular among the Jerusalem and Palestine Christians, he wrote this work but did not sign his name to it, lest his name would prejudice his readers, and that he wrote it from Rome, during his first imprisonment (13: 24). Timothy was with him when it was written (13:23).

Some believe that Paul wrote the

epistle originally in Hebrew for the Jerusalem and Palestine Christians and that Luke later translated it into Greek for Jewish Christians and Gentiles throughout the world. But later scholars point out that Hebrews is not *translated* Greek, but original Greek; it is the nearest to the classical Greek of any book of the New Testament. This largely lays the older theory to rest and certainly favors Apollos as the author, since he was a highly trained Alexandrian, well versed in Greek.

Scholars have been about half and half in the division for and against Pauline authorship. Some of the greatest minds in early and later Christianity have been listed on both sides of this question.

To date, no discoveries have been made which would give us positively certain knowledge as to just who did write this remarkable book. We must therefore conclude that there is, as yet, no final answer. The style is certainly different from most of Paul's writings; yet, it is *possible* for him to have written it, as numerous expressions in it sound very Pauline. However, we rest the case by saying it could *possibly* be that Luke, Apollos, or someone else wrote it for Paul.

This much is certain: We do not know who wrote it, but we are sure that it is *inspired by the same Holy Spirit who inspired all the other Scriptures,* whoever its human author may have been. It is one of the most beautiful and powerful books of the New Testament.

This book may be divided into two parts:

I. The Superiority of Christ and Christianity over the old Levitical system, 1-10

II. The Christian way of life through Christ, 11-13

GREAT TRUTHS IN HEBREWS

1. The key word of this book is "better." It is used thirteen times in the thirteen chapters.

Christ is the center of the entire argument of this work. He is compared to the old system as being infinitely *better* in every respect. Note briefly that Christ is shown to be *better* than: the angels (1-2), Moses (3), Joshua (4), and Aaron (5-10). Christianity offers a better covenant (8), a better rest, a better priesthood, a better altar, and a better sacrifice.

The word "better" (11:16) means "heavenly." The Jewish religion provided an *earthly* altar, *earthly* sacrifices, and an *earthly* tabernacle; but Christ has brought to Christians the *heavenly* and spiritual realities of all these, fulfilled in Himself. We no longer have the symbol, the type, and shadow, but the reality of all these in Christ.

2. Angels are guardians of real Christians (1:14). This is the same truth as the Psalmist declared (Ps. 34:7) and should be a most comforting thought to Christians. To believe that angels watch over God's children is to rest from fear of evil happening to them outside of God's will.

This does *not* mean that accident, sorrow, or even death in accident may not overtake a true Christian. But it does mean that God watches over us, allowing only what He sees best for us to occur.

3. To *neglect* salvation is pointed out as a dreadful thing (2:1-4). This warning should be heeded by young and old alike, for none can know the time of his death and his last opportunity to prepare for it.

4. Christ has identified His followers who are totally committed to Him as His "brothers" and is not ashamed of

ARCH OF TITUS. *Titus, a Roman general, serving under Vespasian, besieged and captured Jerusalem. It was at this time that the Herodian Temple was destroyed (A.D. 70). Emperor Domitian erected this monument to commemorate the taking of Jerusalem. Titus became emperor of Rome and ruled the Roman Empire from A.D. 79-81.*

them. He will at last present them with great joy to the Father (2:11-14; Jude 24).

5. The powerful work of God's Word is described as being "sharper than any two-edged sword" (4:12), accomplishing its mission in human hearts. Just as the skillful surgeon saves life by the painful knife, so God saves from eternal death those who will accept His operations of grace in their hearts.

6. Two important points about Christ's life are pointed out (5:7, 8):

(1) He offered supplications to God with "strong crying and tears." This may suggest a pattern for our praying. Too much Christian praying is little more than the sickly whine of a child or the

pious repetition of well-worn words. There is little about it that is akin to mighty, prevailing prayer! Though He was the Son of God, yet He prayed as if *all* depended upon prayer. How much more should we as earthly creatures pray!

(2) It is said, "Though he were a Son, yet learned he obedience by the things which he suffered" (5:8). Suffering is no sign that one is not a true child of God. Quite to the contrary, God "scourgeth every son whom he receiveth" (12:6). Young Christians are often perplexed by sometimes feeling as if God were displeased with them and punishing them, as if their conscience were painfully aware of some sort of *inward whipping.* Sometimes this is after some thoughtless word or deed, or upon discovering that they have acted in some unbecoming way. This is sometimes confusing, but it is sometimes God's way of "chastising" one and drawing him closer to God. God, too, like parents, must sometimes take His children aside and "paddle" them! This is especially true with the younger ones, who are just learning to walk in the way and often need *correction.* This is not because God no longer loves them; just the opposite — it is *because* He *does* love them.

7. Christ is our Anchor, both "sure and steadfast" (6:17-20). This is a most beautiful promise of God's undying love and grace. "Sure and steadfast" has also been rendered "which can neither break nor drag." This Anchor is forever trustworthy. Whatever storms may sweep the Christian's life, he need never fear; Christ, the Anchor, will hold.

8. Christ offers to His followers an "uttermost salvation" (7:25). The Greek here rendered "to the uttermost," literally means *perfect; complete; throughout*

all time; ever. Christ needs nothing added; and none can subtract from His glorious salvation offered to all who will "come unto God by him."

Good works certainly accompany salvation as a by-product, arising out of a grateful heart, but as such constitute no part of it. Christ provides complete, perfect redemption from sin, through His atoning grace alone. This was a death blow to salvation by works, or by observance of the law.

9. The seriousness of rejecting this atoning work of Christ is set before the believer in the most drastic language (10:26-30). This passage shows what to expect if one refuses Christ as Savior and Lord. The terrible consequences of turning from Christ to Judaism are pointed out to the ancient Christian Jew. To the modern Christian, it speaks the same language. Modernism rejects Christ as Savior and Lord.

Young people must make sure that their faith is anchored in Christ as personal Savior and Lord and never allow any man with "vain philosophy" to destroy this faith. Modernism, secularism, humanism, rationalism, evolutionism, or any other "ism" or theory does not have the answer to mankind's needs. It can be found only in Christ and His redemptive plan.

10. As I Corinthians 13 is the great love chapter, Hebrews 11 is the glorious faith chapter. It opens with this simple definition of faith: Faith is the "substance" — *standing ground* or *confidence* — of things hoped for, the "evidence" — *conviction* or *witness* — of things not seen (11:1).

Upon this simple definition and its reality the Christian can build everything, both for life and for eternity. Everyone should memorize much of this chapter. It is rich beyond compare. Study it with a commentary for further explanations.

11. The Christian is exhorted to seek peace and pursue it, to follow after holiness of heart and life, for without this none may expect to see God (12:14). This is the acme of Christian experience, for which all God's children should strive. It is the moral and spiritual health of the soul. Just as one is said to be healthy when he is free from all disease, so one is spiritually healthy when his heart and life are made pure and clean by total commitment to Christ and the abiding presence of the Holy Spirit.

12. Christian contentment is exhorted (13:5), and with it is given the promise that God will never leave nor forsake us. What consolation in times of deep sorrow, reverses, and trouble to know that God has said, "I will never leave thee, nor forsake thee." The Christian can then shout triumphantly, "The Lord is my helper, and I will not fear what man shall do unto me" (13:6).

13. The eternity of Christ — His eternal Sonship and Saviorhood — are most beautifully set forth in sublime, though simple, language (13:8). Everyone should memorize this verse as a precious gem.

When the storms of life are beating in maddening fury, as they will; when the winds of adversity blow unbelievably hard; when loved ones die, friends forsake, fortune takes her flight, health fails, and the grave yawns in one's face, he can rest upon this blessed truth: *"Jesus Christ the same yesterday, and today, and for ever!"*

14. The grand climax of this wonderful book is reached in the final exhortation to the Christian: that since Christ has provided uttermost salvation, we should follow Him onward, bearing whatever reproaches are necessary to obtain His eternal favor (13:12-16). We have here no permanent home, he says, but "we seek one to come." It is our business then, to be daily praising the Savior and so living that all men may know that we are His followers.

Memory Verse
"Jesus Christ the same yesterday, and today, and for ever" (13:8).

The General Epistles

James

The general epistles are so called because they are not written to any particular church or person, but to the whole Christian church in general.

The first of these, the Epistle of James, is so named because of the person who is supposed to have written it. In the New Testament, James is the English equivalent for "Jacob," the Old Testament name.

TO WHOM

The opening address indicates that it was written to the Jews only (1:1). This may have referred to the Christian Jews of Palestine, but more likely to Christian Jews universally.

PURPOSE

Quite a justifiable purpose for such a book could well be the intention to bind the Jews more fully into the total Christian church, since so many Gentile converts were then flooding it. In this light, it would be originally written to the Jews alone, but ultimately to all Christians.

This book is the most Jewish of all the New Testament books. It makes no mention of Gentile Christians, and in fact, it makes only two references to Christ as Lord and Savior (1:1; 2:1). Some have thought it may have been intended as a sort of connecting link between the old Jewish system and the new Christian way, which had sprung

from it through Christ. It makes no mention of the miracles or teachings of Christ, but it does reflect the wisdom literature of His ministry. For example, if one will read the Sermon on the Mount (Matt. 5-7), then read James immediately, he will find in James many similarities to Christ's teachings. It has been thought of as the introduction to the principles of Christ's message, but without His very words and deeds.

A further purpose may have been to show the *practical side* of the Christian religion, as compared with the theological side, presented so ably by Paul. Its exhortations to good works and practical religion, as over against Paul's emphasis upon salvation by faith, make it sound at first as if they were contradictory. But examination does not prove this to be true. It was this phase of James' epistle which made Martin Luther, coming so recently from a church where salvation by "works" had been greatly overemphasized, almost reject this epistle as false. Because he failed to reconcile James' emphasis upon goods works with Paul's emphasis upon salvation by faith, Luther called James "an epistle of straw." He failed to see that both have their proper place in any system of true Christian religion because he had been so recently delivered from the error of salvation by good works alone.

TIME

There has been much difference of opinion as to the time at which this epistle was written. If it is the earliest of all New Testament books, as some affirm, then its date would be about A.D. 45. Those accepting the view of its much later writing generally place the date about A.D. 60-63, since according to tradition James, who was most likely

THE STAR OF BETHLEHEM. *This common flower in Palestine is now called the "Star of Bethlehem" because it has six points. James likened a rich man to "the flower of the grass."*

its author, was martyred about A.D. 63. Probably A.D. 60-63 is the more likely date of its writing.

AUTHORSHIP

Considerable difference of opinion exists here, too. There is no final and absolutely certain knowledge as to who wrote this work. The writer himself was content to state simply that he was "James, a servant of God and of the Lord Jesus Christ" (1:1).

There are no less than four persons called James in the New Testament. To establish *which* of these Jameses wrote this book is the problem. Two apostles bore this name: the brother of John, and the son of Alphaeus (Matt. 10:2, 3). Jesus' oldest brother, also named James (Matt. 13:55), is recognized as the leader of the Jerusalem church (Acts 12:17; Gal. 1:19). He has been com-

monly regarded as the writer of this book.

Some think the writer was James, the son of Alphaeus and the sister of Christ's mother; this would make him a *cousin* of Jesus. He is called the "Lord's brother," simply as a common usage of that day, when cousins were often called brothers by the Jews. The writer may have been Mary's own son, born to Joseph and Mary after Jesus' birth, and therefore, truly the "Lord's brother." This is thought by many to be the case.

It will be noted that this James, the "Lord's brother," was the most prominent of the church leaders at Jerusalem. Peter reported to him upon his release from prison (Acts 12:17). At the first church council in Jerusalem he gave the sentence of authority as to the conduct of the Gentile Christians (Acts 15:13-29) and so far as we have record, he either wrote or authorized the first pastoral letter sent to Christian churches, (Acts 15:13, 23-29). At Jerusalem Paul took his advice (Acts 21:18-26). and later he clearly mentions him as the main leader of the church (Gal. 1:19; 2:9, 12). This James would, therefore, be the logical person to have written such a book as the "link" between the Jews and the Gentile Christians in those early days.

Clement of Alexandria called him "James the Just." He was noted for his deep piety. Josephus, a non-Christian Jewish historian, mentions him as "the brother of Jesus, who was called Christ, whose name was James," and his appearance before the Jewish Sanhedrin to be condemned to death. But, he says, the Jews revolted against the High Priest for this act, deposing him, because of their regard for James. One tradition refers to his having calluses on his knees, from much prayer, like the calluses on a camel's knee. It is further stated that he was martyred in Jerusalem by the unbelieving Jews in A.D. 63. But there is no historical certainty of this, though the tradition has prevailed from very ancient times.

In this book, religion almost leaves the field of theology and centers itself in the fields of ethics and practical living. Yet, one is not to suppose that James did not appreciate doctrine. He was merely emphasizing the *practical* side of religion.

James may be outlined as follows:

    I.   Opening greeting, 1:1

    II. Temptation and its value, 1:2-18

    III. Hearing and doing the Word, 1:19-27

    IV. Caution about partiality, 2:1-13

    V. Faith and works, 2:14-26

    VI. The tongue and its use, 3

    VII. Dangers of pleasure and pride, 4

    VIII. Final admonitions, 5

GREAT TRUTHS IN JAMES

1. Christians are to ask for *wisdom* from God (1:5) for all their daily living. If more Christians followed this pattern, many heartaches would be avoided.

2. Double-minded Christians are exhorted to bring themselves to total commitment to Christ and to rid themselves of this hindering element, so that they may have the real victory of normal Christian living (1:8; 4:8).

3. Temptation, when faced properly and overcome, is shown to be a servant rather than a master (1:12, 13). It is in the *yielding* that trouble comes. One grows in grace as he resists temptations; he loses ground as he yields.

4. Victory in Christ is always by *obedience,* not merely by hearing the Word (2:14-26). Paul emphasized the matter of faith for salvation as an experience to be received; James emphasized obedience as the means of allowing this salvation experience to work out in life. They are both important.

5. James bears down on the right use of the tongue (3:1-10). What personal troubles and sorrows in broken homes, divided churches, torn communities, and even among war-torn nations could be averted if only people would *control their tongues!* "How great a matter a little fire kindleth" — and what a world of trouble a little misuse of the tongue can bring! One should early establish the habit of never allowing the tongue to be misused. Half the sorrows of the world could be saved, if people would only control their tongues.

6. Prayer is often not answered because the *pray-er* either asks for the wrong things or prays with the wrong attitude (4:2-10). One should study this passage well, for it is the groundwork for successful praying. When one asks for anything primarily for selfish reasons — "that ye may consume it upon your lusts," pleasures — he may be sure his prayer will not be heard. Prayer must at all times arise out of an unselfish heart, for good motives, if it is to be answered (5:16-18).

7. Where it is God's will to heal one healing of the body is still available for those who fervently pray and meet the obligations laid down by James (5:13-18). "All things are possible to him that believeth."

Memory Verse

"For as the body without the spirit is dead, so faith without works is dead also" (2:26).

I Peter

This book is also named for its author. When Andrew brought his brother Simon to Christ he renamed him Cephus, or Peter. The Greek form of the word Peter means "a stone" (John 1:40-42).

TO WHOM

The opening address indicates that it was sent to the Jewish Christians — "strangers" — throughout Asia Minor. It may also have been intended for the Jewish Christians all over the world. In the original Greek the term *diaspora,* for "strangers scattered abroad," refers to Israel in dispersion — a term widely used by them in ancient times. It may have referred to the Christians scattered abroad from Jerusalem.

Some think this epistle was sent for encouragement to the churches of Asia Minor which had been founded by Paul. Although not stated in the New Testament, it is likely that as a general apostle, especially to the Jewish element of the church, Peter may have visited these churches sometime in the last days of his ministry.

PURPOSE

The purpose of its writing seems quite clearly to have been to encourage the Christians during the siege of persecution which was beginning to sweep over the churches.

About this time Nero, the infamous Roman emperor, had started a furious persecution of Christians in and about Rome — upon pretext that they had set fire to Rome, a deed which he had done or directed. There was no empire-wide persecution at this time, but local authorities were doubtless encouraged in their persecutions of Christians by the emperor's acts. It is clear from the general tenor of this epistle that it was a time of "manifold temptation" and "fiery trial" (1:6-9; 2:19-24; 3:13-17; 4:12-19; 5:8, 9).

It is evident that the writer wished to comfort the suffering, strengthen the weak, and give general directions how to act under persecution and supreme testings. Doubtless then, this epistle came as a great boon to many. In times of trials, testings, and extreme persecu-

NERO. *Christians were severely persecuted by Nero, who was the Roman emperor from A.D. 54-68. Tradition includes Peter and Paul as martyrs under Nero's persecution.*

tions, it has served to bless millions in all Christian ages. It is the book to read when passing through times of trouble and distress as well as times of persecution or extreme trial.

TIME

From the very nature of this epistle, it is clear it was written during a time of extreme persecution. It is suited to the period from about A.D. 64 to A.D. 67. It breathes an atmosphere of encouragement in great suffering. It may have been written around A.D. 64.

AUTHORSHIP

Where the epistle was written is not certain. Some think the reference to "Babylon" (5:13) is mystical and refers to Rome. Babylon was used to disguise the actual place of its writing, they say, although the Christians would have understood the meaning.

Others say, however, that since no other epistles use figurative or mystical language, it is unreasonable to suppose it is used here. Peter, a wide traveler, they say, may have indeed written the letter from near the ancient site of Babylon, where he could have been evangelizing. The weight of tradition, however, favors Rome as the place, but there is no historical evidence to prove it.

From the most ancient times the church has assigned the authorship of this epistle to Peter, our Lord's apostle. In the opening salutation he assigns it to himself (1:1), and there is no reason to doubt.

Peter is recognized as one of the foremost of the apostles of Christ. He was among the first to start following Him (John 1:40-42). He was an active follower of Christ to the end, although he denied Christ at His trial (Matt. 26:40-

42). He was graciously restored by Christ and commissioned by Him as a leader among the apostles (John 21:15-17). He may be called Dean of the Apostles. Peter was the chief preacher at Pentecost (Acts 2:14-40); he is the leading figure in the first twelve chapters of Acts.

It was Peter who opened the doors of the church to the first Gentiles (Acts 10; 11:1-18; 15:1-12); he also took a strong hand in settling the debate over admitting Gentiles into the church (Acts 15:1-31). He is seen later with Paul at Antioch (Gal. 2:11-14). After this he drops from sight in Acts, as Luke carries the rest of the story concerning Paul and his work.

While the Petrine authorship stands undisputed, the whereabouts of the apostle Peter during his last years must forever remain shrouded in some mystery. Why this should be is not clear, when he was one of the most outstanding of the apostles.

Tradition (and some among the early Church Fathers) has given him a place at Rome, but no reliable historical proof has ever been given for this tradition. He is never mentioned by Paul in any of his epistles written from Rome, nor was he mentioned in Romans, which Paul addressed to the Roman Christians before he went there. Had Peter been there then, it is practically certain that he would have been recognized in the references to persons there. Peter does not refer to ever having been at Rome — unless the reference to *Babylon,* from which he wrote his first epistle (5:13), is a mystical or figurative reference to Rome. Some believe that the whole tradition about Peter ever being at Rome is more fiction than fact, since there is no historical evidence of it.

If we accept the strong tradition, however, we may believe that Peter possibly went to Rome in his last days. From here he wrote his epistles and shortly thereafter suffered martyrdom. His martyrdom at Rome has been a long-standing tradition, backed by many notable persons throughout the Christian centuries. It will be remembered that Christ foretold something of his martyr's death (John 21:18, 19). Tradition says that he was crucified with his head downward, feeling unworthy to die as did his Lord, in ordinary crucifixion. There the case must rest, as there is no further evidence or historical note concerning his last days.

This epistle may be divided into two parts:

I. Privileges and duties of believers, 1-3
II. Suffering with humility and faith in God, 4-5

GREAT TRUTHS IN I PETER

1. In Christ, Christians have an unfading inheritance awaiting in heaven (1:4). Earthly fortunes fail, houses and lands are lost, but he who has heavenly wealth is never poor. Early Christians were often of the common class, but they were said to be rich in grace and in the goodness of God; their future was most attractive.

2. Christians are to abstain from all things which "war against the soul" (2:11). Young Christians need to watch for and avoid these same things. Whatever will dampen your ardor or quench your zeal for Christ should be avoided.

3. Throughout his epistle, Peter admonishes quiet confidence in God and a no-striking-back attitude when suffering persecution and trouble at the hands of others. Jesus showed the right atti-

tude toward persecution at Calvary: "Father, forgive them: for they know not what they do" (Luke 23:34; also 2:20-24; 3:14-18; 4:12-22).

4. The believer is to be ready to give an "answer to every man that asketh you a reason of the hope that is in you with meekness and fear" (3:15). Far too many young Christians do not know *why* they believe *what* they believe. Just as any salesman should know his product, or any teacher his subject, so every Christian should know the *reaons* for his faith in Christ.

5. Young Christians especially, will meet with "fiery trials" and sometimes the most pleasant temptations to do wrong (4:12). This is not because they are not truly Christ's, but because they are new in the way, and Satan uses every trick and alluring thing he can to turn them away from Christ. One good way to shun temptation is never to willingly go where you know it will be present; you can avoid it and still do your Christian duty.

6. "If any man suffer as a Christian, let him not be ashamed" (4:16). This is the last of the only three times the word "Christian" occurs in the Bible (King James Version). One never needs to be ashamed of suffering for Christ. It is a high honor to be accounted worthy to suffer for Him. Always be glad to take your stand, even if it means persecution, misunderstanding, and suffering. When you suffer for Christ, you honor God.

7. Disobedience to God is a fearful thing. Judgment must begin among God's people. If *they* "scarcely" escape, what will be the end of rebellious sinners? (4:17, 18) It is a solemn thought that only by God's grace will the righteous be saved — by no merit of their own.

If with all their obedience, faith, prayers, and sufferings for Christ, they barely escape damnation, how dreadful must be the end of those who never even bowed the head in repentance!

8. "As a roaring lion" the devil seeks to destroy people, but God's grace is ever sufficient, and the Christian need never fear (5:8, 9). You have but to "resist" Satan with all your heart, and victory will always be yours.

9. The words "make you perfect" (5:10) mean *bring you to maturity*. Involved here is help to develop into a full-grown Christian. There are far too many "dwarfs" in the church now — don't be another one! God wants *mature* saints — experientially, emotionally, and socially.

Just as parents would be grieved if their children never grew to maturity,

THE COLOSSEUM. *This Roman amphitheater, which seated almost fifty thousand people was built on part of the grounds Nero used for his Golden House. Christians were persecuted here.*

---

so God is grieved with people who retain their religious childhood for years. Make it your goal to *"grow up"* in Him.

This is the special book for the suffering saints, whatever the cause of their sufferings. Read it again and again for wisdom, comfort, and help against the enemy of your soul.

Memory Verses

"But sanctify the Lord God in your hearts, and be ready always to give an answer to every man that asketh you a reason of the hope that is in you with meekness and fear: Having a good conscience; that,

whereas they speak evil of you, as of evil-doers, they may be ashamed that falsely accuse your good conversation in Christ" (3:15,16).

II Peter

Like the former one, this epistle was named for its famous author. (See notes on I Peter).

TO WHOM

It is quite clear that the same persons who received I Peter are also addressed here (3:1). Reference to his section in the notes on I Peter will give this information. This epistle becomes wider in scope, however, than the former one, for it embraces all of "like precious faith" (1:1) and was doubtless meant to be a *general* epistle for the whole Christian church.

PURPOSE

Its purpose seems to have been similar to I Peter, although with some added reasons. Since the same persons are addressed here as in the former epistle, it is evident that they could not have been too far apart in their writing. The admonitions are similar, though this one takes on some extra coloring (3:1, 2).

In this epistle the full name Simon Peter is used. Simon was the Jewish name while Peter was the new Greek name Christ had given him; it was the word for "stone." It may be that in this epistle he intends to appeal more widely to both Jewish and Gentile sections of the church.

This also seems to be a "warning" epistle, as well as one of comfort. In the former, persecution and suffering had a major role. In this he reminds the readers that this is not to be forgotten, but he adds touches of warnings: against failure (1:2-12); against false prophets and teachers, who would destroy their faith (2); against unbelievers and scoffers; and against the danger of losing the faith (3).

Doubtless his purpose here is to prepare the readers against the heresies which were beginning to swoop down upon the church. He wished that after his voice was silenced in death, they still would have his message to guide them (1:14, 15).

TIME

The best scholars generally agree that this epistle likely was written about A.D. 67. It is known that the Roman Emperor Nero died in A.D. 68, and tradition says he ordered Peter's execution, which must have been very shortly before Nero's death. This epistle breathes the very atmosphere of a man facing his death (1:14).

AUTHORSHIP

It may seem strange that there has been as much debate about whether Peter actually wrote this epistle as that about the authorship of almost any book in the New Testament.

While there is abundant evidence from the early Church Fathers that I Peter was accepted as the genuine work of the apostle, for some strange reason this cannot be said of II Peter. It was a long time before this book became fully recognized as the writing of Peter; the church councils finally agreed, however, that it was a genuine epistle, and so included it in the New Testament canon of Scripture.

Why the argument? Quite largely because of the very great difference in the original Greek in the two epistles. I Peter is in good, smooth Greek, with much in style that is close to classical Greek, while II Peter is in rough, terse, broken Greek, more of the common language type.

This has been explained by the fact that, apparently, Silas, Paul's traveling companion ("Silvanus," I Peter 5:18), wrote I Peter at Peter's direction, probably using his *own style* It is likely that as a tra eling companion of the highly-educated Paul, Silas would have had a very proficient use of proper Greek terms and language, the reason for the smoothness of that first epistle. It is apparent, too, that II Peter was written by Peter himself, with no assistant, as no one is mentioned as ever being with him. He likely wrote this epistle in haste, a short while before his death, possibly while in prison, and therefore, with no secretary. Futhermore, it is just the type of Greek to be expected from Peter, a Galilean fisherman.

Further internal evidence is that the writer mentions his presence with Christ on the Mount of Transfiguration (1:17, 18) and having been told by Christ of the way he should die (1:14). He refers to his first writing (3:1) in such a way as to make anyone believe the readers are the same people. Now, had some writer written this epistle several years after Peter's death and placed Peter's name to it, as some modern critics claim, he certainly would not have placed the above references in his work. Forgers always fail to include the genuine atmosphere of another person's personality, as this epistle most certainly does. There can be no doubt that this epistle is the genuine work of Peter.

Some striking things occur in this epistle: It refers to the rising false doctrine of Gnosticism in the reference to the false prophets and teachers (2). "Following in the way of Balaam" (2:15) probably refers to the same thing to which John refers in Revelation 2:14 and 15, where John also refers to the *Nicolaitans,* a sect of Gnostics that took its name from *Nicolaus.* In both cases, note that idol worship and fornication are warned against (2:13-16; Rev. 2:14).

Peter also mentions that at the end-time in the changing order of this planet, "the elements shall melt with the fervent heat" (3:12). This appears to be the first mention of this fact in the New Testament. The "new heavens and earth" (3:13) are, of course, also referred to by John (Rev. 21, 22). As Noah predicted a flood, so Peter predicts here a fiery baptism for the earth, melting everything we now know.

Paul is referred to as "beloved brother Paul," and his epistles are compared with the "other Scriptures" (3:15, 16).

This rather strange but powerful epistle is filled with things concerning the "last days," which are of the utmost interest. It has a number of warnings Christians will do well to heed. Sinners should shudder to think what is coming upon the unsaved, as predicted here, and repent.

This book may be outlined briefly as follows:

   I.   Opening salutation, 1:1-2
  II.   Exhortation to grow in grace, 1:3-21

III. Warning against false teachers, 2
IV. Dangers of the last days, 3

GREAT TRUTHS IN II PETER

1. "Exceeding great and precious promises" and "partakers of the divine nature" are wonderful truths which every Christian should grasp with rejoicing. God's promises are always "exceeding great and precious." And how wonderful to know that every child of God, through faith in Christ, has been made a "partaker of the divine nature" (1:4). This relationship makes Christians sons of God, heirs of God, joint-heirs with Christ

COINS OF VESPASIAN. *Following the suicide of Nero, Vespasian was proclaimed emperor of Rome. He ruled from A.D. 69-79.*

(Rom. 8:17). It is the most important transformation and change of relationship possible. When a girl marries, she changes her name and her relationship and becomes heir with her husband to the new estate. But the divine relationship reaches far beyond this and is a far deeper, more wonderful relationship than any earthly one can ever be. It should be held sacred by everyone.

2. The Christian's *addition* list is set forth (1:5-9). These seven basic things should come to every Christian as he walks with God. The apostle makes it clear, however, that these do not "add"

automatically. Rather, he says, "Giving all diligence, add to your faith virtue. . . ." It is understood that *you* do the adding. These are not the graces of the Spirit bestowed in conversion, but rather the graces of Christian growth and progress in grace.

Note the special warning in verses 8 and 9. *If* these abound in you, fine; but he that *lacketh these* is in a bad way! Read these verses carefully.

3. God's Word did not come by enthusiasm, a personal desire on someone's part to "write some Bible," or by unscrupulous men who were interested in forwarding some opinion of their own. No! It came as "holy men of God spake as they were moved by the Holy Ghost" (1:21). This includes every book in the Bible. For our day, every moral and spiritual truth which these books teach is binding upon Christians. We are not under the old ceremonial laws of the Jews, as they were only shadows and types of what God has given us in Christ. But every New Testament truth is binding upon every Christian.

4. Chapter 2 is a serious warning against immorality, false teachings, and the negligence of personal Christian living. One should study this well and heed its admonitions. Note especially what is said in verses 9-11; 14-17; 20-22. Chapter 3 is filled with the most important warnings about the last days (vv. 3-9) and predictions of the end of this present earthly order. If possible, secure a good commentary on the Bible for study of this most wonderful passage (3:10-14).

Memory Verse
"The Lord is not slack concerning his promise, as some men count slackness; but is longsuffering to us-ward; not willing that any should perish, but that all should come to repentance" (3:9).

I JOHN

This is the first of three letters of the beloved apostle John. It is named for him.

TO WHOM

There is no address in the opening chapter, as in most epistles. His oft-repeated references to "my little children" and "my children" make it evident he refers to Christians. It could have been a local congregation or church with which he was most familiar (2:19) to which he wrote. But this also could refer to the Christian church as a whole. It is more than likely that John had in mind the universal church. At his advanced age, and having visited much of the Asian church, it would be only reasonable for him, the last remaining apostle of our Lord, to refer to the Christians as his "children."

Once there was an opinion that since John refers to "light" and "darkness" on several occasions, this epistle was written for the Christians in the Persian section of the ancient world. The doctrine of *dualism* — that all things are made of two forces, good and evil, darkness and light, in constant opposition to each other — was strong in Persia then. But this is very similar to the Gnostic system of dualism, which it is certain he wrote to correct, and therefore, this opinion is not valid. The book was doubtless meant for all Christians as a statement of the truth about God and

Christ, in relation to the doctrines of Christianity.

PURPOSE

The purpose of this epistle was, as stated, to combat error and teach the real truth of Christianity. The twofold purpose, then, would be to establish the Christians in the truth of God in Christ and to correct the false teachings against this truth.

At the time of this writing Christianity had become a world wide religion with considerable prestige and marvelous power to bring men into its fold. As it rose, there appeared false religions which tried to attach themselves to it or take its teachings and apply them to their own in such a way so as to profit by them.

One of these false cults were Gnosticism. It taught that there are two separate systems in the world — spirit and matter. Spirit is totally good and matter is totally evil. The Gnostics said matter was a series of *emanations* — or emissions — coming forth from God, but that these were really bad in themselves. In some unknown fashion these "emanations" brought about matter, such as the earth and men's bodies. Since God was supreme good, He could not have created the evil earth and men's bodies; He created only the spiritual things. Therefore, Christ could not have been the Incarnate Son of God, for His body would have been evil. Since this could not be, then His body, they said, was not *real* — it was just a *phantom,* a shadowy something which *contained* His spirit.

As one can see, if this were true, then there could be no true redemption wrought by Christ. A *phantom* body could not die and be resurrected; it could contain no "blood" to shed in atonement for sin! Another phase of Gnosticism was that it claimed superior knowledge to all other men. The very word *Gnostic* is derived from the Greek word meaning "to know."

Armed with this attitude and this doctrine, the Gnostics aimed to make Christianity a part of the Oriental mysticism and Greek philosophy of which Gnosticism consisted. They intended to reduce it to a religion of mystical naturalism.

Now, one of the most terrible things about the results of this heresy was this: Since spirit was totally good and material and body were totally evil, one could be good in spirit, enjoy wonderful visions of God, and in the Spirit, do great things; yet, at the same time he could live in the worst of sins! He could be living an *immoral, licentious,* deliberately wicked life *in the body,* but be pure, good, and holy *in the spirit!* This was, of course, very appealing to people who wanted all the *follies* of sin, but all the *benefits* of religion.

This was the wicked doctrine and practices which John wrote to condemn. Quite likely this is also what Peter referred to in II Peter 2.

TIME

Concerning the time at which this epistle was written there has been some difference of opinion. Some have assigned it to a time before the destruction of Jerusalem in A.D. 70, possibly about A.D. 65 or 68. Others, however, feel that there is evidence for a much later date, probably as late as A.D. 80, even as late as A.D. 96. It was probably written sometime between A.D. 80 and 90. Tradition has always thought the place of its writing to be Ephesus, where John min-

istered for many years and spent his last days.

AUTHORSHIP

While his name is not attached to it at any place, tradition and history have always assigned this epistle to John.

Placed alongside the Gospel of John, of which there is no question of authorship, this epistle bears very striking resemblances in several ways. He emphasizes Christ as the Son of God, says much about love, faith, and the life of God in Christ, and refers to the work of the Holy Spirit, much as he did in his gospel.

Tradition long received in the church says John made his home at Jerusalem, where he cared for Jesus' mother until she passed away, some fifteen years after Christ's death and resurrection. After the destruction of Jerusalem, he moved to Ephesus, where he was minister of the church for many years.

During his long stay at Ephesus, John became tutor to three young men whose names have become famous in early church history — Polycarp, Papias, and Ignatius. These men became bishops of the churches at Smyrna, Hierapolis, and Antioch, respectively. Their lives carried well over into the second century A.D., helping to establish much of the history we have about the early Christian church. Tradition says that during John's later days at Ephesus, a man named Cerinthus also lived there, who apparently was a leader of the Gnostics of that area. It may be to him and his followers that John refers in chapter 2:19. These may also be the persons to whom John refers in his blasts against "antichrists" already working in the world (2:19-22; 4:1-3).

Key words used in this epistle are *know, light, life, believe,* and *love.* These John uses to show the living realities in the

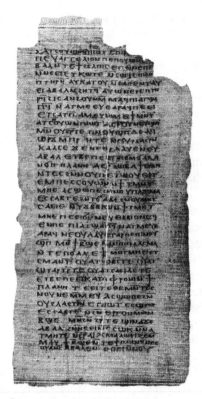

Courtesy, Rascher & Cie Verlag

Photo by James M. Robinson

THE NAG HAMMADI TEXTS. *Digging in an old cave for bird manure to enrich their fields, Egyptian peasants discovered hand-written manuscripts in book form. They had evidently been collected by a group of Gnostics or someone interested in the movement. The site of the discovery was Nag Hammadi, a town on the Nile River, sixty miles north of Luxor. Shown here are the entrance to one of the tombs, a page from the GOSPEL OF TRUTH, and an untitled manuscript. A total of fifty-one treatises were discovered.*

Photos from THE NAG HAMMADI GNOSTIC TEXTS AND THE BIBLE
© Baker Book House

Courtesy, Deutsches Archaeologische Institut

Christian's life, made possible by Christ's redemptive work.

Following is a brief outline of II Peter:
I.   Introduction, 1:1-4
II. God, the Source of all light, 1: 5—2:29
III. God, Source of all spiritual love, 3:1—5:17
IV. Concluding remarks, 5:18-21

GREAT TRUTHS IN I JOHN
Special Note:

Much of this epistle is directed against the pernicious, evil doctrine of dualism (see above — Gnosticism). John makes it abundantly plain that this teaching is wrong. Probably the reason for his strong statements about believers sinning is his desire to warn true Christians that one cannot live a spiritual life and at the same time live in willful disobedience to the laws of God, as the Gnostics taught. "He that committeth sin is of the devil" (3:8), nor can one love God and not love his fellowmen (2:9-11). He who is truly Christian in spirit is trying to live the pure life (2:6; 3:2, 3). In case a believer may sin there is mercy and forgiveness for him (2:1), for Christ is the *Advocate* of the Christian, always interceding for him. Even when one willfully sins and turns away from God, he may repent and return; but there is no provision made for living a life of willful sinning and at the same time enjoying the Spirit's presence and blessing, as Cerinthus, a Gnostic, would have had people believe (3:4-10).

Gnosticism insisted upon the evil of the body; if so, Christ could not have been incarnate, or born of Mary, as a holy being free from sin. Upon this notice was based the "phantom" idea of the body of Christ. John strikes at this when he opens his epistle by saying he was one who had "heard" Christ's words and "seen" Him.

He writes of that which "hands have handled, of the word of life" (1:1). Clearly the intention here was to state that he had personally known Christ to such a degree as to make any "phantom" idea of His body impossible.

Throughout the epistle John calls Christ the Son of God and refers to God as Father and Christ as Son in such a way as to make plain that the truth of the Fatherhood of God and eternal Sonship of Christ was basic to Christian doctrine. The name of God is used some sixty times, most of which refer to Christ or Christian living in such a way as to establish the doctrine of the Sonship of Christ. John, more than any other gospel writer or New Testament author, faces the rising heresies of the last part of the first Christian century and does his best to destroy them and establish the Christians in the true faith.

1. Walking in the light of obedience to God brings fellowship with God and other saints, cleansing, and peace (1:7). Rebellion can bring only heartache; obedience, with faith, knows only purity and fellowship. "Walk" here carries the thought of active obedience to God. This is the way of Christian victory.

2. When mixed with true repentance and faith, confession of sins on the part of sinners never fails to bring forgiveness (1:9). John uses the "we" here, not in the sense that he *himself* was a sinner, but in the same way it is often used today by speakers who *associate* themselves with their audience, or as the editorial "we" used in writing. Those who deny that they have ever sinned and therefore need no forgiveness, he says, make God a liar (1:10; Rom. 3:23).

3. Placing Christ as the example which all should follow, John raises a high standard of conduct for Christians. Those

who confess Him and yet do not keep His commandments are sternly dealt with (2:4-6). Perhaps the greatest damage to the church today is not from unbelievers outside, but from the failure of believers on the inside to live the vital Christ-like life. Young people should determine never to *betray Christ in His own name* by bringing a reproach upon His cause!

4. Christians are to "love not the world," with its sinful indulgences, nor to follow after its alluring ways; all who do so have not God's love in them (2:15, 16).

The word "world" here is from a Greek word which means *order, beauty, arrangement, embellishment,* or *decoration.* Do not allow your affections to fasten themselves onto the showy, the gaudy, the sensual, and the fleshly attractions of this life and man's sinful ways. Seek not to be satisfied in mind and body by those fleeting fleshly lusts and earthly things which can bring no help to the soul. Christians have far higher satisfactions than these.

5. Christians are sons and daughters of God, and with this comes all the inherent blessings of being in the family of God (3:1-3). What a high and glorious honor to be in God's great family!

Sons of God, then, should so conduct themselves as to bring credit to their heavenly Father, just as children should so live as to honor earthly parents. This may not always be the easiest way at the moment of temptation, trial, or persecution. But in the long run it will prove the easiest and best way.

6. What blessed knowledge Christians have — as evidenced by the devout love of other Christians, "they have passed from death unto life" (3:14). This is not the only evidence, but it certainly is one of the marks of a real Christian. He who

loves God loves also His children; the loss of this love is the saddest evidence of failure to God.

7. "Blessed assurance" of answers to prayer and of the fact that God is pleased with one's life come to one whose heart "condemns him not" as he fully trusts in Christ (3:19-22).

8. Christians can test the truth or error of every doctrine by its relation to Jesus Christ. If it denies Him as Lord and Savior, it is wrong, no matter how appealing (4:1-4). Sometimes, as in many "cults," this denial is securely hidden under a raft of popular views. But if one asks enough pointed questions, it will come out. At heart almost every "ism" denies the basic truth.

9. God's love, made perfect by the indwelling Spirit in the believer's heart, casts out the fear of worldly men, of persecution, of cross-bearing, and even of death. Why should one who loves God with all his mind, heart, soul, and strength dread to go to be with Him whom his soul adores? (4:16-18). No, it does not remove the *natural dread* of death — no one wishes to die, especially he who is young and full of life. The fear that is removed by God's indwelling Spirit is that of God and the results of facing Him without being prepared for it. The best replacement for the dread of what's beyond death is constant victory in Christ!

10. Overcoming victory through Christ can be had by complete trust in God (5:4). There is no reason for Christians to be living a "defeated life" when through Christ there is plenty of grace, courage, and strength at hand to live victoriously. Paul even saw that out of *weakness* he could be made strong (II Cor. 12:9); almost in the same breath he shouted, "When I am weak, then am I strong."

BASICALLY OF ST. JOHN. *Tradition places the apostle John in Ephesus in the latter years of his life. A large basilica was erected by Justinian over the tomb where the apostle is said to have been buried. Shown here are the ruins of that basilica.*

11. Christians have the inward witness to their relationship with God. What a word of comfort this is: "He that believeth on the Son of God, hath the witness in himself" (5:10).

This witness is far more than an emotional overflow of good feeling. It is a deep-down *consciousness* inside one that he has been reconciled to God, and is, therefore, His child. It is not a boastful self-secured knowledge but the result of God's Spirit witnessing to the human spirit that one is God's child (Rom. 8:16).

12. The Word of God also furnishes further witness to the redeemed soul that he is God's child and has eternal life through Christ (5:13-15). When one is truly God's child his spirit rejoices in the Word of God and finds comfort in it. And this is true even when that same Word may chastise and condemn him for some momentary thing in which he has erred. He will rise to the task, correct his way, and have God's smile upon him for his obedience.

With reference to man's direct relationship to God through Christ, this is one of the most spiritual books of the epistles. One should read it often and memorize many of its passages.

Memory Verse

"He that believeth on the Son of God, hath the witness in himself: he that believeth not God hath made him a liar; because he believeth not the record that God gave of his Son" (5:10).

II John

This epistle bears the name of its author, as does the last one, although his name is not listed in its contents. The "elder" doubtless is his way of signing his name here.

TO WHOM

"The elect lady and her children" mentioned in the opening words (1:1) probably refers to the church and its members. Note that in verse 5 there is the reference to a person — "lady" — but in verse 8 the plural form is used "Look to yourselves . . ." By these references he doubtless refers to the church and its membership as a whole.

PURPOSE

The purpose of this book appears to have been twofold: (1) to *admonish* the *elect lady,* whoever she was — a person, possibly a church meeting in a home, or the entire church itself — to be faithful to sound doctrine and to walk in obedience to God's commandments, and (2) to *warn* against false teachers and their evil doctrines.

This is still a good and sufficient reason for this epistle's place in the Bible, for it is needed again today.

TIME

It is generally believed that it was written in the apostle's last days. There is no information in the epistle itself by which one can fix a date. From the best

sources it seems wise to say it may have been written at Ephesus between A.D. 80 and 90.

AUTHORSHIP

For a long time the authorship of this epistle was questioned, the early church fearing it may have been a forgery. But by the time the New Testament canon was finally established some three hundred years after Christ's death, it was included. It has since been universally received as a true writing of John the beloved.

While this is next to the shortest book in the New Testament, it contains some important truths closely akin to all of John's other writings.

This epistle may be outlined as follows:

I.   Opening salutation, vv. 1-4
II. Admonitions to faithfulness, vv. 5-7
III. Warning against false teachers and their doctrines, vv. 8-11
IV. Closing remarks, vv. 12, 13

GREAT TRUTHS IN II JOHN

1. Obedience to God brings joy that is not only personal but also that which reaches others. Just as the aged apostle was made happy by the good reports of this person and the church with which she was associated, so older Christians are always made to rejoice when we who are younger live the victorious life. God rewards Christian labor with the joy of seeing others established in His grace.

2. As seen in verses 4, 5, 6, and 9, three key words in this book are *walk, love,* and *abide.* These words echo what we saw in I John and in the Gospel of John. The language of this epistle alone would go far to establish it as a writing of John. This is what we call in Bible study and theology "internal evidence."

These key words are all verbs which show the activity of genuine religion. To "walk" in God's commandments means to *obey* them. John was again warning against the evil doctrine which held that as long as the spirit is saved, it mattered little what the body did. This was the wicked doctrine of the Gnostics that is also mentioned in I John. This is a dangerous position and Christians should never accept it. It *does* matter tremendously *what* we do after we are saved! God demands obedience to His Word.

There is no greater power in the universe than "love." We serve God because we love Him, but most of all, because He *first loved us* and through Christ has brought into our hearts a desire to love Him. When one truly *loves* God, he does not serve Him merely to escape punishment for sin, but because he deeply desires to please Him in all that he does. We long to *please* those whom we dearly love.

Finally, John exhorts his readers to "abide" in the doctrine of Christ as the way to complete victory. One is reminded of John 15:7-16. From its original meaning, this word suggests to *remain* or *continue* and carries with it the thought of the person's acting his part in this matter.

No one can separate another from Christ except the believer himself. No amount of persecution, disappointment, or outward circumstances can in any sense separate a person from his Savior (Rom. 8:35-39). The only person who can effect a drift away from Him is the individual himself (Heb. 2:1, 2). Only one's own will to drift, or the carelessness attached to failure to remain stedfast ever takes one away from the Savior. This is a form of negative willing — action in default of positive willing.

3. Christians never should bid Godspeed to anyone who teaches a false doctrine (vv. 10, 11). In doing so, that person is encouraged in his evil work, and thereby the Christian becomes a partaker in this evil. John is very strong and explicit here. When convinced that one is teaching some evil doctrine which denies the Sonship and Saviorhood of Christ, the Christian's duty is to refrain from any encouragement. If possible, such a person should be courteously and graciously pointed to Christ as Savior and shown the error of his way. The ideal time to become established in sound doctrine is that of youth.

Memory Verse

"Whosoever transgresseth, and abideth not in the doctrine of Christ, hath not God. He that abideth in the doctrine of Christ, he hath both the Father and the Son" (v. 9).

III John

As with the former two books this little book carries the name of its author.

TO WHOM

In the opening salutation the writer names Gaius, his well-beloved friend, as the person to whom he writes. The epistle is addressed to Gaius, and evidently to the church with which he is connected.

Some think Gaius was the pastor of a church in the general Ephesus area, one of the numerous churches over which

John now presided as the chief leader. He is four times called beloved; he may have been one of John's converts.

PURPOSE

Concerning the purpose of this epistle, note the following facts:

As there were no seminaries for training ministers in those days, the leaders of the church had to gather and train the young ministers under their own oversight. It is thought that John had placed Diotrephes as pastor of one of these churches, but that he had turned against John's leadership.

Evidently there had been some missionaries or evangelists sent out by John to visit these churches for their benefit, but Diotrephes had refused to allow them to visit his church or even to be entertained by the members of the church (vv. 9, 10).

As Gaius was a neighboring pastor, the letter is addressed to him, possibly with the intention that he is to get word to

TOMB AREA OF ST. JOHN'S BASILICA AT EPHESUS. *Supposedly the tomb of St. John is underneath the floor of the basilica.*

that church of the Apostle's intended visit, since Diotrephes will not even accept a letter from the apostle. He informs Gaius that when he comes, he will take the matter up with the church and put Diotrephes in his place again.

This, with the fact that he wishes to encourage Gaius in his good work, seems to be the heart of the purpose of this epistle.

TIME

It is likely that this epistle was written about the same time as the former two epistles — probably between A.D. 80 and 90, at Ephesus.

AUTHORSHIP

It is certainly clear from the language of them that whoever wrote II John also wrote this one. Along with II John, it had some difficulty being formally recognized by the church. It was finally admitted into the New Testament canon just as the other one. (See the notes on the authorship of II John.)

GAIUS

There is considerable discussion as to who the Gaius was to whom John writes. The name was very common in those days, and there are several persons by this name mentioned in the New Testament.

Some believe he was the Gaius who lived at Corinth (Rom. 16:23; I Cor. 1: 14), who was host to the Corinthian church and certainly a very influential man. But he was apparently Paul's convert, not John's (I Cor. 1:14). Another Gaius is mentioned in Acts 19:29; he was Paul's travel companion and was with him at Ephesus. There was a Gaius of Derbe (Acts 20:4), also a fellow traveler of Paul's. Apparently neither of these latter two are the same as the one at Corinth.

The second one mentioned, the Gaius of Macedonia, could hardly be the one to whom John wrote, as John planned to visit the church in this area — an almost impossible trip for an old man of John's age, a trip from Ephesus to Macedonia. Nor is it clear that the Corinthian Gaius is the person; for John even a trip to Corinth would have been very strenuous. However, the Diotrephes mentioned seems much like some of the stubborn Corinthian church pastors who had even rejected Paul's apostleship. Some believe the situation applied to churches of the Corinthian area and that John, as a former *fisherman*, would undertake the sea voyage.

It may be more likely that the situation

which John describes existed in or near Ephesus, and if either person is the Gaius referred to, it was the one who was Paul's travel companion and was with him at Ephesus, probably being left there by him to work in the church. Likely this Gaius was one of John's converts whom he had trained and settled as a pastor. As for Diotrephes, there likely were several such ministers in the church then, just as today!

This third letter of John may be outlined as follows:

I. Opening salutation, vv. 1-4
II. Commendation for well-doing, vv. 5-8
III. Disgust with Diotrephes, vv. 9-10
IV. Admonition to right-doing, vv. 11-12
V. Personal matters, vv. 12-14

GREAT TRUTHS IN III JOHN

1. Christians should always cooperate in soul-winning efforts. John was encouraged that Gaius had opened his church doors to his ministers and was helping them with their work (vv. 5-8). It is hard enough for unbelievers to understand Christianity, let alone when we of different denominations, who believe the same Christian truths, refuse to cooperate with each other in Christian efforts. Young people should learn early to appreciate the fellowship of other Christians, even though there may be some differences in small matters of doctrine or church operation.

2. Good men are not always wise. Note that John does not accuse Diotrephes of "heresy," or false doctrine, but of *insubordination* — being unwilling to work under the leadership of a higher authority. Diotrephes ruined his good name for all time by having it placed in the Bible because of his *stubborn* actions

and character! Some people may be surprised to find others in heaven whom they felt would not be there due to some of their faults. They may be good at heart, but their actions have cost them much in Christian influence. Even if one must take a stand for a certain Christian conviction, he should do it with grace and humility, not with stubbornness and self-will.

3. Perhaps the key word of this epistle is "truth." It occurs six times in the book (vv. 1, 3, 4, 8, 12). This is a special word with John. He used it over twenty times in his gospel, nine times in I John, and five times in II John — about forty times in all.

Christians are always to "love in the truth" (v. 1), to "walk in the truth" (vv. 2, 3), to be "fellow helpers to the truth" (v. 8), and to *witness* to the truth (v. 12).

Memory Verse

"Beloved, follow not that which is evil, but that which is good. He that doeth good is of God: but he that doeth evil hath not seen God" (v. 11).

Jude

Because of its place in the New Testament, this epistle, though short, has given its author immortal fame.

TO WHOM

The opening greetings seem to indicate that it was intended for all Christians (v. 1). It is beyond doubt one of the books known as "general epistles," intended for the church universal. Some think the writer had in mind the same general areas of the church as those to which the two epistles of Peter were sent. This is not certain, however, as there is no specific mention of areas in the address itself.

PURPOSE

Verse 3 of this letter sets forth its purpose as a defense of the Christian faith. It has been thought from verse 4 that the writer may have intended at first to write a longer work, but news of the work of false teachers caused him to hasten his work and send it in shorter form out to the churches to help combat these errors.

Since there is now no way to know to what particular area of the church this epistle was sent, if any, there can be no local situation which caused Jude to write it. But since the rise of false teachings was more widespread in the western sections of the church, where the Greek language and culture prevailed, it is most likely that the writer had this area in mind when he wrote.

The purpose, then, is most clearly that of defending the church against false teachers and their evil doctrines. The early church had both to combat error and establish its members in the truth of Christianity. Almost every epistle has for its purpose the correction of some unwholesome situation in the local churches of an area, the combatting of some false doctrine, or the stating of the true Christian doctrinal position. In this way the church became established in the truth of the Gospel, as well as ridding herself of erroneous teachings.

The whole epistle is taken up with illustrations of what happened to those false teachers and disobedient people who took the way of evil and with encouraging the believers to always follow that which is right.

TIME

Regarding the time at which this work was written, there is no evidence whatsoever in the book itself. Nor is there much in history or tradition to help settle this question. It is, of course, tied in with its authorship. The best authorities now believe it was written before the destruction of Jerusalem (A.D. 70), or else this tragedy would most likely have been used as a late illustration of God's punishment of sin, since it was a fulfillment of Christ's prophecy. It was probably written about A.D. 65.

The place of its writing is totally unknown both to history and tradition.

AUTHORSHIP

The authorship of this epistle has been the subject of much debate. For many years it was not accepted as part of the inspired writings of the New Testament, but by the time the canon was finally established, it had gained general acceptance as an inspired writing.

The New Testament mentions several Judes and several Jameses. The author's bare reference in his opening words to himself as "Jude . . . brother of James" is not at all sufficient to tell us exactly who he was. *Which* Jude is still an unanswered question. Evidently this epistle did not make an immediate impression upon the early church, at least not sufficient enough for the earliest Church Fathers, such as Polycarp, Ignatius, and others, to establish its authorship with certainty. It has come down to us with incomplete identification.

However, look at these facts for a moment: If the author of this epistle were the Lord's brother, he probably would have identified himself as such rather than "the brother of James." The reference to James is certainly an identifying reference, even though it is subject to various interpretations. Had he been the apostle Jude, it would have been much more meaningful to have said, "Jude, an apostle of Jesus Christ."

There was another Jude, a brother of James, who was sometimes called James the Just or James the Great to distinguish him as the first presiding officer at Jerusalem. The reference, "brother of James," seems to point to this James. Identifying himself with James the Just would have given the author of this epistle considerable prestige, especially among the Jews. James the Just was held in high esteem throughout the church. It is likely, then, that this Jude is the author of the epistle under consideration. He was one of the Lord's followers but not an apostle.

We must not overlook the fact, however, that there is a tradition, generally well accepted, that the Jude who wrote this epistle was one of the Lord's brothers. Eusebius, an early church historian, seems to lend some credence to this tradition. If so, the Jude of this epistle would be the one referred to in Matthew 13:55.

There the matter must rest, for no one knows for certain just *which* Jude was the author. The important thing is that, from all internal evidences, this epistle was inspired of God; it is therefore important to us today.

One will discover in this book a marked similarity to II Peter, especially to the second chapter of that book. There has been considerable discussion upon this point. Because of this similarity, some believe Jude's epistle was based upon II Peter, especially chapter

2. Few have accepted this notion, however. The early followers of our Lord were well known to each other and doubtless discussed many of the same things. Jude's epistle, like Peter's, is the reflection of the man's own convictions of Gospel truth, plus the Holy Spirit's inspiration. What is to hinder the Holy Spirit from inspiring two separate epistles which have much in common? This would only serve to strengthen this truth. Jude is beyond doubt a fresh, original book, inspired by the Holy Spirit.

The book deals with false teachers, rebellion against God, and the need for the faithful to hold steadfastly to the doctrines of Christ and to Christian experience. The reference to the contention between Satan and the archangel Michael is entirely new in the New Testament. It is thought to have been taken from a book, *The Assumption of Moses,* written by a Jew in Palestine about the time of Christ's birth. It was never received as *inspired,* although possibly it was widely read by both Jews and Christians.

The book is a "fiery" treatise and may indicate that its author was something akin to Peter in his preaching ministry to Christians. In its warnings it has much material of value.

The closing part of this book has been called one of the "most beautiful benedictions in the New Testament."

Jude may be outlined in the following way:

I.   Opening greetings, vv. 1-2
II. A defense of the common faith in Christ, vv. 3-4
III. Illustrations of the punishment of the wicked, vv. 5-16
IV. Admonitions to building up faith, vv. 17-23
V.   Benediction of blessing, vv. 24-25

GREAT TRUTHS IN JUDE

1. Christians are to "earnestly contend for the faith" of Christ in its purity and power (v. 3). The term "once delivered to the saints" may better be rendered "once for all delivered." This strikes a blow to the idea of *continual revelation,* even down to our day.

No church or group of people has the right to assume that they may still receive original revelations from God. When the New Testament's last penman wrote the Revelation and laid his pen down, revelation of God to man was complete. We should be thankful that the early church was so very watchful against admitting various books into the collection of the New Testament. To be selected, books had to stand the most rigid test. There were about seventy-five so-called *gospels* of Christ — with some similarity to the four gospels — offered to the church in early times, purporting to be proper and correct accounts. These were all rejected because they did not show internal proof of inspiration. They had errors, contradictions, and foolish side notes; these forbade them even the smallest bid for inspiration.

Besides these there were untold numbers of *epistles* which had to be rejected. Many of them were excellent reading, such as the *Epistle of Clement,* the *Shepherd of Hermas,* the *Teachings of the Twelve,* and a great host of others. Some of these are useful for historical reference, but all fall far short of the truly inspired standard. Had the church accepted all these, the real *truth* of the Gospel would have been so hidden within this mass of mediocre chaff and human opinion, that it would have been difficult to preserve, if not lost entirely! How wise were those early Fathers, who were doubtless guided by the Holy

Spirit in their selection of these books. Thus we have our Bible, a complete, finished revelation of God, sufficient for all men, for all time.

2. Warning is given against "turning the grace of God into lasciviousness" — immoral practices (v. 4). One cannot turn grace into sinfulness. The meaning, then, is that of using the church and its fellowship for a cloak under which to do sinful things. Young people need to be warned that sometimes in the midst of religious fervor and emotion, Satan can take the advantage of one, causing him to become too free with those of the opposite sex. When religious fellowship brings two people very close together, it is sometimes easier to go beyond the "conventions" and take liberties which are not right. Persons who allow themselves to make religion a cloak for immoral purposes are about the lowest people upon the earth!

3. Three solemn warnings are given to those tempted to turn back and follow a false doctrine. Still good for today are the following warning illustrations: (1) God's judgment upon the rebellious Israelites in the wilderness (v. 5); (2) the angels who by disobedience fell into sin (v. 6); and (3) Sodom and Gomorrah, which were destroyed for their sins, after rejecting Lot's preaching (v. 7). Of these, two groups had been in fellowship with God, the others were outright God-rejecters. One should study this passage carefully.

4. Another trio of disobedients were listed as a further warning (v. 11): (1) "The way of Cain." Rejecting *God's way,* Cain brought his own sacrifice, which God rejected. This represents utter selfishness and man-made religion. (2) "The error of Balaam."

This represents *covetousness* — wanting to get ahead at all costs, even though it means a sacrifice of religious principles. Balaam, when he could not curse Israel, advised immoral practices by which they would be defeated. (3) "The gainsaying of Core." Korah of the Old Testament rebelled against Moses and divine leadership. After plenty of stern warning, he persisted in his way, and perished (Num. 16).

Young Christians should let these warnings sink into their hearts, lest in older years they fall into such sins by neglect of this truth.

5. "Building up your faith" by praying in the Holy Spirit (v. 20) is one of the Christian's most sacred duties. None can build up faith without prayer. Only as prayers are prayed "in the Holy Spirit" — that is, with the Spirit of God directing the *pray-er* — can one hope for an answer. Too many people want to pray "pocketbook prayers, and expect encyclopedic answers," as one has aptly put it.

6. "Keep yourselves in the love of God" (v. 21). Just as one must eat, breathe, and exercise for himself, so one must *keep himself* in the love of God. This is the human side of the way of salvation. Only *God* can give us grace; but only *man* can furnish the necessary obedience to keep in this grace. God cannot keep us unless we obey Him. On our part this requires faith, activity, resistance to temptation, and obedience to God.

Memory Verses

"But ye, beloved, building up yourselves on your most holy faith, praying in the Holy Ghost, keep yourselves in the love of God, looking for the mercy of our Lord Jesus Christ unto eternal life" (vv. 20, 21).

The Revelation

Revelation

This book is sometimes called "The Revelation of St. John the Divine," but it is really the revelation of Jesus Christ to John.

The name of the book — the *Revelation* — comes from a Greek word *transliterated* into English as *"apocalypse."* It means a *revelation* of something heretofore *concealed* or *hidden*.

TO WHOM

It is addressed to the "seven churches in Asia" (1:4). Like the Gospel of Luke, it has a special introduction — only two books in the Bible are so opened.

Beyond doubt the message of the Revelation, though originally directed to these Asian churches, was intended to be universal in its ultimate scope. It has had a message for the church in all ages, and especially for the church of the end time.

PURPOSE

The purpose of its writing is of considerable importance. Written so largely in symbolic language, its purpose may not be easy to discover. It seems, however, to have been fourfold:

1. The writer intended to show the ever-existing struggle between right and wrong, with right finally triumphing. God, Christ, the Holy Spirit, holy angels, and righteous people are seen in combat with the devil, evil spirits, and wicked men in the age-old struggle of right to conquer wrong.

2. A specific set of messages was intended for the seven Asian churches of that day. This section has been thought also to have some message for the church in all ages. Some think it represents the church in various stages of its historical progress through the centuries.

3. The section devoted to the heavenly visions doubtless gave support, comfort, and encouragement to the Christians of the early church, amidst their terrible persecutions. It would also serve this purpose for Christians meeting such conditions in any age.

4. Without question it was to serve as God's last words to man in the revelation called the Bible. It is the crowning work, the final invitation to salvation, and the last word about the rewards and judgments of mankind. Without this book the Bible would have been incomplete, like a story without its proper ending, a task unfinished, or a house which had not been completed in some of its most important parts.

TIME

Much discussion has occurred among both the ancient church leaders and modern scholars as to when this book may have been written. Some have thought it to be as early as A.D. 50; others as A.D. 68; still others as A.D. 79. None of these dates, however, has ever been seriously considered by most of the best scholars.

The most commonly accepted theory is that John was banished to Patmos during the last part of the reign of the Roman Emperor Domitian. Domitian died soon afterward, and the Emperor Nerva succeeded him. He had John recalled to his home in Ephesus, possibly to win the favor of the Christians as soon as he came to power.

It is thought that about A.D. 95, John was banished to Patmos where he saw the visions of the Revelation, and that he then wrote the book upon his return to Ephesus. This opinion is strengthened by John's saying, "I was in Patmos" (1:9), meaning it was there that he saw the visions, but that he was writing the book afterward. The weight of evidence favors a date about A.D. 95.

AUTHORSHIP

Twice in the introduction the writer states that this work was written by John. The only identifying words there, however, are "his servant," meaning Christ's servant. He does not list himself as an apostle of Christ. However, this is peculiar to John; while Paul often styled himself the apostle of Christ, John did not. In his gospel he merely refers to himself as "the disciple" (John 21:24); in his first epistle he makes no reference to himself at all; in his second and third epistles he identifies himself as "the elder." Mention of himself in the introduction of the Revelation is in keeping with his normal style.

From the most ancient times the authorship of this book has been credited to John, the apostle of Christ, author of the gospel and the three epistles bearing his name. Though some have argued for a later writing by a presbyter named John, and others for several apocalyptic writers whose writings were joined into one piece, there is no evidence to support such claims.

While the imagery of the Revelation is vastly different, there are, nonetheless, resemblances to John's other writings. His references to Christ as the Lamb of God (5:6; 12:11; 22:1), for example, echo his gospel language. So also the idea of witnessing to Christ (12:11) is characteristic of John's other writings.

Some have argued that the different character of the Revelation points to a different author. This, however, is not any great difficulty. Take Daniel, for instance. There we have both history and apocalyptic literature in the same volume. The idea of two Daniels has never been accepted by the best scholars. Neither do they suggest two Ezekiels because we find both historical writing and apocalyptic visions in Ezekiel. This difficulty vanishes at once when we remember that John did not *coin* this book; at God's orders he merely wrote down what he *saw* in his Patmos visions.

THE MEANING OF THE REVELATION

Since it is the most unusual book of the New Testament, a word about its *interpretation* seems necessary. Four theories as to its meaning have been offered:

1. The *preterist* theory says it was meant largely for the peoples of its times — Christianity's struggle with the Roman Empire and predictions of final triumph.

2. The *historical* theory makes it designed merely to cast a foreview of the church's whole history. Different periods and struggles within these periods are said to be shown by the various happenings or events in the visions.

3. The *futurist* interpretation claims the book describes largely the events clustering about the Lord's second coming, the closing scenes of this age in which we now live.

4. The *spiritualistic* theory teaches that the imagery of the book has no reference to any historical events on earth, but is rather a highly pictorial

presentation of divine government or of other spiritual lessons to the saints.

These interpretations and theories leave the young person pretty much in the fog, wondering which of these really *is* the right one! Young people want something *definite*, not just a guess. Well, this is a good place to learn, once for all, that there are many things in life, and some very important things in the Bible, for which there *cannot* be a simple, ready-made answer with all the explanations. But hold on a moment — there *is* an answer.

Throughout the Christian centuries this book, more than any other, has elicited two things from mankind: a fascination for its grandeur and difficulties, and a very great, wide range of interpretations. This may be partly because much of it is in language which is not easy to understand.

There may be some truth in each of these theories. Possibly the best method of interpretation is to take the view that

RUINS AT LAODICEA. *This once prosperous city was an important commercial center since it lay on one the busy Asian trade routes. It was also surrounded by fertile land. Products manufactured in the area were wool garments and medicinal salves.*

much of it has a *twofold* meaning. The messages to the seven churches had for that day an original charge; but they also contain warnings and encouragements for our day; they may well be applied to churches and even individual Christians of our day.

Possibly, if we accept a combination of the *historical* and *futurist* views, with the larger share of the visions yet future, we may not be far from the truth. A good Bible commentary is recommended for further study on this important matter.

As to where John received the Revelation, it will be remembered that he

Courtesy, Berlin Museum

RECONSTRUCTED ALTAR OF ZEUS. *The first triumph of German excavators at Pergamum was the discovery of the great Altar of Zeus. It had been built in the second century B.C. With stealth, the valuable archaeological find was transported to Germany and reconstructed. During World War II it was hidden, but after the war it was again set up in East Berlin. Some think the apostle John had this altar in mind when he spoke of "Satan's throne" at Pergamum.*

says it was "in Patmos" (1:9). Patmos was an island in the Aegean Sea, some thirty miles off the coast of Asia Minor. It is about fifteen miles in circumference and is now very rocky, rough, and bar-

ren, as it most likely was then. It produces very little in vegetables, but has many birds and rabbits, and some fruit and nut trees. During those ancient times, Patmos was used by the Roman government as a prison island for bad criminals. During the persecution under Emperor Domitian, John had been banished there as a prisoner of the Roman government.

The Revelation may be outlined as follows:

I. The prologue, 1:1-3
II. Letters to the seven churches, 1:4—3:22
III. The apocalyptic visions, 4:1—22:5
IV. The epilogue, 22:6-21

GREAT TRUTHS IN THE
REVELATION

1. This is the only book which opens
with a pronounced blessing upon its
readers (1:3). This indicates the importance of its message. Blessing is always associated with reading God's
Word, from whatever book one reads.
The Psalmist said it is a "lamp unto my
feet and a light unto my pathway" (Ps.
119:105); he also said, "The entrance of
thy word giveth light" (Ps. 119:129).

Young people can do nothing better
than to fill their minds and hearts with
the Word of God. It will bring blessings
throughout a lifetime.

2. "I John . . . was in Patmos . . . I
was in the Spirit" (1:9, 10). Here one
sees a true duality of life; it is physical,
mundane, visible, tangible, and earthly
— *I was in Patmos*. But it is more: it is
spiritual, invisible, intangible, and heavenly — *I was in the Spirit*. Man is both
body and spirit; in quality he is both
transient and eternal.

The unseen — that which we cannot
take hold of or feel with our hands, the
spiritual part of life — is far more important than the merely physical. Take
love, for instance. It cannot be measured, weighed, bought, sold, or seen
by the eye, but it is the most important
thing in the universe.

Religious life, though it cannot be
seen or tested by the senses, is no less
real. It is by far the most important
thing in life. It is this quality that lifts
mèn above circumstances and makes
them victors over the difficulties of life.
Note that there are twenty-two chapters
in the Revelation. In the first one, John
mentions Patmos; but after he says, "I
was in the Spirit," he does not mention
Patmos again in the remaining twenty-
one chapters. This was merely a his-

torical note, stating where he received
this revelation. But his life in the Spirit
symbolically lifts him above his earth-
bound life on Patmos so that he has
such victory over it that he mentions it
no more. The Christian may have
such victory over life's difficulties that
he does not whine about them!

3. To look up in a Bible dictionary
each of the seven churches is a rewarding experience. Then read carefully the
messages to each church. Each message,
except one, has both a commendation
and a condemnation portion in it. Philadelphia — the church of brotherly love,
where no rebuke was needed — is the exception.

These seven messages have sometimes
been thought to be suited to the seven
major periods of church history, beginning with John's own days and the
Ephesian church — the church age of
• cooling love and zeal for Christ. On this
scale the Philadelphia church probably
represents the Reformation period and
sometime following. Laodicea, the last-
mentioned church may be listed for our
age. This is only one of the rather popular theories *of historical* interpretation,
but it may be used as a good illustration.
If not taken too strictly, it has been
found that it is very well suited to the
various periods.

4. "Be thou faithful unto death" is
the challenge to the church at Smyrna
(2:10), and it is most suitable for us today. God rewards the Christian for
faithfulness, not merely for success. It
is nowhere admonished, "Be thou *successful*," although God puts no premium
upon failure. But faithfulness is much
more likely to bring success, more likely
than the mere aim at success alone.

5. "Behold, I have set before thee an
open door, and no man can shut it" (3:

8) is the promise to the church at Sardis. Possibly this can be said to be the promise to any church or individual which meets God's full requirements for victorious Christian living. Total dedication and full commitment to Christ of all there is in one's heart and life as a Christian prepares oneself for the utmost of God's choices and uses of oneself in this life. The highest goal of God for man in life is to do His will!

6. Now the scene changes: it is Christ who says, "Behold, I stand at the door and knock," promising communion with God to any who will allow Him to enter (3:20). This is the last sad word to the Laodicean church. Do you not suppose Christ still may knock at the door of some churches where the fire of His love has gone out, where His deity, Sonship, and Saviorhood have been denied? Ah, the sad state of any church or person when Christ is no longer adored, obeyed, and honored as Savior, Lord, and Master.

7. In his visions John saw the devil defeated and cast out of the heavenly place, and there followed great rejoicing. "And they overcame him by the blood of the Lamb, and by the word of their testimony; and they loved not their lives unto the death" (12:11). The victory hinged upon the atoning blood on Christ's part and the "word of their testimony" on the part of the saints.

This matter of Christian testimony is tremendously important. Every young person should learn early that his testimony is a vital part of his Christian life. One must always live, pray, and keep up-to-date victory over evil so he can anytime and anywhere witness for Christ without condemnation.

8. "Blessed are the dead that die in the Lord" (14:13). This marks the ideal of the Christian, not only in cases of extreme persecution, as here predicted, but any time. The saints have everything to gain and nothing to lose in death.

One of the greatest attractions and most powerful appeals of the Christian religion is that its true followers die triumphantly. Christians have nothing to fear from death, for Christ has already conquered it and taken away its bitter sting for them (I Cor. 15:54-57).

9. It is very important that everyone knows that his name has been written in the "lamb's book of life" (20:12; 21:27). Jesus admonished His disciples that it was more important that their names were "written in heaven" than that devils were subject to them (Luke 10:17-20).

One's name is written in the Lamb's book of life when he comes to God through Christ and receives forgiveness of sins and the witness of the Spirit that he is a child of God. God receives him into His kingdom. He then becomes a son of God (John 1:12; Rom. 8:16, 17) and a joint-heir with Christ of God's vast and indescribable riches. There is nothing in all the world so wonderful as to be a son of God! (I John 3:1-4).

10. Among the most glorious scenes which John saw in his visions was that of the Holy City, the New Jerusalem, the future home of God's redeemed children (21:1 — 22:5). This is a word picture of the beautiful heavenly home. We might say that this Four-square City is the home of God and the angels, and possibly the "many mansions" in the Father's house of which Jesus spoke (John 14:1), as well as the "place" which Jesus said He was going to "prepare" for His disciples (John 14:2). As it is described as having certain dimensions (21:15-17) and called a "city," we

THE ASCLEPION. *A world-renowned health center known as the Asclepion was located at Pergamum (top). Included in the complex of installations was a theater which accommodated five thousand people (center) The entire Asclepion centered around worship of Asclepius, the god of healing. Entwined serpents (bottom) were the symbol of Asclepius.*

SARDIS. *This ancient capital city of Lydia in western Asia is mentioned in The Revelation. One of the seven Christian churches was at Sardis. Sardis had been the residence of the wealthy King Croesus. His fortress was on the acropolis (background, above). Excavations from 1910 to 1914 brought to light the huge temple of Artemis, the Greek goddess (center and bottom).*

may infer that it represents the capital city of the celestial universe, much as Washington, D.C. is the capital of the United States. Now, just as any country is far and away many times larger than its capital, so the heavenly "country" of the redeemed may be expected to exceed this beautiful city untold times. Heaven is referred to as both a "country" and a "city" (Heb. 11:16). Let the imagination rove for a moment into sidereal space and all its immensities and one can begin to glimpse only the slightest bit of the glorious inheritance of the saints. One should read this total description carefully and think deeply about the heavenly home.

We are assured in the Scriptures that God's children will finally inherit the whole universe, whatever belongs to God. Paul said the saints are "heirs of God, and joint-heirs with Christ" (Rom. 8:17) and that "All things are yours" (I Cor. 3:21-23). If God gave His Son for our salvation, Paul reasoned, "how shall he not with him also freely give us all things?" (Rom. 8:32). "The inheritance of the saints" is beyond all human imagination, "an inheritance incorruptible, and undefiled, and that fadeth not away, reserved in heaven for you" (I Peter 1:4).

One can bask long in the unfading splendor of this immeasureably vast, indescribably glorious eternal home of the children of God. Whether one is young or old, this wondrous city of everlasting glory never ceases to hold him in fond admiration of its celestial delights.

It is altogether fitting that the Bible, which opens with the sad story of how man lost his home in Eden's paradise through sin (Gen. 3), should close with the eternal paradise of God restored to all who will come to God through Christ.

Let every reader of the Bible encourage everyone else whom we can interest to become also a reader of this, the greatest book ever written, that he may learn for himself the most fascinating and greatest story ever told!

Memory Verse

"And the Spirit and the bride say, Come. And let him that heareth say, Come. And whosoever will let him take of the water of life freely" (22:17).

Bibliography

Bible Versions

American Standard Version. New York: Thomas Nelson and Sons, 1901 and 1929.
Amplified Bible. Grand Rapids: Zondervan Publishing House, 1958, 1962, and 1964.
King James Version. London: Oxford University Press.
Moffatt's Translation of the Bible. New York: Harper and Brothers, 1954.
New Testament for English Readers. Chicago: Moody Press, undated.
New Testament in Four Versions. New York: Iverson-Ford Associates, 1963. Includes the King James Version, the Revised Standard Version, *The Bible in Modern English* by J. B. Phillips, and *The New English Bible.*
Weymouth's New Testament in Modern Speech. New York: Harper and Brothers, undated.

Books

ALLIS, OSWALD T. *The Five Books of Moses.* Philadelphia: Presbyterian and Reformed Publishing Co., 1943.
ANGUS, J. *The Cyclopedic Handbook of the Bible.* New York: Fleming H. Revell, 1907.
BARNES, ALBERT. *Barnes' Notes on the New Testament.* Grand Rapids: Baker Book House, 1958.
BLACK, M. *The Scrolls and Christian Origins.* New York: Charles Scribner's Sons, 1961.
BREWER, J. A. *The Literature of the Old Testament.* New York: Columbia University Press, 1933.
BRUCE, F. F. *The English Bible.* London: Oxford University Press, 1961.
BULTMAN, RUDOLPH. *The History of the Synoptic Tradition.* New York: Harper and Row, 1963.
BURTON, E. D. *Records and Letters of the Apostolic Age.* New York: Charles Scribners, 1912.
Catholic Encyclopedia. New York: Encyclopedia Press, 1913.
CLARKE, ADAM. *Commentary on the Holy Bible.* An abridgement by Ralph Earle. Grand Rapids: Baker Book House, 1967.
COLLETT, SIDNEY. *All About the Bible.* New York: Fleming H. Revell, undated.
DIBELIUS, MARTIN. *From Tradition to Gospel.* New York: Charles Scribner's Sons, 1953.
DODS, MARCUS. *The Bible — Its Origin and Nature.* New York: Charles Scribner's Sons, 1904.
DAVIDSON, FRANCIS F. (ed.). *New Bible Commentary.* Grand Rapids: William B. Eerdmans Publishing Co., 1953.
DOWNEY, DAVID G. and others. *Abingdon Bible Commentary.* Nashville: Abingdon, 1929.
DRIVER, R. S. *Introduction to the Literature of the Old Testament.* New York: Charles Scribner and Sons, 1900.
EARLE, RALPH (ed.); H. J. S. BLANEY; CARL HANSON. *Exploring the New Testament.* Kansas City: Beacon Hill Press, 1955.
EVANS, WILLIAM. *The Pentateuch.* New York: Fleming H. Revell, 1916.

FILSON, FLOYD. *Which Books Belong in the Bible?* Philadelphia: The Westminster Press, 1957.

——————, *Understanding the Old Testament.* London: Oxford University Press, 1953.

FULLER, R. *The New Testament in Current Study.* New York: Charles Scribner's Sons, 1962.

GOODSPEED, J. E. *The Formation of the New Testament.* Chicago: The University of Chicago Press, 1926.

GRANT, R. *The Gospels: Their Origin and Growth.* New York: Harper and Brothers, 1957.

GREGORY, R. *The Canon and Text of the New Testament.* New York: Charles Scribner and Sons, 1907.

HALLEY, H. H. *Halley's Bible Handbook.* Grand Rapids: Zondervan Publishing House, 1962.

HUFFMAN, J. A. *Progressive Unfolding of the Messianic Hope.* New York: George H. Doran, 1924.

——————. *A Guide to the Study of the Old and New Testaments.* Marion, Indiana: The Standard Press, 1926.

——————. *Redemption Completed.* Marion, Indiana: The Standard Press, 1903.

——————. *Voices from Rocks and Dust Heaps of Bible Lands.* Marion, Indiana: The Standard Press, 1928.

The Interpreters' Bible. Nashville: Abingdon-Cokesbury Press, undated.

JAMIESON, ROBERT; A. J. FAUSSET; and DAVID BROWN. *A Commentary on the Old and New Testaments.* Grand Rapids: Zondervan Publishing House, 1957.

KENYON, F. G. *Our Bible and the Ancient Manuscripts.* London: Eyre and Spottiswoode, 1939.

KLASSEN, WILLIAM, and GRAYDON SNYDER (eds.). *Current Issues in New Testament Interpretation.* New York: Harper and Brothers, 1962.

Life and Works of Flavius Josephus. Translated by W. Whiston. Philadelphia: John C. Winston Co., undated.

McCLINTOCK, JOHN and JAMES STRONG. *Cyclopedia of Biblical, Theological and Ecclesiastical Literature.* New York: Harper and Brothers, 1891.

MORGAN, G. CAMPBELL. *Living Messages of the Books of the Bible.* New York: Fleming H. Revell, 1912.

NICOLL, W. R. (ed.) *The Sermon Outline Bible.* Grand Rapids: Baker Book House, 1958.

OWEN, G. F. *From Abraham to Allenby.* Grand Rapids: William B. Eerdmans Publishing Co., 1939.

PATTERSON, JOHN. *The Goodly Fellowship of the Prophets.* New York: Fleming H. Revell.

PEMBER, G. H. *Earth's Earliest Ages.* New York: Fleming H. Revell, undated.

PFEIFFER, R. H. *Introduction to the Old Testament.* New York: Harper and Brothers, 1941.

PURKISER, W. T. *Exploring the Old Testament.* Kansas City: Beacon Hill Press, 1958.

RAMM, BERNARD. *Protestant Biblical Interpretation.* Boston: W. A. Wilde Co., 1956.

RAVEN, J. H. *Old Testament Introduction.* New York: Fleming H. Revell, 1910.

RIMMER, HARRY. *Modern Science and the Genesis Record.* Grand Rapids: William B. Eerdmans Publishing Co., 1945.

ROBINSON, G. L. *The Twelve Minor Prophets.* Grand Rapids: Baker Book House, 1962.

ROBINSON, JAMES. *A Quest for the Historical Jesus.* London: SCM Press, undated.

ROBINSON, JOHN A. *Twelve New Testament Studies.* Naperville, Illinois: Alec R. Allenson, Inc., 1962.

ROBINSON, W. H. *The Old Testament*: *Its Making and Meaning*. Nashville: Abingdon-Cokesbury Press, 1947.

RYLE, J. C. *Expository Thoughts on the Gospels*. New York: Baker and Taylor, 1873.

SELL, H. T. *Studies of Great Bible Cities*. New York: Fleming H. Revell, 1927.

SPENCER, H. D. M.; E. J. EXCELL. *The Pulpit Commentary*. Grand Rapids: William B. Eerdmans Publishing Co., undated.

WATSON, JOHN. *God's Message to the Human Soul*. New York: Fleming H. Revell, 1907.

WRIGHT, W. F. *Highlights of Archaeology in Bible Lands*. Chicago: University of Chicago Press, 1955.

YOUNG, J. E. *An Introduction to the Old Testament*. Grand Rapids: William B. Eerdmans Publishing Co., 1949.